SPEAKING
TWO
LANGUAGES

SUNY Series in Medieval Studies
Paul E. Szarmach, Editor

SPEAKING

TWO

LANGUAGES

TRADITIONAL DISCIPLINES
AND CONTEMPORARY THEORY
IN MEDIEVAL STUDIES

✳ ✳

EDITED BY
ALLEN J. FRANTZEN

State University of New York Press

Published by
State University of New York Press, Albany

Printed in the United States of America

For information, address State University of New York
Press, State University Plaza, Albany, N. Y., 12246

Library of Congress Cataloging-in-Publication Data

Speaking two languages: traditional disciplines and contemporary
   theory in medieval studies / edited by Allen J. Frantzen.
        p.   cm. — (SUNY series in medieval studies)
     Includes bibliographical references (p.   ).
     ISBN 0-7914-0505-2 (alk. paper) . — ISBN 0-7914-0506-0 (pbk. :
alk. paper)
        1. English literature—Old English, ca. 450–1100—History and
criticism—Theory, etc. 2. English literature—Middle English,
1100–1500—History and criticism—Theory, etc. 3. Literature,
Medieval—History and criticism—Theory, etc. 4. Civilization,
Medieval—Historiography.   I. Frantzen, Allen J., 1947– .
II. Series.
PR176.S65   1991
829'.09—dc20   90-9638
                                                        CIP

10 9 8 7 6 5 4 3 2 1

Contents

Acknowledgments   vii

Preface   ix

1. Prologue: Documents and Monuments: Difference and Inter-
    disciplinarity in the Study of Medieval Culture
    Allen J. Frantzen   1

2. On Reading Eve: *Genesis B* and the Readers' Desire
    Gillian R. Overing   35

3. *Beowulf* and the Origins of Civilization
    James W. Earl   65

4. The Plot of *Piers Plowman* and the Contradictions
    of Feudalism
    Britton J. Harwood   91

5. The Language of Transgression: Body, Flesh, and Word in
    Mystical Discourse
    Karma Lochrie   115

6. Texts That Speak to Readers Who Hear: Old English Poetry
    and the Languages of Oral Tradition
    John Miles Foley   141

7. Working with Patristic Sources: Language and Context in Old
    English Homilies
    Clare A. Lees   157

8. Medieval Textuality and the Archaeology of Textual Culture
    Martin Irvine   181

9. Epilogue: *De Scientia Interpretandi:* Oral Tradition and the Place of Other Theories in the Graduate Curriculum
    Adam Brooke Davis   211

Notes   225

Contributors   289

Index   291

Acknowledgments

Speaking Two Languages has been supported by Loyola University of Chicago, the Loyola Endowment for the Humanities, and Loyola's Research Services; Timothy R. Austin, Thomas J. Bennett, Francis J. Catania, and James L. Wiser have been enthusiastic about the project and generous in funding it. It is a pleasure to acknowledge support for *Speaking Two Languages* from the institutions of the contributors: Georgetown University; Miami University; the University of Missouri; the University of Oregon; Randolph-Macon College (Clare Lees has since moved to Fordham University); and Wake Forest University. Dewaine Beard and Deborah Frisby assisted in organizing a seminar at which the essays were discussed, and I am grateful for their help.

The contributors to this volume have earned the editor's special thanks. They enthusiastically embraced the experimental nature of the project and agreed to address essays to the "two languages" motif at an early stage of its development. Each of them has enlarged, refined, and inflected the concept; the intensity of their convictions is matched by the diversity of their views. In addition to undertaking an essay tailored to our motif, the contributors not only critiqued the essays but traveled to Chicago midwinter to discuss them at length (rather than to deliver them) and persuaded their institutions to share in the expense of doing so. Early drafts of their essays were rich in thanks for the assistance they received from one another, but with their permission those internal acknowledgments have been removed; without their collaboration and willingness to give and accept criticism this volume could not have become a reality.

With the authors I thank Paul E. Szarmach, general editor of the series in which this volume appears, for the opportunity to undertake it, and Carola Sautter for supervising our dealings with the SUNY Press efficiently, effectively, and enthusiastically.

Preface

The changes that have swept all areas of the graduate and undergraduate curriculum in recent years have slowly become apparent in medieval studies. Books "introducing" theory to general readers have been legion for a decade,[1] and essay collections about the role of contemporary theory in medieval literary criticism are now appearing.[2] The Medieval Academy of America recently devoted a special issue to the question of the "new philology," indicating that concern about the relevance of medieval studies has reached the highest institutional levels. Medievalists who wish to respond to new developments in their discipline while retaining their commitment to traditional analytical methods are concerned about the implications of contemporary theory for traditional critical practice. Many essays in the medieval collections offer stimulating rereadings of familiar texts, but few of them address the problems of articulating tradition and contemporary theory. The articulation of tradition and contemporary criticism is the subject of *Speaking Two Languages*.

The collection differs from other collections in two ways. The first, reflected in its title, is this volume's interpretation of critical methods as consciously chosen and spoken "languages"; each essay identifies distinct theoretical methodologies and explores the consequences of combining them and, hence, speaking two (or more) languages. The second, and related, difference is the volume's collaborative development: the number of essays was kept small so that each could be drafted in response to the "two languages" motif, developed at length, and discussed by all the contributors. That discussion took place at a seminar at Loyola University of Chicago in February 1989; it was designed to examine the languages chosen and to explore the problems involved in relating them; the essays were then reworked with the seminar discussions in mind. Aimed at the reader new to theory, as well as at the reader already engaged with contemporary criticism in some way, each essay concludes with a critical bibliographical note pointing to further reading in the languages it employs.

Contributors to *Speaking Two Languages* were educated in Old and Middle English literature programs devoted to traditional methods. They represent a variety of approaches current in the 1970s and 1980s, including

ix

patristic criticism, the New Criticism, linguistics, philology, and literary history, and their recent work shows them moving beyond those approaches. Each contributor was asked to identify two methods or critical traditions and to conceptualize them as languages that were combined in his or her critical practice. Some essays in the collection that resulted identify two more or less traditional languages; others articulate traditional approaches with distinctively postmodern concepts.

Gillian R. Overing employs feminist theories of reading to read critical desire and its effects on Eve in *Genesis B*. Neither claiming that Freud is a "contemporary" critic nor reading Freud through Jacques Lacan, James W. Earl uses a psychoanalytic discussion of the theme of origins in *Beowulf* not to argue for a psychoanalysis of the text but to argue instead that the text psychoanalyzes its audience. Britton Harwood's discussion of feudalism and *Piers Plowman*, an inquiry into literary, economic, and political history, returns the poem to the material history of its point of production and simultaneously reidentifies the literary-historical tradition to which the poem is assigned. Karma Lochrie employs Kristeva's concept of abjection to discuss the body in medieval mysticism. John Miles Foley's essay opens the critical idiom of oral tradition to an examination of the aesthetic implications of Iserian reception for Old English verse. Clare A. Lees integrates language theory and sociolinguistics with patristic analysis of Old English homilies. Martin Irvine proposes an archive of discourse to be used in analyzing Latin and Old English texts in manuscript contexts. Because Adam Brooke Davis was requested to take Foley's place at the Loyola conference, he was invited to make an independent contribution in which he viewed the "two languages" motif and the larger issue of contemporary criticism in the graduate medieval studies curriculum. His essay serves as an epilogue to the collection, to which mine is a prologue. Since I could not presume to "speak" all the languages spoken by the contributors through an editorial language seeking to assert thematic coherence, I do not attempt the customary gesture of linking contributions or asserting their complementary nature. Instead, I raise the issues of the collection in a broadly institutional perspective and examine the often-invoked need for interdisciplinarity in the context of traditional disciplines, difference, and identity.

The order in which I have described the essays is the order in which the essays appear. Although that order is not entirely arbitrary, neither does it reflect a systematic spectrum, suggest a unifying syntax, or posit the existence of a larger order that the sequence of essays makes manifest. I could not hope to match Stephen Nichols's assertion that the essays he edited for the special issue of *Speculum* formed a continuum.[3] Indeed, the continuum in the *Speculum* volume is a disadvantage, since most of the contributions emphasize Old French and romance philology (four of six, two historical, two literary; the others concern Middle English). The volume, which resembles other collections concerning medieval French studies and edited by Nichols, focuses like them exclusively on the later medieval period, defining medieval as "1000 to 1500."[4] The *Speculum* volume is not a statement about the "new philology" so much as a statement about the impact of certain kinds of criticism on Old French literature and, more generally, historiography.

The essays in *Speaking Two Languages* do not form a continuum of any kind that I can see. They are written to be read in any order the reader wishes; their interconnections and collective disjunctions will be apparent no matter what sequence is followed in approaching them. The collection is unusual in that it emphasizes Anglo-Saxon texts and problems more heavily than texts from the Middle English period. The emphasis on Old English is intended. Some collections contain no Old English at all;[5] the neglect of Old English is particularly conspicuous in the *Speculum* volume, in which Germanic philology barely surfaces. Our volume does not attempt to cover major figures, to balance studies of poetry with prose, or otherwise to scatter its subjects in "interdisciplinary" paradigms in the hope of providing something for everyone. Textual and literary cultures predominate, but they are broadly defined to include economic, sociolinguistic, and spiritual as well as artistic dimensions of medieval life.

Scholarship in languages other than English—in medieval French and Italian in particular—has responded more rapidly to the new critical climate than either Middle or (indeed, especially) Old English. But it cannot be said that recent discussions of Dante or French lyric and romance are without a parochialism of their own. The Medieval Academy volume illustrates this parochialism in two ways, ignoring Anglo-Saxon as well as early Latin literature and steering strangely clear of feminist criticism while taking to task more than once the political limitations of New Historicism. In many collections, it is to the Renaissance that medievalists look for guidance in their critical practice. While it would indeed have been desirable to present a collection attending to texts in other languages as well as in English, it proved more productive, in a collaborative experiment, to bring together scholars who already spoke one common language—that is, who recognized the major traditions in Old and Middle English literary and historical criticism—in the hopes that a shared sense of tradition would promote discussion of the need to revise and review that tradition. Eventually, I trust, scholars in other medieval languages will collaborate on collections that theorize particular areas of the medieval spectrum, and although there are limitations to the formation of such collaborations around languages— the emphasis on Old English in *Two Languages*, on Old French in the *Speculum* collection—it is also clear that the work of several scholars in one area is required to theorize the history and the future of different scholarly traditions. When the historical formation of these traditions is more fully examined, cooperation among the traditions is more likely to take place.

The protocol of this volume is not thematic but problem centered and oriented toward praxis. In asking how medievalists present and future can use critical self-consciousness to extend the boundaries of medieval studies, we ask how new attitudes toward speaking, reading, and writing—whether they are Derridian, Lacanian, or Foucauldian—relate to the traditional study of the Middle Ages. While all the essays in this collection "read" literary texts, they do so in order to see texts as the embodiment of cultural forces that criticism can identify, dislodge, and scrutinize. But none of the essays simply applies a method to textual material or seeks to saturate a text (canonical or uncanonical) with details in order to produce a new reading. Most of the essays are concerned with several texts and with textual categories; essays that do concentrate on major texts—*Piers*, *Beowulf*, and *Genesis B*—avoid conceptualizing "theory" in one place and "text" in another, and "applying" the theory"to" the text to produce a reading. All the essays recognize that if a theoretical approach functions as a given, as an already-formed tool used to make sense of literature, its own hermeneutic and constructed nature is shielded from analysis. Our concern is not to "apply" theory to texts of recognized importance or to use theory to challenge the status of texts of "recognized importance" and assert the importance of others. Rather, our goal has been to identify and test the flexibility of theoretical paradigms.

As Ruth Waterhouse has reminded us, an innovative or "contemporary" approach to medieval culture does not remain separate and isolated from the texts or objects it studies; instead, it is modified by them. "Often the theories are developed with a particular period or type of literature in mind," she writes, "and when they are tested against other periods or types of literature, they are seen to require modification or re-thinking in some way or other."[6] Her point is worth some elaboration. Scholars are used to describing their work as looking *at* texts *through* theory; we are less accustomed to describing our practice as viewing one theory through another or looking at theory through texts. The dual-language motif of the volume requires several theoretical operations: the critic may look at two theoretical languages in complementary or contradictory ways but may also use one theory to modify another, look through theoretical constructs at texts, and consider the effect of texts on theoretical propositions about them. These perspectives permit the critic to test one theory against another, not to determine which is the better but to show that either, in isolation, is inadequate.

While it is obvious that all critical methodologies are based on assumptions and values that determine what the methods can be used to achieve, those methodologies are not all obviously hermeneutic. Marxism and feminism are easily identified as politically interested, while scholarship that results in a "definitive" edition or historical study is, by definition, perceived as objective and scientific. Criticism of the latter sort enjoys the status of "scholarship" that is prior to interpretation, which is seen as subjective and secondary. But the hermeneutic nature of textual criticism has long been acknowledged, even by some of its most traditional practitioners (for example, Richard D. Altick and James Thorpe),[7] and revisionist textual critics, especially Jerome McGann, have demonstrated the benefits of ideological analysis on textual criticism.[8] Hermeneutic and interested functions are likewise important to patristic exegesis, the New Criticism, literary history, oral studies, and any traditional method that seems to offer a neutral approach to the "data" of texts and contexts.

Just as traditional analysis holds the "new" to the level of a supplement, a second language added to current parlance, it holds theory to a secondary level of "interpretation," implying that access to unreconstructed, uninterpreted data is somehow accessible in medieval scholarship. "Speaking two languages" is a trope that brings contemporary criticism to parity with traditional methodology, but not as a step toward replacing the old with the new. Instead, our essays recognize methodological choices as individual critical acts that lead to the continuing and mutually modifying exchange between innovation and tradition, an exchange between already accepted and emerging critical constructions.

Speaking Two Languages includes no call for sleepers to awake. At the end of 1990 such a call is hardly necessary. It is true that some medievalists continue to resist innovations in critical tradition, overlooking the covertly theoretical nature of their own discourse while dismissing overtly theoretical work as a passing fad. And we can already see evidence of the predictable response of those skeptics who believe that, jargon apart, contemporary criticism offers nothing "new." Arguments incorporating contemporary criticism (in any age) are liable to be recognized, as Peter Travis has recently put it, as "the redeployment of various linguistic problems and the replication of certain medieval philosophic issues"—in other words, as old wine in new bottles. Citing Travis's remark, a recent review notes that "a tradition for which it was an article of faith that 'now we see through a glass darkly, but then face to face' is not going to be shattered merely by hearing the Derridian litany, 'Difference, Presence, Absence'"; the reviewer adds that the real test of theory is whether "it can teach them [medievalists skeptical about theory] something new about the literature they study."[9] Traditional scholars may take some pleasure in defanging the monster of contemporary criticism, thinking that if there is nothing new, there is nothing to fear and reassuring one another that the chaff may change, but that the fruit will stay the same (the phrase is Karma Lochrie's). Hans Robert Jauss and Michel Foucault seem to have become among the most easily appropriated contemporary critics; "reception" is a term that seems almost self-explanatory to those who have not thought about it, and the relationship of power to knowledge likewise seems clear. One can, it would seem, refer to reception theory or discursive formations without the inconvenience of having to learn about the complexities that either concept entails. Through such glibness the antitheoretical can acquire a sheen of theoretical awareness, but that polish is too superficial to disguise either the plodding positivism of certain scholarly practices or the dismaying and even self-congratulatory sureness with which some scholars seek to establish the "linguistic facts about poetic style" upon which mere critics may be permitted to construct interpretations.[10] In an age in which scientific theories are constantly being revised, perhaps even linguistic facts may change.

Even if they dismiss new theorists as interchangeable, medievalists who confront the complexity of critical theory in its historical situation, "poststructuralist" or not, can hardly rest assured that the real test of theory is whether "it can teach them something new about the literature they study." The object of criticism is not only to teach literature, but to teach critical paradigms, their transformation, and the business of the critics who activate them. The essays in *Speaking Two Languages* do not assume that the objective of theoretical inquiry is the production of new interpretations; rather, they assert the importance and the consequences of critical self-consciousness.

Many medievalists are concerned with the techniques and approaches offered by poststructuralist thought; graduate students and faculty who are acquainted with contemporary criticism see the future in articulating tradition and innovation, not holding them apart. That articulation is the purpose of this book. Conscious of critical diversity and the tensions it creates, we have tried to keep in mind our role as medievalists educating one another and as future medievalists in an ongoing institutional reexamination of longstanding convictions about a plurality of methodological approaches and of the meaning of "pluralism."[11] The premise of this collection is not that pluralistic responses to contemporary theory mean a "fall" into relativistic chaos, in which all methods are seen as equally effective, or equally ineffective. Rather, it is that two languages—two paradigms—are better than one, and that both "languages" should be chosen rather than inherited, selected rather than given.

The discussions before, during, and after the "two languages" seminar have been opportunities for candid and sustained exchange. We invite our readers to join our discussion of the implications of speaking two languages and to join us in learning how academic practices guided by tradition can continue to thrive in a critical climate that challenges tradition. All medievalists are affected by this challenge; all have an interest in meeting it.

Chapter 1

Prologue: Documents and Monuments: Difference and Interdisciplinarity in the Study of Medieval Culture

✳ Allen J. Frantzen ✳

Medievalists who today resist the "contemporary" maintain a skepticism about innovation that is itself a tradition. In 1833, brimming with philology and mythology as practiced by the Brothers Grimm at the University of Göttingen, John Mitchell Kemble returned from Germany. His contemporaries in England were slow to acknowledge the significance of the scholarly revolution he had joined. Kemble crossed swords with many of them, denouncing both historians (Sharon Turner) and linguists (Joseph Ritson and F. M. Madden) who failed to measure up to the new system he championed. His letters to Jakob Grimm boasted of his success in insulting his old-fashioned opponents.[1] Barely forty years later, Henry Sweet complained about the German domination of medieval studies, but England's most formidable "philologer" also recognized the benefits of the new professionalism. Made anxious by the productivity of the Germans, Sweet calmed himself by looking out over the wide "fields of linguistic science," where he saw many regions "as yet uninvaded by dissertations and programs."[2] At the end of the nineteenth century Anglo-Saxon studies constituted a scientific field, and the scholars who surveyed it had divided up the territory. The Department of English as we know it was still taking shape, but the scientific basis of the discipline was widely recognized. Kemble's revolution had passed into orthodoxy.

The methodological debates that engaged Kemble, Sweet, and other nineteenth-century medievalists are important to the critical debates of our own time. As we witness the challenge to traditional criticism posed by postmodernism, we do well to understand how, in the early years of the discipline, new practices became traditional and, once orthodox, were in turn confronted by innovation. Philology was once the center and only subject of the Department of English; it now resides on the fringes, a curiosity manifest in the exclusively linguistic introductions to edited medieval texts

1

whose "literary" or "historical" interest is either dismissed or denied.[3] Historical criticism emerged to counter the narrowness of philology and its neglect of context, but the account of context offered by early historical criticism was naive and reflectionist; it was constructed on biographical lines and sought to contextualize medieval texts by relating them to specific occasions.

Exegetical criticism, in the form of patristic scholarship and source study, moved away from attempts to historicize texts in this particular way but offered unacceptable generalizations in exchange. The problem with exegetical criticism was not that it asserted the place of dogma in medieval literature—an assertion that could hardly be denied—but that it proposed scriptural interpretation as the only authentic mode of historical criticism. With historical analysis thus defined by historicity that was unacceptably narrow and by exegesis that swept all before it, scholars influenced by the New Criticism gladly assumed the duty of asserting the artistic autonomy of texts.

Patristic scholarship and formalist analysis, whatever their theoretical differences, soon settled into a harmonious relationship. The former discovered sources and allusions that related medieval texts to Latin writing, supplying information complementary to the hard data of textual criticism. The latter, in an appreciative mode, extracted from such discoveries the elements needed to confirm the historical authenticity of interpretive patterns generated by close readings of the texts. I do not want to exaggerate the cooperation of formalism and exegesis; a recent essay by Lee Patterson casts exegesis and the New Criticism in a sibling rivalry and categorizes their differences as humanist and antihumanist. But despite their differences, it seems apparent that the two approaches in fact worked extremely well both in the classroom and in the study.[4]

Exegetical criticism and the New Criticism were once innovative. Both are now seen as dominating and even totalizing critical practices. "Traditional" in a negative sense, both are under considerable pressure from postmodernist forms of historical and textual analysis. Deconstructive and oppositional in emphasis, these modes assert political and social claims against the models of exegesis and the New Criticism in an attempt to expose the scientific pretenses of the former and the alleged aesthetic neutrality of the latter. The postmodern challenge to traditional critical practice in medieval studies presents an opportunity for rethinking the paradigm in which innovation confronts tradition.

The passage of innovation into orthodoxy suggests that criticism and scholarship are caught in a cycle of obsolescence. But professional (professorial) custody of the past is not a task with constant values or certitude. Our methods are time-bound rather than timeless, and their timeliness—

their inevitable obsolescence—is neither vice nor virtue. They remind us that we speak, write, and teach in our own time and as our own persons, and that we choose our critical languages accordingly. Scholars do not embody unchanging values of a transhistorical establishment but instead express and debate the changing values of the institutions in our power, the institutions we establish and renew in our teaching and research. That our work is rooted in its time and place—which Gillian Overing's essay (quoting Alice Jardine) identifies as "the place from which we speak"— neither ennobles nor demeans it. Valorization is an empty gesture, and self-deprecation, in a profession in which leadership and communication with others different from us ought to be the main tasks, is as hollow. If it is the business of the critic to speak, it is the business of criticism to make a place for the critic and the activities of reading, writing, and teaching. This business means that every generation of critics, approaching tradition with new perspectives and new issues, will be engaged in reestablishing and renewing tradition even as tradition is overtaken, and taken over.

The roots of the tradition now being challenged are not particularly deep. Patterson has reviewed the debate in Chaucer criticism.[5] Anne Middleton has surveyed the same territory in the critical history of *Piers Plowman*.[6] John P. Hermann has discussed the critical tradition of Old English poetry, and I have traced the effect of patristic scholarship and source study on the history of Anglo-Saxon scholarship.[7] The first phase of patristic exegesis in medieval scholarship is bracketed by two essays published by D. W. Robertson, Jr. in 1951[8] and responses to them by R. E. Kaske and E. Talbot Donaldson that appeared in 1960.[9]

Donaldson argued that historical critics put the requirements of their thesis before the artistic nuances of their texts. This is a charge that could be—and has been—lodged against almost any critical method, and Donaldson did not take into account the recourse to self-validating procedures that his own method shared with that of his opponents. Donaldson did, however, memorably demonstrate that the exegetes had failed to make poetic sense of poetic texts. In reply, Kaske asserted that the writings of the Fathers were "a sort of massive index to the traditional meanings and associations of most medieval Christian imagery," thus confirming the disquieting impression that "Robertsonianism" did intend Church Fathers to speak for all medieval people.[10]

Dissatisfaction of a fundamental and more explicitly theoretical kind than Donaldson's came from R. S. Crane. Describing what he called the "high priori road," Crane challenged the unitary and totalizing force of patristic exegesis and its insistence on characterizing an entire period in terms of a handful of assumptions about literary culture, as, for example, Robertson's assumption that medieval literature was "always allegorical."

Crane pointed out that scholars confused the capacity of a hypothesis to account for the facts ("almost any hypothesis will do this in some fashion," he wrote) with the more difficult, and more significant claim, that "*only* if it [the hypothesis] is true, could the facts, in their totality, be what they are."[11] One can stop well short of Crane's criteria and note how rarely a "ruling hypothesis"—for example, the dependence of medieval texts on Augustinian theology—is subject to scrutiny by those who insist on its validity. Traditional critical discourse stresses the capacity of a hypothesis to account for facts but does not address the incapacity of the hypothesis being advocated or subject it to Crane's severe (and certainly positivist) test that a hypothesis must be analyzed independent of the "theoretical or other general reasons that may have suggested it."[12]

Views predicated, in proleptic fashion, on assumptions about the "always-allegorical" nature of medieval literature accommodated only texts and parts of texts that conformed to them; texts that did not conform were either ignored or revised (through editorial emendation) to establish conformity. The consequences of this exclusivity were obvious. When patristic criticism recast *The Nun's Priest's Tale* in the paradigm of the Resurrection—a provocation of the theological subtext of the poem—Donaldson dismissed the allegorical reading on the grounds of artistic integrity. Cautioning that "one ought to trust the statistics of great poetry rather than those of critics," Donaldson claimed that if Chaucer had wanted us to see the tale as an allegory he would, in the fashion of a medieval preacher, "have warned us to heed the *sensus* before extracting the *sententia*."[13] The historical assumptions of patristic criticism excluded the social history of the period and the social ambiguities of the text, including its idealized portrait of poverty, which Derek Pearsall has recently characterized as Chaucer's "masterpiece of patrician condescension."[14]

Certainly the New Criticism could not be troubled to examine Chaucer's lighthearted reference to the English rising (the so-called "Peasants' Revolt") of 1381,[15] or to note how insignificant the event seems when compared to the catastrophes that matter so much to the tale's narrator, including the burning of Rome, the fall of Troy, and the destruction of Carthage.[16] Chaucer's response to the rising continues to serve as a revealing test of the politics of Chaucer criticism. Even David Aers, who has done more than any contemporary medievalist to assert the social text of the medieval text, has been faulted for failing to historicize Chaucer's treatment of the episode.[17] The impact of patristic criticism for Old English literary culture was equally devastating. *Beowulf* was made safe for the ages when its controlling theme was traced to Gregory's *Moralia in Job*, and the same critical operation then performed on *Judith*.[18] But patristics influenced Anglo-Saxon studies as more than literary interpretation, since it spawned a host of projects seeking to demonstrate the Latin source of every text—and eventually every line—of Old English.[19] Valuable though patristic exegesis remains and useful though source studies are, it is nonetheless true that exegetical analysis only confirms in texts the attitudes toward Latin sources that scholars project onto a literary culture too narrowly imagined.

Crane saw patristic criticism as self-determining or proleptic. Similar observations have been made about criticism more generally. In a discussion of the rising of 1381, Pearsall points to a critical gesture he calls the "preconditioning of expectation," in which both the process and the result of inquiry "are deeply affected, if not determined, by the questions" the scholar asks.[20] Pearsall points out that it is impossible to examine an event from a position that is not an *interpretation* of the event. Indeed, Siegfried Wenzel regards the observations that interpretation precedes investigation and that "one's question will determine the answer one gets" as "fundamental even if by now banal."[21] The observation may have become commonplace, but its implications remain unappreciated. It is clear that scholars cannot recover or analyze texts "in their own terms," but it is not clear what alternatives are available. My suggestion is that the hermeneutic circle is not the dead end it seems to be. Critical self-awareness can be used as an excuse for abandoning method and discipline—the threat that theory, self-consciously applied, poses to some traditional scholars. But it is also a way to explain how "the preunderstanding of the reader," in Giles Gunn's terms, is used to obtain "a postunderstanding of the text."[22] If we consider that neither text nor reader is stationary and fixed, and that the exchange between them is open and the results of their interchange always incomplete, we will agree that claims to neutrality cannot be validated. One of the major differences between traditional and contemporary critical practice (inside or outside medieval studies) is that whereas traditional criticism maintains faith in the objectivity and neutrality of its procedures, contemporary criticism aggressively identifies the interests of scholars with the critical procedures to which they have recourse. It would, therefore, seem possible that prolepsis is not only an inescapable feature of critical discourse but also a strength rather than a weakness. If we regard critical methods as acts of remembering and, concomitantly, acts of forgetting, we can see how prolepsis can create an opportunity to assert critical difference against disciplinary identity.

Discipline and Identity

Traditional methods assume rather than assert an identity, not only for their subject matter but for the scholars who study it. They bestow value by remembering certain procedures and the texts to which they are applied;

they withhold value by forgetting, as if by accident, and thus prohibiting other procedures and consideration of the texts that evoke them. The preferences that dictated these acts of remembering and forgetting have constituted scholarly practices for so long that we are utterly habituated to them. The elaborate systems that codify and help to teach dead languages and extinct cultures seem to be natural developments so intimately connected to those languages and cultures as to determine what they will say to us.

Built on and out of traditional methods, traditional disciplines institutionalize the acts of remembering and forgetting that the methods dictate. Traditional disciplines seem to be free of subjectively determined value, however, and the oft-repeated point that they derive from theoretical assumptions of their own is an abstract, impersonal way of saying that these disciplines incorporate and instantiate the beliefs and preferences of persons. Recognizing the theoretical bases on which those disciplines rest requires that we examine their history and relate them in new ways not only to the cultures they abstract for purposes of academic inquiry but to the persons who presided over those abstractions. The wish of contemporary critics to find a place from which to speak, therefore, is also a desire to identify traditional criticism as a place from which others have been speaking. As we trace a discipline to the scholars who presided over its foundation, we move from a scholarly system to the personal status of those who created it out of the fabric of their own history and social experience.

The connection of scholar to scholarly subject and critical act is rarely obvious in traditional critical discourse. It is easy to see why this has been the case. An inquiry into the patristic sources of an Anglo-Saxon homily, for example, takes place only after a scholar has assigned some value to the text and thus motivated the search for its origins; eventually the results are formulated into verbal statements and published. This inquiry involves several theoretical decisions (about the use of one's time and creativity, among others) that are consolidated when the finished text is offered for publication; that consolidation elides motives and desires and other "subjective" characteristics of scholarship and subordinates them to the "objective" and externally verifiable features of scholarly publication. In this move from the private to the public the details of the private moment are shielded. Although it represents only part of the inquiry that produced the publication, published work is a paradigm for other scholars, a standard against which all work will be judged. The paradigm suits the established scholars who are accustomed to the discursive conventions of the profession. But scholars whose private decisions about the value of scholarship and criticism differ from the norm may find traditional public forums inhospitable and (rightly) seek another place from which to speak.

Many forms of contemporary criticism focus on the relationship between private and public networks of ideological and social values. Feminist
models of criticism, to take obvious examples, relate the subordination of
women in literature to masculine domination of professional criticism.
Marxist criticism undertakes the equally ambitious task of explaining how a
culture's resources are consumed as aesthetic pursuits reserved for the plea-
sures of a few (including scholars whose mission it is to explain high culture to the social classes that can afford to purchase and participate in it).
But these are only the obvious examples. Less specific projects, such as
reformation of the canon, likewise require focus on the relation between
preferred texts and the social status of those studying them. The unmasking
of critical identity is part of the rhetorical process of defamiliarizing academic and social institutions; that process is one of the demands made by
critics who seek to explain how the preferences of a few have come to
constitute the possibilities of the many.

The personal identities of individual scholars represented in the form
of class have played a conspicuous role in the establishment of the scholarly
disciplines medievalists observe. The conditions in which traditional disciplines were produced (that is, thought up or invented) in the last century
ensured that the disciplines themselves could not be too dissimilar, not only
because they were secured under the umbrella of humanities but because
the humanities were secured in the hands of a few scholars. So much discussed today, the humanities have unfolded into their complex modern
shape, Gunn argues, from three sources: Francis Bacon's attempt to define
"three knowledges"; later Renaissance associations of humanism with
knowledge of the classics; and post-enlightenment ideas of history as the
development of human perfection.[23] The vocabularies of various disciplines
within the humanities became increasingly distinct as the disciplines became professional, but the disciplines themselves, in large part because of
the circumstances of their historical development, continue to reflect and
reinforce the classification systems and class attitudes of their founders. We
can see these attitudes emerging in history, English, and philosophy in the
United States in the last century.

The early stages of the development of professional historiography in
the United States were powerfully influenced by "patricians," gentlemen
scholars who published important histories of the nation; among them were
Theodore Roosevelt and Henry Adams. The first professional historians who
assumed the role of these disciplinary founders like them "entered through
the gates of the modern university into the earnest and confident world of
the aristocracy of culture" and espoused the same "high-minded conservatism of the patrician historians."[24] Gerald Graff, Richard Ohmann, and
others have demonstrated how language departments, including the English

Department, took shape under the guidance of a few influential scholars whose moral and social outlook shaped the professional endeavors of generations.[25] These developments were not unique to American education, of course; R. Howard Bloch has shown comparable features in the development of Romance philology and Old French.[26] The focus on aristocratic culture that until recently dominated medieval studies is, I believe, in considerable part due to the aristocratic views of their own culture that the founders of the disciplines shared.

The disciplinary founders had more on their minds than conservatism, nationalism, and cultural elitism. They were also motivated by fear of the institutional power of the natural sciences and took defensive measures to professionalize and organize their own disciplines accordingly. English and history were not alone. In a persuasive critique of the limiting effects of professionalization on academic inquiry, Bruce Wilshire has recently demonstrated how reaction to the professionalization of the natural sciences helped to structure the American Philosophical Association. Scientists exchanged views and examined research at annual meetings, thereby demonstrating progress in their work. Professionalism directed the attention of the disciplines away from the university (the meeting place of the disciplines) toward a national audience of scholars unique to each discipline.[27] Annual meetings eventually became central to the professional activity of all the disciplines, but as marketplaces for jobseekers, not as markets for ideas. The demand for interdisciplinary studies that has characterized the last two decades testifies not only to the success with which the disciplines within the humanities have been narrowed as they have been professionalized, but to the sterility of the results.

Disciplines in the humanities are excellent examples of discursive formations that conceal the conditions and interests that preside over them.[28] They are systems of valuation that have become standardized. Drawing attention to the social conditions outside literary study that precondition interpretation (that is, that determine interpretation in proleptic fashion), Marxist critic John Frow identifies a "sleight of hand by which particular class-specific discourses of value elevate their criteria of judgment into universally normative principles which can be appealed to against the criteria of other, contradictory discourses of value."[29] The exclusiveness of the "class-specific discourses" of literary criticism is most obviously manifest in the proportions between the number of texts available for analysis in any given literary period and the number critics actually write about and teach. Likewise the procedures of criticism are designed to exclude certain responses and styles of writing that were set aside in my education because they were "personal" and "subjective." These are the very kinds of writing that reveal identity; by suppressing them—the classic example, perhaps, is the use of the first person pronoun in professional writing—the discourse of the disciplines forces writers to speak in a communal, institutional voice rather than in voices of their own.

The individual nature of each discipline is not established by the individuality of the scholars who practice it; rather, the distinguishing features of the discipline are its specialized vocabulary and the limits of its subject area. Each is a field with its own procedures and with a governing hierarchy to enforce its exclusiveness. "Instead of constructing arguments for their general relevance," Gunn writes of the humanities, "humanists have mounted arguments for their special uniqueness."[30] Such arguments were necessary for institutional reasons, if for no other. In order to justify their places, disciplines obviously had to demonstrate their differences from each other. One of the last to do so in the humanities was literary criticism. The classical assertion of the independent status of systematic criticism is perhaps Northrop Frye's. "The first thing the literary critic has to do," wrote Frye in *Anatomy of Criticism*, "is to read literature, to make an inductive survey of his own field and let his critical principles shape themselves solely out of his knowledge of that field. Critical principles cannot be taken over ready-made from theology, philosophy, politics, science, or any combination of these." Frye's demand that critical principles be derived from literature itself plainly asserted a claim of scientific status for criticism. In search of the "scientific element" in criticism, he wrote, "The presence of science in any subject changes its character from the casual to the causal, from the random and intuitive to the systematic, as well as safeguarding the integrity of that subject from external invasions."[31]

Frye's emphasis on systematic criticism and on the defense of one's territory from invasion recalls both Kemble, the first English Anglo-Saxonist to believe in system, and Sweet, the besieged scholar wary of invasion and protective of his territory. Frye's statement demonstrates the weaknesses of both the territorial imperative and the belief in system. The disciplines he conceptualized were to be distinct, each constituting a field and an independent realm. Two problems trouble his claim for a scientifically based literary criticism. The first is that disciplines must rely on assumed interdisciplinary differences in order to maintain their individual identities. Yet those differences were created by nothing other than the identifying procedures of the disciplines themselves.

The second problem is lack of historical consciousness. The disciplines seem to transcend time and place, always to have existed as distinct areas that could be (or must at some time have been) named by those able to stand outside of them and to see them collectively as a unity of knowledge. But there is, of course, no such place in which to stand or from which to speak: no one could, a century ago, see the disciplines arrayed like so many patches in a quilt on a clothesline or like so many fields in a landscape viewed from aloft. Everyone who identified a discipline was already speaking from within a discipline or construct of knowledge, even if it had yet to find a name (as literary criticism had yet to do). Frye could imagine disciplines as isolated but contiguous fields only because he thought he spoke outside the limits of any of them. He was writing in 1957, a point at which the failure of the disciplines to achieve integrated views of knowledge was widely recognized and also a point at which the romance of interdisciplinary studies had already begun.

Interdisciplinarity and Difference

In a recent essay tracing the application of the word "interdisciplinary" from its apparent beginnings to the present, Roberta Frank notes that in the beginning "interdisciplinary" was a vague concept that a few people used tentatively. In the present, clearly, it is still a vague concept, but it is now used—resolutely—by nearly everybody. The term "interdisciplinary" was coined in the 1920s to describe the lofty ideal of cooperation in intellectual ventures; by the mid-1980s, it had become far more basic. A writer in a Canadian journal declared that "life" itself was interdisciplinary, while the Association of American Colleges, not to be outdone, announced that "real life" had achieved the same status.[32] Since the Middle Ages themselves were interdisciplinary, medieval studies were particularly ripe for interdisciplinary study.[33] Thus a term created to promote the cooperation of various scholarly specializations was, as these specializations became more and more elaborate and more remote from one another, inevitably reduced to the pious asseveration that specializations should work together in the *academy* because they worked together in *life*. In life? This self-congratulatory folly shows how scholars can use the signifying practices of theory and method to create what they study and then try to justify those practices by insisting that they have a reality outside and independent of that which has just been created for them.

Calling attention to the artificiality and hollowness of interdisciplinary claims, Frank points to scholarly preference for the word *discipline* over *field*. This preference is explained, she says, because *discipline* sounds precise and scientific, while a *field*, with its "mud, cows, and corn" does not.[34] But the "field" significantly contributes to the false security of "interdisciplinary" work, for the "field" image illustrates the basic misconception at the heart of interdisciplinary claims. That misconception is that different academic subjects are different in essence because they are different in name. Their differences in name, however, are little more than the result of history; there is nothing essential about them. In only a few decades, Anglo-Saxon England has been divided up and parceled out according to what we now recognize as disciplines: objects to archaeology, illustrations to art history, some texts (artistic) to literature, others (utilitarian) to history, behavior to sociology, and so forth. Middle English culture, thus subdivided and categorized, was soon recognizable only as belonging to individual disciplines whose differences it is the duty of the interdisciplinarians to overcome as they reintegrate the fields and the vocabularies.

The academy both insists that the disciplines are different and laments that they are not more similar. This illusion of difference is perpetuated by Graff's principle of "coverage," according to which each discipline claims a different territory and controls it with "fieldspeak,"[35] a technical language that sustains the illusion of disciplinary difference at a profound, even scientific level. "Fields are constructed by an initial attention to the borders which demarcate them," Frow writes; "but the visibility of limits then tends to be replaced by the details of rules derived from the founding principles."[36] As individual disciplines turned inward to debates about methodology determined by, but also taking for granted, borders already established, the stuff of internecine warfare became their real if not their ostensible subject. The result was that each discipline's discourse became ever more rarified and remote not only from that of other disciplines, but also from the world of lived experience, past or present.

The need to break down disciplinary barriers is widely acknowledged, and so is the general failure of traditional cooperative ventures between disciplines to achieve interdisciplinary learning. Seeking an alternative for Anglo-Saxonists, I have chosen two disciplines that constitute "two languages" as this volume uses the motif. They are literary criticism and archaeology, which I will use to show how the analysis of material culture and social relations in literary texts can bring literary critics and archaeologists together. Archaeology and literary criticism both study and produce documents and monuments; documents and monuments create the disciplinary paradigms common to both forms of inquiry and demonstrate the relationship between them in the last century, when these disciplines were taking shape. At that time, scholars began their careers in Anglo-Saxon studies as "antiquaries" interested in archaeology. Archaeology was not regarded as scientific; instead, it was defined as the analysis of ancient monuments in their artistic aspect. It was an aesthetic evaluation that followed geology, paleontology, and anthropology.[37] Archaeology was a way to focus on first impressions of material culture that inspired later work with language and texts. This paradigm of amateurism and professionalism, which also juxtaposes analysis of physical remains and literary records, speaks to us most pointedly in Kemble's life, for he reversed it, beginning as a philologist and ending as an archaeologist and an antiquary.[38] The divorce between texts and objects, the untheorized conjunction of documents and monuments, is as apparent in Old English scholarship as the connections between them are obvious in the corpus. The most famous case is the text of *The Dream of the Rood*, found both on the Ruthwell Cross and in *The Vercelli Book*. Humbler examples are abundant: the writing on the Franks Casket, inscriptions on doorways, runes on pieces of wood, and some tapestries are both texts and objects, documents as well as monuments. But bound by disciplinary traditions and modern ideas of genre, Anglo-Saxon literary criticism has yet to find a way to deal with writing on objects, including runes. The standard bibliography of Anglo-Saxon scholarship omits studies of runic and non-runic inscriptions, of detached (as opposed to continuous) glosses, and of genealogies. The authors cite as justification the view of Richard Wülker who, in 1885, excluded from his history of Old English literature certain texts "because they have no independent interest."[39] Texts having no "independent interest" are those whose interpretation depends on extra-literary evidence. Wülker was not, obviously, anticipating a kind of criticism that did not "go outside the text," but his remark about independent interest reinforces the separation of literary from nonliterary texts. The differentiation, articulated within the field of Anglo-Saxon literature, effectively cuts off from consideration a part of the corpus of writing in Old English; that act reinforces a distinction between "literature" and "text," or even "writing," with significant consequences for our understanding of Anglo-Saxon culture.

Archaeology and Deconstruction

As a theoretical stimulus to rethinking the disciplinary missions of both literary criticism and archaeology through the concept of cultural studies, I will look at recent attempts by archaeologists to interpret literary theory. Michel Foucault's contrast between documents and monuments offers a way to negotiate the difference between the materiality of texts and the textuality of objects. I will then use the case of *Beowulf* and the Sutton Hoo ship burial to focus on the conjunction of literary and archaeological disciplines.[40]

Recent studies of the theory of archaeology show how the language of literary theory is useful in describing material cultural formations. Ian Hodder's *Reading the Past*, for example, indicates kinship with literary theory in its title and examines Habermas, Adorno, and others. Hodder's is merely a sketch of theoretical problems, but its argument for theoretical self-consciousness is strong.[41] C. J. Arnold's criticism of the "artifact-based" nature of Anglo-Saxon archaeology also notes the beginning of theoretical discussion amid traditional art-historical emphasis.[42] But among the current books manifesting a revision of traditional archaeological theory none is more striking than a pair by Michael Shanks and Christopher Tilley; both works analyze the relationship of disciplinarity to identity and difference.[43] In order to distinguish a discipline from an interdiscipline, they consider the relationship of identity to difference and show that disciplines focus on the identity of objects and texts within their own categories. Like archaeologists, as they sift and classify data, scholars in all disciplines fit their materials into abstract categories or typologies. In this operation, the identity of a specific typological category will require that some data be left to one side as contingent. "Such a typological framework systematically excludes *difference* and instead asserts *identity*," Shanks and Tilley write. The identity of all members of one class allows them to be differentiated from other classes. "However, difference is not to be derived from the supposed identity of differential social forms—it makes these abstract categories possible in the first place."[44]

Whether they are seen as neutral categories ("scientific" in the modern sense) or categories that correspond to features inherent in the material being categorized and described (and hence historically related to the cultures under study), typologies are cultural paradigms within which historical data are reconstructed. Our notion of the "Anglo-Saxon king," the "Anglo-Saxon hero," and the Old English elegy are all products of such categorization. It is important not simply to call these terms "categories"; they are systems of organizing data and texts that are themselves part of larger social constructs. Each typology requires and indeed demands an attitude toward the history and cultures of the past; each conceals an attitude toward the scholar's own time.

Although the construction of disciplinary identity is only possible in the presence of recognized difference, difference cannot, Shanks and Tilley note, be derived from the identity it makes possible. The idea of "difference" as part of disciplinary identity deconstructs the possibility of rigid intellectual categories, not only difference within a given discipline but difference between two disciplines, the difference that *defines* them. In order to assess the meaning of scholarly self-reflexivity, we can use the concept of typologies to describe both the *methods* by which all disciplines sort and classify evidence and the *historical development* of those methods. How did an individual discipline know what was proper to it and what was not? How did the discipline decide what belonged to it and what did not? The answer I have suggested above is that no one knew, but that someone somewhere began to take action, to classify and to label, and that his (I am sure of "his") decisions, made public, were repeated once, then many times, and finally came to constitute both a professional vocabulary and an institutionalized norm.

Discussing the typology used to explain evolutionary theory, Shanks and Tilley write that it casts history as "an overall intelligible unity and continuum," or what I would call a unified concept conforming to the paradigm of progress.[45] This notion of progress, the idea that human history moves forward without a significant disruption from age to age, changing inevitably as new discoveries are made, posits the very harmony and logic to the study of the past that study of the past is supposed to interrogate. Belief in the inevitability of progress shines forth from records of meetings of the Modern Language Association and from the works of numerous nineteenth-century American historians.[46] The disciplines of Anglo-Saxon studies cooperate so well because they share the same underlying assumptions about history and culture. The most important of those assumptions is that Anglo-Saxon England was a culture on its way to becoming our culture. That is why it made progress from pagan to Christian, from oral to lettered, from illiterate to literate, from chaos to order.

Some of the most powerful typologies are virtually identical across the disciplines of medieval studies and can therefore been seen as homologies. The common methodological base of the disciplines in the humanities is one reason why they bear out interpretive paradigms matching in structure, position, and character. Rather than several disciplines that do different things, the humanities are a vast network of homologous enterprises that do the same thing in several ways. Disciplines are inadequate not because none of them can include all evidence relevant to certain issues; indeed, such limitation—that is, difference—is the very reason disciplines are perpetuated. Rather, the disciplines that together study medieval culture are inadequate because they all do the same thing, which is to bear out the views of the founding fathers, as it were, and all likewise fail to do other things, in particular to examine their first principles and their histories as disciplines. Traditional disciplinary versions of the Middle Ages re-created, over time, homologous systems of warfare, chivalry, aristocratic entertainment, shared (communally accepted) spiritual values, and consumption without production. The reigning syntheses favor aristocratic values and indeed have created the impression that chivalry itself *was* the Middle Ages, a time of lords, ladies, tournaments, and religious piety. Whether courtly love was a social phenomenon or a literary ideal matters less than that the paradigms of "courtly love" are uniformly identified by literary critics and historians. What scholarship debates is the reality of the phenomenon; the patterns in which it dispersed social and sexual energy are agreed on. Even the most astute studies of courtliness, in my view—for example, C. Stephen Jaeger's *The Origins of Courtliness*[47]—investigate the difference between courtly lit-

erature and the "reality" of courtly ideal within unquestioned and traditional social hierarchies. The difference between sources and the "reality"
they reflect, a subject of endless dispute, seems almost invariably to matter
more than that traditional disciplines all construct the same hierarchical
models. "Interdisciplinary" research conducted in the presence of such disciplinary identity and homology—that is, in the absence of difference—is
redundant if not tautological. It is not unexpected we must turn to Marxist
critics to find challenges to such inquiry. An example is Michael Nerlich's
Ideology of Adventure, which traces the development of romance to mercan-
tilism and warfare and shows the mutually determining effect of literature
on a social class—knights whose profession was becoming obsolete—and
representation of that class's status in literature.[48]

Scholars of Middle English are familiar with the power of *The Knight's
Tale* to create aristocratic views of Chaucer's time. In matters of social
representation, medieval texts are less exclusive than their traditional readers. The texts represent multiple cultural forms—whether they draw our
attention to them or not—and sometimes even assert them against each
other. We can take, for example, that point in the tale when Arcite, who
wished to return to Emily in Athens, "chaunged his array, / And cladde
hym as a povre laborer." Accompanied by a squire "disguised povrely as he
was," he came to Athens to carry water, chop wood, and rise in the Athe-
nian court. It was lucky for Arcite that his nobility of character survived the
illusion he perpetrated; he received the income to which he was accustomed
("men broghte him out of his contree, / From yeer to yeer, ful pryvely his
rente").[49] Exiled from love, he reappeared as a laborer, only to complete
the facile correlation of happiness with social standing by reclaiming love
in triumph, however brief, as the knight he really was, and without having
to bear for long the inconveniences associated with the life of manual labor
he feigns.

An appreciation of material production and the regulation of labor in-
tensifies the reader's awareness of the artificial isolation in which the tale
suspends its aristocratic subjects, isolated from the broad social spectrum in
which they are situated and which, as in the example I have given, sometimes asserts its complexity anyway. Aers notes the power of a Chaucerian
commonplace in the *Parlement of Foules*: "For out of olde feldes, as men
seyth, / Cometh al this newe corn from yer to yere." Just as Chaucer describes agricultural processes as purely natural, without demands on the
necessary human agents (that is, describes production without labor), Chau-
cerians, Aers says, complete a comparably authoritarian gesture by failing
to recognize Chaucer's obvious indifference to the processes of production—the productivity, after all, from whence Dryden's "God's plenty"
stemmed.[50] Criticism of *Beowulf* and archaeological discussions relating the

poem to the Sutton Hoo burial mound also reveal a focus on aristocratic levels of culture, as I will show.

In their effort to disrupt these comfortable typologies, Shanks and Tilley theorize archaeology and the archaeological tradition in terms of Gadamerian hermeneutics. They point to a framework valuable to scholars in both disciplines who wish to integrate the study of texts with the analysis of material culture. In *Re-Constructing Archaeology,* Shanks and Tilley explore the "rhetoric" of archaeology as "re-creation" of the past and as "textual discourse." They describe archaeology as hermeneutic, "something done in the present" that establishes a relationship with what happened in the past. Re-creating the past, they write, "is a practice which reveals the author, the subject in the present." Denying the possibility of reflecting the past "as exactly as possible," they argue that to "reproduce the past 'as it was', to relive the past as a reflection is to produce an image which hides the observing present." But they note that archaeologists often do not seek to relive the past in order to reproduce it; instead, they observe the past in order to write about it.[51] The same observation must be made about those who study the literatures of the past: they do so not to relive them or re-create them but to render them as critical texts. The texts can then be analyzed within disciplinary boundaries that conceal the identities of those at work observing in the present.

Documents and Monuments

In their attempt to reconceptualize archaeology as a discipline that is both oppositional and political, Shanks and Tilley seize on Foucault in order to distinguish the "*universalizing* intellectual" who speaks from within the discursive tradition from the "*specific* intellectual" who struggles against tradition.[52] Both archaeology and literary criticism must be seen as academic disciplines within the larger field of discourse, not simply as methods for disclosing truth but, in the Foucauldian sense, as attempts to construct truth. In *The Discourse on Language,* Foucault includes disciplines among the principles that limit discourse. Since my subject is the exclusiveness of the disciplines that constitute medieval studies, I will define exclusion in terms Foucault used to discuss the systems that regulate discourse. Foucault sets his statements about disciplines not among the external forces governing discourses, although that is where, among the "prodigious machinery of the will to truth, with its vocation of exclusion," the disciplines could be located, but among the internal forces that constrain discourse, rules that concern "the principles of classification, ordering and distribution" and hence limit "the hazards of discourse." These rules are three: commentary (the creation of new texts out of old texts); the author ("he who implants, into the troublesome language of fiction, its unities, its coherence, its links with reality"); and disciplines, which act in opposition both to authors and to commentary.[53]

Commentary demands the repetition of meaning and statements about texts; the author principle limits discourse by imposing individual identity on it. Disciplines limit discourse differently. The rules of a discipline do not require an author, since they constitute "a sort of anonymous system, freely available to whoever wishes, or whoever is able to make use of them [the discipline's rules and methods], without there being any question of their meaning or their validity being derived *from whoever happened to invent them*" (emphasis mine). Unlike commentaries, which require repetition, disciplines take as the point of departure "that which is required for the construction of new statements. For a discipline to exist, there must be the possibility for formulating—and of doing so ad infinitum—fresh propositions." But disciplines require that propositions "fit into a certain type of theoretical field" so that they can be recognized as belonging to a particular discipline.[54]

"Disciplines constitute a system of control in the production of discourse, fixing its limits through the action of an identity taking the form of a permanent reactivation of the rules," Foucault writes.[55] Disciplines constrain, although not by fixing the number of statements that may be made within them. Rather they do so by ensuring that new statements can continue to be made and recognized as relevant to the discipline, but only so long as they fall within recognized parameters or paradigms. The discussion of monuments, documents, and "archaeology" by Foucault in *The Archaeology of Knowledge* undertakes "the questioning of the *document*." My interpretation of Foucault focuses on his analysis of cultural memory, an idea with romantic potential as a humanist ideal that Foucault, not unexpectedly, firmly resists. History "has taken as its primary task, not the interpretation of the document, nor the attempt to decide whether it is telling the truth or what is its expressive value, but to work on it from within and to develop it," analyzing it minutely and organizing it into series and relations. Thus the document "is no longer for history an inert material through which it tries to reconstitute what men have done or said, the events of which only the trace remains; history is now trying to define within the documentary material itself unities, totalities, series, relations." Historians have become accustomed to using documents as a memory bank from which to reconstitute the past, "an age-old collective consciousness that made use of material documents to refresh its memory."[56]

In juxtaposing the document to the "monument," Foucault suggests that traditional history "undertook to 'memorize' the *monuments* of the past, transform them into *documents,* and lend speech to those traces which, in themselves, are often not verbal." He adds that "in our time, history is that which transforms *documents* into *monuments*" and tries to organize "a mass of elements" into groups and relate them to one another "to form totalities":

> There was a time when archaeology, as a discipline devoted to silent monuments, inert traces, objects without context, and things left by the past, aspired to the condition of history, and attained meaning only through the restitution of a historical discourse; it might be said, to play on words a little, that in our time history aspires to the condition of archaeology, to the intrinsic description of the monument.[57]

Unities of thought—all the significant developments or "turning points" that give the shape of progress to the history of ideas—should not, then, be seen from the outside, where the historian, at the end (or culmination) of the story, stands. Documents should not be humanized or be said to "speak" for the past but should be seen internally instead; archaeology, a metaphor for seeing from within and looking inside, is the basis for "intrinsic description." Foucault sees the document as an impersonal monument—Mark Poster calls this his "strategy of dehumanization"—and makes the familiar (that is, the easily recognized type or pattern) appear strange.[58]

In order to make history appear strange, the historian must see its discontinuities. "For history in its classical form, the discontinuous was both the given and the unthinkable: the raw material of history, which presented itself in the form of dispersed events," which had "to be rearranged, reduced, effaced in order to reveal the continuity of events."[59] The reductions that made possible the writing of history in the past are themselves made possible by the forms that language gives to consciousness in any era; they simultaneously enable speaking certain things and prohibit speaking other things. "Speaking is a repressive act," writes Hayden White in an important commentary on Foucault, "identifiable as a specific form of repression by the area of experience that it consigns to silence."[60] The continuities of traditional history have been created by suppressing the elements that contradicted them. In order to approach the monument from the inside, and to read the documentary record from the inside, one must enter into the epistemological assumptions used by historians in various epochs to constitute truth, harmony, and the intellectual and social progress that shaped "the continuity of events" as they would come to appear from the outside. In other words, before we can describe traditional disciplines as they are internally constituted, we must attempt to discover those elements repressed when the disciplines were formed.

I would like to juxtapose Foucault's discussion of monuments and documents with the statements about documents and monuments made by John Earle, who published *The Deeds of "Beowulf"* in 1892, accompanying his prose paraphrase of the poem with a splendid history of criticism up to Earle's time. Earle described the impression of the first English critic of *Beowulf*, John Josias Conybeare, who regarded *Beowulf* as a text written long after its hero's death. Earle described the scholar approaching the poem:

> So, like a wise antiquarian who scans some huge and heavy monument of Pre-historic date, he feels that this strange and lonely relic belongs to a world of ideas with which he is unacquainted, that within the range of his knowledge there is no pedestal for it—he may describe, delineate, he may wonder, and even enjoy, but he cannot explain it. There is, however, a difference between a monument in stone and a monument in language. Of the latter we can at least say to what race it belongs, it bears in each lineament the family stamp.[61]

Beowulf, in Earle's mind, was knowable because it belonged to *his* language family. Earle regarded the physical monument—the archaeologist's focus—as an unknowable relic from "a world of ideas with which he is unacquainted," a relic lacking a "pedestal" that would allow him to fix, gaze up at, and finally explain it. Earle's comment reverses Foucault's relation of the document and the monument; Earle used language (documents) as vehicles of familiarization and did not equate documents and monuments as indices of Anglo-Saxon culture: for him, the document was familiar, the monument strange. The forms of language could be recognized; they could make consciousness clear. This is not so for Foucault; he did not wish to read monuments through documents (which seems to have been Earle's wish) but to see documents as monuments in order to depersonalize them and make them unfamiliar, "unvoiced," even authorless.

Earle, let us recall, thought that the literary critic was less limited than the scholar of material culture, and he was, in the main, right: the textual scholar can be unencumbered by the world if he or she chooses, but this does not mean that the object (the text) is not tampered with. Archaeologists seem well aware of the reconstructive dangers of discipline. As Martin Biddle reminded Anglo-Saxonists visiting an excavation at Repton in 1985, archaeology not only records the importance of what it studies but also "inevitably removes and destroys" the evidence it awakens to new life.[62] Martin Carver, however, stresses that the archaeologist can no longer "afford to disturb the bones of our ancestors under the mantle of serendipity or academic intuition."[63] That is, monuments (buried or otherwise) cannot be sacrificed to produce (explanatory) texts; yet how else are they to be known, in the Foucauldian sense, through internal or archaeological description? We know that even texts are not safe. Textual monuments are less likely to be scraped than added on to: textual editing more frequently patches its monuments, making them comprehensible by filling their gaps and smoothing their irregularities. One can take the editorial history of almost any medieval text—*Beowulf, The Canterbury Tales, Piers Plowman*—as a case in point.

Foucault's monument and document, impersonal and unromantic, prohibit the ideal seen in Earle's image of the remote, inaccessible monument and the accessible document. We cannot experience a postmodern repetition of the nineteenth-century paradigm in which material culture and literary culture were so closely related that scholars versed (so to speak) in one also knew the other. Scholarly specialization has seen to it that literary criticism and archaeology moved apart, but only a certain distance apart, and that they continued in parallel rather than converging directions. Critical theory offers the opportunity to rejoin these disciplines at a significant level, to examine their intersections and connections; theory offers us a beginning in the physical objects that archaeology and literary criticism study.

Beowulf and Sutton Hoo

An example of how archaeology and literary criticism have cooperated in the past in interdisciplinary endeavors that produced identical results emerges in the Sutton Hoo ship burial and its impact on criticism of *Beowulf*. This interaction of material culture with a text resulted not in interdisciplinary investigation but rather in the confirmation of an aristocratic paradigm already existing in homologous relationship in the two disciplines. The evidence of Sutton Hoo has been read narrowly by both archaeologists and literary critics, with selective attention if any to social and cultural agency and power relationships.

The most famous and influential example relating archaeology to literature is C. L. Wrenn's essay on *Beowulf* scholarship up to 1958 in his revision of Chambers's introduction to *Beowulf*. Wrenn regarded the discovery of Sutton Hoo as "the most important happening" since Thorkelin made a transcript of the *Beowulf* manuscript and first published the poem,[64] a significant equation of textual and material evidence. Wrenn reads *Beowulf* in the light of Sutton Hoo and reads Sutton Hoo in the light of *Beowulf*, a classic version of the hermeneutic circle, but not the first in Anglo-Saxon studies. The 1910 discovery of the burial mound of Ottar Vendel-Crow prompted Birger Nerman, and then R. W. Chambers himself, to use archaeological evidence to explain the struggles between the Geatas and the Swedes in *Beowulf,* and then used the chronology of *Beowulf* (none too certain!) to establish the position of Sweden as "the oldest of all European kingdoms." It was not Wrenn in 1958, but Sune Lindqvist, in 1948, who established the most important relationship between the poem and the find; Lindqvist enthusiastically remarked of *Beowulf* and Sutton Hoo that "both become the clearer by the comparison."[65]

It is not easy to see how either of two things can become clearer by comparison only to the other; there must be a third term in this equation, a place where they are brought together, compared, and found compatible. The "third term," as I will call it, is a typological concept created by the critic and influenced by his or her "preunderstanding," to use Gunn's term for it, that produces the "postunderstanding of the text" (whether material object or written).[66] The typological preconception is a classification system shaped by the social conditions of the scholar. Those conditions, whether analyzed as ideology (and pursued through Marxism) or desire (and pursued in a Foucauldian or psychoanalytic way), are not neutral; unlike intellectual preconceptions, which can be seen as "commonplaces" or "traditions" or "paradigms," social conditions are social relations, specific and individual and historical. Typologies emerge from intellectual and social conditions. It is important to understand that they answer questions before they are asked: they explain problems proleptically (that is, before they are recognized as problems). It is equally important to understand that as they create expectations for patterns of change and continuity, and assist scholars in establishing the relationships of pieces of evidence to one another, they express the interests of larger social schema.

Wrenn, Lindqvist, and others found the evidence of the poem and of the burial compatible because both the poem and the archaeological evidence already conformed to overriding ideas of Anglo-Saxon England and its culture that these scholars accepted—and, one wants to say, that "accepted" them, or at least received their imprint. The typology of Anglo-Saxon culture most familiar to us, since it was preferred by many of the culture's early historians and archaeologists, is the world of the epic, of aristocracy, of Germanic antiquity folded into monastic learning, of pagan and Christian combined. The Sutton Hoo artifacts point to aristocratic culture; *Beowulf* points the same way. That is why so many of these comparisons focus on armor and decoration and gold, with the splendor that these objects imparted to the words in the poem. Sutton Hoo furnished "the lavish world of the poem," as Patrick Wormald calls it, with "the material deposits of seventh-century Britain."[67]

The treasures of Sutton Hoo are still a powerful temptation to furnish Anglo-Saxon kingship with splendors described rather generically in

Beowulf. The ideological force of a magnificent material culture, even incompletely represented, is difficult to resist. Eager to redeem Anglo-Saxon England from its reputation for barbarism, we glory in the regalia that testify to sophisticated taste and craftsmanship. We trace treasures to the aristocratic milieu of *Beowulf,* whether or not they illustrate it, as Wrenn thought them to do, and use them to reinforce the gaze of the poem itself on the highest levels of the culture. Swords, helmets, royal standards, drinking bowls, and the little harp are the objects that Wrenn lavishes attention on, all because they are also important in *Beowulf.* Best of all, the artifacts are abundantly multicultural (and therefore interdisciplinary): silver spoons in Greek majuscule attesting to Christian belief, Merovingian coins, Swedish work on the sword, and so forth. Sutton Hoo supplies evidence for nearly every cultural perspective on Anglo-Saxon England that has been taken, and so fuels contradictory arguments about the poem's genesis (not to mention the culture's), new statements, in the Foucauldian sense, desired because they attest to professional progress without generating new paradigms. The neglect of the rest of the culture, and of theoretical development in particular, is nicely summed up by Arnold's comment that ''the Sutton Hoo harp has been played while the archaeological world burned.''[68]

Reconceptualization of disciplinary thinking is made possible if disciplines are seen as ways of reading rather than as collections of fact on which interpretations or readings rest. If we are not satisfied with the thoroughness and variety of the traditional readings enacted by traditional disciplines, we must have recourse to other ways of reading and of seeing both medieval evidence and the systems that evaluate and interpret it; we will have to defamiliarize the reigning syntheses with languages that are newly acquired. In order to make the familiar strange—not merely to make it ''new,'' but to show that the familiar is more exclusive and limited than we have thought—the familiar must be re-learned and the familiar languages of traditional disciplines must be disrupted. Informed by poststructuralist criticism, cultural studies has the potential to accomplish what interdisciplinary studies promised; it can achieve a rethinking of disciplinary limits both because it examines the history of disciplines and because it is oppositional in aim. Cultural studies focus on the political nature of the structural, structuring effects of the relationship between scholars and their subjects. The disruption of disciplinary discourse, the avowed objective of cultural studies, is achieved by asserting difference in place of identity and diversity against disciplinary uniformity.

In order to see medieval studies as a form of cultural studies, it is necessary to look from the uniform rules of disciplines to the moments of their formation and institutionalization of the preferences and interests of those who created them. Exploration of the history of the disciplines is, I submit, the only way to balance the power of these founding scholars and to make their paradigms responsive to the interests of new readers. I take interest to mean both curiosity about something and an investment of ego in exploring it; this interest needs to be identified both as it is, and has long been, expressed and enacted in the texts we discuss, and as it is expressed in our scholarly methods and choice of subjects. We cannot uncover interest at either level by staying within the field of English literature and criticism, however. Rather than pursue the argument in terms of the rules of this discipline, I would like to stop at the border between this criticism and archaeology—a line of contact at many points—in order to examine statements about the line between criticism and cultural studies. This is the line between a field that analyzes texts and defines contexts in opposition to texts, and a field in which the construction of such oppositions is more important than the oppositions themselves.

In "What is Cultural Studies Anyway?" Richard Johnson elaborates on the relationship between cultural studies and literary criticism.[69] Cultural studies, he thinks, can reach outside the narrow limits imposed on texts by either traditional historical critical methods or contemporary criticism. Johnson recognizes the usefulness of textual concepts as paradigms for cultural criticism. At the same time, he points to the limiting effect of such analysis and its capacity to abstract texts from cultural moments and cultural relations and to transform them into objects for reading and interpretation. Cultural moments and concrete aspects of culture "disappear into a reading of the text." Johnson objects to the narrowly textual interpretation of both traditional and contemporary methods. He criticizes both formalism, which he describes as "the abstraction of texts" from other moments in culture, and "structuralist foreshortening," a term he uses to designate ways in which texts can be reduced to certain literary paradigms and isolated from social contexts. Of structuralist and poststructuralist methods, he says,

> They are limited, in a very fundamental way, by staying within the terms of textual analysis. In so far as they go beyond it, they subordinate other moments *to* textual analysis. In particular they tend to neglect questions of the production of cultural forms or their larger social organisation, or reduce questions of production to the "productivity" (I would say "capacity to produce") of the already existing systems of signification, that is the formal languages or codes. They also tend to neglect questions of readership, or subordinate them to the competencies of a textual form of analysis.[70]

It is necessary to remember that the text is a powerful and active force only because it is a cultural phenomenon. Thus the object of cultural studies, Johnson writes, is not "the text, but *the social life of subjective forms* at each moment of their circulation" in the text (his emphasis).[71] Literary criticism—"textual analysis"—memorizes and textualizes only certain features of the culture it studies and is therefore reductive in ways that are political and hence culturally important. Certain social factors to which texts attest are eliminated from consideration and "forgotten" because they do not speak (or, rather, are not heard), in relevant ways, to (or by) dominant interests. But that process of elimination is rationalized because those factors are set outside the field of criticism: they belong to other disciplines and hence can be ignored. Literary criticism narrowed the scope of medieval studies by limiting its terrain to texts and by conceiving of texts in the most reductive way possible, as generic containers for language. Cultural studies require that we seek out the material reality that literary criticism has transformed and textualized.

Frow writes usefully about what Johnson calls "the social life of subjective forms." For Frow, "all social systems are semiotic systems." These systems transform information and impart to it exchange value that, in turn, endows "qualitatively different commodities with a symbolic equivalence and so permits their circulation as signs within a generalized equation."[72] Cultural studies not only see such systems operating within literature but see literature as part of them. Like Johnson, Frow stresses the "exemplary value" of literary study to other "discursively based disciplines." He quotes Leo Bersani's claim that "literature may not *have* much power, but it should certainly be read as a display of power" and seen as a "model of that play of complicity and resistance which characterizes the innumerable local confrontations of power in human life."[73] Frow's remark suggests a way to connect textual transformations of context to cultural displays of power. An example is Clifford Geertz's famous discussion of the Balanise cockfight, which he called a "means of expression" that neither relieved nor aroused passions but displayed them.[74] That texts (literary or otherwise, written or otherwise) neither merely relieve nor arouse passions but display power is a proposition that medieval studies, practiced as a form of cultural studies, will be able to explore. But first medieval studies will have to grapple with the theories of representation that, as both Gunn and Frow have demonstrated, connect aesthetics to the study of social forms and that show how power displays itself in texts.[75]

Cultural studies teach the meaning of dialogical modes of understanding that complicate the represented truths of monological discourse of our separate disciplines. "Once dialogism and polyphony are recognized as modes of textual production, monophonic authority is questioned, revealed to be characteristic of a science that has claimed to *represent* cultures."[76] The monologic voice of the scholarly discipline stands in sharp contrast to what we know, even while hearing them only partially, were the many voices of medieval culture. In the past philology has served to impose a single voice on scholarship in the present and hence on the past it studied. It could do so because as a discourse of power it was itself univocal: educated men of a single class, participating in a new cultural venture, were not likely to produce variety. Those who remembered English literature and who institutionalized their memory excluded that which differed from them and those in whom such memories lived, for those ideas and those persons seemed to belong to other parts of the social system and to have no place in Departments of English or History. As those interests were dismissed, the human actors they involved were silenced; the voices and interests of those silenced agents and acts constitute what I mean by "difference": they were deposited outside disciplinary boundaries during the process of disciplinary formation, the initial phases in particular. Scholarly aloofness, resting on the confident assumption of scientific principles that take form in disciplinary practices the critic has mastered, serves to keep the professional memory pure and to maintain the silence imposed on rejected principles and personal histories.[77] Scholarly objectivity, in other words, disguises the subjectivity of our predecessors and maintains their dominance. Thus it is that we speak, as traditional scholars, in the language and through the paradigms of the first academic professionals.

Academic disciplines can be seen as fixated on certain genres (epic), social levels (aristocratic), forms of memory (myth in particular), and the construction of massive, all-encompassing theories of knowledge. Cultural studies, by contrast, are rooted in ethnography, the study of diverse and remote cultures; keenly aware of the structuring effect of the scholar on his or her subject; and particularly concerned about "non-literary" genres and discourse.[78] Cultural studies address problems that traditional disciplines have ignored—or rather, that they have forgotten. Just as they assert the power of those who were, in traditional paradigms, both forgotten and powerless, women's studies and ethnic studies demonstrate the *in*adequacy of traditional disciplines, not their adequacy. This demonstration of the inadequacy of tradition undergirds and gives great strength to the cultural studies programs that undo them. What these programs undertake is not to duplicate the homologous structures reproduced within the paradigms of traditional disciplines, but to assert new paradigms against tradition.

Rather than study culture within only one "paradigm" and speak about culture in only one "language" (whether it be Marxism, patristics, source study, feminism, or codicology), we should investigate the potential for textual disciplines to explore material culture. We can make constructive use of the limitations of our discipline if we explore its border with another. We cannot speak of culture or academic discipline in only one language effectively because individual paradigms, self-explanatory and self-satisfying, have been constructed in order to eliminate the points of view that challenge them. Those paradigms may consist of syntheses of various critical approaches, but if all those approaches exclude material conditions from consideration, their focus is on the discipline's own rules rather than on a challenge to those rules and to the social and political views of the critics who practice them.

The City and the Village

We are, Paul Zumthor writes in *Speaking of the Middle Ages*, not tourists but archaeologists in the city of the Middle Ages. Zumthor's romantic claim is that our job is to piece together and to speculate on the relationship of such things "with enough sensitivity to discern where that now broken line was leading, to see which way was pointed that sculpted arrow you just picked up among the thorns."[79] This evocation of a literary critic's speculation about contact with material culture is striking in its use of an urban reference for medieval culture and a weapon as an object of interest. Cities and courts are much more impressive than whatever was around them and outside them, and their activities were recorded while others' were not. Zumthor's comment suggests a project in which the urban and aristocratic signs that fascinate medieval studies would be interpreted in the context of cultural sign systems in which aristocratic consumption and urban variety were joined to the manual labor on which they were based.

Such a project, realized as a seminar, would rest on double concepts, with aristocratic evidence inseparable from its social relations and various relations of production. These relations would replace the typological formations that have up to now so often subsumed concrete data (objects or texts) into abstract systems. Traditional disciplinary concepts posit social systems around objects and texts, but often with little reference either to the constructedness—the unexamined historical character—of the system (the history of the discipline) or the "social life" in which the texts and objects functioned as displays of power. Inquiry into "aristocracy," as the concept is constituted by history, archaeology, literary criticism, and political science, would include more than kings and queens: it would direct our attention to nonaristocratic levels and manual labor without which the aristocracy could not have survived. We would examine the political theory of kingship; we would examine narratives of royal force, including chronicle, genealogy, history, and epic; we would discuss the objects of the aristocracy, as well as their religion, laws, and recreation. Beginning with an object, for example, a crown or a helmet, we could pursue various directions concerning its production: its origin, including the antecedents for design and the craftsmanship required to carry it out, and comparable models from contemporary and related cultures; its cost and its value; its relation to texts referring to the object; and its material and symbolic or spiritual value, not only to the aristocracy, but to those outside aristocratic spheres. Such an inquiry would demand immense and varied expertise; no single discipline could undertake it; the history of no single paradigm could account for it; the voices of no single generation of scholars could speak for it.

The seminars needed to realize this exploration would emphasize how the assumptions of each discipline cause it to structure the evidence it purports to study; the seminar would examine the similarities between that structuring of evidence from disciplines to discipline. Such a project, I believe, would not be a contest to see which construction was correct. Instead it would be a comparison of the relation of truth claims to fundamental disciplinary theory and method. The point is not that one discipline has more truth at its disposal than another, or that the signifying practices of one are better than those of the other; the point instead is to examine the relationship of constructions leading to truth claims to those who construct them. Archaeology and literature, compared in this way in the assessment of *Beowulf* and the Sutton Hoo ship burial, would be seen as two disciplines juxtaposing the continuity of language with the obvious discontinuity of material culture and using language to decode and contextualize objects.

Cultural inquiry organized around the idea—and the ideology—of aristocracy in Anglo-Saxon England would help us to defamiliarize our notion of aristocracy and aristocratic culture. There are precedents for such inquiry, of course, and it is only the exclusivity of our critical tradition, and our habitual dismissal of earlier critical voices (excepting, of course, the voices of certain philologists), that causes us to consider oppositional criticism as distinctively "contemporary." In 1898, Vida Dutton Scudder wrote as follows about *Beowulf:*

> In this precious ancient poem, through which the Teutonic race sees dimly its heroic past, a village, slightly mentioned, lies to be sure somewhere in the background, but eyes are fixed on noble Heorot Hall, gold-timbered, fiend-ravaged, where the heroes feast and brag. In battle, the common people hardly exist, even to be slain; in revel the queen herself is cup bearer, for no vulgar hand may minister to the princely warriors. Into this society, fiercely respectful toward the fighter with a pedigree, contemptuous toward the nameless churl, the chanting monks of Augustine, and earlier the Celtic missionaries with a Christianity of more childlike type, introduced a new ideal.[80]

Speaking of the view of medieval culture she strove for in survey courses she taught, Scudder some forty years later observed that the "phenomena of the collective life determined by economic conditions are always implicit as a shaping force, they are the background even when the foreground is occupied by private reactions." She added, "One need be no Marxist to recognize this, though as Marx helps us increasingly in our understanding of life and its movements, I hope and expect that such courses as I feebly sought to initiate are likely to multiply."[81] Scudder's attention to material culture and economic conditions would still be productive for Anglo-Saxon studies, and, in 1990, no less than a revolutionary alternative to the preoccupations of our critical histories.

The impact of Sutton Hoo cannot be observed only by reading what Wrenn and others wrote after the find. Equally interesting is what was thought about Anglo-Saxon civilization before the treasure was discovered, uncovered, and recovered during World War II. E. T. Leeds's 1936 publication on the primitive Saxon village at Sutton Courtenay is as far from the material splendor that Wrenn writes of as one could hope. He describes small huts, ten by twelve feet, with little headroom, sometimes with postholes for looms that took up even more of the scant room available. (The importance for narrative theory of these looms—sites for story-telling and fabric-making—in the middle of these huts, not apart from the domestic dwelling in weaving sheds, awaits attention; Anglo-Saxon looms deserve the scrutiny so far lavished only on harps.)

> In such cabins, with bare head-room, amid a filthy litter of broken bones, of food and shattered pottery, with logs or planks raised on stones for their seats or couches, lived the Anglo-Saxons. The fact that the house described above [i.e., here] represents the most pretentious effort among thirty hardly leaves hope that at first even the chieftains could provide themselves with much greater comfort or luxury.

Of course, *Beowulf* is not about a primitive culture; and Leeds did find a "more pleasing picture" in Kent.[82]

Leeds's remark invites us to juxtapose the lowly and the lofty. His comment calls to mind John Ruskin's comment about the lovely sixth-century church on Torcello, the inconspicuous island whose modesty is overwhelmed by the splendors of nearby Venice. Ruskin notes that the pillars and arches seen on the approach to the church of Santa Fosca lift it only "to the height of a cattle shed"—not very promising—and adds that "the first strong impression which the spectator receives from the whole scene is, that whatever sin it may have been which has on this spot been visited with so utter a desolation, it could not at least have been ambition."[83]

Ruskin's juxtaposition of the modest and the mighty engages a number of homologies that medievalists will recognize in their own criticism. An enormously influential art, art history, and architecture critic, Ruskin was also a philosopher of labor (after a fashion), deeply concerned about material production and material culture.[84] Ruskin deprecated simple material culture because it failed to rise to the pleasing image he desired. For Ruskin, to look on Venice was to look on a fallen ideal, and perhaps a palimpsest. The fall of Venice to the East was, for Ruskin, the corruption of the medieval virgin into the Renaissance whore. In this paradigm Ruskin found much. Venice and Torcello were stages for the play of his psyche. "Mother and daughter," he wrote, "you behold them both in their widowhood—TORCELLO, and VENICE."[85] To look on Venice was to look on sexual knowledge and on the knowledge of his own failed sexuality. Ruskin had, as Richard Ellmann wrote, "more trouble than most people in allowing that he was himself the product of his parents' intercourse." Alone among historians, Ruskin dated the fall of Venice to 1418 (rather than 1423), a date four hundred years before his conception, rather than before his birth. Ellmann explained this oddity by showing that "In Ruskin's mind his mother had immaculately passed from a maid to mother without ever becoming a wife."[86]

But it was not only his mother's sexuality, or his own, that obsessed him. The Middle Ages were corrupted by commerce, Ruskin believed, in much the same way that industrialization had destroyed English life. In "The Nature of Gothic," another essay from *The Stones of Venice,* Ruskin wrote, "And now, reader, look around this English room of yours, of which you have been proud so often, because the work of it was so good and strong, and the ornaments of it so finished." He continued, "Alas! if read rightly, these perfectnesses are signs of slavery in our England a thousand times more bitter and more degrading than that of the scourged African, or helot Greek."[87] Ruskin linked the mechanization of labor in his time with the idealization of labor in the Middle Ages; this medieval ideal was, for him, destroyed by commerce, just as modern life was degraded by it.

Ruskin's view of Venice and Torcello is, ostensibly, merely a sentimental correlation of commerce and sexual experience with an idealized desire for a simpler past. His critical paradigm, self-consciously economic and at least subconsciously sexual, demonstrates how his study of medieval texts and artifacts was heavily invested—layered over with—class preferences, sexual history, and social ambition. Those whose statements and remarks about the Middle Ages have, over the last two centuries, risen to the level of truth systems, if not to truth itself, were as much like Ruskin as different from him; the disciplines these scholars helped to construct embody more than their mental operations. Digging into and under their statements—which is what archaeological analysis and interdisciplinary studies demand—brings us into contact with more than intellectual and intellectualized constructs: it brings us into contact with their personal histories and identities.

The connections between scholars and their subjects are personal and social, as well as professional and seemingly impersonal. We are, I believe, intimately bound up with the critical systems within which we operate. Our social relations play a part both in what we remember and in the ways we remember it; our social relations should, therefore, be a conscious part of our critical practice. It is through social relations that we can renew important connections between person and profession, between scholar and critical language, and between academic disciplines and individual history. Critical theory, consciously acknowledged, calls attention (whether we welcome it or not) to personal investment in the issues we study: who we are, why we are doing this, and why we are here.

The methodology of cultural studies is welcome because it posits a relationship between a scholar and his or her subject and emphasizes the role of the scholar's personality in structuring the subject. Reference to the personal experience of scholars and to the impact of their personalities on "objective" scholarly practices may seem unacceptable. But philologists, who shaped their discipline in conjunction with other disciplines, should, like scholars in those disciplines, begin to learn from the history of their discipline. In anthropology, for example, the onset of professional, detached ethnography was welcomed because it was seen as putting an end to personal accounts, travel memoirs, and other journalistic forms as sources about alien cultures. Now those outmoded forms are being newly appreciated.[88] Anglo-Saxonists and medievalists in general can benefit from this example and reconsider the discourse of the "amateur" scholars, including women writers of the nineteenth century and all earlier writers whose thoughts about and experience of the Middle Ages the philological tradition of the last century has so completely displaced and devalued.

Cultural Criticism

A rereading of Ruskin's criticism and philosophy discloses the inclusiveness of critical acts that, seen as scholarly disciplines and intellectual paradigms, seem remote from individual identity. Contemporary criticism disrupts those closed structures and "remembers" what has been "forgotten" or "lost" to professional memory through them. The early alliance of postmodernism with political criticism has demonstrated that questions of production, agency, and identity such as those raised by Johnson, are questions about culturally-determined and culturally-expressive forces, what Johnson calls "questions of the production of cultural forms or their larger social organisation."[89] Sympathetic to his larger aims, I have many differences with him, in particular with his insistence on politicizing theory in a single (leftward) direction. One of the reasons that theory is resisted today is not that it has been politicized—for politicizing is unavoidable, even when approaches are said to be detached from history and from the individuals who practice them—but that it has been politicized into an orthodoxy of the left. This is, I believe, unnecessary, exclusionary, and reductive; advocacy of contemporary theory, seen as revolutionary fervor, is easily dismissed as an attempt to wrest power from the establishment for one's own interests.[90] Johnson's essay worries periodically about co-optation of leftward theoretical prerogatives by the right; this is one consequence of his sometimes-simplistic polarization of the critical universe and his alignment of "contemporary theory" with political movements, a gesture also made by Terry Eagleton, Edward W. Said, and others.[91]

It seems that contemporary critics rarely write about their tradition without calling for its overthrow. For example, Paul A. Bové writes that the intellectual should use criticism and theory to resist the pernicious effect of institutions on society and to prevent the institution from enlisting the individual in its hegemonic efforts. "The goal should be to challenge and change specific forms of power by encouraging and furthering local struggles," he writes.[92] Johnson strikes a similar note in his manifesto for academic change; so do Frow and Shanks and Tilley.[93] But it is difficult to see why oppositional criticism needs to totalize the institutions it seeks to undermine. Deconstruction and cultural studies are obviously oppositional in a constructive sense, but they hardly require the kind of political affiliation that Eagleton, Bové, Johnson, and so many others demand of their followers. The kind of research I wish to participate in closely resembles that of the Institute for Social Research (sometimes misnamed the "Frankfurt School"), but I can hardly agree to the "radical socio-political transformation" that, according to Douglas Kellner, is necessary to distinguish traditional, ineffective interdisciplinary work (which, Kellner says, brings individuals together "to chat") from "supradisciplinary" research, the right stuff from which a better future will spring.[94]

To insist that we can have interdisciplinary, "supradisciplinary," or culturally contextualized learning only from a revolutionary perspective is only institutionalization of another sort. Although analysis that challenges received ideas and typologies is what we must undertake, we can hardly expect traditional critics or their institutions to agree to step to one side merely because the material prerogatives of the next generation are being asserted. Kellner, like Bové, Said, and others, moves from asserting difference against disciplinary identity to demanding a new identity of his own. But all who find Said's cultural criticism stimulating, and who share Foucault's conviction that social institutions repress truth as they exercise the will to truth, do not necessarily, on the basis of that shared understanding, have to identify with the political agenda offered by these scholars. To assert difference against identity is not simultaneously to impose a new identity of difference on one's colleagues. Scholars dissatisfied with the sterility of our professional endeavors and their isolation from contemporary cultures can make an effective beginning by acknowledging and trying to bridge the gap between the personal and professional in their teaching and research. Much of the ineffectiveness of scholarly research (not only in medieval studies) results from fear of change, strident defense of traditional methods, and intolerable insistence that those on whose shoulders we supposedly stand were giants, pedestals for our monuments, foundations to be upheld because they hold us up.

As the languages of contemporary criticism disrupt (and disturb) disciplines and institutions frozen in nineteenth-century paradigms, those languages are creating continuity by reshaping traditional culture. The demands of contemporary critical theories are demands to be heard made by new voices that address the inadequacy of paradigms and procedures available to readers and writers of all persuasions, and pluralistic, in that sense, in a very old-fashioned way. Those who refuse to acknowledge innovation, which they see as revolution and rejection of tradition, inevitably lose theoretical battles. But the failure of dialogue between the current and the coming likewise works to the disadvantage of the innovators. If the former forget that tradition was once innovation, the latter forget that innovation will one day constitute tradition. The onset of orthodoxy, like the onset of old age, cannot be resisted. The continuity we maintain makes demands of its own. Chief among them is familiarity with the research skills that shaped traditional paradigms. Those skills include knowledge of Old as well as Middle English, familiarity with classical as well as medieval Latin, and understanding of material culture. These are skills needed to study documents as monuments, and monuments as documents; without such skills we cannot undo the harmonious models of high culture, assert the presence of cultural conflict against them, or identify the complacent influence of tradition as tradition is revised.

The belief that the skills of a discipline are neutral methods rather than complex systems of representation encourages the illusion that disciplines, which are skill-centered, are themselves different; the belief also devalues the skills. It has been my aim to show that the skills of traditional medieval scholarship—the essence of the tradition now confronted by innovation— are not timeless, transhistorical, and unchanging. Rather, they are the products of the ages in which they were devised and are personal as well as professional ways of speaking; contemporary criticism, likewise, is not only a new collection of critical languages but also a new group of persons speaking languages of their own. The traditional skills of our disciplines, which are the means of maintaining discipline, cannot be dispensed with; nor can the history of the scholarly disciplines that they have shaped be ignored. The skills must be renewed and the history must be deconstructed or "dismantled" to enable "a more intimate kind of knowing"[95] in which we find another way of knowing ourselves and our predecessors, and of speaking their languages, as well as our own, in the conversation through which we know the Middle Ages.

Chapter 2

On Reading Eve: *Genesis B* and the Readers' Desire

✳ Gillian R. Overing ✳

On Reading

On the title page of *The Rudiments of Grammar for the English-Saxon Tongue,* written in 1715, which she prefaces by an "Apology for the Study of Northern Antiquities,"[1] Elizabeth Elstob makes several claims: she will take back the Saxon language from those who have reviled it as barbaric and unclassical, and she offers herself as particularly well qualified for the task. As a woman she may be excluded from the "patrimony" of material privilege, but she claims privileged access to language: "but the language that we speak is our Mother-Tongue; And who so proper to play the Criticks in this as the Females." Her claim is mediated by the fact that she herself does not assert this justification; it has been made on her behalf by another, more supportive, patriarchal authority, "a Right Reverend Prelate." As she defends both the Saxon tongue and her defense of it, and rejects the traditional authority of Latin as a linguistic function of patriarchy, she plays one version of authority off against another. This is to say that she may not speak the first language, but will speak in and for her "own" language, and in so doing she will lay some implicit claim to the first.

Elstob does not yet overtly identify this "mother" tongue as a further linguistic function of the patrimony, whose authority she will go on to challenge in such scathing rhetoric later in her preface. Rather, she defends the honor of its paternal genealogy, and aims "to shew the polite Men of our Age, that the Language of their Forefathers is neither so barren nor barbarous as they affirm, with equal Ignorance and Boldness."[2] Neither did Elstob have to contend with the language of critical theory. Nonetheless, she experienced the necessity of bilingualism and of tenuous and mediated access to the languages of patriarchy. And the stance and dilemma of this early trespasser in the closely guarded territory of the "Saxon tongue" re-

main relevant to women using the language of theory to translate and interpret not only that same tongue but also that of its male translators and
interpreters.

Elstob's situation as female critic raises the still-central issue of mediation. It is an issue that connects Elstob and me as critics, and that will
connect us both, as I shall argue throughout this essay, to Eve as a first
female speaker, translator, and interpreter. Both Elstob and I, like Eve,
came on the scene after Adam had named the animals.[3] Elstob commanded
two languages certainly—Latin, the language of patriarchal authority, and
its ostensible challenger, the vernacular whose origins were celebrated as
unclassically Saxon. We might also include the skills of translation and interpretation as additional fluencies, but for the sake of initial clarity and the
overall scheme of this volume I shall limit her to two languages. But which
of these two spoke *her?* Notwithstanding the important question of whether
any language may give unmediated expression to self, male or female, we
may observe the problem of mediation more acutely when the female voice
is articulated via masculine forms, via languages whose subject is male.
The feminist speaker, reader, or critic must learn not two, but (at least)
three languages, and the third is by far the most difficult to articulate, even
as it problematizes and threatens fluency in the other two.

How to speak this "other" language, how to speak the female self,
how to articulate a response as a female reader to a patriarchal text,
whether or not this is accessible of articulation through language, these are
central issues in feminist critical discourse,[4] which intersect with the task of
reading and articulating a response to an Old English poem—and especially a poem such as *Genesis B*. The feminist critic who uses masculine
discourse, whether this be traditional and philological or contemporary and
epistemological, is faced with several choices: "a renewed silence, a form
of religion (from mysticism to political orthodoxy), or a continual attention—historical, ideological, and affective—to the place from which we
speak."[5] This latter choice is one that I propose to examine, and to practice. The self-conscious questioning of habits of interpretation, an idea outlined by C. S. Peirce over a century ago, demands of the feminist reader/
critic the additional task of questioning and revealing the ways in which
that self has been constructed, within and without the text. In other words,
learning to speak the third language requires a continual engagement with
the other two, and an engagement predicated on resistance.

Recent studies of gendered reading practices take the feminist critic/
reader beyond the stance of "resisting reader."[6] If we are to pay effective
attention, for example, to the place from which we speak, the premises
and promise of reader-response criticism take us only so far. Patrocinio

Schweickart calls attention to the essentially utopic nature of reader-response criticism, where the projected reading experience takes no notice of the passionate realities that might attend it, of factors such as gender, race, or class.[7] While the readers' role in the production, experience, and enactment of meaning is not questioned, the issues of control and identification in the transaction between reader and text become more complex when that text may control, remove, or work overtly or covertly against the readers' desire. Schweickart contends that in order to avoid the "immasculated" bifurcated response of the woman reader to the androcentric text, that is, reading as a man via androcentric paradigms, or reading as a woman and confirming her position as other, the feminist reader/critic must assume control of the reading experience. This entails "reading the text as it was *not* meant to be read, in fact, reading it against itself."[8]

Far from destroying or summarily dismissing the text in this process, a feminist theory of reading participates in the utopic energy of reader-response criticism; it empowers and foregrounds the text while rejecting its power to "immasculate" the woman reader, to engage her complicity in her own disappearance as subject. Christine Froula rereads Eve and Adam's nativity scenes in *Paradise Lost* in such a way that "the invisible becomes visible; the transcendent, historical; the sacred icon, a cultural image."[9] Milton's "bogey" may lose its power to terrify as it becomes a ragged scarecrow figure, but the power of the text is rediscovered, expanded, celebrated; when read "against itself," Milton's poem "no longer shuts out the view."[10] Moreover, Schweickart maintains that Milton's quintessentially patriarchal text retains its fascination for female readers precisely because it engages a utopic desire; it is a male text that adumbrates "authentic desires" before appropriating them to the process of immasculation.[11]

Schweickart does not elaborate on what constitutes the authentic or the utopic, however, and leaves these notions in the mysterious and rather murky terrain of fundamentally human desires and desire for human origins. Positing a common desire for a common understanding of an originary moment, Milton's text thus exercises a fascination over male and female readers. But the problems of circularity attending any search for origins—authentic, utopic, or otherwise—are those that the feminist reader/critic will do well to remember and, indeed, to engage and include in discussion in order to pay continual attention to the place from which we speak.

Despite and because of the fact that the very "genesis of Genesis" is the repression of the mother,[12] I set to reading *Genesis B*—or, to be more precise, I set to reading Eve and the passages of the poem that focus on her. This Saxon poem particularly merits and demands a dual hermeneutic: a negative hermeneutic that unveils the text's androcentrism and "a positive hermeneutic that recuperates the utopian moment."[13] I think that this might quite literally be a moment in this poem—somewhere around the time when Eve is persuading Adam to eat the apple—and I include the possibility that this may be my moment, an expression and vehicle of my own desire. If I set to looking for Eve, to identifying a female subject and its desire where none has been identified before by reading this poem against itself, I run the risk of finding myself as reader and creating a doubly fictive Eve. Or worse, if I don't, I run the risk of renewed silence.

The problem of identifying and making a connection with Eve as separate female self, as a cultural presence rather than a literary character conceived within a Saxon (or modern) poetic fiction, is essentially a linguistic problem of several dimensions. Although Elstob and I might not have shared the language of critical theory, communication remains possible through forms of social, historical, and linguistic reconstruction. With Eve, the communication problem is enormous, and quite possibly insurmountable. We know little enough about the eventfulness of language in general in Anglo-Saxon society, and even less about an actual female speaker's or reader's relation to it, let alone that of a fictional character. Other essays in this volume are beginning to explore the material and cultural contexts of writing, reading, and speaking:[14] what I want to establish here is rather an acknowledgment of the problems facing real female readers of fictional female speakers, of the persistent and particular opacity of language. In reading, after all, "one encounters only a text, the trail of an absent author,"[15] and though, to borrow Adrienne Rich's description of her attempt to enter the mind of Emily Dickinson, "the scent is very powerful,"[16] the woman is still absent. If the only possible connection with the woman in the text remains metaphorical, let us continue to examine and rework our metaphors. My sole strategy for expanding communication will be to keep trying; by this I mean paying a thoroughgoing attention to language, to it forms, conditions, resonances, silences, to its speakers and readers within and without the poem. My essay will therefore be as much about how we read what happens to Eve in the poem as it is about what happens to her, and it will focus as much on textual criticism as it does on the text itself.

I also set to reading *Genesis B* for a number of more tangible reasons connected with the purpose of this volume. This Old Saxon/Anglo-Saxon poem is so neatly, confusingly, and abundantly paradigmatic on such a variety of levels that it challenges and engages all three languages that the feminist reader/critic must learn and might also serve as a means for a conversation among them. The poem deals with several issues that engage traditional, theoretical, and feminist viewpoints, three of which will be my ongoing concern in the following sections and which I will briefly outline here. These are the poem's "difference," its preoccupation with language, and my primary focus, its construction of Eve.

Many of the interpretive critical essays on this poem begin with a statement regarding how remarkable and/or different it is, and its difference is then accounted for, explained (away), or claimed by a certain theological or cultural viewpoint. The poet emerges as either a slightly confused, faintly Gnostic Christian or a crack Germanic storyteller who thinks doctrine is less important than the reason why. More on these viewpoints in the next section, but I note here that the specter of the "Christian/pagan dichotomy," which has haunted Old English scholars for so long, is still present in some measure in critical views of *Genesis B*. The poem foils this "dichotomy" and nicely problematizes traditional critical patristic method; the poem's relation to scriptural authority is both a source of its difference and a measure against which we understand its difference.

We know that *Genesis B* is not an Old English poem.[17] We experience the text as a translation of a translation, and neither its beginning or conclusion are known to us. In addition to these paradigmatic attractions for the (post)modern critic, the poem is, as I have said, much preoccupied with language. It is largely about words: words and The Word, divine, satanic, masculine and feminine words—a multiplicity of signifiers set adrift after the introduction of the transcendent Word of God. It is both convenient and fortunate for my discussion that the poem "begins" with God speaking, with the resounding inderdiction that all other speakers must speak around and against. There is no way to follow this act, in terms of a credible match of signifier and signified; all satanic and human signification will blur, must be turned loose in comparison. But if meaning is measured against this enacted/enunciated and thereby incarnated divine signification, if this version of Incarnation—the "Word made flesh" appearing via God's disembodied voice in the poem—authorizes the relation between signifier and signified and "guarantees their correspondence,"[18] and if this Word is fully perceived as an origin, then the feminist reader/critic must ask what kind of body contains and shapes this controlling metaphor of signification.

We come up against the body in a variety of ways, as the poem involves not only incarnate language but food also; it's about speaking *and* eating, and the boundaries between what we ingest and what we speak or spit back as a result. These will be the concerns of the third section, where in order to speak against or through masculine incarnation in language, it will become necessary to begin before the Word to examine the bodily conditions of symbolicity, to take a journey back from the Word via metaphors of body.

The third issue I will be addressing intersects with the first two. Another of the paradigmatic theoretical attractions of this Saxon rendering of the Fall myth, which in any of its multiple versions remains a "master narrative"—context, pretext, and metatext for patriarchal ideology—is its construction of the figure of Eve. It presents the feminist reader/critic with the challenge of finding Eve, or at least reconstructing the terms of her disappearance. This is where *Genesis B* reveals another source of its difference. Between the traditional mother repression and woman-as-root-of-all-evil inherent in the Fall myth and the poet's variously interpreted so-called exoneration of the human pair and especially of Eve, between these apparent extremes, there lies a map of desire through and against which we may begin to read Eve. We can recover her trace in the configurations and intersections of desire that shape her within and without the poem. The following sections will attempt a close reading of this map of desire, engaging readers of the poem, readers in the poem, and me as reader, with the explicit premise that my own desire as reader is for a recovery or discovery of how Eve might read and speak.

On Reading Eve

> "and pat (s)he comes, like the catastrophe of the old comedy."
>
> Shakespeare, *King Lear*

If, as I claim, the text of *Genesis B* generates some crucial and paradigmatic theoretical issues, it must also be acknowledged that the text itself is similarly generated; it is a two-way process. *"Insofar as we are taught to read,"* Annette Kolodny writes, *"what we engage are not texts, but paradigms. . . .* We read well, and with pleasure, what we already know how to read; and what we know how to read is to a large extent dependent on what we have already read (works from which we have developed our expectations and learned our interpretive strategies)" (Kolodny's italics).[19] I set to reading Eve in *Genesis B*, then, by first examining some critical paradigms and assumptions that give the poem a portion of its reading context, and my aim here also will be to read these texts "against themselves."

My attempts to find and read Eve through a critical history of *Genesis B* were largely unsuccessful because often the critical readings of Eve controlled and substituted for, or became synonymous with Eve reading. Eve emerged as creation and creature of masculine representation. It became far more interesting and revealing to chart this map of the critical readers' desire in terms of the degree and nature of complicity in her disappearance, of the variety of strategies of representation employed to produce the same missing sign. Moreover, this approach can contribute to our multilingual conversation in that some of the same strategies will recur in the next section as means of (re)configuring the absent sign.

In the past twenty-five or so years, a good deal has been written on *Genesis B*, much of it inspired by and derived from the early work of J. M. Evans and Rosemary Woolf. Approaches to the poem tend to fall into three often overlapping categories, or camps: the source hunters, those which focus on single phrases/motifs/passages, and those which take on the problems of "moral" interpretation and the business of guilt.[20] This last group will be my primary concern. The poem's doctrinal peculiarities suggest some quite drastic changes, if not apparent reversals, in the organization and distribution of guilt,[21] and a reconfiguring of forms of moral and aesthetic representation of the Fall myth. The most pressing questions raised by the third category of critics have been why such restructuring, and where does the guilt originate and finally settle in the shuffle.

In pursuit of Eve, I initially tried to divide critical viewpoints into those that argued more or less for a greater or lesser degree of exoneration of Eve. The pro-Eve and anti-Eve lists soon began to merge, however, and the distinction became irrelevant. Those who set out to redeem her finish by damning her with faint praise or condescension, while those who set out to find her more guilty by virtue of the poet's unorthodoxy vacillate between the explanatory poles of stupidity and evil. The Germanic "rescuing" of Eve, moreover, involves interpreting her in terms of the female peace-weaving role, and this, as I shall argue, complicates matters further while contributing to Eve's disappearance. So instead of trying to divide critics into pro or con factions, I am going to look briefly at a dozen or so of these recent critical arguments, loosely grouping them under the more Christian aegis of Rosemary Woolf or under the more Germanic aegis of J. M. Evans. My focus in this survey will be on common and intersecting themes, on contradictions that are not, on discovering ways of constructing and representing Eve that reveal not Eve but rather the readers' desire, and specifically the workings of masculine desire.

Let me begin with Rosemary Woolf's influential essay, "The Fall of Man In *Genesis B* and the *Mystère d'Adam*," where, as her title implies, she argues that the Saxon poem is not as strikingly original as some critics have suggested. She also takes exception to a prevailing sympathetic view of Eve, which she believes undermines rather than recognizes the true artistry of the poet: "Unfortunately the psychological subtlety of the author of

Genesis B has been obscured by the common assumption of modern critics that Eve in this poem was unfairly deceived and utterly blameless."[22] The poet is to be credited with rescuing Eve, who only "acquires her stature through the poet's compassion."[23] The important question for Woolf is "whether or not the devil's disguise was impenetrable."[24] Juliana, in the Old English poem of the same name, was able to penetrate the disguise of her diabolical emissary, and why then, the argument follows, could Eve not do the same? Woolf states clearly, moreover, that the devil "should have been recognized by Eve."[25] His speech is one aspect of his disguise that may be penetrated by "*a clear moral understanding*" (my italics).[26] Does Eve, then, possess this? The logic of Woolf's questions also, to an extent, frames the answers.

The nature of this clear moral understanding remains obscure; Adam is somehow able to see through the devil's speech—"*almost perhaps* by a philosophical understanding that God cannot contradict Himself" (my italics).[27] Eve's lesser mental powers, "the traditional *wifes wac geþoht,* so much stressed by the poet," might explain how she was unable to make "the simple logical deduction so lucidly apparent to Adam,"[28] so in order to fully explain Eve's now-inevitable guilt, Woolf takes a different approach: "To prove the point therefore that Eve was to blame, it is necessary to show that her moral sense as well as her reason failed her."[29]

Without clarity, or morality, or understanding on Eve's part, only desire, apparently, remains. And here Eve's desire is translated into self-aggrandizement and narcissism. As the nature or source of Adam's philosophical abilities escapes definition within the poem, so too does Eve's moral disability, in that this must be provided and defined from without. I suggest that when Woolf, using the masculine standard she has set for Adam, deduces that the devil's disguise was in fact penetrable and that "Eve listened with a willful credulity springing from a nascent vanity,"[30] she evidences a logic formed by her own desire as reader, and in some respects informed by stereotypical constructs that are both doctrinal and cultural. From a view of Eve as "vain and silly" under the duress of temptation, it is but a short step to Woolf's vision of her persuasion of Adam as prefiguring "the nagging wife of Medieval literature."[31] What emerges from Woolf's reading is a familiar pattern of displacement of guilt rooted in misogynistic religious and social tradition.

That Eve becomes an object of both pity and contempt, only to be rescued by the poet's good artistic graces, is one aspect of Woolf's argument taken up by John Vickrey. Woolf and Vickrey also invoke the presence and raise the issue of audience within and without the poem. As Eve becomes progressively more guilty via the artistic and structural development within the poem—in Woolf's view, this is charted by way of Eve's misreading of the devil's speech, while Vickrey traces Eve's misapprehension of her vision—an audience, or readers with their wits about them, would be aware of all that is escaping Eve. In Vickrey's argument, Eve is seen to be quite spectacularly and drastically misinformed: the vision she describes to Adam when she has eaten the fruit is typically that of the Day of Judgment. Vickrey suggests that the configuration of angels, God's throne, and its southeastern location would have been an obvious and immediately recognizable apocryphal description and, hence, a powerfully ironic "reminder of that day which must conclude human history, as, in a sense, Eve's temptation of Adam begins it."[32] Eve's "immense error" and her subsequent use of her mistaken vision to persuade Adam would have evoked a strong response from a ninth-century audience, one of "exasperation, indignation, perhaps even derision and scorn."[33] Hence the poet's expressions of sympathy—his insistence, for example, that she acts in good faith and through a "loyal heart" ("holdne hyge" [708])[34]—are there to rescue Eve in the eyes of this audience, "perhaps not well disposed to womankind";[35] she must eventually emerge, Vickrey argues, a notch ahead of Satan, and therefore "cannot be allowed to fall too far in our esteem."[36]

Vickrey notes that modern critics have "not expressed any shock, or even much surprise, at the vision of Eve"[37] and have wrongly construed the poet's sympathy as showing a "primary intention to exonerate."[38] The question of who, indeed *how*, to blame is raised again. Moreover, Vickrey's own vision of Eve as a pitiable dupe is only one extreme method of constructing her as a straw figure, which is consistent with other subtler and more complex representations of her absence that Vickrey also depicts. What Eve sees may not be what she thinks it is, and the irony the vision encompasses may well make her look slightly ridiculous, but whether she cannot, may not, or will not interpret her vision correctly never becomes a real issue. Her own interpretation of what she sees is irrelevant. She becomes a representation of the tempter's representation, a double fiction that Adam then interprets.

Alain Renoir adds several more layers or levels of representation to this construct: he maintains that the tempter is deceived into tempting Eve by Satan and that the temptation is "actually an act of self-deception on the part of the Tempter."[39] With so many forms of lies and deceptions, of representations of representations intervening, we could say that Eve is but a shadow of a possible self, a facsimile far removed from an irrecoverable original. Interestingly, Milton's Eve shares this interpretive conundrum and must read and be read in a similar hall of mirrors, as Maureen Quilligan points out: "To say that Eve inhabits a mirror world of successively mediated figurations of divinity is to suggest the sheer difficulty of her interpretive situation."[40] The Saxon Eve's relation to her own experience and her degree of responsibility/guilt becomes moot when she is not identified as a reading, interpreting subject but as representational object, the text or sign ("tacen" [714]) that is read, interpreted by Adam. I shall take up these points again in the next section; here, I want to emphasize that Eve has effectively been removed as subject and has become a creature of representation—a process participated in by the tempter, the audience, Adam, and the critic.

Two essays by Robert E. Finnegan appear to be less rigorously condemnatory of Eve. Finnegan addresses directly the "bad press"[41] Eve has received as a result of Woolf and Vickrey's arguments. He finds "nothing in the poem"[42] to support their assertions that Eve could have seen through either the devil's disguise or the details of her vision. In fact, he hints at the intrusion of critical desire when he suggests that Woolf "perhaps . . . interiorizes Eve's temptation"[43] to a point beyond the reach of objective psychological investigation and that the poet is a "less stern"[44] moralist than his critics. Although his rejection of Woolf and Vickrey's *means* of finding Eve guilty leads Finnegan initially back to a view of the poet's heterodoxy, his argument then turns to Augustinian doctrine as a possible orthodox rationale for judging Eve. He finds Eve "guilty enough, but not of vanity or pride,"[45] but rather of "vincible" or "culpable ignorance."

Finnegan's argument begins to appear more parallel to those of Woolf and Vickrey as he lists carefully the many linguistic and thematic details that Eve could have spotted, draws attention to the tempter's "rhetorically flatulent"[46] words, which are calculated to offend even a moderately aware aesthetic sensibility, and demonstrates how the poet "manipulated the very substance of his art to indicate to the audience outside the artistic frame the duplicity of the tempter within."[47] We have the same framework of those "outside the artistic frame" knowing, seeing and understanding more than those within it, but the distance between inner and outer is not gauged in terms of the blindness of vanity or pride—"the least attractive quality of human nature"—but in terms of simple stupidity: Eve "simply cannot see."[48] Nor, we might note, is her aesthetic sensibility offended, and thereby registered, by so obvious an affront. The Saxon poet rejects the "nasty vice" of pride and the Miltonic conception of a power-hungry Eve in favor of a "more human, and humane, redaction of the myth."[49]

Finnegan returns to the matter of Eve's "human" failings in a second essay; again, he emphasizes the nature of the tempter's rhetoric, here identified as *cræft,* a "certain superficial skill with words, almost a low rhetorical cunning,"[50] that convinces Eve despite its dubious aesthetic qualities and despite the fact that "she has enough material to form her conscience correctly."[51] Eve's lack of discrimination, however, or, in Finnegan's earlier argument, her simply "human" failings, here also enables her to become another variety of objectified vehicle; as she becomes "infected by *deofles cræft*," and an "instrument" for it, her words and the action of the narrative are both choreographed by the tempter.[52] And if, in Finnegan's construction of Eve, there is this rather scary disappearance of Eve as subject, it is compensated for at the end of the poem by an "improved" reappearance. "Eve contritely accepts her responsibility for the disaster with far more dignity than Adam can muster."[53] When she tells Adam that no words of his may blame her more than she already blames herself (824–25), she gains affirmative identity by taking responsibility for her own victimization. If dignity is to be discovered in what might also be seen as self-flagellation, such discovery might also conjure the presence, and point to the hand, of the critical wizard who makes Eve appear and disappear.

One final argument merits attention under my very loosely "Christian" aegis. Margaret Erhart's apparent focus is the intricate verbal artistry in the poem, though her argument also offers another means of constructing Eve's limitations from without the poem. She interprets the fall as "an instance of disciples listening to the wrong teacher"[54] and etymologically argues that discipleship connotes not subjection but learning, acceptance and understanding of teaching.[55] Erhart charts the poet's skillful manipulation and the changing connotations of the word "lar" (counsel/teaching) in the poem, showing how Eve, a patently unsuccessful Christian disciple, fails to perceive the tempter's teaching as misteaching in the face of blatantly repetitive hints, which "Eve should have noticed."[56] Whether Eve is judged to be fast learner of bad teaching or a slow learner of good teaching, however, is beside Erhart's point, as Eve is once more held accountable for not seeing or reading that which is obvious to outside readers of the poem, for not being in and out of the text at the same time. The more artistry Erhart discovers in the poem, the more excluded/absent Eve becomes.

Eve's multiple failures and ways of failing undergo a kind of makeover—certainly a renaming—under the scrutiny of the more or less "Germanic" critics. This group would seek explanations for the poem's difference in secular rather than sacred terms; they stress psychological, social, and sexual behavior and assess blame in the context of underlying assumptions and definitions of what constitutes acceptable moral "human" behavior.

J. M. Evans was the first critic to adopt this more secular approach, which ostensibly creates a somewhat "better press" for Eve. Evans's re-evaluation of Eve, moreover, is a function of his overview of the text as culturally produced and determined. This approach has some interesting implications both for my present argument and for the argument of the next section, and thus Evans's premises will warrant some additional scrutiny and discussion. The first part of his influential two-part study takes up the issue of sources, but Evans's approach problematizes this traditional originary pursuit and its stance of scholarly objectivity.[57] The nature of the poem's difference has been misunderstood: "the extent of its peculiarities has been blurred by haphazard comparisons"[58] with an ill-assorted group of source texts, Evans argues. Certainly *Genesis B has* sources, but these too are different; *Genesis B*'s difference may be understood in the context of writers such as Alcuin and Raban Maur, whose mode of adding, subtracting, or borrowing from traditional Augustinian teaching on the Fall mirrors that of the *Genesis B*-poet. Difference breeds difference, then, as the *Genesis B*-poet might have relied on "rather more esoteric writings on the subject"[59] to formulate his account of the Fall, and Evans provides an impressive array of these esoteric possibilities.[60] These choices, Evans goes on to argue, are in turn products of cultural difference in its broadest sense, of a different desire for a different narrative, operating on the part of the poet and of his audience.

Evans claims that the poet was "a man less interested in doctrinal niceties than in telling a vivid and moving story"[61] in the tradition of Germanic epic, and also that "an audience familiar with Germanic epic would expect to be told why"[62] things happened as they did. This emphasis on figuring out "the reason why" and on the nature of the readers' expectations connects the distant "Germanic" audience and poet with Evans and me as readers of cultural information—we all want to know the reason why, perhaps especially in the case of this story of our communal fall from grace, wherein we might find ourselves doctrinally or culturally implicated and identified—even as it must reveal a certain circularity in the source-hunting project itself while this connection remains unacknowledged. Evans does hint at the connection only to dismiss it with a caution against the intrusion of the "subjective" when he remarks that "it is, of course, only too easy to over-read a poem such as this."[63] My questions remain of to what extent and how this "different" narrative is a product of the readers' desire, and how Eve is constructed by its writers and readers.

How, then, does Eve fare under the secular critical banner? How does her "humanness" improve her press? To get at the answers to these questions, I also question the standards of acceptable human moral behavior, how they are determined, and what kinds of assumptions underlie this determination. When Evans discusses the events of the Saxon poem and their relation to Germanic narrative technique in the second part of his study of the poem, he points out many ways in which the style, structure, and point of view of the poem invoke a military, heroic *comitatus* ethic. His analysis culminates in a view of the stages of the temptation as "strategic manoeuvre rather than moral enticement."[64] And at the center of this Germanic social militaristic nexus stands the hero. Evans's overview of the temptation scenes necessitates the structural assumption that this is Adam's story: "In a manner very reminiscent of Grendel's approach to Heorot, the camera 'swings' from Adam to the Devil, back to Adam, then off to Eve, and finally back to Adam. The central dilemma of the hero is put into perspective by glances at the psychological forces surrounding him, and each 'shot' brings him closer to the terrible deed itself."[65]

Adam as hero is a man trying to make decisions, though in this case they are based on incorrect or inadequate information for which he is not held accountable. The important and interesting part for Evans is the process of trying. He applies a similar approach to Eve and claims that the poet maintains a "continual contrast between the catastrophic nature of the actual deeds and the goodness which inspired them."[66] Eve's "goodness" here is measured not in theological but in social terms; she is cast as a well-meaning, devoted wife, acting upon misinformation for which she is not held accountable. Her motives are "love for her husband" and desire to "protect her husband."[67] Evans does not codify these motives and methods as those of the formal female social role of peaceweaver, as do later critics, but he makes it abundantly clear that Eve is doing what she is supposed to do, what is expected of her, and therefore is not *morally* to blame for the Fall. He does not call attention to the possibility, as I shall do later, that it is precisely this set of expectations that programs her own—and everybody else's—downfall.

In Evans's view, both Adam and Eve are guilty of making only too human mistakes: "their errors are errors of judgement, not sins."[68] Eve is not singled out as the more "human" one of the pair; instead, their mutual humanity, their human failings and dilemmas are perceived as the source of artistic power in the poem, if not as a force for exoneration. In this view Eve may appear to be the object of less condescension or derision, but it does not make way for an emergent subjectivity that might do away with the problem of objectification itself. What motivates, rationalizes, and defines Eve's behavior as human is her relation to Adam. It is a relation of marginality paralleled to the Germanic narrative structural centrality of the hero that Evans earlier invoked, where we see Eve, and Satan too, as players in Adam's drama—a narrative characteristic I shall take up again in the next section. Her role is to assist in realizing the dimensions of Adam's essentially human and psychological dilemma, to amplify his role as subject. Eve's humanity and Satan's evil are seen then as marginal attributes dependent on a masculine center.

Later critics move Evans's overall argument more squarely into the
arena of Germanic social roles and relations, and Eve is cast as a thoroughly and even laudably loyal Germanic woman. Michael Cherniss offers
a wholesale rejection of Woolf's condemnation of Eve and contends that
"while the temptation of Adam was founded upon a direct lie, the temptation of Eve is founded partially upon the truth of her duty to Adam."[69] The
willful or nascently vain Eve is replaced by a woman acutely conscious of
the demands of social and familial roles:

> One cannot argue with Miss Woolf's theology, but theology plays a mini-
> mal part in this poem, and in heroic terms Eve's duty, like that of any
> queen in Germanic heroic poetry, is to serve and advise her husband, and
> to protect him, if possible, from the dangers which might beset him as the
> result of a wrong decision. No one, after all, criticizes Wealhtheow for
> urging Hrothgar to give generous gifts to his visitors at Heorot.[70]

This much improved vision of Eve places her in noble company and
offers an eminently respectable social rationale for her behavior, though it
too does not recognize the paradox of this female activity of peaceweaving.
Also, that the vision resides at least partially in the eyes of the beholder is
made plain in a further interesting detail of critical divergence. In another
stark contrast, Cherniss rejects Vickrey's apocalyptic view of Eve's vision
and identifies its descriptive elements in Germanic heroic terms as a vision
of the Lord surrounded by his *comitatus*.[71]

Evans's and Cherniss's more favorable views of Eve are grounded in
the socially based moral assumption that she is only doing or, more specifically, she is only trying to do what a woman should do. Before moving on
to discuss Jane Chance's study of Eve's "trying," I want to examine this
assumption and point out some of the inherent contradictions and compli-
cations attendant upon this socially sanctioned female role.[72] The role of
peaceweaver appears to assign and enable female identity, and to provide an
arena for the possible autonomous development of female subjectivity. But
one of the consistent characteristics of the peaceweaver, especially as we
see her in *Beowulf*, is her inevitable failure to *become* a peaceweaver in any
ongoing or permanent sense: the task is never accomplished, the role is
never fully assumed, and the woman, therefore, is never identified. In the
world of *Beowulf*, peaceweavers are assigned the role of creating, and also
embodying, peace in a culture where war and death are overriding, privileged values. Female failure, or nonsignification, is built into the system,
where woman's primary social role is essentially untenable, predicated on
absence and paradox. I do not think such absence is absolute, however, and
have argued elsewhere that we can discover traces of female signification in

Beowulf; that Hildeburh's particularly spectacular failure in the role, for example, serves to expose its paradoxical demands and to indict the system that ostensibly champions her as its cause, and that her silence and absence at the end of her story are far from passive.

But what of Eve's efforts at peaceweaving, the first woman to try out, as it were, for the role? Jane Chance examines Eve's prototypical performance and outlines a master pattern wherein Eve continually tries and continually fails. Chance nicely diagrams the paradoxical, nonfunctional function of the role. Satan has represented eating the apple to Eve as part of an attempt to make peace between God and Adam, and when Eve agrees to intercede she is accepting her role as peaceweaver, which, according to Chance, also necessitates her ultimate failure in that role. Eve's inability to resist temptation—her "weaker thought"—is a function of the role: "Thus Eve fails here not because she is unintelligent or inferior to Adam but because she has not been trained to resist, to fight, to remain strong against an adversary, and because this 'best of women' in an Anglo-Saxon society would have been trained instead to concede, to ameliorate, and to harmonize."[73] In other words, Eve is programmed for failure.

There is nevertheless some virtue to be extracted from this no-win situation, since Chance thinks that "the poet exonerates Eve, to a certain extent, because she faithfully pursues her role as peaceweaver."[74] She is seen to be trying, though failing, and this dogged persistence is what is important and praiseworthy. Such praise for Eve from the Germanic group might also evoke the monumental futility of the task, and affirm and facilitate Eve's disappearance as subject, while it calls attention to the impossible conditions of female subjectivity.

Chance also points out that Eve continues to try to assume the role when she weaves clothing for herself and Adam at the end of the poem (845–46), an act that prefigures the "heavenly weaving," or intercession, of the Virgin Mary.[75] Eve, Mary, and the Germanic woman are all located in a continuum of perpetual aspiration to fulfill the role of peaceweaver: the Virgin's relative success may spur on "the peace-weaver who has failed but who will continue in succeeding centuries to toil for peace between family members and between tribes, weaving through words and offspring what the First Peace-weaver attempted through her disobedient eating of the fruit and her later weaving of leaves into suitable covering for the pair."[76]

In answer to Chance's overarching vision of Eve as precursor of female failure, which will historically resound and repeat itself, and to Evans's, Cherniss's, and Chance's assessment of the poet's approbation for Eve on the grounds that she *is* trying, though failing, I want to point out something that they and other critics have overlooked, though perhaps the poet has an inkling of it, and in doing so I will anticipate one of the arguments in the next section. Eve does—in fact, in word, in action—*succeed*. If ever a peaceweaver accomplished the task she set out to do, it was surely the Saxon-poet's Eve. This notion of success is by turns incredible, staggering, unacceptable, repulsive, impossible for a variety of reasons. One of the most interesting issues it raises is that of female subjectivity; as the role is assumed, the woman is identified, she achieves an identity as subject. Her words and actions are no longer empty or ceremonial signifiers; they have an effect in the material world—indeed, they materialize her. When Eve as subject threatens to come into being, we witness one form of the hitherto unnameable and unexpressible entering representation, and such births or entries, Derrida reminds us, are usually attended by horror, appearing only in the "terrifying form of monstrosity."[77]

Monstrous or otherwise, Eve's subjectivity and its conditions, emergence, or disappearance are not specifically considered by the Germanic group of critics, who find her "human" or "womanly" qualities praiseworthy in some measure. Chance effectively removes the "problem" of Eve's success and the consequent possibility of identity by changing the rules of the game just as Eve appears to be winning. In her persuasiveness, Eve oversteps the limits of the female peaceweaving role and trespasses in a masculine domain: "Eve has arrogated for the peace-weaver the duties of the retainer"[78] and has assumed "too much responsibility in dealing with the Tempter."[79] It is hard to determine whether she fails at being female by adopting a male role, or whether her success at being female may be rationalized only in masculine terms. Often the latter is the case, where Eve's behavior and the ways in which she is human are gauged according to essentially masculine standards.

I include here in my Germanic group two critics who, although arguing from a more or less doctrinal basis, emphasize the human aspects of the story, and in so doing reveal this identification of the human with the masculine. In fact, my distinction between Germanic and Christian categories breaks down completely here when we look at the larger pattern of prescribed roles, whether social, moral, and/or religious, and Eve's relation to them. Thomas D. Hill places the actions of the human pair in a worldly context, although the world of human relations remains structured by biblical allegory. Hill seeks to develop Vickrey's argument where he claims that Eve is more exonerated than Adam by virtue of her inherited allegorical characteristics: "since Eve had come allegorically to represent sense and reasoning was not her forte, it follows that some perhaps, and among them the *Genesis* poet, might have come to view her lapse with a kindly eye."[80] Hill, however, uses the same allegorical basis to create a distinction between the human and divine worlds, and between the nature of human and angelic transgression. Allegorization is the key to a "fundamentally hierarchical understanding of the fall. That is, if Adam represents reason, Eve sense, and the serpent temptation, the Fall involves a subversion of hierarchy rather than Promethean overreaching as the biblical text itself would suggest."[81] So the situation in the poem involves more mundane, more characteristically human elements, notwithstanding the fact that these have doctrinal rather than Germanic antecedents.

But the application of a schematic hierarchy that dictates sexual roles has some predictable results, among which are the centrality of Adam as protagonist and another variety of disappearance for Eve. Eve is exonerated and negated at the same time; one appears as a function of the other. The crucial moment is Adam's yielding to Eve: "When this subversion of hierarchical order is achieved, the fall has occurred, but the burden of guilt rests with Adam rather than Eve."[82] Hill goes on to suggest that this hierarchical view "provides a model for all human sin,"[83] but when Hill concludes that "Eve is in effect subjectively innocent"[84] we might also agree that she is indeed innocent of any hint of subjectivity.

One final view of the poem[85] is worth noting here for its explicit acknowledgment of Adam's centrality, which presents a rather puzzling and ironic contrast to the study's declared focus—the development of psychologically realistic female characterization. Anne L. Klinck firmly maintains that this is Adam's story: "the treatment of Adam and Eve is handled so as to bring out to the full the dramatic possibilities of a tragedy in which Adam is the victim and Eve the vehicle of the catastrophe,"[86] and, furthermore, "the poet has attempted to recreate the situation in which the temptation of Adam would be most potent and tragic, and the result is his characterisation of Eve."[87] What is becoming psychologically realized here is the pattern of female passivity and dependent identity.

We might compare Klinck's assessment of the "artless simplicity of Eve's words"[88] to Woolf's implication of artifice, willfulness, and manipulation—Eve as the "nagging wife"—and consider that we have come full circle; neither view brings us much closer to the shadowy identity, psyche, motivations, or subjectivity of Eve. Adam remains the subject of both critical stories, the Christian and the Germanic. Whether Eve is found more or less guilty or innocent in terms of being only "human," such humanity is measured against a masculine model of behavior. Eve emerges consistently as a fiction written into these critical stories, a representation of a variety of desires unclaimed by her, the pantomim(et)ic figure at whom everyone is yelling "behind you." She becomes in effect an almost comic dupe, the production of her critics. She herself remains a "blank page,"[89] upon and into which we may read the history of her creation.

Eve meets Oedipus, or

> . . . the undecidable possibility of a few truth-effects
>
> Julia Kristeva, *Powers of Horror*

When Eve is judged and found wanting—though not absent—her lack is understood in relation to two different but essentially patriarchal logics. Being too "human" may be far more culpable in Christian than it is in Germanic terms, but the spectrum of guilt is a variety of speculum, Irigaray's image for the mirror of patriarchal investigation that reflects most clearly upon itself. The juxtaposition of Christian and Germanic orders does not offer a choice, especially to the feminist reader/critic. Although some critics hold to a mutual exclusivity—the poet's lack of "theological competence" supports the view that it is an "essentially Germanic heroic work,"[90] for example—the notion of "dichotomy" here, as I have stated, is foiled by this poem, as it is by most Old English poems. The Christian and Germanic elements of this poem, which in this section I am aligning with broader notions of the sacred and the secular, have a fundamental rhetorical and metaphorical relation of coexistence. What is of most interest for the feminist reader/critic is how Eve is situated in this juxtaposition of overlapping and coexisting orders and the possibilities that this Saxon reconfiguration of the Fall myth offers of glimpsing Eve between the cracks of its symbolic logics. Such "slippage" is recoverable in the failure, or confusion, of metaphors, moments in the poem when the metaphors of masculine body that underpin language and the conditions of symbolicity no longer seem either *appropriate* or *logical,* moments when body, language, sin, food, and Eve collide—such as when Eve herself becomes, embodies, temptation, holding one apple in her hand and nursing another in her heart (636–37). These moments create and require some different critical paradigms, which I want to set forth briefly here.

Let me first ask what kinds of metaphors of body underpin the twin discourses of the poem and (re)turn to Oedipus, or more specifically, to two recent reconstructions of the oedipal metaphor. The oedipal critical paradigm, insofar as it is reworked by Teresa de Lauretis and Julia Kristeva, has several attractions. It offers another perspective on the poem's "difference," on its preoccupation with language and signification, and another way of approaching the Augustinian relation of sin and ignorance, which concerned Eve and her critics in both Germanic and Christian groups.

De Lauretis argues that all narrative and narrativity—its work and effects—are inscribed by oedipal desire, and this, she is careful to point out, is historically developed: "the Oedipus of psychoanalysis is the *Oedipus Rex*, where the myth is already textually inscribed, cast in dramatic literary form, and thus sharply focused on the hero as mover of the narrative, the center and term of reference of consciousness and desire. . . . The desire is Oedipus's, and though its object may be woman (or Truth or knowledge or power), its term of reference and address is man."[91] Eve, then, like the Sphinx or Medusa, is seen as inscribed in someone else's (Adam's/God's) story—a narrative pattern that may also be inscribed or written by readers/ critics, as we have seen in the previous section. The specifics of Oedipus's own story become paradigmatic in the narrative structure of the movement of quest/subject/question toward object/answer. De Lauretis further contends that although Oedipus's crime of incest is one that destroys differences, myth and narrative work together to produce Oedipus:

> The business of the mythical subject is the construction of differences; but as the cyclical mechanism continues to work through narrative—integrating occurrences and excess, modeling fictional characters (heroes and villains, mothers and fathers, sons and lovers) on the mythical places of subject and obstacle, and projecting those spatial positions into the temporal development of plot—narrative itself takes over the function of the mythical subject. The work of narrative, then is a mapping of differences, and specifically, first and foremost, of sexual difference into each text.[92]

Developing the metaphors of Propp, Lotman, and Girard, de Lauretis textually metaphorizes body—within and without the text—in terms of "male-hero-human" as subject, and "female-obstacle-boundary-space" as other than subject.[93] We might map the *action* of the *Genesis B* narrative according to these poles of reference; certainly its narrativity, that is, the work and effects of the narrative, can be plotted to some extent by the examination of the working of external desire attempted in the previous section. We can point to the pretextuality or rhetorical relativity of Eve as artlessly innocent or as nagging wife, and we can also see the poem's difference, especially as Evans constructs it, that is, as a different *cultural* desire for a different narrative, in the context of de Lauretis's "cyclical mechanism" of cultural/textual coproduction of the mapping of sexual differences. But I shall also argue that the Saxon poet's reconfiguration of the Fall myth temporarily confuses these subject and object boundaries that keep the oedipal narrative structure in place, that Eve trespasses in Oedipus's space and thereby reviews the criteria for masculine subjectivity. In other words, we get a glimpse of the emergence of female subjectivity.

De Lauretis's schema outlines a masculine narrative map that Eve does not appear to follow, and in order to talk about the ways in which she redraws the contours of the map, however briefly, or confuses its boundaries, I must look beyond or before language in the poem. The nature of the confusion Eve gives rise to is hard to find in language: the end product, the codified result of a process that describes the conditions of masculine symbolicity and subjectivity. It is especially hard to find in language in *Genesis B*, where such symbolicity is already achieved in the incarnate Word of God, where the divine dictates human, which dictates masculine signification. In order to read the poem "against itself," to map this territory of confusion where Eve might be found, to read the "blank page," we must begin *before* language, before the Word, and look at the process of Oedipus becoming and at Kristeva's examination of the oedipal paradigm.

Oedipus's desire is achieved in narrative/language at some cost, described by Kristeva as varying levels of estrangement from self, of "abjection."[94] While I am not going to try to define a term that Kristeva uses as a process, I am going to borrow some pieces of the concept that connect body, food, and sin—all places where we might find Eve. The abject, like the object, is that which opposes the "I," but unlike the object it is also within the self, undetachable and unobjectifiable; it is essentially ambiguous, it holds the subject in a "vortex of summons and repulsion,"[95] which begins with elementary forms of food loathing and culminates in the "always already" of the abject subject who produces language and culture. Food loathing is a version of the repulsion of death and decay, both viscerally associated with the maternal body, and it is in the rejection of both bodily processes and the maternal body that psychoanalysis discovers the conditions of symbolicity; language is a form of autonomy from the maternal entity.

The Saxon poem engages the abjection thesis in some puzzling and fascinating ways; we recall, for example, the obviously repulsive aspect of the forbidden fruit, where the taboo is wholly visually comprehensible; or the point in the poem where Eve *becomes* the fruit (636), which I shall examine in more detail. What is particularly interesting about the concept of abjection in an examination of metaphors of body underpinning the twin discourses of *Genesis B* is Kristeva's distinction between secular and sacred logics of abjection and the role Oedipus plays in both challenging abjection and heralding the subject's entrance into the symbolic. Christianity changes the location of abjection; the external abjection of food loathing or dietary taboos is interiorized, and one is defiled not by what goes in but by what comes out of the body. As Eve embodies, speaks (or is spoken by) both metaphorical bodies and straddles both logics, we can ask whether she is partaking of defilement, that is, imbibing the fruit and giving off/spitting back language, or whether abjection lodges within: "Not that which goeth into the mouth defileth a man; but that which cometh out of the mouth, this defileth a man" (Matt. 15:11). And we must also ask how this relation to defilement is complicated when the man is a woman. Moreover, Kristeva's formulation of secular and sacred logics of abjection both parallels and helps reformulate some of the same questions about the genesis and location of evil and guilt that concerned Christian and Germanic groups of critics.

Kristeva returns to Oedipus to examine the connections between body and language and levels of abjection, but unlike de Lauretis, she is more concerned with the Oedipus of Colonnus, to whom Freud paid much less attention. When this subject Oedipus (that is, one who is no longer king) states his ignorance of the Law and, hence, his innocence before the Law, he confronts abjection, *declares* himself estranged from self. Kristeva glosses his admission thus:

> *I do not know the Law, the one who solves logical enigmas does not know the Law,* and that means *I who knows am not the Law.* Thus a first estrangement is introduced between knowledge and Law, one that unbalances the sovereign. If the Law is in the Other, my fate is neither power nor desire, it is the fate of an estranged person: my fate is death.[96]

At Colonnus Oedipus heralds the advent of the symbolic: his is "*transgression* due to a *misreading* of the Law," and the result is that abjection can henceforth be *interpreted* as "I am abject, that is, mortal and speaking."[97] It is via Oedipus at Colonnus's acknowledgment of the symbolic that we might "recognize ourselves without gouging out our eyes. . . . Incompleteness and dependency on the Other, far from clearing a desiring and murderous Oedipus, allow him only to make his dramatic splitting transmittable—transmittable to a foreign hero, and hence opening up the undecidable possibility of a few truth-effects."[98]

In many respects Eve shares this oedipal role; in the Saxon poem critics argue that her connection to the Law is much attenuated by ignorance, whether this be blamed on her "weaker thought" or rationalized according to Augustinian notions of "culpable ignorance"; her deed, or rather her consumption of the fruit, sets words finally adrift from the Word. In *Genesis B*, Eve provides passages into the symbolic: she makes language possible. And it remains to ask, *what is transmittable* as a result, what are the terms of this contradiction when the maternal body, linguistic antimatter, as it were, meets language—when Eve meets Oedipus.

Working with these two metaphors of the masculine body that underpin both secular/Germanic and Christian/sacred discourses of the poem—

oedipal desire as narrative center and propulsion, and Oedipus as abject subject of language, enabling the masculine entry into the symbolic—I want to begin as the poem does, with the Word, but with a clearer understanding of the terms of its symbolicity as these concern Eve. I have stated that the poem is much preoccupied with language, with the relation of words to the Word, with the development of disconnection and the reassertion of connection of signifier and signified. On the level of simple verbal repetition, phrases concentrating on the idea of "honoring the word" ("word weorðian") recur insistently, resonating with many variations—holding, trusting in, breaking, changing, or overturning the word.[99]

That the opening words of the poem are held up to be "divine" language—albeit a masculinized incarnation of the Word, and a highly arbitrary place to begin—poses an immediate challenge to nondivine language, in fact, to the poem itself. They are a resounding interdiction against both eating the fruit and human language. There is no discussing these divine words, no further or different representations of them are possible; the divine Word, with its absolute guarantee of correspondence of signifier and signified, precludes and disallows the ambiguities of representation. Satan, of course, begins the prohibited discussion, "feala worda gespæc/se engel ofermodes" (271–72, "the angel spoke many words of pride") with the express intention of robbing the divine Word of its absolute significance by persuading the human pair "þæt hie þæt onwendon þæt he mid his worde bebead" (405, "so that they overturn what he had commanded with his word"). The poem's many references to changing and breaking the Word chronicle the onset of representation, a process that is well underway before Eve's eating of the fruit. This is, after all, only one further representation of the collapse of divine signification.

Satan words and the progress of the poem itself irrevocably open the door to representation and the play of signification. Adam's first response to the tempter is to recall the divine voice and its command (523–31) and then to confess utter incomprehension: "Hwæt, ic þinra bysna ne mæg, / worda ne wisna wuht oncnawan / siðes ne sagona" (533–35, "Indeed, I cannot recognize at all thy commands, words or ways, nor thy mission or sayings"). But his rejection of the tempter is clinched because he has received no sign ("tacen" [540]) that will convince him. If Adam possesses, or is possessed by, absolute signification, we might question why he needs *another* sign of it. Adam here seeks, appears to need representation, and has already moved beyond a quiescent state of inarticulate belief.

My point here is that by the time divine desire as it is incarnate in the Word is ostensibly broken by Eve ("heo þa þæs ofetes æt, alwaldan bræc / word and willan," [599–600, "she ate the fruit, broke the word and the will of the Almighty"]), the perfect mesh of divine signification has long been destroyed. We are wholly in the realm of representation. As Renoir's argument cited in the previous section makes clear, Satan deceiving himself deceiving the tempter into deceiving Eve depicts a scenario of layered representation in which Eve will either interpret or become a representation herself, a "tacen," or text, for Adam to interpret.

The events of the Fall of the human pair parallel the human—here opposed to divine—movement into language, the emergence of nondivine desire and the reconnection of signifier and signified according to a situational subjectivity. Eve's role in this process is essential, though her incipient subjectivity is eventually subsumed by the reclamation and reassertion of the masculine subject, the realignment of the divine/masculine with the human/masculine. One of the most interesting, and problematic, aspects of Eve in this Saxon poem, which contributes both to the incipient formulation and dissolution of her subjectivity, is that the poet holds her before us in an unrelentingly double perspective. Everything about her is ambiguous; the poet does not let us organize her on any level. There is the repeated contrast, noted by so many critics, between motive for and consequences of her actions, between her "holdne hyge" (707, "loyal thought or intention") and its terrible results ("hearma swa fela, / fyrenearfeða" [705–6, "so many evils, sinful woes"]).[100] There is the insistence on her great beauty even as she consumes and embodies the most repulsive of fruits (626–27, 700, 701, 704), and even in her fallen state (821–22). Such contrasts, as we have seen in the previous section, can be variously interpreted as exoneration, sympathy, contempt or apology, according to Germanic or Christian interpretive frameworks. But we can also see them as contrasts and try to maintain the poet's double vision.

That Eve is both sincere and deceptive, ugly and beautiful, that she has a "weaker mind" ("wacran hige" [590]) and the passion and power to persuade are perhaps the clearest elements in a semantic confusion that surrounds her, one that may not be wholly accounted for by traditional ambivalence rooted in misogyny. Something far more complicated may be happening. In the Saxon poet's construction of Eve, definitions of many kinds lose their discreteness, and boundaries, especially those marking inner from outer, subject from object, eating from speaking, are dissolved. This last distinction is particularly important, for while we must keep in mind the tempter's key role as organizer and facilitator, we must also pay close attention to the relative autonomy of the distinguishing metaphor of the human fall, that of bodily process, and the Saxon poet's remarkable account of it. Eve's vision begins to dissolve and confuse semantic boundaries in earnest, toppling meaning, and forms of representation, into temporary chaos. As she eats the fruit, physical consumption is semantically equated with linguistic denial:

> forðon heo æt þam laðan onfeng
> ofer drihtnes word   deaðes beames
> weorcsumne wæstm.

(592–94)

(Thereupon she received from the loathsome one against God's word the
painful fruit of the tree of death)

The doubling of the acts of eating and speaking, as in rejecting, is repeated
a few lines later, when Eve's consumption of the fruit "breaks" the word of
God (599–600). Eve's experience of the fruit is realized on several levels. It
is not only edible, a function of physical consumption, but visible and pal-
pable as well. Her visual range is increased (600), her aesthetic sensibility
deepened as the world becomes more beautiful ("eall þeos woruld wliti-
gre," [604]), and the radiance that surrounds her may be touched ("nu þu
his hrinan meaht" [616]). It remains to be seen whether or not, and how, Eve
can translate her cross-sensual experience, which overturns divine meaning,
into alternative linguistic form.

The cross-significatory consequences of "eating words" are a particularly human, nonangelic aspect of fall and rebellion, which recalls the
traditional doctrinal problem of gnosis; Froula points out that the individual human claim of experience of the divine via self-knowledge, so often
dubbed as heresy, poses an essentially political challenge to scriptural
hierarchy and authority.[101] The poet's account of Eve's vision hovers between a replication of, and therefore an obvious and heretical challenge to
the divine, and an unfolding recognition of the physical conditions of
subjectivity.

Let us remember that, however we eventually rationalize Eve's experience of the fruit, the poet holds it before us as synonomous with Eve's
actual physical presence. After imbibing the apple, she becomes it. The
poet insists on her terrible beauty as she moves toward Adam (626–27),
carrying and embodying the fruit within her:

> Sum heo hire on handum bær,   sum hire æt heortan læg,
> æppel unsælga

(636–37)

(One of the wicked apples she bore in her hand, one lay in her heart)

Eve also evokes a cross-sensual fusion of inner and outer perspectives in her
representation to Adam of her experience: "þis ofet is swa swete, / bliðe on

breostum'' (655–56,"this fruit is so sweet, blithe in my breast"), and "Wearð me on hige leohte / utan and innan siðþan ic þæs ofætes onbat" (676–77, "light comes into my mind from without and within since I tasted of the fruit").

It is curious that the obviously forbidding and repulsive aspect of the tree of death (476–79), one of the many distinctive details in the Saxon poet's version of the Fall story, matters little in the account of Eve's consumption of its fruit. When this dietary taboo so closely associated with death is transgressed, the overcoming of food loathing is barely noticeable in the overwhelming emphasis on Eve's transfiguration. Food and body—in this case, the maternal body—become inseparable functions of each other, not yet rejected or undifferentiated by the symbolic. It is hard to determine the level or stage of Eve's abjection here, when Eve's speech, her representation of her experience, is indistinguishable from presence as embodiment of experience. We might paraphrase some of the questions raised by critics in the previous section in Kristeva's words and ask whether Eve is defiled by what comes out of her mouth, according to the Christian (New Testament) or sacred logic of abjection, or whether she defiled by what she has taken in, according to secular or Germanic logic.

The answer is at once neither and both, and if the question ceases to make sense after a while, this may also be a result of an ambiguity in Kristeva's argument, where she hedges between the dual locations of "sin" in the Fall story. When she asks whether sin is "owing to God or woman" she points out that although "the brimming flesh of sin belongs, of course, to both sexes" it remains the case that "its root and representation is nothing other than feminine temptation."[102] Root and representation, story and storytelling, if we recall de Lauretis's formulation, become one, functions of each other, in the ongoing production of narrativity.

What we are up against in this poem—from the point where Eve eats the fruit to just before this act is represented or read by Adam—is that how Eve is represented, what she signifies, eludes these masculine terms of representation. If abjection, and its attendant continual displacement of defilement onto the maternal body, is imagined in masculine terms, how then do we imagine or metaphorize the maternal body as distinct from the process of defilement and represent an abjection that may not be solely female, but more inclusively human? By confounding categories of sin, food, speech, and beauty in his vision of Eve, by arresting the readers' (and Adam's and God's) decisive or judgmental representation—no one may say that this means this at any point in this passage—the Saxon poet effectively puts these forms of masculine representation on hold.

How, we must still ask, does this delaying tactic contribute to identifying Eve as a subject, and how will Eve's entire experience be transmitted into the symbolic? Let me return for a moment to the Germanic role of peaceweaver as one means of metaphorizing subjectivity. When Eve agrees to eat the fruit she assumes a role, which, as I have already suggested, is predicated on both absence and paradox. I also maintain that she is consummately successful. In her transfigured state, where boundaries between inner and outer have been dissolved, she enacts *and* embodies the role. The woman who performs as peaceweaver is the physical pledge of peace, her words and her presence coalesce. The Saxon poet's vision of her is also a powerful account of the process of becoming identified in the achievement of the task. Eve's desire in and for the role becomes increasingly evident, and inseparable from her body and manifested by it. As her verbal persuasion becomes more intense—a *materialization* of desire so acutely evoked by the poet's choice of "thickly" ("þicce," [684], and "þiclice" [705])[103] to describe her persuasion—the poet reminds us of her great beauty (700, 701, 704). The peaceweaver's success and identity are achieved in the assertion, recognition, and ratification of her desire, which parallels and verges on replacing oedipal desire as the central structuring point of the narrative. The poem chronicles Eve's success in just these terms, as a triumphant and irresistible overflowing of desire. Adam is convinced as he identifies with her desire:

> oðþæt Adame   innan breostum
> his hyge hwyrfde   and his heorte ongann
> wendan to hire willan.

(715–17)

(Until within Adam's breast his thought turned, and his heart began to change according to her desire).

The fruit, one physical manifestation of Eve's desire, begins to provide a similarly cross-sensual experience for Adam, as it comes within him and reaches his heart ("Swa hit him on innan com, / hran æt heortan" [723–24]), but his experience is cut short in two highly dramatic ways. The first is that the poet cuts abruptly away from the human pair and focuses on the laughter and delight of the tempter. And the second is that Eve's incipient subjectivity ceases to elude forms of masculine representation. Her experience is read, named, assigned signification. In a passage that provides a stunning analogy for the process of representation itself, the poet effectively clears up the semantic confusion surrounding Eve and restores some boundaries of signification:

> He æt þam wife onfeng
> helle and hinnsið,   *þeah hit nære haten swa,*

ac hit ofetes noman   agan sceolde;
hit wæs þeah deaðes swefn   and deofles gespon,
hell and hinnsið   and hæleða forlor,
menniscra morð,   þæt hie to mete dædon,
ofet unfæle.

717–723, my italics)

(He took from that woman hell and death, *although it was not so named, but had to possess the name of fruit;* nonetheless it was the sleep of death, the devil's bond, hell and death and warriors' destruction, the murder of men, that they ate as food, unholy fruit.)

While I can think of few more riveting instances of variation in Old English poetry, I also think that part of the power of this passage comes from my equal fascination and horror at the closure it designates. The confusion of metaphors crystallizes into poetically powerful but nonetheless familiar images of death and destruction—especially familiar and ironic when we recall the inevitable failure of the peaceweaver to signify in a death-centred Germanic heroic world, where her success is outside signification. Eve's experience, and the readers' experience of Eve, are thus represented. The apple has a "new" name.[104]

When the poem returns to the human pair after the tempter's long rejoicing speech, Adam is (re)established as narrative center, as oedipal subject/hero contending with the feminine as obstacle and object. Although Eve has brought about, "marked out" for them, an evil path ("yfele gemearcod / uncer sylfra sið." 791–92), it is Adam who is afraid, hungry, and thirsty, who recriminates, who fears the worst, who assigns blame, who tries to take control of the future by action, who offers to swim the deepest and widest ocean to prove his good faith (830–35), and who introduces shame: "Ac wit þus baru ne magon bu tu ætsomne / wesan to wuhte' ("but we two must not be together thus naked" [838–39]). Adam is both the subject of the story and the means and force for its representation. Eve's short remaining speech shows her both bereft and deprived of words, removed from words in the face of Adam's barrage of words, though her presence lingers in yet another reminder of her beauty (821–22). Her few words also contain an intimation of the failure of Adam's words to represent her experience:

"Þu meaht hit me witan,   wine min Adam,
wordum þinum;   hit þe þeah wyrs ne mæg
on þinum hyge hreowan   þonne hit me æt heortan deð."

(824–26)

("Thou might accuse me, my dear Adam, with thy words, though it may not trouble thy mind worse any worse than it does my heart")

That Adam may not speak what is in Eve's heart concludes the poem's journey through representation, as it also bears witness to Eve's silence and disappearance as subject. I have suggested that the poem offers a challenge to itself, to human language, and I shall conclude now with some observations on the ways in which the poem resolves its own questions, and reclaims signification. It begins with the "divine" Word, which claims an absolute correspondence of signifier and signified—there really is no need for discussion, for further representation. But the play of representation— and this of course involves the poem itself—begins immediately, and poetic, satanic, masculine, and feminine words unleash a multiplicity of signifiers that set meaning adrift. The poem progresses toward a reassertion of connection of signified and signifier, a reclamation of meaning via the positioning of the human subject in language. And I have also argued that this reclamation is a reidentification of the masculine subject, a realignment of the divine/masculine with the human/masculine, that the divine and human word are both metaphorized via the masculine body. How, then, does Eve, whom the Saxon poet places squarely at the oedipal crossroads of this unusual poem, who carves out a passage into the symbolic, who makes human language possible, how does she disappear as subject?

When Oedipus discovers his terrible mistakes, he begins human interpretation. His abjection, his estrangement from self is formalized, understood, manifest through language. The revelation of abjection—that he did not know the Law and "that the Law is in the Other"—does not exonerate him in the least. Blame and guilt are not at issue here, but rather what may be learned, transmitted, via his experience. Kristeva suggests that we might recognize ourselves in Oedipus "without gouging out our eyes. . . . Our eyes can remain open provided we recognize ourselves as always already altered by the symbolic—by language."[105] The "truth-effects" glimpsed via Oedipus's dilemma reveal above all that he is (and we are) mortal and speaking.

In *Genesis B* Eve bears the terrible burden of ignorance of the Law, a burden painstakingly and methodically constructed by the poet, who tells us in so many ways that she did not know what she was doing, did not comprehend the true consequences of her present actions. Throughout her period of ignorance, the poet offers a vision of her that confuses and escapes the boundaries of representation as these had been laid out by the divine Word. As readers of the poem, we temporarily do not know what she means. She doesn't fit into oedipal, masculine constructions of narrativity or subjectivity.

But as I return to, and conclude with, the question of *what is transmit-table* as a result of the revelation of her ignorance—and indeed of our ignorance of her—I draw a blank. It is Adam who makes sense, makes language, out of her dilemma. In her transfigured state, Eve comes to finally represent the "tacen" Adam had required from the beginning of the poem. He assesses the *"tacen"* as a signified but later learns his mistake and reassigns it status as a mere and false signifier. Adam, in effect, takes over the oedipal role. We learn that *he* is mortal and speaking. And if Adam has become the estranged Oedipus, the one who makes language possible and who solves riddles, Eve then *becomes the riddle*. When Adam's words fail to speak what is in Eve's heart, the mystery of Eve's subjectivity deepens into silence; she becomes mortal, but spoken.

✳ ✳

Further Reading

Women's relation to language, as both readers and writers, is one of the central issues in current feminist critical discourse—and also one of the most variously debated. I refer here to some studies that will present an overview, not a summary, of this debate. Annette Kolodny introduces some important revaluations of the reading process in "A Map for Rereading: Or, Gender and the Interpretation of Literary Texts," *New Literary History* 11 (1980): 451–67. Elizabeth Abel's *Writing and Sexual Difference* (Chicago, 1982) takes up the issue of women's relation to deconstructionist difference, a question also addressed by Elizabeth A. Meese in *Crossing the Double Cross* (Chapel Hill, NC, 1986); see especially chapter 1, "Sexual Politics and Critical Judgment." For a discussion of the French feminist connection of writing and the female body, see Hélène Cixous and Catherine Clément, *The Newly Born Woman*, trans. Betsy Wing (Minneapolis, 1986) and Ann Rosalind Jones, "Writing the Body: Towards an Understanding of *l'Ecriture Feminine*," in *The New Feminist Criticism*, ed. Elaine Showalter (New York, 1985), 361–77. *Gender and Reading Essays on Readers, Texts and Contexts*, ed. Elizabeth A. Flynn and Patrocinio P. Schweickart (Baltimore, 1986) offers a good selection of theoretical and applied discussions focusing on women as readers; also of interest is Pamela Caughie's review of this and other recent publications in this area, "Women Reading/Reading Women: A Review of Some Recent Books on Gender and Reading," *Papers on Language and Literature* 24, no. 3 (Summer 1988): 317–35; Caughie provides a useful survey of works that challenge "sexually neutral assumptions behind our aesthetic and critical theories" (318).

Chapter 3

Beowulf and the Origins of Civilization

✻ James W. Earl ✻

Two Languages

This essay will suggest the relevance of psychoanalysis to the study of *Beowulf*. It offers a model for understanding heroic literature, and epic in particular, as an idealization of a certain sort, inviting certain forms of psychological identifications in the audience—socially desirable identifications, to be sure, but necessarily effected in the individual. In the case of *Beowulf*, these identifications are facilitated by vast silences in the text that are analogous to the silence of the psychoanalyst, another facilitator of such identifications. In this way, heroic literature produces an analyzable psychological effect in the audience, much as tragedy does with its catharsis.

Also, insofar as *Beowulf* is a Christian poem, I would like to restore the psychological dimension to our discussion of the Anglo-Saxon conversion, which is central to our understanding of Anglo-Saxon culture and literature but always treated as if it were a purely ideological phenomenon, a more or less simple matter of shifting alliances, reforming institutions, and substituting terms. But Christianity, with its cultivation of guilt in the individual, and its institutionalization of a cultural superego in the Church, imports its own psychology along with new social structures and doctrines.

This Christian psychology invites psychoanalytic interpretation, so its historical origins in the conversion should be analyzable too.[1] The notoriously difficult relations between Christian and pre-Christian traditions and values in Anglo-Saxon culture, and in *Beowulf* in particular, can be understood historically and theologically, of course; but they can also—and perhaps even better—be understood psychologically, as an interesting case of ambivalence at the cultural level.

As I read *Beowulf* and other heroic literature, I am led to wonder about the relation of individual to social and cultural psychology. Like Freud, I am tempted to analyze culture as if it were an individual—to speak, for example, of its growth, its mourning, or its ambivalence, or of myths (and to some extent literature) as its dreams. But how can such analogies be defended—how can *psychoanalysis* be defended—among today's compet-ing critical ideologies, many of which have renounced both the concept of culture (a "facile totalization," as Fredric Jameson would say, at best only a dominant culture repressing myriad subcultures struggling for expression), and the concept of the individual (a bourgeois fabrication built on a human-istic conception of human nature, the myth of the autonomous ego)? And even if those concepts could be retained, could we discover a clear train of linkages between them, to account for all their tempting analogies?

If we pragmatically dismiss these philosophical objections (and I do),[2] at the very least we will wish to clarify those areas of psychoanalytic the-ory where the linkages between the individual and the group must lie—the theories of identification and the superego. Not to forget the text itself— so easy in theoretical discussions like this—I will point to certain passages in *Beowulf* characterized by silence and ambivalence, the psychological signatures of Anglo-Saxon heroic and elegiac poetry. But I am not so much interested in "psychoanalyzing the text" as in understanding how the text, with its deep, uninterpretable silences, might be said to sit in the ana-lyst's place and psychoanalyze its audience—then and now—by acting as a screen for its projections.

This approach hardly replaces earlier approaches to the poem (the first of this volume's "two languages") and, in fact, builds heavily upon them; in the end, psychoanalysis being the omnivorous hermeneutic that it is, it interprets them, and itself, right along with the poem. In this instance our two languages are not exactly inimical, but they are not exactly complemen-tary, either. Psychoanalysis is concerned with all of the mental states rele-vant to the poem and its understanding, and therefore our "first-language" responses to the poem are an important part of its subject. When I come to grapple with particular problems in the poem, it will be seen how "second-language" theoretical judgments tend to grow out of philological, textual, literary, and historical first-language analysis, considered along with our more immediate psychological responses to the poem.

Nor can psychoanalysis, at least as I invoke it here, claim to interpret the poem better or more comprehensively than other contemporary ap-proaches. I certainly do not consider psychoanalysis an "ultimate horizon" (Jameson's term again) or a programmatic hermeneutic. I can claim to ad-dress only the sorts of psychological questions that the poem prompts in a student of Freud. But these are important, if not ultimate, questions. They primarily concern origins: not only the origins of civilization, but the ori-gins of the poem and the origins of our critical attitudes toward it. These questions turn out to be related psychologically. The individuality of the author and the reader, I would like to suggest, is one issue that binds them into a single problem.

For the philologist, the folklorist, the New Critic, the oralist, the post-modernist, and the New Historicist—that is, for just about every scholarly reader—the author of *Beowulf* is decentered, erased, ignored, diffused into a web of preexisting traditions and historical forces, or evaporated into the ephemerality of oral culture. On the other hand, if I am right, the author was a highly original genius, a strong poet who in large part shaped those traditions, at least as we perceive them now.[3] Why is this position, which I find almost inevitable, so at odds with most traditions of *Beowulf* scholarship? What is it about the poem that invites such resistance to the idea of authorship, at least in those who have set about to conquer the poem intellectually?

It is partly because the roots of *Beowulf* scholarship lie in folklore and philology: the idea of an author never had a chance. Today it is orality and ideology. The poem does invite this response, I must admit, by passing itself off as traditional—even though it is demonstrably unique and original in many important respects, and even though there is scant proof of its traditionality outside its own claims and our uncommon willingness to believe them.

These two readings of the poem (the traditional *Beowulf* and the original *Beowulf*) imply not just ideologies but critical psychologies as well; for if the poem sits in place of the analyst, much of our response to questions of origin and authorship will be influenced by our dispositions toward the authority of the text, and toward authority in general. The ideology served by our interpretations may be humanism, or romanticism, nationalism, Marxism, or feminism; but weighed psychoanalytically, our interpretations will always be to some extent vicissitudes of the family romance, operations of the ego, expressions and sublimations of our own narcissism. We are social beings; but reading the poem here at the desk late at night remains an extremely private, individual act. That individuality is not insignificant, nor is it imponderable, and it might be factored right into our interpretations.

Our attitudes toward authorship and the authority of the text will be the inverse of our attitudes toward the autonomous ego, the self. If these are ideological commitments—humanism, Marxism—they still have psychological roots and can hardly be dissociated from our conceptions of ourselves as relatively free individuals, or as members and representatives of groups, or as expressions or victims of historical forces. Such self-representations are largely characterological, hammered out in childhood; so, as the poem sits in place of the analyst, the analyst ultimately sits in place of our parents. Epic especially may be said to serve with singular devotion that universal (though not ultimate) ideology that Lacan calls *the Law of the Father* and that Freud explored in his theory of the superego.

The theory is a good description of the Anglo-Saxon concept of Fate, *wyrd*. Thus our own highly individualized relations to the superego are bound to inform our interpretations of a poem like *Beowulf*.

The role of psychoanalysis in critical thinking today is largely determined by the ideological drift of other schools: its role is to reassert the value and legitimacy of the individual (whether the author or the reader) as a focus of critical attention, and the importance of the unconscious and the irrational in interpretation—and in mental life generally. Psychoanalytic readings of texts, psychobiographies of their authors and psychohistories of their contexts notwithstanding, however, the greatest contributions of psychoanalysis to literary criticism are probably just the internalization of the simplest Freudian insights—unconscious intention, for example, or the overdetermination, condensation, and displacement of meaning, or art as sublimation. Another obvious example is Harold Bloom's realization that literary influence is not just a matter of one poet having learned from another like a student from a teacher, but more a matter of the deeply "agonistic" relations of son to father.

The anxiety of influence is not just a matter for poets. Every reader's relation to a text is similarly complex, if we treat reader-response responsibly in light of Freud. The common reader's response is also oedipal to a degree. That is the simple insight I would like to internalize here. Psychologically, the suspension of disbelief is not rational, nor entirely willing; it is a complicated, spontaneous act of projection and identification. That is where we must start; though in the end, projection and identification will lead us, like the Oedipus complex itself, back to the theory of the superego.

As a genre, epic is involved with the task of superego construction, at the individual and at the cultural levels. Freud summarizes: "Strengthening of the superego is a most precious cultural asset in the psychological field. Those in whom it has taken place are turned from being opponents of civilization into being its vehicles."[4] That strengthening is one of the tasks of epic, the poetic accompaniment to the birth of civilization.

But the epic cannot discriminate among its audiences: it sets about constructing our superegos as well as its original audience's. So in the case of epic especially, interpretation is likely to express our own invaded psychologies as well as the author's. In this regard, *Beowulf* is an extreme, and therefore an extremely interesting, case.

Why *Beowulf*?

Beowulf has a bad reputation: Woody Allen advises English majors, "Just don't take any course where they make you read *Beowulf*." Despite its foreignness and its difficulty, however, and its funereal obsession with death, *Beowulf* is now commonly taught to ninth graders, along with the *Iliad* and the *Odyssey,* as if these were adventure or fantasy stories. This trivialization accounts for some of the poem's bad reputation, but not all of it.

Beowulf is a difficult text. Its language, style, and values seem as distant and strange as those of Homer and the Greek tragedies. Like them, *Beowulf* opens up a metrical world parallel to our own, different but strangely akin, throwing our ideas and attitudes, some of them unconscious, into new light. But our kinship with the world of *Beowulf*—our perspective in this new light—always remains hauntingly out of focus. Today a good reader of *Beowulf* has to be an expert time traveler and mystery unraveler, an expert scholar and interpreter; but even so, it remains uncertain what we can learn from the poem that is not wholly contingent on our own attitudes and beliefs. It is not at all clear that a "clean" interpretation is possible. This may be true of all texts to a degree, but again, *Beowulf* is an extreme case.

The poet and his first readers already had something of the same problem, however. The world of *Beowulf,* set in the heroic past, was already distant from them, akin to but strangely different from their Christian Anglo-Saxon world. Between the world of the poem and the world of its poet lay not only the gulf of meter but the complex transformations, social and psychological, of the development from tribe to state, and of conversion to Christianity. The relation of the Germanic tribal elements in the poem to Christianity has always been its most notorious crux and the driving force of its criticism. *Beowulf* is an ethical poem of the Christian Anglo-Saxons, but its ethics are not Christian, and its hero is not an Anglo-Saxon; so it is not clear how the poem's ideals might actually have functioned in the actual world of the audience.

Many scholars meditating on this problem have concluded that an Anglo-Saxon audience could not have accepted the poem's non-Christian ("pagan") ideals, so it is commonly argued that the poem's heroic warrior virtues are actually metaphors for Christian ones. Lately it is even commonly said that the poem's greatness may lie precisely in the way it subtly *undermines* those heroic ideals—in effect, undermines itself.[5] These are modern readings of *Beowulf.* They are not entirely false, but they are unlikely simplifications, because they still leave many questions unasked. A few questions I like to ask are: (1) How do the psychologies of tribal and civilized societies differ? (2) What are the psychological dynamics of the transition from one to the other, and of religious conversion? (3) How and why do we idealize the past? and (4) How do we identify with and internalize a work of literature? In any case, we can assume from the start that *Beowulf* bore a complex, indirect, and nonmimetic relation to any historical reality, including the Anglo-Saxon ethos either before or after the conversion.

I have mentioned our kinship with the poem, and also the Anglo-Saxons' kinship with it; but then there is a third kinship, ours to the Anglo-Saxons. We still live in a largely Anglo-Saxon world, and even over a millennium the child is father to the man. Different as we have become from the Anglo-Saxons and from each other, in our cultural origins we still sometimes see stark enlargements of our deepest traits, which otherwise now go unobserved—though they have hardly disappeared for all that. The hall may have become the office, its rituals a system of contracted salaries, duties, and taxes, the wars corporate (or even academic); but the relations of such traditionally male-dominated institutions to women, the family, and religion remain as teasingly unresolved as ever and are still the subject of much of our literature. So too the broken oath, the failed promise, the conflict of loyalties, the silent hero, the alienation of the individual from society, and the problematic roles of women and kinship in social life.

These are the great Germanic themes—Germanic, more than biblical or classical. Our modern English-speaking world is indebted to those three traditions equally, and the Germanic leg of this cultural triad is firmly rooted in *Beowulf*. It is perhaps the oldest, most ambitious, and most deeply resonant text in that tradition; it is the nearly inaudible, Germanic basso profundo of English and other Germanic literature. For all its Christian elements, it is still our most pregnant Germanic text. *Beowulf* is not just another poem. It seems to lay bare our Germanic, our Anglo-Saxon origins.

But the investigation of our own origins has to be fraught with all the usual perils of self-reflection—nearsightedness first of all, blindness to what is too close; also ambivalence, denial, avoidance, and vague fears of what might be discovered beneath the mask—in short, anxiety and guilt. As a result, *Beowulf* both reveals and disguises some surprisingly familiar structures of our cultured Germanic, Anglo-Saxon, English-speaking minds: antifeminism, repression of affect, materialism, and denial of death.

This system of relations—of us to *Beowulf*, of *Beowulf* to the Anglo-Saxons, and of the Anglo-Saxons to us—constitutes the meaning of *Beowulf*. There is not much agreement about this meaning, though the poem's best students do like to claim that *Beowulf* is a poem for our day. But it has always been a poem for the day. That is because silence was a positive virtue to the Anglo-Saxons. Thus *Beowulf* (like the Old Testament, but unlike the classical epics) has its deep silences—so much is left unsaid!—in which we can hardly help but read our selves, and out of which we draw our interpretations. Like the sagas, the poem seldom speaks, for example, of its characters' motivations or feelings; so it is easy to assume they are like us, or like our stereotyped ideas of them. Not only speech, but heroic behavior is also typically restrained. Behind this restraint, can we assume great passions are being repressed? Which ones? Fear perhaps, hiding behind all of its predictably heroic reaction formations?

Family and economic life are wholly invisible in the poem too; and the poem's attitudes toward women, and toward themes as fundamental as religion and heroism, are famously ambiguous. The poem might be said not to articulate its themes at all, leaving the reader a wide range of interpretive freedom. Thus the heroic, or the overreaching, or the sinful, or the existential, or the Christian, or the Christ-like Beowulf—the folk-Beowulf, the kingly Beowulf, the monastic Beowulf: like *Hamlet, Beowulf* supports with its silence whatever reading we most wish, and modern readers seem to wish many things of it.

Interpretation is not a science even in straightforward cases, and *Beowulf* is a rock on which interpretations are easily broken. The history of *Beowulf* scholarship (like Anglo-Saxon scholarship generally) has been a history of the projection of cherished beliefs upon the poem, both individually and collectively. They form the great tradition of Protestant, English, Gothic, Pan-Germanic, romantic, Victorian, and modern readings of Anglo-Saxon culture—a tradition of cherished beliefs, that the Anglo-Saxons were really Protestant, or democratic, or noble savages, or Aryan folk, or anxiously self-contradictory, existential Christian warriors.

The modern interpretation of *Beowulf* was born in Tolkien's analysis of its martial heroism in 1936:

> While the older southern imagination has faded for ever into literary ornament, the northern has power, as it were, to revive its spirit even in our own times. It can work, even as it did work with the *goðlauss* viking, without gods: martial heroism as its own end. But we may remember that the poet of *Beowulf* saw clearly: the wages of heroism is death.[6]

This is in fact a very wise—and very modern—interpretation, one that genuinely makes *Beowulf* a poem for Tolkien's day; only three years later the great ship burial at Sutton Hoo was exhumed and immediately reburied to protect it from the Germans. Tolkien was not in a position to romanticize Germanic heroism or to trivialize it. To him the poem's theme is obvious: the poet saw clearly that the wages of heroism is death. (One might say just as easily, of course, that the poet saw clearly that the wages of heroism is victory, or glory, or peace.)

Unbelievably, only a half-century later, Tolkien's Christian existentialism, which has served so many interpretations well, and which is so moving in itself, looks almost sentimental to postmodern eyes, like Churchill's posturing. Tolkien's own fiction is in some measure responsible for the reduction of *Beowulf* to adolescent literature. We await a postmodern *Beowulf*; for surely, our more complete disillusionment is bound to discover itself even more forcefully in those same poetic silences.

This essay does not deliver a postmodern *Beowulf*. My title, "The Origins of Civilization," is Freudian in spirit and, therefore, distinctly old-fashioned in the postmodern climate. By the suspicious totalization *civilization* I mean a stage in social evolution characterized by cities, as well as by literacy, statutory law, and civil government—as opposed to an earlier stage characterized by villages, orality, revenge, customary law, and kinship structures. These are well-worn anthropological concepts, still useful since Freud's day, though they will never be precise enough to resist philosophical attack, because the development from one "stage" to the other involves large and complex areas of overlap. But is it necessarily reductivist or essentialist to define such structures contingently, within the numberless historical accidents we call a society, or the ceaseless flow we call history? Must it be mean spirited, patronizing, or romantic to explore the otherness of tribal societies still struggling on the margins of civilization, or to explore, as in this case, the deepest roots of our own civilization?

For our generation has witnessed this holocaust: civilization's eradication of tribal societies everywhere. We are bound to mourn this loss forever. We share this mourning with the *Beowulf* poet, and it is one of our deepest ties to the poem. For now especially, in this generation, the relation of civilizations to the "primitive" societies that preceded them, and from which they developed, remains an urgent issue in the great tradition of Montaigne, Rousseau, and Freud. My focus is the transition in England. For the English-speaking world, and for much of the rest of the world too now, Anglo-Saxon England (along with early Greece and ancient Israel) was one of those formative stages, determining the direction of future development; and it remains one of our earliest cultural memories, traces of which can still be found deeply embedded in the present.

Interestingly, the Anglo-Saxons themselves, like the Greeks and the Jews before them, once they had entered into the stream of civilization were immediately obsessed with their own origins, with the transition they had just endured. *Beowulf* was not written in the heroic past, but about it, and in particular about the trauma of its loss. In large part the poem creates that heroic past retroactively, thematizing cultural origins and the transition to civilization. Like the Pentateuch, and like Homer and the Greek tragedies, *Beowulf* and many of its companion poems in Old English dwell on the origins of civilization, mourning the loss of the prehistoric tribal past, now redefined as a heroic age. This mournful obsession defines the *heroic*, the *epic,* and the *elegiac* generally, and the Anglo-Saxon case with special clarity.

More than my title, of course, is Freudian in spirit, as I think through this mournful obsession, the audience's psychological relations to that imaginary heroic world, and its identification with those consoling idealizations of what has been lost. Criticism too has its psychological component: the greatest inhibitions to interpretation, in literature as well as life, seem to me to be psychological before they are philosophical, and they are barely open to "critical" discussion at all, because they occur at the personal (and in fact unconscious) level, even if collectively. These are the inhibitions Freud called projection, resistance, and transference and countertransference.

I have already mentioned *projection* as a special problem in reading Old English poetry, because of the ethical value the Anglo-Saxons placed on silence; and our unconscious *resistance* to perceptions that pose a threat to us. *Transference* and *countertransference* are more specifically psychoanalytic terms. The first refers to the projections of the analysand upon the silent analyst; the second refers to the limitations placed on analysis by the analyst's own neuroses, which necessarily cloud and distort interpretation unless he or she is aware of them. That is why the analyst must be analyzed. Countertransference is the specific mechanism of projection and resistance in the psychoanalyst, but the concept might easily be extended to interpretation in general.

In short, who we are means quite a lot to our interpretations, and the best we can do is account for ourselves every step of the way. In this regard, the neuroses I bring to *Beowulf* are neither religious nor heroic; but scholarship has its own neuroses, so it might be pertinent here to report two recent dreams.

Falling asleep recently while thinking about *Beowulf,* I dreamed of a sphinx, not quite buried in the desert sand; in fact, no matter how hard I tried to bury it, one eye always remained uncovered. The sphinx is *Beowulf,* of course; but it is also my superego. I had the second dream the night before delivering a conference paper on the poem. I dreamed about a little girl who had a fascinating, unusual doll, every part of which—arms, legs, head, torso—seemed to be made from other dolls, all of different colors and proportions. I knew where it had come from: the little girl's brother had collected all the old, broken dolls he could find around the neighborhood, and he had loaded them into his red wagon and pulled them home behind his bicycle; then he had made a single doll out of all their parts and had given it to his sister. Far from thinking it was junk, she thought it was beautiful and loved it—first of all because it was unlike any other doll, and yet like them all; also because it was so interesting, and also because her brother had made it for her, and because he had made it so well.

The doll, of course, is *Beowulf;* I am the little girl, and the poet is her brother. In the construction and the meaning of the doll may be seen something of my understanding of the poem's genesis and the relation of its traditions to its originality. Perhaps because I first studied *Beowulf* while also reading Levi-Strauss, in the dream I represent the poet as a *bricoleur.* When I fall asleep, it seems I am still a structuralist.

So I am the little girl; but the dream is in the third person, because I am also the brother, piecing together (like the poet) my own bricolage, my effigy of *Beowulf* constructed from past scholarship; and you are the sister I am trying to please. In scholarship as in poetry, practice tells me, originality is still mostly bricolage, a new and loving reconstruction of the materials we have inherited from the past. Among other things, the dream tells me that as a scholar I do not identify so much with the hero of the poem as with the poet, and with others who have made this identification. I take this dream, like the sphinx dream, as a good sign.

My double identification in the dream, with both the girl and her brother, illustrates certain features of identification—its shifting ambivalence and overdetermination—which will become important later in our interpretation of the poem. The most important of these features is that insofar as I am a reader of *Beowulf* I identify with the girl, but insofar as my reading is itself a creative act, I identify with her brother, the artist. This is how overdetermination works.

Actually, the situation is much more complex, the images more overdetermined, than that, for the characters in the dream are clearly modeled on my wife and her older brother (she was my *Beowulf* student, he is a craftsman), as well as my earliest memories of me and my own older brother (an inveterate scavenger with his red wagon). My scholarship is never entirely free of even the most intimate themes of my life. Enough said about that.

Like the poem, then, the dream is richly overdetermined and deeply ambivalent. In fact, the neatness of all this splitting makes me think that ambivalence itself is probably the dream's latent thought and that *Beowulf* has unconsciously become a symbol of it for me. Thus the ambivalent image of the poem itself: it is only a junk doll, but a unique, beautiful, and meaningful one.

The dream also brings rather delicate problems of gender to consciousness. *Beowulf* is a markedly antifeminist poem, and making it a gift to the little girl is my attempt at compensation, though necessarily condescending: she is still being strongly marginalized, after all. I do not see any way around that, since the poem so strongly marginalizes the female reader already. My simultaneous identification with her, however, indicates my deep ambivalence about the patriarchal project of the poem and the patriarchal project of its criticism (not to mention the patriarchal structures of professional life, teaching, and marriage). Beyond that, moreover, the bond of love between her and her brother, both of whom I identify with strongly, though in different ways, indicates how far from such ideological criticism my psychoanalytic responses to the poem really are.

The fulfilled wish of the dream is the harmony of opposites, *concordia discors*. Pursued long enough, the analysis would come to rest in the thought that although I am a child, I am also a parent—a form of the original oedipal paradox ("What walks on four legs in the morning?" and so forth). Much unresolvable conflict and ambivalence is harmonized in the manifest dream, and the junk-doll *Beowulf* is an overdetermined symbol of this harmony.

The ease with which the problem of understanding *Beowulf*, more than other poems, shades into the problem of understanding myself suggests to me (naturally) that the high indeterminacy of the poem provokes strong psychological responses, which may well be a clue to its raison d'être. Just such an indetermincy in the Greek tragedies seems intended to provoke catharsis. What does *Beowulf* intend for us in this way? If the overdetermined symbols and vast silences of the poem function like the silence of the analyst, the poem will function as a screen for our projections, which can be manipulated by the plot and predictably drawn toward resolution.

I have already mentioned the psychoanalytic term for such carefully controlled projections: the transference. The psychoanalytic encounter itself is often described as a drama (so why not an epic?) of transference and countertransference. Perhaps then our understanding of the psychoanalytic situation is applicable to our encounter with works like *Beowulf*—and it is we who are on the couch, being affected purposefully by these identifications.

Identification of one sort or another is essential. Our relations to poetry are always highly personal. Even Keats's negative capability is only the heightened ability to make identifications without the interference of transference and countertransference. When statements about art claim to be impersonal, objective, and scientific, we are probably in the presence of resistance. The compulsion to objectivity is both a denial of affect and a exaggerated claim of importance—"my thought, my theory, my method is universal, ultimate, transcendental"—two sides of the same neurotic coin. There is still a lot of positivistic and rationalistic scholarship being produced about *Beowulf*, in a spirit of resistance to the more modest and self-effacing claims of both modernism and postmodernism. I am finally coming to see the necessity and the value of what Bloom calls a "strong misreading."

Thus objectivity is not exactly the goal of my interpretation; objectivity is not what is left when the psychological inhibitions to interpretation are finally overcome. *Disillusionment* strikes me as a more useful, less impersonal concept. This disillusionment is not necessarily negative or morbid; like the reality principle, it is an agent of the ego, something close to an active psychological force. Perhaps it is a version of Freud's death instinct, progressing naturally, though against resistance, from infant narcissism to the bier. Perhaps it would be more comforting to think of it in Socratic terms as the self-effacement that naturally comes with self-knowledge.

Not surprisingly, the silences of *Beowulf* seem to me symptomatic, or proleptic, of even these latest developments in our cultural and personal histories. I see *Beowulf* as an artful, cagey, and defensive last stand against disillusionment with both heroism and religion; affirming and denying the comforts of both those illusions at the same time; postheroic, Christian but secular. That is not the same as saying that the poem undermines its own ideals, though: ambivalence is not the same as ambiguity. Ambivalence is a psychological term pointing to the attitudes, conscious or unconscious, of the author and the audience, as well as to the poem. Ambiguity is a hermeneutic problem involving the critical faculties, whereas ambivalence is a vicissitude of the passions, requiring a certain amount of disillusionment for its appreciation. This is one of the qualities ninth graders do not bring to *Beowulf.*

I suspect that behind the silence and restraint of Germanic heroism there are indeed great passions being repressed, and therefore great ambivalence. The elegies, especially "The Wanderer," tell me so:

> Ic to soþe wat
> þæt biþ in eorle   indryhten þeaw,
> þæt he his ferðlocan   fæste binde,
> healde his hordcofan,   hycge swa he wille.
> Ne mæg werig mod   wyrde wiðstondan,
> ne se hreo hyge   helpe gefremman.
> Forðon domgeorne   dreorigne oft
> in hyra breostcofan   bindað fæste;
> swa ic modsefan   minne sceolde,
> oft earmcearig,   eðle bidæled,
> freomægum feor   feterum sælan. . . .

> (I know for a fact
> In an earl it is always a noble habit
> To seal fast the soul's chest,
> The treasure chest, think what he may.

The weary mind cannot withstand fate,
Nor a troubled spirit be of assistance.
Eager for glory then, often he binds
Unhappiness fast in his life's locker.
Deprived of home, far from family,
So I in misery my own spirit
Must often seal in chains of sorrow. . . .)

(11–21)[7]

The Wanderer's psychology is neither Christian nor Roman, nor even consistent. It is easy enough to understand the masculine, stoic, "noble" impulse to lock sorrow away in the silence of the heart, to repress it; it is more difficult to understand that doing so might actually cure the troubled spirit. To the Wanderer, the mind is weary only if its weariness is spoken, but he is certainly a bad advertisement for this assumption. As in the other elegies, his hoarding of language in silence is overfilled and broken even as it is being described and affirmed. The elegies are speech out of silence, expressions of the inexpressibility of loss, absence and grief, emotional contradictions of their own stoic assertions—masterpieces of ambivalence.

Readers cannot decide, therefore, whether the Wanderer is at peace or in despair, whether he awaits God's grace or has already achieved it, or gains it in the course of speaking—or whether the conflicting attitudes in the poem can even belong to a single voice. The poet could have made such issues plain, but rather he invites these questions, perhaps because he cannot answer them, perhaps because he cannot even ask them. We are thrust into his ambivalence regarding them as soon as we accept the irreducibility of the poem to a set of true or untrue statements. Strong arguments for any one of the interpretations I have listed are to some extent, then, projections of the reader's own attitudes, various rationalizations of the same provocative inkblot. And *Beowulf* presents us with an even greater screen than "the Wanderer" upon which to project our fears, desires, and ambivalences.

Hero to Hero

In 1983 I published an essay in *Psychiatry* magazine, which included the following argument among its several conclusions:

The endless debate over whether Beowulf behaves correctly at the end of the poem is thus beside the point; what matters in the context . . . is how Beowulf's *troops* behave. . . . Whether or not Byrhtnoth should have let

the Vikings take position at the Battle of Maldon is similarly beside the
point to the men who sacrifice themselves for him after he has been
killed.[8]

A year later Colin Chase reviewed the essay in the *Old English Newsletter,*
taking issue with this particular point of mine:

> Despite his claim that psychoanalytic anthropology is both "universal and
> particular," Earl is quick to dismiss particular literary problems if they
> clash with his general theory. Having classified Beowulf as an "ego
> ideal," for example, Earl dismisses the question of whether Beowulf's be-
> havior at the end of the poem is in fact ideal as being "beside the point."[9]

I would like to answer this criticism by considering the psychoanalytic relationship between the two heroes, Byrhtnoth and Beowulf, in some detail.
The conceit of this argument is that Byrhtnoth represents the epic's intended
audience; and so we might explore his identification with Beowulf as a sort
of thought-experiment.

I like to imagine Byrhtnoth as a reader of *Beowulf;* I even like to imagine *Beowulf* inspiring the English at the Battle of Maldon, as Henry Adams
(following William of Malmesbury and Wace, in *Mont-St.-Michel and
Chartres*) liked to imagine the *Chanson de Roland* inspiring the Normans at
the Battle of Hastings. It makes a certain sense, even if it never happened.
For all we know, *Beowulf* was written *after* the Battle of Maldon and was
influenced by it; for all we know, *Beowulf* never had any readers at all. But
even these possibilities do not detract from the interest of our thought-
experiment: how might Byrhtnoth have read *Beowulf*? Not in the sense of
Bolton's question—how Alcuin might have interpreted *Beowulf*[10]—but in
psychoanalytic terms, what would the structure of Byrhtnoth's identification with the epic hero have been?

Identification with the hero is not a simple matter, considered philo-
sophically or psychologically. The hero is an idealization, and both idealization and identification are complex areas of psychoanalytic theory.[11]
What exactly is the hero an idealization of? Do I identify with him as a
representation of my ego?—or what I would like to be, or what I should
be, or even (the possibilities are endless) what I most fear or hate? What if
the hero, like God, were an idealized parent figure, with all the conflicted
feelings *that* could involve? These and other questions suggest themselves.
Nor is there any reason the possibilities should not be mixed; as in my
dream of the *Beowulf* doll, so with mental representations generally: overdetermination is the rule.

Identification could be defined roughly as a failure or refusal to distinguish the self from an object. But which part of the self is being extended

in this way—the id, the ego, or the superego? And most important, what results are to be brought about by such identifications, especially with a literary character? My first thought is that whereas the tragedy aims at relieving, in its oddly negative way, certain feelings in the audience temporarily—like taking a laxative, as Aristotle put it—the epic is more positively ambitious: it aims at structuring and reinforcing prevailing social relations, by creating and maintaining certain shared attitudes in the audience. Identification is the means to this end, but it is indirect and complex; it is certainly not a matter of encouraging everyone in the audience to imitate the hero—for what kind of society would that be?

According to Aristotle, the epic hero (Achilles) is flawed like the tragic hero (Oedipus). The flawed hero—an idealization conspicuously short of ideal in some regard—presents special problems of identification. Our identification implicates us in the hero's flaw and the guilt that it symbolizes. Certainly in the case of the tragic hero, who is being conspicuously punished by the gods for his hamartia, identification with him either produces, or is produced by, feelings of guilt in ourselves, the audience. The hero's death then brings cathartic relief from these feelings, as a form of self-punishment. To some extent at least, we go to the tragedy to punish ourselves and feel the better for it.

I have always resisted the common notion that Beowulf has such a tragic flaw, because I do not want to confuse epic with tragedy or encourage the elucidation of this flaw as the aim of criticism; but Beowulf and Byrhtnoth do raise questions of this sort. There is an especially puzzling contradiction encoded in the Anglo-Saxon version (perhaps the Germanic version generally) of the heroic ideal, and in our responses to it. In both *Beowulf* and *The Battle of Maldon* this contradiction appears as a suicidal logic of unresolvable conflicts, complete with easy rationalizations of unarticulated ambivalence. These rationalizations (for example, "the conflict of loyalties," or "Christian vs. Germanic") have been the traditional subject of literary criticism, so here we must take a long first-language detour.

If we come to *Beowulf* primarily through its Germanic background, we tend to see Beowulf's fateful decision to face the dragon alone as exemplary of Germanic heroism; the dragon evokes the Midgarth-serpent, an apocalyptic symbol of fatality itself. On the other hand, if we come to the poem from a Christian angle, we tend to find Christian wisdom in it; the dragon is a symbol of *malitia,* evoking the Beast of the Apocalypse, and Beowulf's defeat is a flawed moral action: he is brought low in the end by his pride and avarice. Which is only to say, perhaps, that from a Christian point of view, Germanic heroism looks a lot like a combination of pride and avarice.

Whatever our perspective, the result of Beowulf's fateful decision is the same: his people, vigorously berated for abandoning him in the hour of his greatest need (though he did insist on going alone, didn't he?), are certain to be destroyed also, now that he is dead:

> "Forðon sceall gar wesan
> monig morgen-ceald   mundum bewunden,
> hæfen on handa,   nalles hearpan sweg
> wigend weccean,   ac se wonna hrefn
> fus ofer fægum   fela reordian,
> earne secgan,   hu him æt æte speow,
> þenden he wið wulf   wæl reafode. . . . "

> ("So spear shall be
> Many a morning-cold fast in fist,
> Upheld in hand—no sound of harp
> Waking warriors, but the black raven
> Impatiently calling out over the doomed,
> Telling the eagle how he fared at the feast,
> When he and the wolf stripped corpses. . . . ")

                                                        (3025–31)

After this grim prophecy, Wiglaf delivers his terse summary judgment:

> Oft sceall eorl monig   anes willan
> wræc adreogan,   swa us geworden is.

> (Often for the will of one, many an earl
> must suffer punishment: so it happened to us.)

                                                        (3077–78)[12]

But is this moral judgment, or simple wisdom? The first clause reads like an Old English maxim, almost as matter-of-fact as "frost shall freeze" or "a king shall be on the throne." It is difficult to believe that Wiglaf is actually criticizing the dead Beowulf here; but it is just as difficult to understand how this could not amount to criticism, especially of a king. Did Beowulf insist on going against the dragon alone, or did his men abandon him? Is his heroism exemplary or cautionary? Is the dragon evil, or the hero cursed for opening the hoard? Is Beowulf wise, over the hill, kingly, proud, or foolish? As with "The Wanderer," and even more so, the meaning is very much our making.

The Battle of Maldon comes with a similar wrinkle. Byrhtnoth's "ofermod" is either "great courage" or "overweening pride," depending on your attitude (and your glossary)—much as the word *pride* today has two morally opposed meanings: a secular virtue, a religious vice. "Ofermod" may be the sin of Satan in *Genesis B,* but it is difficult to accuse Byrhtnoth of that. After all, *Maldon*'s famous climatic wisdom (again in maxim form), which no one has ever thought to criticize, is "mod sceall þe mare" [*mod* must be more]. But then again, is Byrhtnoth not responsible for the lives of his men? And does he not condemn them, by the heroic code's expectation that a warrior fight to the death when his lord has fallen?[13] Could not his men also have complained,

> Often for the will of one, many an earl
> Must suffer punishment?

The two cases are different, of course. Whereas Beowulf is an entirely fictional character, Byrhtnoth's action is historical and not just literary—though to what extent we will never know. Since Byrhtnoth too is a literary hero, it is hard to know how to proceed with this thought. It is hard to know if the anachronisms in the poem belong to the hero or the poet. Both *The Battle of Maldon* and *Beowulf* are composed in an archaic style, including an archaic social structure and code of behavior. Did Byrhtnoth really have a *comitatus* like an ancient Germanic warlord? Did tenth-century soldiers really feel the force of the heroic code defined by Tacitus nine hundred years earlier?

If we answer in the post-heroic, pre-feudal terms of the tenth century we will say both yes and no. But in order to understand Germanic heroism in whatever form it takes, we must always start by going back to Tacitus. His famous formula has not yet yielded all its secrets.

> It is shameful for the lord to be excelled in valor, shameful for his companions not to match the valor of the lord. Furthermore, it is shocking and disgraceful for all of one's life to have survived one's lord and left the battle: the prime obligation of the companions' allegiance is to protect and guard him and to credit their own brave deeds to his glory: the lord fights for victory, the companions for the lord. . . . Banquets and provisions serve as pay. The wherewithal for generosity is obtained through war and plunder.[14]

This passage illuminates the problem I am raising in our poems—the contradiction in the Germanic heroic code—quite brightly. The heroism of Wiglaf and of Byrhtnoth's companions is self-evident, set as it is in high relief against the flight of others. Their heroism is essentially their obedience—faithfulness to their oath, willingness to die for their lord, no matter what the cause, no matter how hopeless. Byrhtnoth's men die for him and for honor, not for the king, or for England, or Christendom; and their more immediate *treow*—which seems to be the chief point of the narrative—is certainly offered as exemplary.

But how do we judge the behavior and the heroism of Beowulf and Byrhtnoth themselves? Their valor and generosity—the only lordly virtues mentioned by Tacitus—are not in question. It is not their *fortitudo* but their *sapientia* we doubt. On this subject Tacitus is curiously silent, as are our poems. The "literary problem" which is, in Colin Chase's words, "whether Beowulf's behavior at the end of the poem is in fact ideal," reflects a problem in the heroic ideal itself, and cannot be solved.

The most Tacitus offers by way of a motive for lordly heroism is victory, in the pregnant formula, "The lord fights for victory, the companions for the lord." Perhaps if we could hold on to this thought, we could still charge our heroes with entering battle with something else than victory in mind. But in this little formula, "The lord fights for victory, the companions for the lord," we can see the deeper problem of Germanic heroism: there are *two* heroic codes, one for the lord and one for his companions; and whereas the ethical principles pertaining to the latter are perfectly clear, even to Christians, no principle at all is educed to explain why a lord fights—except to win, to prove his valor, and to acquire the wealth needed to pay his men. No wonder it looked like pride and avarice to Christians. Even Tacitus saw the self-perpetuating circularity of violence in the structure of Germanic society, for which war was an economic system requiring valor and obedience, but not necessarily nobility of purpose.

Nevertheless, the ideal of the obedient thegn prohibits criticism or contradiction of the lord, no matter what—with the result that lordly heroism, in poetry and life, could operate in relative freedom from ethical constraints. Though we would like to derive a consistent code of honor from the behavior of Beowulf and Byrhtnoth, Gunnar and Njal, Sigmund and Sigurth, the most important trait they share is that like Greek tragic heroes they resist such criticism and analysis. In both of our poems the result of this lordly freedom is suicidal annihilation—which pushy Christians (like Alcuin) might fairly interpret as a moral judgment, but which seems rather to operate more like a law of physics in the secular world of the poems. Heroic action is emphatically not practical action; nor is it necessarily imitable, or even ethical, much less moral. Most important, no one tells the hero what to do; he *knows* what to do, and who is to gainsay it?

Now we may return to our "second language." The sort of idealization I have been describing, one demanding obedience and resistant to criticism—requiring, that is, the submission of the ego—is very well known to psychoanalysis. In *Group Psychology and the Analysis of the Ego* (1921), Freud analyzed the military as a typical group, and connected it to his "scientific myth" of the Ur-group, the "primal horde." In the primitive family, according to this myth, the father tyrannizes his sons, who eventually join together to kill him. Thereafter, their shared guilt for this primal crime holds the group together; that is, the dead father is not really eliminated but is internalized in the members of the group as a tyrannical voice of authority, the ego ideal or superego.

The theory has its problems; but interpreting it has become something of a glamour area for thought.[15] For Freud it was a way of illustrating the relations between the Oedipus complex and group psychology. His conclusion, that "the group appears to us as a revival of the primal horde," lets us take his account of the horde simply as a metaphoric description of strong groups: "A primary group . . . is a number of individuals who have put one and the same object in the place of their ego ideal and have consequently identified themselves with one another in their egos.[16] This insight hardly depends upon the myth.

The myth goes on to suggest that it is the epic poet who first forges the collective ego ideal, in the form of the hero.[17] This is to say, a propos of our argument, that the hero is defined by the audience's shared guilt in relation to him. The heroic ideal, then, is not simply a model of excellence or virtue to be imitated but is also a forbidden and unattainable desire, highly defended against, sharply distinguished from the ego itself, and highly critical of it. Mutually exclusive as these two descriptions may sound, the superego is definitively both at the same time.

> Its relation to the ego is not exhausted by the precept: 'You *ought to be* like this (like your father).' It also comprises the prohibition: 'You *may not be* like this (like your father)—that is, you may not do all that he does; some things are his prerogative.'[18]

At the behavioral level, the result of this quite normal ambivalence is a guilt-ridden obedience to the ideal. In a warrior society, where obedience must be installed as a cardinal virtue, this effect can be amplified by the construction of an artificial superego to be shared by the group. This is the sort of ideal we are identifying with in the epic hero—or rather, we are identifying with each other in our egos, by means of our shared identification with him as our common superego. Two sorts of identification are involved. Regarding the latter especially, we must not forget that "identification, in fact, is ambivalent from the very first";[19] so the idealization of the hero, which frees him from criticism, is accompanied by self-criticism among his followers—and the audience.

Thus the faithful Wiglaf's speech excoriating the unfaithful companions is not anticlimactic after Beowulf's death, nor is the messenger's speech prophesying the nation's extinction. These speeches have the effect of chastising the audience, whose shared guilt in relation to the hero, it turns out, is one of the most important bonds holding the warrior society together, since it is the basis for the identification of the members of the group with one another. And thus also, Wiglaf's implicit criticism of the hero ("Often for the will of one . . . ") remains only implicit. Its restraint, which to us seems an uninterpretable ambiguity, actually masks his (and our) ambivalence toward the hero.

Because the hero is an ideal of this sort, however, he is invulnerable to our criticism. He need not be exemplary to retain his authority. The endless debate over whether Beowulf behaves correctly at the end of the poem is thus beside the point—because consciously at least, we are expected to identify our ego with the thegnly, not the lordly, hero. Our identification with the lordly hero as superego will remain largely unconscious, like so much of the superego's activity, and to that extent be felt only as anxiety or guilt.

The hero's invulnerability to criticism—including *our* criticism—has behavioral and psychological repercussions within the poem, and critical repercussions for us. Just as we detected two sorts of heroism in Tacitus's account, Freud discovered two psychologies in his account of the group:

> From the first there were two kinds of psychologies, that of the individual members of the group and that of the father, chief, or leader. The members of the group were subject to ties just as we see them today, but the father of the primal horde was free. His intellectual acts were strong and independent even in isolation, and his will needed no reinforcement from others.[20]

For some reason, *Beowulf* criticism has chosen not to respond to this heroic freedom but to respond instead to the group ties, as if they applied to the hero as well. So *Beowulf* criticism is always passing judgment on Beowulf, good or bad, which the poet and his world would probably have found presumptuous and irrelevant.

It is easy to see the social function of such an ideal of heroic freedom, for it corresponds not only to fatherhood but to lordship in the real world. In the late tenth century, warriors like Byrhtnoth were eldermen, officials of the king's government, responsible for the well-being of large areas of England. It was obviously in their interest to promote the principle that although the lord is responsible *for* those below him, he is not responsible *to* them. It was to this audience of warrior-aristocrats like Byrhtnoth and his men that heroic poetry was traditionally addressed.

Most men in this audience, being of the thegnly class, would have identified with Beowulf in the first part of the poem, insofar as he is an utterly exemplary thegn. Beowulf serves both Hygelac and Hrothgar faithfully, without any ambition to supplant or even succeed them, and totally without consideration of their conspicuous faults. But in the last part of the poem, this audience would probably have shifted their identification to Wiglaf, who comes to occupy the position of the faithful retainer. Beowulf himself, then, at the end of the poem, would be a representation not of the ego, but the superego—inspiring, but terrifying in his heroic freedom and superiority; revealing by his very existence our inadequacy, and punishing us for our inability to be like him. (Christianity has its own language for the same thought, of course, and Christ is often portrayed as just such a hero in Old English poetry.)

When we consider Byrhtnoth in particular as the audience, the situation is complicated by the fact that he is at once both thegn to King Ethelred and lord to his own men. Thus insofar as he is the king's man, he too would shift his identification to the faithful Wiglaf. The lesson that you defend your lord at all cost without judging him had some relevance in the reign of Ethelred the Unready; it has a special self-defeating urgency in the reign of any bad king, when criticism is most tempting. *But it is never your place to criticize your lord:* for by definition that amounts to challenging his lordship, and thus lordship generally, including your own. Unquestioning obedience is essential to the system.

But it is not so simple, of course, not to criticize a bad king. Byrhtnoth has something of the same problem as Kent in *King Lear*: his devotion to the *ideal* of the king could easily be interpreted as criticism of the reality. Accordingly, the focal question in "Maldon" scholarship seems recently to have become whether Byrhtnoth's action praises or criticizes Ethelred. Wiglaf too has something of the same problem: he can only help his king by disobeying him. ("Gebide ge on beorge . . . nis þæt eower sið" ["Wait on the barrow; it's not your adventure"], Beowulf had said [2529–31].) Thus Byrhtnoth's identification with Wiglaf would have led him to the excruciating outer limits of the ideal of obedience, where it becomes heroic by becoming its opposite.

But insofar as Byrhtnoth himself is a lord, he would also maintain his identification directly with the hero, right through to the end of the poem. That is, his identification would become split—much as in my dream I was able to identify simultaneously with both the girl and her brother, though in different ways. In fact, it is this doubleness of vision in the poem that lay behind the doubleness of the dream; the repeated splitting of identification in the poem became associated in the dream with other nodes of ambivalence, like child-parent, male-female, passive-dominant, and self-other.

These may not be neatly parallel, but they all reflect the theme of my individuality in relation to the determining structures of history and society—that is, the relation of the ego to the superego.

The problem of our individuality in relation to the group cannot be solved; the contradictory relations of our freedom to necessity cannot be solved; the ego's relation to the superego is destined to be ambivalent. These are antinomies we learn to live with. Not fortuitously, this lesson is an epic as well as tragic theme, and so a deep theme in *Beowulf,* which is a hymn to the individual hero as much as it is a hymn to the group he belongs to—and which he transcends, at least in desire. Insofar as I wish to be autonomous (and this wish is indestructible, being infantile)—that is, insofar as I actually wish to *be* the superego, rather than be governed by it—I will identify (perhaps unconsciously) with the hero himself; but insofar as I must always remain an agent of history, I will retain my conscious identification with the loyal thegn. The end result is guilt, the fuel of obedience. Christianity could only have clarified and deepened this already amplified dynamic.

At the Battle of Maldon, Byrhtnoth stumbled into one of those rare moments of lordship's terrible responsibility when, even in his highly codified world, he was free actually to choose between desperate alternatives, to fight or not, to die or not, to commit his men to death or spare their lives, to dare to be more valorous and heroic even than the king. In his freedom, Byrhtnoth could identify with Beowulf himself. That secret infantile wish came true: in the most crucial moment of his life, he finally got to *become* the superego.

What kind of behavior would such a thrilling identification recommend? What could Byrhtnoth learn from Beowulf? Be generous, be valorous; not much beyond that. It is true that a code of honor—minimal, contradictory, and extremely subtle—can be deduced from heroic poetry. It is seldom articulated, though, because its first rules seem to be silence and restraint. It is a Hemingway heroism of power, generosity, valor, restraint, *treow,* revenge—and occasionally the nobility of spirit to forgo revenge. But this loose, unformulated code provides little guidance at the heroic moment, when unresolvable conflicts arise and a decision must be made, when responsibility and power fall to you. When you are the hero, there is no one to tell you what to do.

In epic, this heroism is usually tested against death, because the real issue of heroic behavior is how to engage necessity with freedom. Epics as diverse as *Beowulf, Njalssaga,* and *The Niebelungenlied,* as well as the ancient cycle of poems in the *Edda,* all offer us primarily models of heroic dying. It might fairly be said that in identifying with these heroes Byrhtnoth would have learned little else than how to die well—that is, how to embrace his fate freely and without fear. What could he have learned from Beowulf, then, except to plunge toward death against all odds, without the interference of complicating practical or moral considerations? And as Beowulf had said to his companions,

> "Nis þæt eower sið,
> ne gemet mannes nefne min anes."

> ("It's not your adventure,
> nor any man's measure but mine alone.")

(2531–32)

As the French said of the Charge of the Light Brigade, "C'est magnifique, mais ce n'est pas la guerre." But as readers—and as thegnly readers at that, most of us—ours is not to reason why. The forms of identification these poems invite from us do not invite us to question whether Beowulf and Byrhtnoth behaved correctly or not. Rather, they invite us—try to coerce us—into an identification with our fellows and an unquestioning obedience to the hero's authority.

I must admit that my pleasure with this understanding of *Beowulf* and its effects on the audience sits rather uneasily with my own individuality, and my own resentful attitudes toward authority. The oedipal failure the poem tries to enforce is intended to socialize us into a radically authoritarian world. It is balanced, thank goodness, by the spectacle of the hero's awesome, if unobtainable, freedom. This freedom may often choose to express itself traditionally, but it is still freedom, feeding our most infantile desires even as it punishes us for them. For the reader-as-critic, like us, caught in the poem's thoroughgoing ambivalence, it is the hero's and the poem's freedom from all of our reductive interpretations, and from our demands that they be simpler or other than they are.

One would think modern, if not postmodern, readers, would be interested in this freedom from criticism—but no. Not content with stressing the hero's traditionality, his allegiance to established values, or his role as an ethical or moral example, *Beowulf* criticism has proceeded to reduce even the poet to a cultural vector field as well. This common attitude to the poem amounts to a two-pronged attack on its most real authority, the autonomy and authenticity of its author, who created the hero and (as Freud put it) "had in this way set himself free from the group in his imagination." "At bottom," Freud concludes of the epic poet, "this hero is no one but himself."[21] Recent advances in oral theory do not dissuade me of this, at least in the case of *Beowulf*, this most original poem with its invented hero.

The Oedipus complex tempts us to parricide, but that is not its best resolution! Criticism, having too little interest in our unconscious response to the poem, has set out to kill off both the hero and the poet in revenge for their power and superiority. In trying to fulfill this wish, criticism only rebels against the poem's authoritarian intentions like an adolescent, declaring itself victor prematurely. But you can't fool the superego. The poem will survive all of our depredations.

The Riddle of *Beowulf*

And now I see the meaning of my dream of the sphinx whose eye could not be covered. The sphinx is, as I knew immediately, the riddle of *Beowulf,* and the eye is the ever-observant, omniscient superego. They are identified in such a way that the poem looks down through the ages to criticize me, even as I am in the act of criticizing it. My criticism seems, at least when I am asleep, only like so much sand heaved futilely against the truth.

But I am scholar enough to have a second, reflexive association with the sphinx, whose riddle is, of course, the riddle of Oedipus, the riddle whose answer is Man. I did not yet understand, when I had the dream, that my reading of *Beowulf* could be largely determined by oedipal themes—as I have come to discover. Not only is the reader's relation to the author always oedipal to a degree, in the sense that Bloom suggests; but in the case of *Beowulf* the poem invites a meditation on the unconscious themes of our own individual and cultural origins—invites it with that same silence of the psychoanalyst, who allows us to relive and reformulate our own oedipal dramas, but consciously this time, by loudly plucking the deepest chords of ambivalence within us.

* *

Further Reading

I strongly recommend that those interested in psychoanalytic criticism begin with Freud. The *Standard Edition,* in twenty-four volumes, is a lifetime's study. Peter Gay's *Freud Reader* (see note 4) selects eight hundred pages from the *Standard Edition,* providing a solid minicanon for beginners; I have quoted from it in this essay whenever possible. Also essential for grasping Freud's work is Gay's *Freud: A Life for Our Time* (New York, 1988), which, like the *Reader,* is attentive to the many changes in the developing theory.

Loewald's *Papers* (see note 11) are an excellent example of the development of the classic theory since Freud. Chasseguet-Smirgel's *The Ego Ideal* (see note 9) explores and develops Freud's ideas on that topic in ways relevant to this essay. The debate over Freud's anthropology is represented in Muensterberger's *Man and His Culture* (see note 15) and surveyed by Edwin R. Wallace IV in *Freud and Anthropology* (New York, 1983).

Elizabeth Wright surveys the literary field in *Psychoanalytic Criticism: Theory in Practice* (New York, 1984). William Kerrigan's *The Sacred Complex: On the Psychogenesis of Paradise Lost* (Cambridge, 1983) sets the standard for future work in psychoanalytic literary criticism and thus deserves wide study.

Chapter 4

The Plot of *Piers Plowman*
and the Contradictions of Feudalism

✳ Britton J. Harwood ✳

In the century and more since Wright and Skeat made it available again to a reading public, *Piers Plowman* may have come closest, of any poem in the traditional English canon, to eliciting historical interpretation only. Yet little of this has been materialist.[1] Critics have found many earlier ideas, topical allusions, and formal conventions in the text. But the text as conjoining these—the text as the product of Langland's personal and class interests and traditional and emerging textual forms—has hardly been explained.

Even if he had chosen to try, Langland could no more have succeeded in detaching himself politically and economically from his society than twentieth-century medievalists can lead disinterested lives of their own. Because a writer's sense of value is determined by his place and time, Langland's Christocentric text is also ideological.[2] His text is not sometimes Christocentric, sometimes ideological. It is always both. He adapted textual forms for his theological, perhaps ethical reasons; yet in so doing he necessarily reflected, in one way or another, the limitations of a historical position. Forms change—have a history—because writers are in history. Langland's ideology, which became a project of writing for him, necessarily exerted pressure, like any unconscious motive, on whatever existing forms of expression he hit upon. The specificity of *Piers* as a layering of conscious question and unconscious project, as a torsion of existing forms, seems to be worth further attention.[3]

While Pierre Macherey chiefly analyzes nineteenth-century novels, medieval texts too can be read in what he has called a "double perspective."[4] Langland has both a historical moment and an ideological version of it. Ideology, however, is not to be found pure in *Piers* or any poem. Rather, the Langlandian history that can be taken up from Macherey's first perspective is itself double. First, it includes literary forms in their own historical development: while the poet's ideology has no way of making itself felt without them, literary conventions mediate and determine ideology, no less than any material sets limits to the work that can be done with it. Second, this history includes political and economic history. Otherwise, materialist critics, while encased in ideologies of their own,[5] could have no way of discerning what is ideological in poetry—how it offers a version that displaces and reduces contradiction.

Consequently, I am not proposing here to link one of the disciplines traditional in the study of medieval literature with later theory. Doubtless such links can be made. Jacques Derrida, for example, in deconstructing Rousseau's *Essai sur l'origine des langues,* takes pains to examine, in quite traditional ways, the timing of the *Essai* in relation to Rousseau's so-called second *Discours.*[6] To the contrary, if a "second language" is spoken here, that will happen only when two traditionally autonomous histories—the history of texts and political and economic history—are brought into relation with each other.

Before attempting to illustrate how that might be done in the instance of *Piers,* I believe it may be worthwhile to identify some consequences when criticism keeps the history of texts and political and economic history apart from each other.

1

In recent years, Anna P. Baldwin has made important identifications of political allusions in *Piers.* She has argued persuasively, for example, that Lady Meed is tried in one of the "prerogative courts" that English kings came to rely on to protect equity.[7] Yet when Baldwin moves to the economy in her latest essay, certain difficulties arise: "historical facts begin to lose their hardness, although historians . . . have used *Piers Plowman* to discover the conditions of the time. This use of a literary work depersonalises and defictionalises it."[8] It is hard to tell whether she regrets the limited usefulness of a poem in recovering "historical facts" or the effect of such attempts upon the poem. She may regret both. Concentrating on the poet's social attitudes, she does not question the relation between allusion and event—fiction on the one hand and, on the other, "the conditions of the time." While she indicates such fictive moments as Langland's "apolitical" solution to the injustice of the law courts,[9] she allots no space to relating these to Langland's larger fiction. Intending not to "defictionalize" *Piers,* she excludes altogether the place of it within literary history.

As a consequence, literary history enters unbidden, in Baldwin's uncritical adoption of a piece of medieval ideology as the structure of her essay. If Baldwin had seen her task, in part, as deciding what she had to do to keep *Piers* "fictional," she might have been led to distinguish fiction from ideology and thus been at a remove already from Langland's ideology. While fiction is an ideological practice it is not simply an ideology.[10] Instead, fiction and ideology vanish together, the latter because Baldwin has internalized it.

Baldwin invokes feudal ideology at an early point: "In the traditional model of society the peasants who 'work for all' are placed at the bottom, below the clergy who 'pray for all' and the knights who 'fight for all' (and we might add, rule all). By centering his poem on a plowman Langland is, in effect, reversing the model."[11] There is nothing unfeudal, however, about the means this plowman envisages for the "pilgrimage" to Truth. When the knight wishes to learn to plow, Piers tells him instead to "fight for all," keeping "holy kirke and myselue / Fro wastours and wikked men þat wolde me destruye."[12] The knight agrees, "þou3 I fi3te sholde" (6.35). When Piers urges him, "Loke 3ow tene no tenaunt," "Mysbode no3t þi bondeman" (6.38), Piers assumes the feudal relationship between the possessing and the laboring classes. If he has been elevated as director, it is only so that he may reaffirm the place of those who "work for all," first of all himself.

Literary history enters in the form of the framework Baldwin makes for her essay from this idea of the three estates: "That Langland was a chronicler of social change is clear, but that he resisted such change is questionable. He seems rather to define how the individual should respond to it. Accordingly this chapter will use the traditional analysis of society in terms of the three estates in order to demonstrate both Langland's historically accurate perception of how each was developing, and his interpretation of the individual's role within them."[13] Leaving aside the difficulty of how a demonstration of accuracy respects the poem as fiction, Baldwin's reader must deal with the puzzling implication that "social change" will in some way have left the three estates intact as such, so that individuals will continue to have roles within them. This idea of trifunctionality that rules the organization of her text has certain effects.

(1) Baldwin thinks the idea was a device for "analysis" and thus is able to make it her own framework. In this way she ignores its development within feudalism as an intervention. Jacques Le Goff has pointed out that the three-estate theory functions to act upon reality, not reflect it.[14] Tracing this "ternary figure" from the third decade of the eleventh century, Georges Duby has shown how it expressed both "the antagonisms existing within the dominant class" and "the structural complicity" of *oratores* and *bellatores*.[15] Given "a highly stable and wholly polarized two-class community wherein a much elevated class of feudal magnates and knights was confronted with a much inferior mass of rural humanity,"[16] the trifunctional model displaced within consciousness this irreducible opposition: it replaced an opposition that could not be economically mediated with a model

in which the *bellatores* split the difference between clerics and rustics. They were possessionate like the former but secular like the latter. The trifunctional theory, like all ideologies, was developed by one class in its struggle against another.[17] It disguised struggle by draping it with an image of the "concord" arising from mutual aid. This idea of "mutual contract, the 'faithkeeping' which is the basic meaning of the Middle English word 'truth,' "[18] is evidently constitutive of society for Baldwin herself, since she sees "the peasants' new feeling about their changing position" after the Plague as posing "dangers to society."[19]

(2) Because she adopts this trifunctional idea of concord, she rather locates the emergent "wage-economy" represented in passus 6 within the "development of a money economy"[20] than sees it as symptomatic of any fundamental conflict within feudalism itself. She links Piers's payments to laborers on the half-acre with the commutation of labor services that had begun well before the Black Death. However, the linkage is indirect at best. The collection of rent in the form of money apparently did not in itself alter the feudal relations of production;[21] precapitalist rents—whether money or labor—were determined by custom and external coercion, not "the intervention of the laws of commodity exchange."[22] By hiring laborers without reference to any possible customary rights of theirs, Piers is already a capitalist, like the peasant employers who rebelled with peasant laborers in 1381.[23] To speak of the change simply as the substitution of money for custom mystifies the change of devices for the expropriation of the surplus product. Thus, Baldwin writes of hunger as "a natural sanction which affects all men equally,"[24] as if it affected the customary tenant in effective possession of his fifteen acres in the same way it affected peasants who had "no land to lyue on but hire handes" (6.307).

(3) Just as the trifunctional model perdures in her text, so Baldwin understands " 'truth' (justice, loyalty)"[25] as "a Christian virtue not restricted to one social pattern."[26] Consequently, she can understand the Statutes of Laborers as trying "to transfer the feudal principles of 'truth' into a wage-economy": "There was no reason why such relationships should not also have been governed by truth."[27] Neither the statutes nor the idea of trifunctionality serves, in her view, the interest of a specific class.

(4) Just as she separates the Christian virtue of truth from any single "social pattern," she effectually detaches such issues as the papal "provision" of nominees for benefices, disendowment of the clergy, praemunire, and continuation of the Hundred Years War from any basic contradiction within feudalism as a social formation. Political issues come up under "The Clergy" and "The King and the Nobility," economic issues under "The Peasants." Thus, the trifunctional idea enters to affect Baldwin's description of "The Historical Context" itself.

(5) Because "truth" remains an option despite changes in society, individual responsibility for these becomes obscured. Human agents are not those who operate these changes but those who are faithful or not. The peasants have a "new feeling about their changing position."[28] Who have changed it, and how they have changed it, remain hidden. By "wage-economy" and "the new individualism," Baldwin defers the term "capitalism,"[29] just as the claim that the peasants can prevent "their new self-determination" from becoming "mere self-interest" defers the question of the specific determinations of "truth" within capitalism. "Truth" as a traveling idea thus works to displace the historicity of capitalism.

In discussing Baldwin's text, I have meant to show some of the difficulties when criticism begins with the transparency of literature to political and economic history. Criticism that sees the poem as transparent to another historical context, namely, an ideological one consisting of literary, theological, political, or other texts, has become the more common criticism of *Piers* since the 1950s. To consider what happens when the rest of material history accordingly disappears, I should like to take up two recent instances: Myra Stokes's *Justice and Mercy in "Piers Plowman"* and Robert Adams's "Piers's Pardon and Langland's Semi-Pelagianism."[30] Stokes's work invites this question particularly, since she focuses on an idea about commodities: "the kind of exact justice best epitomized in the commercial logic of price and debt."[31]

Stokes contends that this idea had a primacy for Langland, who applied it "to spiritual matters."[32] In her view, the poem moves from a display of equity in the state, enforced by natural law and revelation, to the equitable Christian society organized in passus 19. She implies that "equity" gets some of its meaning for Langland from specifiable relations of production: wage demands in passus 6 are "analogous" to laborers' "forgetfulness of their station." "A society that so jealously guarded hierarchical order" would approve of Langland's having pointed this out.[33] Nonetheless, she abstracts the idea of "equity" from any particular context, making it a notion that floats without change above fourth-century Milan and fourteenth-century Spain in certain passages of Cicero, Ambrose, John of Salisbury, Thomas Aquinas, Robert of Basevorn, Juan Ruiz, and John Fortescue. Immune to determination by its textual environments, this idea never differs in its use; no particular institutions with specific aims ever promote it. It is part of the same ideological practice whether it helps to reproduce slave societies or feudal ones.

There is little difficulty, perhaps, in a critic's heuristic use of ideas that she never explains as ideological practices. This may not be so when, in this bracketing of history, she isolates the poem itself. Literary history begins to lose its own specificity. What are the genres and other conven-

tions that Langland uses? Do they lend themselves without distortion to the
project that Stokes identifies for him? *Piers* seems to exist for Stokes only
as a series of disputed questions, and its form as the particular sequence in
which Langland takes these questions up.

Detaching the poem from the history of representation leads to the
ellision of differences within *Piers* itself. When a poem is interpreted as
transparent to a preexisting idea, it becomes transparent to itself. Uneven-
nesses with the poem, all the fault lines showing that Langland produced
the poem under conflicting historical conditions, vanish. Since *Piers* for
Stokes is a thesis, not also a set of literary means that may affect Langland's point, she can go on to believe that his thesis successfully organizes
his poem in all its significant details. Passus after passus, then, become the
steps of an argument. Equity becomes the substantial form of the poem, a
message made redundant through episodes that must only be deciphered for
the message to be laid bare. Breaks happen just when the poet fails before
the force of his own thesis. For example, remembering that one of the crucified thieves escaped "penaunce of purgatorie" altogether (10.427), Langland breaks off the A text in despair and in B represents himself as having
undergone a crisis.[34]

But *Piers* of all poems does not seem to have this unified character.
Anne Middleton has observed that the relationship of any episode to the
poem as a whole is "problematic," and A. J. Colianne remarks on its
"structural confusion." Steven Justice argues for "discontinuous" generic
choices by the poet. John Norton-Smith spoke several years ago for a number of earlier critics: "The poem, however closely and skilfully annotated
and explicated, seems to lack a convincing controlling *idée*."[35] Although
Piers plainly includes warnings that no injustice will go unpunished, critics
need to explain why Langland also composed lines like the following, from
Anima's complaint:

> . . . Iewes lyuen in lele lawe; oure lord wroot it hymselue
> In stoon for it stedefast was and stonde sholde euere.
> *Dilige deum & proximum* is parfit Iewen lawe;
> And took it Moyses to teche men til Messie coome,
> And on þat lawe þei leue and leten it þe beste.
> And ȝit knewe þei crist þat cristendom tauȝte,
> And for a parfit prophete þat muche peple sauede
> Of selkouþe sores; þei seiȝen it ofte,
> . . . .
> Ac þei seiden and sworen wiþ sorcerie he wrouȝte,
> And studieden to struyen hym and struyden hemselue,
> And þoruȝ his pacience hir power to pure noȝt he brouȝte:
> *Pacientes vincunt.*

. . . . . .
Ac pharisees and Sarȝens, Scribes and Grekes
Arn folk of oone feiþ; þe fader god þei honouren.
And siþen þat þe Sarȝens and also þe Iewes
Konne þe first clause of oure bileue, *Credo in deum patrem*
omnipotentem,
Prelates of cristene prouinces sholde preue if þei myȝte
Lere hym litlum and litlum *et in Iesum Christum filium*. . . .

(15.583–610).

No doubt Anima is pressing the ethical obligation of Christian prelates to proseletyze (15.490–532). And yet the poem simultaneously represents the disaster of failing to believe in Christ: through a white dove, for instance, "Makometh in mysbileue men and wommen brouȝte" (15.410). Although Stokes is perceptive as a New Critic, the poem will have succeeded in silencing history if critics fill in every fracture, as if to defer to a governing poetic intention.

Like Stokes, Adams works with the history of ideas. In proposing sources—Gregory's *Morals on Job,* for example, as the subversive source of Need's speech (20.6–50)[36]—Adams has contributed valuably to Langland studies. When he interprets the poem as a whole, however, he acknowledges no possible discontinuity in the object. Adams's critical procedure in his semi-Pelagianism essay is to unify several episodes in the poem on the basis that they teach the possibility of meritorious action. Human beings are obligated to do their very best ("facere quod in se est"), God having freely committed himself to accept this effort as meritorious and salvific.[37] Piers's "pardoun" in passus 7 underwrites this obligation, making us "respect significant moral differences between those who are productive and those who are not."[38] "The only pardon comes when you try to avoid offending God in the first place."[39] Langland's semi-Pelagian outlook results in the "heavy moralism" of the poem,[40] which is preoccupied with ethics.[41]

The pardon scene forms a totality with other episodes: for example, (1) the emperor Trajan was saved only because he obeyed the best law he knew, with an "effort" of the "whole being";[42] and (2) although the fruits that drop from the Tree of Charity are "under the penalty of death,"[43] Piers's testimony that he has successfully deployed the three staves against the world, flesh, and Devil shows that "natural perfection in virtue is accessible to humanity, at least in theory."[44] This sort of redundancy in the poem gives it a depth. So does a series of texts from the fifth to the fourteenth century that take a semi-Pelagian position. For example, Adams quotes from Robert Holcot's *In librum Sapientiae Regis Salomonis praelectiones*

CCXIII: "Primam concedendo, quod dat misericordia ex et gratia sua pro tanto: quia talem legem misericorditer statuit & observat: sed statuta lege, necessario dat gratiam necessitate consequentie."[45]

Like Stokes, Adams assumes that analysis is (in the language of Pierre Macherey) "the discovery of . . . the secret coherence of an object."[46] Textual disjunctions are penetrated to "a pre-established truth," here the teaching that exegetics has always found in serious medieval poetry, "the obligation to love God above all else." For Adams, the poem shows ("like many theologians") that the "inward knowledge" of this duty is already possessed by all people, unless they willfully obscure it.[47] This message gives *Piers* its "secret coherence." Critical analysis consists in making passages like the pardon scene deliver up a truth, predetermined not only in the critical project of Exegetics but in an unbroken history of semi-Pelagian textuality. ("Langland evidently does not share the modern preju-dice whereby significant art can only spring from fresh insights.")[48] The "message" delivered by Truth, Trajan, and, for that matter, John Cassian in the fifth century has been left unaffected by any sort of specific material condition.[49]

Literary criticism that confines itself to a certain history of texts may attach as little importance to disparities within a text as within that history itself. Thus, reading the Tree of Charity scene, Adams analyzes Piers's claim ("I saue it [the fruit] til I se it ripen," and so forth) to mean that the patriarchs successfully avoided temptation while they lived; the Devil takes away the fallen apples only because, "without the benefit of Christ's sacri-fice, such virtue has no merit in the sight of God."[50] Why, however, should Piers have thought the fruit to be sweet (16.72) if it would make "a foul noise" when the dreamer tried to taste it? Perhaps "natural perfection in virtue" gave the "holy men" figured by these apples who lived before Christ no hope in their dying hour. But Langland may also mean that such natural perfection was not to be found.[51] The dreamer, after all, does not find it now:

> Ac charite þat Poul preiseþ best, and moost plesaunt to oure Saueour
> *Non inflatur, non est ambiociosa, non querit que sua sunt—*
> I seiȝ neuere swich a man, so me god helpe,
> That he ne wolde aske after his, and ouþerwhile coueite
> Thyng þat neded hym noȝt and nyme it if he myȝte.
>
>   (15.156–60)

Adams has little to say about penance, irrelevant to a message on "the natural role of mankind in producing acts of charity."[52] And yet passus 14 and 20 concentrate on it. In the lines of Anima's already quoted, Langland apparently does not propose that Moslems will find grace by persevering in their belief, which is the best law they know. He depicts the Prophet as covetous but his followers as simply credulous. No one in *Piers* tries to argue that theirs is a failure in ethics. When Langland calls the unbaptized Christian child "heþene as to heueneward and helplees to þe soule" (15.458), he gives a different message than that God has committed himself to accept as semimeritorious *(meritum de congruo)* the good deeds that the child may go on to perform. The poem reflects its own division (assuming some passages do argue the adequacy of obeying the best law one knows) in the split between Faith and Hope in passus 16 and 17, which the Samaritan is meant to anneal.

The critical disinterment of a message is conservative, not simply by saving the appearances of the text but in its politics. The difficulty is not that exegetical critics may be politically conservative in the usual sense,[53] but that the homogeneous text as Stokes and Adams produce it, transparent to a series of texts, helps *Piers* itself to silence history. By reading conflict out of the latent meaning of the poem, Stokes and Adams assist ideology in totalizing and thus naturalizing itself.[54] Partly because the object of their attention is a theology lying apart from any specific text, they drive to the critical margin the deformations that occur when a poet's ideology, including his theology, cannot master even literary history, much less the other material conditions within which he writes.

"The concept of the 'author' as a free creative source of the meaning of a book," according to Diane Macdonell, "belongs to the legal and educational forms of the liberal humanist discourse that emerged in the late eighteenth and early nineteenth centuries; it is not a concept that exists within discourses that have developed recently."[55] It does not exist in Baldwin's, Stokes's, or Adams's criticism either—not, however, because their criticism is Lacanian, deconstructive, or materialist. For Baldwin the literary text is transparent to political and economic conditions, while for Stokes and Adams it reflects a traditional idea in ethics or theology. Thus, while both kinds of criticism lay claim to history, they each understand the text as the untroubled result of its (politico-economic or ideological) determinant. Such conservative critics leave little space for "the specificity of the [literary] object."[56]

2

To the contrary, we may begin with the peculiar surface of *Piers*. At the point that Baldwin's work connects with Stokes's and Adams's, the poem itself divides: since the poem is doubly determined—situated, that is,

not less within literary than political and economic history—its surface is
strained and riven. These fractures the critic can take to be symptoms and
trace them in attempting to explain the poem as product. "In narrative
there is no continuity," Macherey has remarked, "but rather a constant
disparity."[57]

Like other Marxist criticism, Macherey's rests on "the conviction that
works of literature can be fully understood only if placed in the context of
the economic, social, and political relationships in which they are
produced."[58] Because poetry cannot cut loose from other ideological uses
of language, the text is influenced by the problems of the writer's existence, which cannot be individual without being social.[59] Nevertheless, the
poem as a project of ideology is also determined by literary convention.[60]
This follows from the two different operations of the writer. "The project
of writing begins inevitably by taking the form of an ideological imperative," because the writer, at a particular moment, speaks from and
for a certain position within a social formation and within relations of
production.[61] But this project "will have to adopt the conditions of the
possibility of such an undertaking." The ideological project exists only as a
project of writing. Hence, writing is a species of production.[62] The means
of expression (means of production, so to speak), the formal devices of
writing, "do not appear instantaneously but at the end of a long history."
Writing, without ceasing to be "the elaboration of ideological themes," has
a history of its own.[63]

Consequently, the means of expression resist the writer's own historical imperatives. On the one hand, theological discourse, whether semi-
Pelagian or neo-Augustinian, is not the secret content of *Piers;* it is a means
of expression that, owing to the pressure of the writer's project, cannot be
appropriated intact. On the other, because *Piers* participates in this history
of representation, ideology—in the sense of the fictive language closest to
the ideological language of everyday life for Langland—remains an alien
presence within the text. The text as a project of writing pushes it to the
margin, together with the rest of the material history of Langland's time.
From the margin, Langland's project within history, like an unconscious
utterance, does not cease to speak; but it does so most of all in its distortions of the means of expression.[64] The disparities in a text that point to a
conflict of meanings are not the signs of an imperfection; rather, they maintain a relationship with what happens at the margins of a text.

To begin to see *Piers* as produced, I would like to take up two such
disparities in the poem, one in a passage that has already come up, the
cultivation of the half-acre, where the poem seems especially to reflect material history; the other a disjunction that pervades the entire text.

Piers claims he needs assistance in plowing just half an acre, when the typical peasant family cultivated a holding that averaged perhaps fifteen to thirty acres. The Statute of Laborers required villagers to work for wages if they possessed less than an oxgang of land (seven or eight acres), with the implication that under that circumstance they would have time on their hands.[65] This disparity, like the fiction that all of society is ready to be organized by a plowman or the one that Piers has filled a long series of occupations (5.547–48), helps to derealize the scene. Perhaps the most interesting disparity in our present context, however, is the economic position that Piers attributes to himself.

The disparity does not lie in his calling himself a *hyne* (servant, member of a household [6.131]), after he himself has planned to hire wage laborers at harvest time (6.113–14). Piers never represents himself as working for wages within human society.[66] At several points, the poem affirms the labor process as a divine imperative. For example, Wit claims that God loves "alle trewe tidy men þat trauaille desiren" (9.107–8). Similarly, Piers knows in his conscience that he should produce (5.540–41). When he does produce, being one of "alle kynne crafty men þat konne lyuen in truþe" (6.68), he has a good conscience—metaphorically, his "hire" every evening (5.552).[67] I emphasize this to suggest that Piers is not unequivocally represented as holding only half an acre. How much more he may hold we cannot know, of course. But "plowman" in literature from the fourteenth and fifteenth centuries signifies not an employee but a husbandman who possesses a plow team and a more or less substantial holding of land.[68] As David Aers has rightly pointed out,[69] Piers is depicted throughout passus 6 as a peasant *employer,* offering laborers ("hise seruauntȝ") the usual "mete and hyre" (6.243, 139).[70] Peasant employers had holdings often "four or five times the size of those of the middle stratum of peasants who were producing mainly for subsistence and only marginally in order to obtain cash for rent, tax, and essential manufactured commodities."[71] In all three late-medieval localities studied by P. D. A. Harvey and his coworkers, some tenants are observed using the land market "to accumulate holdings on a scale that must have placed them in a dominating position within the local community."[72] Such peasant employers were, perhaps, likelier free than servile.[73] In any case, because of the labor shortage in the years Langland was composing the A and B texts (by 1377, the English population had declined some 40 to 50 percent since the 1348 plague),[74] we can be sure such employers had to compete for labor with feudal landowners.[75] The price of corn having fallen, feudal landowners attempted by the Statutes of Laborers to put a ceiling on their labor costs and thus neutralize the demand coming in part from peasant employers.[76]

The intriguing disparity in passus 6 consists in Langland's representing Piers and the "wastours" as opposing each other over the Statutes of Laborers. Langland's laborers curse the king and his council for having enacted "Swich lawes . . . laborers to chaste," complaining when they are not "heiȝliche hyred" (6.318, 312). The mystery arises because Hunger and the law are represented as working toward the same end ("Ac whiles hunger was hir maister þer wolde noon chide / Ne stryuen ayeins þe statut" [6.319–20]), when in fact the statutes were enacted precisely to prevent peasant employers like Piers from hiring labor at the market rates—dictated in part, of course, by Hunger. Peasant *employers* would rebel in 1381 because the statutes gave clear preference to feudal landowners, "who had the first call on their villeins' labor."[77] The economics of the "half-acre" is mysterious for the reason that, in resistance to the statutes in the 1370s, laborers and peasant employers like Piers *were on the same side.*[78]

3

This disparity is local, while the second one I shall argue for is not. Although the second is in no sense hidden (to the contrary, it is, in Macherey's word, "glaring"), it soon becomes visible when *Piers* is considered in light of a literary convention that Langland has adopted. While Langland surely worked in several genres, as Morton Bloomfield and others have shown,[79] the dream-vision opening of *Piers* and the subsequent debate between Conscience and Meed suggest that Langland made use, at least in part, of the generic conventions exemplified by *Winner and Waster.*[80] To invoke *Winner and Waster,* nevertheless, at once introduces a large formal difference.

In the earlier poem, the king from his height acts effectively: the battle is prevented, representatives of both armies are summoned to state their grievances, and the king renders judgment, sending Winner to Rome and Waster to Cheapside. The force of the king acts by prolepsis, so to speak, as a principle that first organizes two armies and then a debate. By contrast, *Piers* begins with a polar opposition between the hilltop castle of Truth and the dungeon in the "deep dale byneþe" (prol.15). However, adjacent to this straight line between True and False is the confusion of the field of folk, which Truth from his height utterly declines or fails to organize. The folk themselves are many of those represented in *Winner and Waster:* in *Piers,* for example, "Somme chosen hem to chaffare; þei cheueden þe bettre" (prol.39). Similarly, in *Winner and Waster,* signs show the presence of drapers, vintners, and other merchants (190). The four orders of friars move through each. Drunkards call for "Wyfe, wedowe, or wenche" in *Winner and Waster* (280) and rise up "wiþ ribaudie" in *Piers* (prol.44). Yet in *Piers*, the imminence of Truth notwithstanding, the field is a "maȝe" (1.6).

I am not assuming that Langland knew *Winner and Waster* and made changes in his source (although it would, of course, be highly important to be able to know such a thing). Indeed, in the "Timeliness of *Wynnere and Wastoure*," the late Elizabeth Salter questioned the grounds for the traditional dating of the composition of that poem to 1352.[81] Rather, the convention that a superior authority can situate and neutralize contending inferiors is represented by *Winner and Waster*. *Piers*, which deforms the convention, is the later poem if in no other sense than that a limitation upon authority depends upon the prior idea of authority itself. (The reverse, that the idea of rule is a development of the failure of rule, is unlikely.) The disparity between an organizing force and a "maȝe" erupting with a multitude of autonomous creatures will run through the whole of *Piers*, because this spatial opposition within the first vision will become temporalized as a certain oscillation within the plot, as I shall try to illustrate. That *Piers*, then, moves from the opening vision and the debate into other genres is not a necessity that befalls the poem. As I shall finally try to show, it arises with an incommensurability between Langland's ideological project and the expressive means, as *Winner and Waster* gives an instance of them.[82]

If there is any constancy in *Piers* as narrative, it seems to be an alternation of a certain kind. This symptom of Langland's unconscious project is not intended as such and thus occurs in no precisely predictable pattern. It consists first in the representation of a decisive moral force as external to the individual, then, to the contrary, its representation as internal. The opposition between something given in sensory experience and something entirely interior to consciousness is itself made explicit in the poem. For example, Anima says that a person's "wordes" and "werkes" can be experienced by other people, but his "wil"—known only to Piers the plowman—cannot (15.210-11).[83] Doubtless this opposition, like any, is deconstructed at certain points. Poverty at the end of passus 14, for instance, does not seem a matter of external circumstance to the exclusion of spiritual poverty: "So pouerte propreliche penaunce is to þe body, / And Ioye to pacient pouere, pure spiritual helpe . . . " (14.284-85).[84] But this is not what I wish to emphasize at the outset. I would like first to review places where the opposition seems to be secure but the plot of the poem moves the locus of decisive force from one pole to the other. Then I would like to conclude by trying to explain this.

The poem begins with Will's taking an initiative, in order to hear "wondres." Then, in the next lines, Langland represents the adventitious: "Ac on a May morwenynge . . . / Me bifel a ferly . . . " (prol.4-6).

Since what happens to him, the "ferly," is what he wants ("wondres"), the whole force of the "Ac," it seems, is to mark the change from inner motive to outer event. Soon after, having reviewed the ways in which various ecclesiastics improve their income, Will perceives "þe power" of the keys, deposited among the four cardinal virtues. "Parceyued" here is metaphoric (prol.100), since virtues—habits of the soul—cannot literally be observed; neither can their power to open the gates of heaven. Langland then points to the substitution of an external force, arrogated by prelates along with the name "Cardinals." And the dreamer observes the power of the commons to elect a king (prol.112–13).[85] This is only the first of several passages in which the poem invokes a secular authority as an organizing force. Holy Church will argue that kings and knights should enforce truth (1.94–97), and the king who appears later in the same vision penalizes those who give and take bribes (2.193–207). A "kyng," according to the character Thought, will be crowned by "dowel and dobet" to secure their compliance with "dobest" (8.100–106). And Clergy foresees a king coming to chastise worldly monks (10.322).

Once Holy Church identifies herself and reminds the dreamer that she has been his teacher, he makes the first of his several demands for an inner certainty that might enable him to change his life: "Kenne me kyndely on crist to bileue, / That I myȝte werchen his wille . . . " (1.81–82). His repeated requirement for a "kynde knowyng" inscribes the assumption of a decisive inner force.[86] Holy Church deals briefly with this power as inner: "loue . . . comseþ by myght, / And in þe herte þere is þe heed and þe heiȝe welle" (1.161–64). But in answering the dreamer, she soon concentrates on a being distinct from him, who wrought all his works with love "as hym liste" (1.150). Finally she has it both ways:[87] love is an (internal) "myȝt" that "falleþ to þe [external] fader þat formed vs alle" (1.165, 166). When the dreamer, making another start with Holy Church, asks about an internal power for knowing the False ("kenneþ me by som craft"), she shows him something on the outside: "Loke on þi left half" (2.4, 5).

Before the *Visio* concludes, there will be two failures like Truth's to organize the field. Each will differ somewhat from Truth's. Reason is represented as preaching and, thus, within the fiction, exists outside those who hear him. In collaboration with Conscience, however, where he is a knowledge of the natural law, he is obviously internal to the multitudes, as habit or faculty. He fails, for the conversion of the folk is incomplete: Envy mistakes contrition for the bitterness he has always felt (5.128), Covetousness misunderstands "restitucion" (5.231–32), and so on. Piers also fails. A cutpurse, pardoner, and others reject his directions to Truth (5.630–42); and after his effort on the half-acre, he substitutes for truth-in-heart as final cause the internal motive of hunger.

The Truth who sends a pardon at the opening of passus 7 seems to be as external a sanction as heaven or hell (7.51–52). Piers will invoke the internal authorities, however, Abstinence and Conscience (7.138–39). In the waking interval after the second vision, Will, searching in objective space for a "leode" named "dowel," meets a pair of Franciscans, who promptly situate "dowel" in subjective space, namely, as "charite," which they claim to possess (8.45). The decisive power, in their view, is "Wit and free wil," given by God to "yeme wel þiselue" (8.53, 52). With Thought and Wit in the third vision, the locale of the plot itself shifts, from London, Westminster, and half an acre of arable to an interior distance where certain capacities of the mind get to speak for themselves. Wit, however, shortly reminds Will of external sanctions like the flood. Dame Study describes herself as a successful authority external to her pupils ("Grammer for girls I garte first write, /And bette hem wiþ a baleys but if þei wolde lerne" [10.180–81]). By contrast, while Clergy does point to the external power of priestly example (10.260–96) and quotes a threat from God to punish sinners in purgatory (10.375), he emphasizes an internal force—belief in Holy Church and in God (10.239, 241; cf. 250, 254). In a similar way, Study had complained of the absence of such a motive, God being in the heart only of poor people in the present age.

The dreamer declares the efficacy of baptism,[88] predestination,[89] and Doomsday, all adventitious events (10.351, 381, 417). Then, for a long while, the poem turns to the power of events internal to the individual. Will warns that reason and conscience will condemn a person to purgatory unless contrition intervenes (11.131–36). Trajan's "leutee" and "truþe" evidently change his fate (11.253–65). Faith is adequate for salvation, Will argues (11.216–21), and shame and "nede" alone can change a person's life, Imaginative asserts (11.426, 432).[90] The dreamer agrees (11.435–37). Will's vision of Middle Earth in an inner dream recapitulates, in a measure, the beginning of his first dream; for again he sees that an external power does not organize the field: God does not interfere when people behave unreasonably (11.370–71).[91] Although Imaginative will go on to grant the power of the adventitious (sights and teachings, Christ's love as the root of clergy, written texts by the Father and the Son, the teachings of Socrates and Solomon), passus 12 focuses on the "imaginative" ability, an inner ability to perform particular operations upon texts.[92]

The power represented in passus 13 also comes from within—the extraordinary capacity of patience to prevail over emperors and popes (13.165–67). Nevertheless, this section closes with Will's urging the importance of environment: "flateris and fooles" are bad influences; the poor, the pious, and the disabled are good ones. And Patience will go on to describe another external power, one who punishes excess (14.80) and apportions rewards: God condemns the pitiless rich (14.132–33), gives an

extra reward (beyond their wealth) to those rich who do pity the poor
(14.147–52), and comforts the destitute with heaven (14.109–10, 175–80,
214–15, 260–61).

The poem will shift again. The Tree of Charity scene, where Anima
will guide the dreamer, concentrates upon the power and the components of
choice just as the quotation from Isidore of Seville early in the preceding
passus bears on the organization of the soul to the end of making choices.
Choice itself—the *liberum arbitrium* replacing Anima in the C text—is obviously internal,[93] like the habits of the soul that follow. *Caritas* is one such
habit, and the dreamer denies that, for him at least, it has ever existed in
external space, any more than Christ has: "I sei3 hym [Christ] neuere
sooþly but as myself in a mirour" (15.162).

Nonetheless, most of Anima's lengthy speech is given over to the force
of examples. Many saints have died "to enforme þe faith" (15.519–20).
Because Antony, Egidius, and other hermits took their food just from birds,
not lions or leopards, ecclesiastics should learn to decline support from
covetous people (15.307–8). Passus 15 is so preoccupied with examples
that it takes up not only good ones (15.261, 266, 268, and so on) but such
problematic ones as Mohammed and greedy English clerics (15.397–411,
434–51). Anima poses the dilemma that the external world must have a
certain character for people to learn to love: folk, he says, are "loþ" to
"louye wiþouten lernynge of ensaumples" (15.473). Yet the existence of a
defect in the soul (15.347–76) makes it doubtful whether *any* example could
bring about a change of heart. Even Christ's miracles could not convince
all the Jews.

After the fruit of charity falls to the devil, *Piers* shifts from the Tree
that grows "amyddes mannes body" to events taking place outside the
body of any sinner—the Annunciation and episodes in Christ's life, including his orders to the "sike and synful" (16.110) and physical retribution he
imposed (16.127–32). At the close of passus 16, where the highly intrusive
event of the Harrowing of Hell is foreseen (16.262–68), the dreamer will
go on to meet *Spes*, "Hope," who displays the Law, the supreme ordering
device, given to Moses, not discovered within him. (Similarly, Conscience
will later report that Jesus taught the Jews the "lawe of lif" [19.45]; and
Conscience himself will give a piece of counsel, "redde quod debes," that
is clearly alien to "al þe comune" [19.383–97].) While the Samaritan concedes that "vnkyndenesse," an internal quality, is strong enough to quench
God's mercy (17.348), passus 18 begins, rather, with the adventitious
power of God: the elements of heaven and earth witness "That swich a
barn was ybore" (18.235).[94] The baby becomes "a geaunt wiþ a gyn,"
beating down all who stand against him (18.252–53), orienting and organizing from the outside: unless the Jews revere his cross and his resurrec-

tion, they will be utterly lost (18.259–60). Passus 18 ends with Will himself submitting to the cross, and passus 19 begins with his pointing out the power of Jesus' name (19.17). When he asks whether "Christ" as a name exerts even more power, Conscience adduces an external force who creates knights and awards lands, teaches the Law, protects, and conquers death. Passus 19 continues to dwell on Christ as an extrinsic organizing power, sought by the disciples after his resurrection (19.163–65), who teaches and cures miraculously. Doubting Thomas responds to him as to an external proof (19.170–75). As his surrogate after Pentecost, Piers deploys a comparable force, binding and unbinding (19.188–89).

By contrast, most of the final two passus attend to events and habits that occupy internal space. The graces distributed at Pentecost and the sanctified cardinal virtues are sown in the soul just metaphorically, for they are psychological habitus. While there are external forces, they are neutral, like the sun, shining alike on the just and the unjust, or failed, like the pope (19.442–45) or the ailments inflicted by Kynde (20.81–85). Unity will be successfully defended so far as contrition, an inner act, is kept lively. If Kynde assists from the outside with reminders of death, there is also a "kynde" on the inside that, as a brewer claims, "wol noȝt be ruled" (19.396). Its allies are likewise interior, the habit of covetousness, "heighnesse of herte," sloth, and despair (20.121–39, 153, 158–60). The ultimate casualty in Unity is an inner one, "drede" of sin (20.379).

The constant shift of focus through the whole poem between outer and inner authority does not cease in the last two lines, in which Conscience prays, " 'Sende me hap and heele til I haue Piers þe Plowman.' / And siþþe he gradde after Grace . . . " (20.385–86). Piers is, as throughout the *Vita*, the object of quest, grace the power that arises within.

The plowman, however, is not simply the external authority who, for example, teaches leechcraft to Jesus (16.103). Perhaps the best indication that Langland recognized at some level the shifts I have attempted to illustrate lies in his conception of Piers. If nothing else, Piers is his author's attempt to overcome this opposition.

4

The two disparities I have tried to illustrate reflect an ideology. As conflicts in the text, they inscribe an "otherness" through which the work maintains "a relationship with that which it is not, that which happens at its margins."[95] "That which happens at its margins" is the nonliterary discourse of ideology: like the rest of political and economic history, it exerts a pressure upon the literary conventions that the poet adopts, just as ideol-

ogy in turn is shaped "by the pressures upon the class which generates
it."[96] Conflicts in the text, the result of an incommensurability of Langland's project as ideological and its expressive means, reflect nothing in the
rest of history term for term; rather they image the contradictions within
the everyday language of ideology that ideology would attempt to hide.
Through the fractures of a text, the contradictions of ideology become visible. In that way only is ideology, in its strict sense, an "otherness" present
in the text. The ideological project that, finally, I want to suggest as the
unconscious of *Piers* presupposes a certain class membership on Langland's part, and I need to make explicit the grounds on which this assumption rests.

However dependent a member, Langland appears to belong to the
landowning class that disposed of the labor of a nonpossessing class that
worked the land.[97] There is a crucial difficulty in defining the exploiting
and the exploited classes of feudal society in such terms, and I shall revert
to it shortly.[98] Putting that aside, an ascription on the last full leaf of Trinity College, Dublin, MS.D.4.1, in a hand that has been authoritatively
dated within twenty years of the composition of B and C, identifies Langland as the son of a gentleman who held land from a Despenser. The ascription is not, in the expert view of George Kane, currently subject to
challenge.[99] In a passage added in C, Langland makes clear that he is not
servile and implies that he is "lordes kyn" and "pore gentel blood."[100]

So far as portions of *Piers* resemble the everyday language of ideology, the greater part of them serve to reproduce the social relations of feudalism and thus would have served the interest of the ruling class. The
poem "is full of approving references to the old, feudal system," as Anna
Baldwin has observed.[101] Exceptions, of course, can be found: possessing
their specific histories and their own problematics, religion, literature, and
the other ideological discourses that Langland works within result in a complex text that can have no single or simple reproductive function.[102] Nevertheless, a certain predominance establishes Langland's class position with
some likelihood. The late E. T. Donaldson's scrupulous study of explicit
political opinions in *Piers* found them to be "conservative and traditionalist."[103] Other kinds of statements also place Langland with the ruling
class. No worthy king ever made a knight, he claims, without seeing that he
had wealth: "It is a careful knyȝt, and of a caytif kynges makyng, / That
haþ no lond ne lynage riche" (11.294–97). Kings create lords by bestowing
conquered lands (19.32). Perhaps the central idea within feudalism is that
land (the chief means of production) comes as a revocable grant;[104] and
Langland uses this idea without comment. Serfdom, which had hardly
passed from existence,[105] does not trouble him. In the course of drawing an
analogy, he mentions villenage without calling its disabilities into question:

For may no cherl chartre make ne his chatel selle
Wiþouten leue of his lord, no lawe wol it graunte.
Ac he may renne in arerage and rome fro home,
As a reneyed caytif rennen aboute.

(11.127–30).[106]

Neither does he question feudal fines (19.37), for which only serfs were liable. The several passages in which the poet urges landowners to be moderate in their impositions on tenants all assume the feudal relations of production.[107]

These same relations are also supported, we should be clear, by Langland's many pleas for charity to the poor. Langland compassionates the poor (14.160–65, 174–79), who he realizes are often victimized by retailers and lawyers, have a special title to heaven (10.346–48, 465–66), and should be especially loved (11.180–84, 231). Time and again, he urges the rich to use their surplus to feed them (7.30; 12.56, 250–55; 13.441–43; 14.145–48; 15.220–21, 342) and rebukes the careless and stingy:

Elenge is þe halle, ech day in þe wike,
That þe lord ne þe lady likeþ noʒt to sitte.
Now haþ ech riche a rule to eten by hymselue
In a pryuee parlour for pouere mennes sake,
Or in a chambre wiþ a chymenee, and leue þe chief halle
That was maad for meles men to eten Inne,
And al to spare to spille þat spende shal anoþer.

(10.97–103)

From the spiritual viewpoint, poverty is the best life: "Whoso wole be pure parfit moot possession forsake" (11.276). Yet Langland never asks about the political and economic conditions for the existence of involuntary poverty, any more than he demands cheap rent, an end to villenage, and labor by free contract only. Dearth comes from a lack of moderation, he thinks (14.71–74), although it is not clear how the poor have a chance to be immoderate. (He elsewhere concedes that poverty greatly tames the flesh.) In the years of labor shortage, the Church, redefining the appropriate object of charity as someone unable to work, served the interest of possessionate clergy, regular and secular, and gentry too. Yet the function of *Piers* in reproducing feudal relationships does not depend on whether Langland supports a charity that would seek out only the disabled, doing no more for "wastours" than keep them alive, or whether he supports an indiscriminate charity toward every beggar. Either view of the poor—(1) those who must work if they can or (2) those who receive alms so that the souls of the rich

might be saved—underwrote feudal relationships, the former by rationaliz-
ing the labor legislation that began in 1349, the latter by the trifunctional
idea of interdependence.[108] For Langland, the poor in either view have
emerged through providence: "Alle my3te god haue maad riche men if he
wolde, / Ac for þe beste ben som riche and some beggeres and pouere"
(11.197–98). He helps to perpetuate feudal relationships by referring them
to the order of nature.[109]

Assuming such a class membership on Langland's part, then, I believe
that the project of *Piers* is to mediate the most critical contradiction within
feudalism as a mode of production. A position within the ruling class
would not exclude such a motive, while the existence of it would explain
some of the formal disparities of his poem.

This crucial contradiction, which the poem itself keeps at the margin,
may have supplied a necessary condition for many social disturbances in
England between the first visitation of the Black Death and the Rising of
1381. It certainly does not account for all of them. The contradiction consists in the fact that, within feudal relations of production, the land is, by
custom and enforceable right, occupied by the direct producer, whether free
or servile. Because titles to peasant holdings were protected by manorial
custom, as labor services were,[110] it must be remembered that "in different
contexts the question, 'Whose land is this?,' would be answered, equally
correctly, by giving the name of the lord, the peasant, or possibly that of
some intermediate tenant."[111] *Piers* briefly reflects this in Wit's likening
Adam's conception of Cain to "an hewe þat erieth nat, [but nonetheless]
auntreth hym to sowe / On a leye-land a3eynes his lordes wille . . . "
(C.10.215–26). The land was in the hands of the peasant to begin with.
"The main factor in most men's standard of living was not what they could
earn but what they could produce."[112] Thus, the peasant family occupying
its fifteen or thirty acres was, to a significant degree, economically independent of its lord. This independence was strengthened by the decline in
population: before the first pestilence in the village of Heworth, for example, each tenant had a separate holding; after the plague, each tenant had
three.[113] "The strength and vitality of the community of the shire," remarked by May McKisack as an aspect of the Rising,[114] is chiefly, it
seems, the political expression of an economic independence.

Feudal relations of production are thus defined by a need for political
means if the lord was to protect a surplus in the peasant's production and
extract some or all of the surplus. They are thus defined by the economic's
never emerging as such, but remaining indissoluble from a political relation, defined in turn solely by the political ascendancy of the aristocracy.
The feudal relations of production *presuppose* this ascendancy. "How does
the landlord prevent the appropriation of the land by the direct produc-
ers? . . . To exact rent supposes not only a general title to property en-

forced by the state, but the political dominance of the landlord class."[115] Rodney Hilton has proposed that, by comparison with French seigneurs, English aristocrats never managed to develop a jurisdictional and political power comparable to the ban. The resulting "relative weakness of the English manor" was a reason for the destruction of feudalism in England nearly a century and a half before the French destroyed it.[116] Capitalism, whatever its own internal contradictions, does not require this dominance,[117] at least within its own logic: an *internal* force—the Hunger that Piers uses for recruiting labor—moves the landless laborer to exchange labor for wages. Labor becomes a commodity exchanged for other commodities. By contrast, precapitalist rent was not an economic relation at all but a political one,[118] and the landlords did not always succeed at collection.[119] Their intensified political efforts helped to bring on the Rising itself,[120] their suppression of which was only a temporary victory.

Thus, an "inbuilt contradiction," in Perry Anderson's phrase, torments feudalism, a contradiction "between its own rigorous tendency to a decomposition of sovereignty and the absolute exigences of a final center of authority in which a practical recomposition could occur."[121] In the unconscious of the text is the project that this contradiction be resolved. The presence of it acts like an invisible mass, exerting its force upon the forms that Langland adopts. With the conventions represented by *Winner and Waster* comes the convention of the centrally powerful judge; but owing to the presence of the contradiction, such an organizing central figure—to which *Piers Plowman* incessantly returns—alternates in Langland's poem with those who claim to find their guidance within themselves. Thus, *Piers* becomes discrepant with its generic tradition (thus creating, perhaps, the need for an accretion of genres) when it becomes discrepant within itself. I do not mean that the alternation in *Piers* between an external force, generally existing within a tradition of theological discourse, and an internal force, drawn from theology also, is somehow allegorical for a contradiction between the political center and the economic margins of the feudal social formation. Nor do I mean simply that the religious sanctions represented in *Piers,* external and internal, often enforce feudalism. Rather, I mean that the religious problematic to which Langland devotes his work—namely, how he might save his soul (1.84)[122]—does not control his text. As he produces his poem, the "project" that remains preconscious—no doubt isolated in his mind from the religious problematic, just as his critics have isolated it (Donaldson, for example, correctly observed that ninety-nine one hundredths of the poem has nothing to do with politics)—the "project," I suggest, determines the theological development of the poem, and determines it as disjunctive and discrepant.

The ideological imperative to resolve the dilemma of the feudal economy results in the detour of religious discourse that consists in Piers himself. On the one hand, Piers is an orienting figure, as on the half-acre (to which I must return very briefly): chosen by the penitents as their guide, he is also the teacher of leechcraft to Jesus (16.103–5), the object of a quest (16.18–19, 168; 18.21; 20.382), the judge and emperor of all the world (19.427). On the other hand, he is moved by some inner force, a certainty about Truth that clearly has not come from travel or external teachers (5.538). This inner force is never more apparent than in his change of direction. Truth sends him a pardon commanding him to do what he has been doing (7.5); whereupon Piers undergoes, for no very clear reason, a conversion: "I shal cessen of my sowyng . . . & swynke noȝt so harde" (7.122). He is said to be able to perceive the will (15.200), but this claim— whatever its validity—inverts the fact that it is *his* will that fascinates the reader.

Piers as this kind of mediator applies the three staves that protect the Tree of Charity. These, however, are themselves undecidably outer and inner, the Persons of the Trinity but also the faculties of the soul organized to make a loving choice. Mediating as the arms in which Jesus jousts (18.22; 19.12), *Petrus* both is and is not "christus" (15.212). Finally, in passus 6, in economic terms that, as I have tried to show, mystify the historical situation, Piers mediates: he resists the mobile laborers and hence is on the side of the landlords of Langland's England. He is a peasant employer of labor himself and hence logically on the side of those who oppose the labor statutes.

Piers resolves at the level of ideology a contradiction insoluble within history.[123] This resolution nevertheless does not put an end to the poem's own disparities. Even at the last moment, Conscience, the inner book, closes Langland's book by setting off to look for Piers, who thus remains in some sense external to Conscience as well as to the poem. The disparities do not end because the resolution is an imaginary one, the projection of an order, in a poem where history is silent: in all the thousands of lines in *Piers,* for example, not one peasant is represented as leaving a manor so that he might work for wages. But the text, composed within literary history, does not cease to function in the rest of material history. In the differences with which Langland appropriates dream vision and debate, the contradictions of feudalism itself become glaring.[124]

✳   ✳

Further Reading

Two recent surveys of Marx's thought are W. A. Suchting, *Marx: An Introduction* (New York and London, 1983), and Jon Elster's longer work,

Making Sense of Marx (Cambridge, 1985). A reliable guide to the history of Marxist literary theory in the twentieth century is Tony Bennett's *Formalism and Marxism* (London, 1979). See also Raymond Williams, "Crisis in English Studies," in *Writing in Society* (London, 1983), 192–211; and Frank Lentricchia, *After the New Criticism* (Chicago, 1980).

Before his death, Williams himself was almost certainly the most influential theorist and critic writing in English within the traditions of historical materialism. His major theoretical work is *Marxism and Literature* (Oxford, 1977). His practical criticism includes such books as *Culture and Society, 1780–1950* (1958; reprint, New York, 1983). With *A Theory of Literary Production,* trans. Geoffrey Wall (Paris, 1966; London, 1978), Pierre Macherey has had considerable influence also—upon Terry Eagleton's *Criticism and Ideology* (London, 1976), for example, and Fredric Jameson's *The Political Unconscious* (Ithaca, 1981). No study of the commensurability of Williams's theory with Macherey's seems to exist yet, although the two are not obviously incompatible. For example, Macherey's analysis of text production may respond to Williams's claim that authorial development "can be grasped as a complex of active relations, with which the emergence of an individual project, and the real history of other contemporary projects and of the developing forms and structures, are continuously and substantially interactive" (*Marxism and Literature,* 196).

Macherey's interest in contradictions within the text (an interest in "symptomatic"reading) and insistence that neither ideology nor the history of aesthetic forms by itself can explain texts (his emphasis on texts as "overdetermined") begin to indicate Macherey's debt to Louis Althusser. Two relevant works of Althusser's in this connection are *Reading Capital,* by Althusser and Etienne Balibar (Paris, 1968; New York, 1970), and "Ideology and Ideological State Apparatuses (Notes Towards an Investigation)" in *Lenin and Philosophy and Other Essays,* trans. Ben Brewster (New York and London, 1971). Important rejections of Althusser include Jacques Rancière, "On the Theory of Ideology (the Politics of Althusser)," *Radical Philosophy* 7 (Spring 1974): 2–15; Alex Callinicos, *Althusser's Marxism* (London, 1976); Edward P. Thompson, *"The Poverty of Theory" and Other Essays* (London and New York, 1978); and Steven B. Smith, *Reading Althusser: An Essay on Structural Marxism* (Ithaca and London, 1984). Meanwhile, a notable work that begins with Althusser is Göran Therborn's *The Ideology of Power and the Power of Ideology* (London, 1980). Michael Sprinker's *Imaginary Relations: Aesthetics and Ideology in the Theory of Historical Materialism* (London, 1987) offers an important positive critique of Althusser.

For readers interested in other Middle English texts that have been read within the traditions of historical materialism, some recent Chaucer criticism would include Sheila Delany's "Politics and Paralysis of Poetic Imagination in *The Physician's Tale*," *Studies in the Age of Chaucer* 3 (1981): 47–60; Stephen Knight's *Geoffrey Chaucer* (London, 1986); Lee Patterson's " 'No man his reson herde': Peasant Consciousness, Chaucer's Miller, and the Structure of the *Canterbury Tales*," *South Atlantic Quarterly* 86 (1987): 457–95; and Paul Strohm's *Social Chaucer* (Cambridge, MA, 1989).

Chapter 5

The Language of Transgression: Body, Flesh, and Word in Mystical Discourse

✳ Karma Lochrie ✳

> One of the insights of Christianity, and not the least one,
> is to have gathered in a single move perversion and beauty
> as the lining and the cloth of one and the same economy.
>
> Julia Kristeva, *Powers of Horror*

The phenomenon of female spirituality during the twelfth to the early fifteenth centuries has been variously recognized and reenvisioned recently by feminist historians, literary scholars, and feminist theorists. In her thorough documentation of the religious significance of food to female mystics and saints during this period, Carolyn Walker Bynum regards this period as the first time in the history of Christianity that women were able to influence and shape piety. With the proliferation of religious roles—monastic, quasi-religious, and lay—available to women, the twelfth century witnessed the first women's movement in Christian history, according to Bynum.[1] In a different vein, the French feminist Luce Irigaray brackets female mysticism as "the only place in the history of the West in which woman speaks and acts so publicly."[2] This conjuncture of feminine publicity and speech is enabled by excess through which woman accedes to the Imaginary, where all subject-other terms dissolve. In decidedly different registers, these two evaluations nevertheless see in female mysticism an articulation of the feminine that is powerful and enabling.

The question immediately arises, however, whether that place in Western history occupied by female mystics in Irigaray's formulation is capable of resisting colonization by the very patriarchal institutions and discourse within which it is situated. That is, does female mysticism in the late Middle Ages radically subvert or surreptitiously reinforce the dominant patriarchal discourse of the medieval Church? Further, is the female mystic able to use her location in the feminine to dislocate the prevailing institutional relegation of woman to the status of Other?[3]

These questions cannot be answered, however, unless we revise the language currently used to study medieval mysticism. Emphasis on the body, physical suffering, and a frighteningly literal understanding of what it means to imitate Christ are all at issue in discussions of female mysticism, feminist as well as historical and theological. While scholars trace this emphasis to the spirituality of Saint Bernard and Saint Francis, it also derives from their own taxonomies of mysticism. Most scholars distinguish between positive mysticism, which is characterized by quite physical mystical experiences, and negative mysticism, which deplores the former in favor of transcending the physical in a process of self-emptying.[4] The alignment of female mysticism with the positive type places it in the realm of the physical, constellating the feminine and the body together. It suffers not only from the judged inferiority of positive mysticism but from the unexamined modern equation of the body and the physical. The identification of the feminine with the body in medieval mystical writings, then, must either be embraced in a feminist essentialism or rejected as untranscendent and even masochistic.

What has been ignored in the evaluation of female mysticism is the historical construction of the body and its relationship to language. That is, studies of the physical in female spirituality already assume the body to be that material, untranscendent, universal, and self-evident given which exists in opposition to the soul. Such a notion does not acknowledge the cultural construction of the body as well as the possibility of historicizing the body. In order to determine what it means to say that female mysticism speaks from the place of the body, we must first consider the theological, medical, and even literary constructions of the body in the Middle Ages. Further, we need to know what the relationship of body to speech and to words was if we are to evaluate the ability of that speech to subvert patriarchal exclusion of women. Whether the place from which female mystics spoke was one of subversion or conscription is at stake in this revisioning of the body.

Such a revisioning is possible through a historical reconstruction of the body and the feminine in relationship to it. By examining Augustinian and Bernardian constructions of the body, we can begin to place the medieval implications of the body for the feminine. Devotional works for women also contribute to this historical reconstructions because they draw upon cultural constructions of the female body in particular. Yet a theorizing of this "new" body's relationship to the word and to language requires itself a new language, one that does not already subscribe to the illusion of the body as self-evident. Such a language is possible using Julia Kristeva's notion of abjection and abject speech as it relates to the body and Christian discourse. Her essay on abjection, *Powers of Horror,* provides a possible point of departure for considering the operation of the feminine and the intersection of body and language in women's mystical writings.[5] The historical reconstruction of the body together with this theoretical discussion of mystical language should work in conjunction to revise our understanding of just what women's mystical texts might claim regarding language, the body, the feminine, and even culture.

Before addressing any theoretical questions, however, it is necessary to map out that place from which female mystics publicly spoke and acted in the late Middle Ages. One of the defining features of female spirituality beginning in the thirteenth century is an increasing emphasis on the humanity, or rather physicality, and suffering of Christ. Conformity to Christ becomes the primary focus of the *via mystica* not only in female mysticism but in the larger movement, affective spirituality, of which female spirituality is usually considered a significant part. This founding of religious life on the identification with and imitation of Christ, rather than on contemplative or monastic models of devotion, accounts for the burgeoning lay spiritual movement that occurred between the thirteenth and fifteenth centuries.[6]

For both the male and female religious, imitation of Christ's suffering could take many forms, including fasting, self-flagellation, and self-defilement. In addition to these seemingly self-generated forms of *imitatio Christi,* others were involuntary, such as bodily effusions and elongations, stigmata, tears, and seizures.[7] While the degree of the individual's control over and manipulation of these somatic enactments of Christ's suffering was often questioned, the distinction between this kind of imitation and the practice of deliberate mortification of the flesh was not. Margery Kempe's "boisterous tears" accompanied by writhing, wresting on the ground, and turning blue as lead, for example, were viewed quite differently from her abstention from eating meat on Fridays. The latter practice annoyed the pilgrims with whom she traveled, but it was her roaring that aroused the censure of church and secular authorities.[8] Finally, there is a third kind of imitation that was more popular with the saints and the Church before the fourteenth century, the imitation of Christ's works through charitable ministry to the poor, sick, and disadvantaged. Such a notion of imitation, most familiarly demonstrated in the life of Saint Francis, was subsumed by those interior models of devotion associated with Christ's Passion.[9]

The centrality of the first two kinds of *imitatio Christi,* particularly to female spirituality, is further complicated by the medieval medical and theological alignment of the female with the flesh, and the male with the spirit.[10] Both Galenic and Aristotelian theories of conception consider the woman's contribution to the fetus to be a material one, that is, the woman provides the matter or flesh to the developing human being.[11] This medieval conception theory carries important theological implications for the Virgin Mary's role in the incarnation of Christ and ultimately for *imitatio Christi*. The Virgin's humanity is celebrated for providing Christ with sinless flesh—the *materia* redeemed from the Fall—in Hildegard of Bingen's idea of her as *tunica humanitatis,* the "clothing of humanity" that Christ puts on.[12] Because "woman signifies the humanity of the Son of God," according to Hildegard, not only does the Incarnation exalt femininity as *materia,* but it feminizes Christ.[13] While Christ became a bridegroom in his divinity, according to Godfrey of Admont, he simultaneously became a bride in his humanity.[14]

In the Crucifixion, the scientific and theological theories of the feminine and the flesh find their most graphic expression. The wounded and bleeding body of Christ, which gives birth to new life for humanity, does so by offering itself as food, as the matter that restores humankind to God. Christ becomes female and mother on the cross when he suffers bodily and when he surrenders his flesh as the *materia* of new life.[15] While the ultimate purpose of the Passion is the redemption of mankind, woman seems to be privileged as the means for this redemption.

Such a privileging of the bodily, the physical, and the female allows for the male *imitatio Christi* a means by which he calls into question his own transcendent status as spirit, and thereby humbles himself. For the female religious, however, the meaning of the *imitatio* is more problematic. While it offers her a valorization of her perceived association with the flesh, it also excludes her from transcendence.[16] Even if her mimesis of Christ's Passion permits her a "privileged communication" expressed through her bodily *imitatio,* it inures her to the patriarchal double binarism that insists that man is to woman as soul is to flesh.[17] Whether the female mystic discovers in her imitation of Christ's suffering a public place from which to speak, as Irigaray suggests, or whether she merely embraces and reinforces her own subjection from a position of masochism becomes the central theoretical issue in recent studies of late medieval female spirituality.

In *The Second Sex* Simone de Beauvoir argues that the flesh and female is invoked in the passivity and victimization of the Crucifixion. Though the woman mystic may be "overwhelmed to see that man, man-God has assumed her role," she hardly achieves more in these Passion visions than the satisfaction of her sadomasochistic fantasies in the glorification of her own subjection.[18] By identifying with the body of Christ, she reifies her own contigent status as lover. Feminist theory provides a more recent argument that the female *imitatio Christi* was encouraged by the medieval Church in order "to reinforce the relegation of 'woman' to a transcendent, mystified and mystificatory sphere where female masochism is spectacularly redeployed in the pose of crucifixion/crucifiction."[19] The female mystic's ecstatic sympathy with Christ's Passion turns out to be little more than transported self-loathing. She never questions the crux of the fiction that "it is the very equation of victimization, passivity, subjection with feminity, that allows the Christian inversion [the valorized humanity] its paradoxical triumph."[20]

The central problem, then, of the study of female mysticism is determining the place from which it speaks, whether from within or without the patriarchal construction of woman, or whether it positions itself somewhere in the borderlands. The focus for this determination is the *imitatio Christi* and its attendant assumptions about the body, in particular the female body. Yet most modern discussions of late medieval spirituality continue to be shaped by modern, not medieval, assumptions about the body and its distinction from the spirit. We take for granted, for example, the self-evidence of the body as "a fact of nature, a constant and universal reality," as Jean-Pierre Vernant has recently argued.[21] Only a few scholars have begun to treat the body as itself problematic, as something that, like gender constructions, cannot simply be taken for granted.[22] Our own positivistic attitude toward the body, shaped as it is by modern science and medicine, deproblematizes the body by reducing it to pure matter more than Aristotelian science ever did.[23] The fact that, as Bynum reminds us "the body itself may actually have a history" is rarely taken into consideration in studies of female spirituality. Further, the Western assumption of the opposition of body to spirit allows us to collapse distinctions among flesh, body, and the senses. Our own conception of the body limits our investigations of the significance of the *imitatio Christi* to female spirituality and ultimately to the theoretical question of its importance toward establishing the place from which to speak.

Medieval assumptions about the female body in particular tend to be subsumed under modern oversimplifications that equate it with sexuality.[24] As a result, the tendency in female hagiography and devotional works for women to emphasize chastity is viewed as evidence of the cultural denigration of the female body and sexuality.[25] Peter Brown has challenged the assumption that female asceticism merely reflected male anxiety over female sexuality in early Christianity, while Bynum has asserted that "medieval images of the body have less to do with sexuality than with fertility and decay."[26] Nevertheless, modern assumptions about the body continue to inform discussions about female spirituality of the late Middle Ages.

Whether female spirituality managed to disrupt patriarchal constructions of the feminine, providing women with a new place from which to speak, as Irigaray maintains, or whether it merely adopted a new forum for the subjection of women is a problem that cannot be answered without an understanding of the medieval theory of the body. One of the great influences on affective spirituality of the late Middle Ages, the Cistercian Bernard of Clairvaux, offers just such a theory of the body with which we may begin to evaluate the female *imitatio Christ*.[27] After examining Bernard's theory of the body, we will then turn to medieval devotional works written by men for women to see how Bernard's theory contributes to a theory of the female body in directives for devotional practice. This devotional model will serve as the basis for a theory of the female *imitatio Christi*.

The Fissured Flesh

Peter Brown traces the changing perception of the body in early Christianity from the frontier between nature and the city to the Augustine's notion of the "fissured flesh" that put body at odds with soul, city, and God.[28] The key to this change was Augustine's insistence on the Pauline distinction between the flesh and the body.[29] As Augustine points out in *De civitate dei,* Paul often uses the term *flesh* as a synecdoche for the entire human being.[30] In addition, Paul locates the source of man's evil in the flesh, rather than in the body. The body's role in human sin is merely that of a sort of lackey to the restless, rebellious, and intransigent flesh.[31] The primary human conflict, as Paul characterizes it in his Letter to the Romans, is one of flesh against spirit or, rather, the life of the flesh against the life of the spirit (7.18–34 and 8.1–13).

For Augustine, the flesh represented "all that led the self to prefer its own will to that of God."[32] The Fall of Man signified a corruption of the flesh and of the soul, which were no longer directed toward the will of God. Augustine is careful to point out that this corruption was caused not by the flesh but by the soul, else how could one explain evil committed by the serpent who has no flesh? Neither is the rupture enacted by the soul and flesh together necessarily bodily in nature, for some vices—such as anger, jealous, idolatry—are not aimed at bodily gratification.[33] The concupiscence of the flesh is the result of the rebellion of the human will against God's will, drawing all to its own private purposes.[34] Hence the concupiscence that had irrevocably fissured the flesh from soul, will, and God included the sum of dark forces or drives which caused discord in the soul and in the city of man. The "urge of the flesh" could be controlled but not necessarily by reviling the body: the "law of the mind" must exert pressure to bring the flesh back into conformity with the will.[35] Augustine uses a telling analogy to explain how the concupiscence is to be monitored:

[C]aro tanquam conjux est. . . . Concupiscit adversus te, tanquam conjux tua; ama et castiga, donec fiat in una reformatione una concordia.[36]

(Your flesh is like your wife. . . . It rebels against you, just as your wife does. Love it, rebuke it; let it be formed into one bond of concord between flesh and spirit.)

Because the flesh implicates both body and soul, it must be mastered by the "law of the mind," just as the wife should be mastered by the husband. The flesh, like the wife, is not by its nature evil unless it is unmastered. Yet it is the site of disruption, the fissure that estranged the human will from God's, human beings from each other, and the law of the mind from the goadings of the flesh. Through his analogy, Augustine places the wife not at the site of the body but at the fissure of the flesh where concupiscence forever agitates against the will, the gap through which the self fell from God and from itself.

Bernard of Clairvaux constructs his mysticism of affectivity on the Augustinian distinction between flesh and body and the vulnerability of the will due to the Fall. The body, for Bernard, is not evil, but is subjected to the raging of the will in conjunction with the senses. In an interesting twist on Augustine's analogy of the relationship of soul to flesh to body, Bernard focuses on the will as woman in collusion with the flesh to eviscerate the soul:

Mitga efferos voluntatis motus, et crudelem bestiam mansuescere cura. Ligatus es: solvere studeas quod rumpere omnino non possis. Eva tua est [vita]. Vim facere, aut eatenus mea offendere nullo modo praevalebis.[37]

(Check the wild motions of the will and take care to tame the wild beast. You are in bonds. Strive to untie what you can never break. The will is your Eve. You will not prevail against her by using force.)

Bernard identifies the corrupted will as that which has been seized by the desires of the flesh, making less of a distinction between flesh and will than Augustine does. Eve is the perverse will that runs riot with the senses. In his powerful treatise "On Conversion," Bernard dramatizes the resistance of the will to reason and the divine will. The will, a little old woman whose hair stands on end, scratches her foul ulcers, grinds her teeth in fury, and infects the very air with her foul breath. In her argument against the soul's remorse, she summons all the fleshly senses to her aid, reminding the soul of the threefold ulcer—voluptuousness, curiosity, and ambition—that afflicts her:

[E]t ab hoc triplici ulcere non est in me sanitas a planta pedis usque ad verticem. Itaque fauces, et quae abscena sunt corporis, assignata sunt voluptati, quandoquidem velut de novo necesse est singula recenseri. Nam curi oscitati pes vagus, et indisciplinatus oculus famulantur. At vanit ati quidem auris et lingua serviunt, dum per illam impinguat caput meum oleum peccatoris, per hanc ipsa suppleo quod in laudibus meis alii nimus fecisse videntur.

"There is not part of me which is free from this threefold ulcer, from the soles of my feet to the top of my head (Is 1.6). My gullet and the shameful parts of my body are given up to pleasure; we must name them afresh, one by one. The wandering foot and the undisciplined eye are slaves to curiosity. Ear and tongue serve vanity, while the sinner's oil pours in to make my head greasy (Ps 140.5). With my tongue I myself supply whatever others seem to have omitted in my praise."[38]

The will's resistance to reason is maintained through the senses, which, though they are not evil in themselves, infect the soul and the flesh. In fact, the senses and the flesh have been perverted by the will, by the threefold ulcer that befouls them and clogs them with filth.[39] The "wild motions of the will"—our Eve—are the urges of curiosity, ambition, pleasure, which enlist the senses in their satisfaction. The state of "living in the flesh" is one in which the body is abducted by the appetites and the ulcerous soul. Bernard construes the relationship of body to spirit to flesh in an interesting analogy:

Our body finds itself located between the spirit it must serve, and the desires of the flesh or the powers of darkness, which wage war on the soul, as a cow might be between the peasant and the thief.[40]

The will, the old woman who rages and picks at her ulcers, the Eve, of Saint Bernard resembles Augustine's association of the Eve with the sensual or the lower reason.[41] In both cases, woman is associated with the perviousness of the flesh, which began with a fissure as a result of the Fall and which has festered into ulcers since. Bernard's bovine body merely finds itself caught in the middle of the war between flesh and spirit.

Woman, then, occupies the border between body and soul, the fissure through which a constant assault on the body may be conducted and a painful reminder of influx that maintains the division between body and soul. In fact, woman represents in Bernard and Augustine influx itself, where the boundaries of body and soul are continually erased. The influx is not, however, primarily induced from the outside. Rather, it is the foul little woman scratching her ulcers which produces the perviousness of the senses. While she is in command, "a mass of bloody pus is flowing everywhere."[42] Thus the soul finds itself contaminated from within and without and vexed by a kind of spiritual vertigo.

Bernard's theory of affectivity, which underlies his discourse on mystical love, is dependent on this same bond between the will and the senses found in his psychology of sin and conversion. The crux of his idea of love is his concept of affect. While this term is difficult to define in Bernard's work, it is not difficult to identify. Every human soul consists of four affects: love, joy, fear, and sadness. These affects are dependent on both the senses and the will for their expression. Whether these four affections bring glory or shame depends on how they are ordered and maintained in the soul. The concupiscence of the flesh is an ever-present evil affect because it is ungoverned. Under the watchful eye of reason, the soul pursues its carnal affection in the contemplation of Christ's Passion.

As attribute of the soul, affect is a complex interaction of external and internal promptings, very much as sin is. As Bernard contends, "Affects, simply called, are found in us naturally, it seems as though they emanate from our own being, what completes them comes from grace; it is indeed quite certain that grace regulates only what creation has given us, so that virtues are nothing but regulated affects."[43] Love is the purified affect that is regulated by grace and guarded by reason. It is, as Kristeva notes, crucial to Bernard's emphasis on the importance of Christ's humanity: "Thus for the Christian, a human being imprisoned in his flesh, the affect of the flesh is already significant; even though it might be the zero degree of our love for the Other, the affect is already dwelled in by Christ."[44] Christ's indwelling in the affect offers the Christian a perviousness that accedes to glory rather than to shame because it is regulated internally by reason and externally by divine grace.

One logic informs both doctrines of sin and of mystical love. The bundle of drives unleashed in the Fall when reason abdicated its regulatory role becomes the means by which man is restored to God.[45] The perviousness of the flesh, which is mark of its perversion, also offers the possibility of redemption.

Does the one imply the other? That is, does Bernard's Eve, an old scabrous woman who rages against reason with the riotous flesh, become converted into the Bride of Christ, whose love begins in carnal affection? Curiously enough, it does not. Our Eve, like fleshly concupiscence, remains unreconstructed. The carnal affections continue to be weighed down by fleshly desires and by a "habit of worldliness." Woman remains associated not with the bodily, which grazes nervously between the peasant spirit and the thieving flesh, but with vile affect: that is, the concupiscence of the flesh and corruption of the senses.[46] Bernard's vision of the *imitatio Christi*

means a binding of the *affectus cordis,* "the affection of the heart," in a
carnal love that is purified of fleshly habits: "to love with the whole heart
means to put the love of his sacred humanity before everything that tempts
us, from within or without."[47] Such a love not only restores the resem-
blance to God in the soul, but it consoles the soul in her exile. Due to the
Fall, the soul forever inhabits a *regio dissimilitudinis,* "a region of
unlikeness."[48] The irony of the *imitatio Christi* is that the striving for re-
semblance to Christ serves to remind one of one's dissimilarity, of the concupiscence that separates the flesh of fallen humans from that of Christ.

If woman occupies the region of deformed dissimilarity, perviousness
of the flesh, its fissure, vile affect, in Bernard's works, what does it mean
for the woman religious to imitate Christ? One possibility, the more radical
one, is that the woman mystic insists upon that dissimilarity, upon the ambiguous, heterogeneous flesh in her imitation of Christ. From and through a
place of disruption, she seeks spiritual perfection. However, this is not how
this configuration of body, flesh, spirit and *imitatio* become scripted for the
female religious. Devotional works written for women do in fact assume
Bernard's anthropology, but they do so by sublimating it in a theory of the
female body. This theory, in turn, serves to suppress the radical possibilities of Bernard's theory of affections. They seek, in effect, to apply a
Band-Aid to the fissure of the flesh with the doctrine of the enclosed female body.

The Sealed Body

Medieval theology constructs its theory of the female body in conjunction with medieval science. According to the physiological model, woman
is identified "with breaches in boundaries."[49] The convergence of the two
is seen in the interesting justification by Heloise (not Abelard, as is usually
maintained) for allowing nuns to drink wine. Based on the medieval theory
of the humors, Heloise appeals to the "nature" of woman as humid and
fumy to argue that women are less apt to become inebriated than men are.
She cites the physician Macrobius Theodosius:

> Aristoteles mulieres inquit raro ebriantur crebro senes. . . . Mulier humec-
> tissimo est corpore; . . . docent praecipue assiduae purgationes superfluo
> exonerantes corpus humore. . . . Muliebre corpus crebris purgationibus
> deputatum pluribus consertum [est] foraminibus ut pateat in meatus et vias
> praebeat humori in egestionis exitum confluenti; per haec foramina vapor
> vini celeriter evanescit.[50]

> (Aristotle says that women are rarely inebriated while old men are
> often. . . . Woman has a very humid body, . . . as is proven mainly by

her continual purgations which empty the body of superfluous moisture. . . . A woman's body which is visited with frequent purgations is fit with several holes so that it opens into passages and supplies outlets for the excess moisture to be dispersed; through these holes the fume of the wine is quickly discharged.)

While this fumosity allows for purgation of toxins such as wine, it is dangerous in its susceptibility to external influences. Women are given to a suspicious superfluity, which makes them prone to sickness and which also helps to make up for their humoral deficiency. Cold and moist, they lack the energy, heat, and consistency of men, who are hot and dry.

This physiological susceptibility to external and internal influences finds its theological equivalent in the moral breaches in boundaries associated with woman's nature. It is no coincidence that chastity is defined for women as a physical and spiritual *integritas,* or intactness.[51] The religious life for women consists primarily in adopting boundaries and maintaining an unbroken body. The author of *Hali Meidenhad* warns his female reader to guard the sign of her chastity: "Ant tu þenne, eadi meiden, þet art iloten to him wiþ mei[ð]hades merke, ne brec þu nawt þet seil þet seileð inc togederes." ("And you then, blessed maiden, who are assigned to him with the sign of virginity, break not thou that seal which seals you together.") This warning refers both to the seal which binds the virgin to Christ and that which signifies her virginity "without breach." The virgin will earn a place equal to the angels with God himself if she leads a life "in the frail flesh without breach." As the sweet balm guards the body from rotting, so virginity preserves the live flesh from defilement.[52]

Borrowing from Bernard's notion of the *regio dissimilaris,* the *Meidenhad* author urges the virgin to preserve her likeness to heavenly nature during her habitation in the "land of unlikeness." Yet her unlikeness is clearly more precarious than is a man's, since her very nature is already situated in the flesh. In an interesting departure from his source, the *Hali Meidenhad* author invites the virgin to savor a special victory over the devil, since he is ashamed to be overcome by a thing "as feeble as flesh is, and namely by woman."[53] The flesh in its feebleness is here named woman, as if the one term were a species of the other generic term. Woman represents the frailty of the flesh, concupiscence, the region of dissimilarity. To borrow from a later analogue in an entirely different context, "Frailty, thy name is woman."

The female body—with all its perviousness to external and internal influences—is the signifier of the frailty of the flesh, including the "fleshly will" and the faculties of sight, speech, kissing, and affections.[54] The sealed body, then, becomes the sign not only of virginity but of the *integritas* of all the senses, particularly speech and sight. When virgins are then instructed not to break that which seals them together with God and with themselves, they are being called to enclosure at many levels. The unbroken flesh ultimately means bodily closure and silence. It is no coincidence that female sanctity during the late Middle Ages was often manifested through miraculous closure of the body.[55] The seal is both boundary and suture to the consequences of the breached flesh.

The English Cistercian Aelred of Rievaulx (1110–67) likewise interprets female chastity in terms of bodily enclosure in his instruction for anchoresses, *De Institutione Inclusarum* (1160–62). The middle-fifteenth-century English translation of this work, MS. Bodley 423, defines chastity as a state of being above "the conuersacion of the worlde." The metaphor of conversation here works at the level of speech and sexuality, levels that Aelred collapses. Condemning the anchoress who thinks it sufficient to "shutte her body betwene too walles," Aelred warns that the intercourse of her thoughts and speech with the world turns her cell into a brothel.[56] The windows of the cell reflect the perviousness of the flesh, while speech in particular betrays the promiscuity of body and soul. Silence is as much a condition for chastity as is sexual renunciation. For Aelred of Rievaulx as for Ambrose much earlier, female chastity preserves the "invisible frontier" between body and world, a sacred space that resists the condition of abjection posed by the "heaving powers of the flesh."[57]

The *Ancrene Wisse* similarly locates the female body at the frontier of the flesh in its justification to anchoresses for fleeing the world. Like the *De Institutione Inclusarum*, the *Wisse* advocates a sealing of the borders, particularly the border of speech:

> Al swa as ʒe mahe seon weater hwen me punt hit [ant] stoppeð hit biuore wel þ[at] hit ne mahe duneward, þenne is hit inedd aʒein, forte climben uppart, ant ʒe al þisses weis pundeð ower wordes, forstop þið ower þohtes, as ʒe wulleð þ[at] ha climben ant hehin toward heouene, [ant] nawt ne fallen duneward, [ant] to fleoten ʒont te worlt, as deð muchel chaffle.

> ("Just as you see water, when it has been firmly stopped and dammed so that it cannot flow downwards, forced to go back and climb upwards, in just this way you should dam up your speech and your thoughts, if you want them to climb and rise up towards heaven instead of falling downwards and being scattered about the world as much idle talk is.)[58]

Conversation with the world in thought and speech as well as through sight, habit, and daily contact diffuses one's relationship with God. As a practice of damming up speech and thought, the *Ancrene Wisse* author recommends meditating on Christ's suffering. In particular, he concentrates on how the recluse should imitate Christ's suffering in the five senses on Calvary. For example, just as Christ's mouth was closed by the blows of the Jews, so "you, for love of Him and for your own great good, close up your chattering mouth with your own lips." Eyes and ears should likewise be enclosed, while anchoresses should take example from the nails of Christ's hands to keep their own hands safe within the boundaries of their cells.[59] In this way *imitatio Christi* for the female religious is incongruously identified with the unbroken flesh and the sealed female body. Christ's wounds, far from signifying the perviousness of the female body, serve to remind women of the need to dam up their own vulnerable bodies. Instead of glorifying the feminine, imitation of Christ forces the recluse to internalize the association of the feminine with the breached flesh. The sealed body finds its complement in seclusion and silence.

Bernard's theory of the flesh and the body has important consequences for the female religious. The identification of the feminine with the fissured flesh, the dark drives in complicity with the senses, and ultimately, the loss of boundaries leads to the emphasis on the sealed body in the rules for nuns and anchoresses. The logic of the *imitatio Christi* is thus a logic of renunciation, of enclosure, of finding in Christ's suffering not an image of woman's own suffering humanity, but a remonstrance to woman as frail flesh. As such, the female religious's imitation of Christ was not scripted to allow her to transcend or to celebrate the "frail flesh" without a certain masochism.

The key to the representation of woman in the Middle Ages, then, was not the body or the physical, per se, but the flesh, the senses, and the recalcitrant will. Woman was the "heaving powers of the flesh," the place of disruption, the breach in the harmonious unity of man and God and the flesh and spirit. Represented in physiological terms, she was windy, susceptible to influences that roamed freely throughout her body; theologically, she is Bernard's ulcerous will who refuses the prompting of God and reason to give reign to the heaving powers of the flesh. She is also that perviousness which consists in the heaving powers, the will, and the senses together. Any potential for subversion is effectively controlled and repressed in the concept of the sealed body, as we have seen in spiritual guides for women.

Yet within the same logic of perfection for the female religious is inscribed a logic of perversion, a potential for disruption. The flesh in its Augustinian and Bernardian senses is neither spiritual nor corporeal, but heterogeneous. It is that which cannot be divided, but neither is it unified or harmonious. It is already impure. The possibility for enlisting the broken flesh into the service of perfection is therefore always present. How can the

female mystic break the seal? Julia Kristeva offers one possible strategy for
disruption in her essay on abjection, *Powers of Horror.* After looking first
at her theory of abjection, I will turn to the example of the fourteenth-
century Italian mystic, Angela of Foligno, to see how the seal might be
broken in medieval female spirituality.

Abjection: The Broken Seal

By definition, abjection is an ordeal of the self in which "nothing is
familiar." It is experienced as a kind of fear and revulsion precipitated by
the loss of boundaries of the subject. The "I" finds itself "ceaselessly
straying" in "unstable territories." The abject is that which "does not respect borders, positions, rules. The in-between, the ambiguous, the composite." An example of abjection is, according to Kristeva, food loathing
that causes retching, a protest of the body. This experience of abjection has
little to do with the qualities of the food itself—its texture, smell, or appearance; instead, abjection comes from the awareness of the internal and
external threats to the border of the self. Corpses, festering wounds, the
smell of decay all have the power to invade the subject/object and inside/
outside borders, making those borders pervious and identity problematic.[60]
Abjection is bound to the sacred in the form of taboo. That is, the
taboo serves to exclude something—say, a food or sexuality—in order to
secure the borders of the subject. At the same time, then, the sacred calls
transgression into being, since it is transgression of the taboo, rule, or law
that gives rise to abjection. The taboos of Judaism and Christianity attempt
to prohibit the threat of the abject by protecting the boundaries of the body.
The main difference between the two, according to Kristeva, is that Jewish
law seeks to protect the pure body from external defilement while Christian
law internalizes abjection by making defilement interior.[61] "Not that which
goeth into the mouth this defileth a man; but that which cometh out of the
mouth, this defileth a man" (Matt. 15.11). Christian subjectivity, then, depends on the crucial division of inside/outside (rather than the pure/impure
boundaries designated by Judaic law).
We can see how abjection is relevant to Ambrose's fear of the "heaving powers of the flesh," Augustine's attention to the "fissured flesh," and
Bernard's analogy of the will to Eve, who permits the "wild motions of the
soul." Abjection is the result of the Fall, whence the boundaries of the
body and soul were violated. Because the flesh is heterogeneous—neither
body nor soul, but carnal and spiritual at the same time—abjection poses a
continual threat to the Christian subject. Yet it also offers a radical notion
of perfection. The excess of drives—those heaving powers of the flesh—

topples over into love of God. The same interior flux or perviousness of the flesh that leads to sin likewise leads to perfection. According to Kristeva, self-abjection requires of the mystic continual avowal of her impurity, yet it is not necessarily masochistic in the usual sense of the word:

> The mystic's familiarity with abjection is a fount of infinite jouissance. One may stress the masochistic economy of that jouissance only if one points out at once that the Christian mystic, far from using it to the benefit of a symbolic or institutional power, displaces it indefinitely . . . within a discourse where the subject is resorbed . . . into communication with the Other and with others.[62]

The spiritual treatises examined so far do not encourage such mystical abjection in the female religious. Such abjection exploits by overturning the medieval effort to exclude abjection and, with it, the feminine from religious experience. The sealed body represents a taboo against that abjection which threatens the boundaries of the soul. If the female mystic (or male mystic) chooses to occupy those borders, to confound them by transgressing them, she exploits the medieval association of flesh and feminine. Like Bernard's thief who steals the bovine body from the peasant-spirit in order to sin, the flesh transgresses the spirit's domain continually in the experience of abjection. If the woman mystic's ordeal of abjection is masochistic, it is not in the service of the self-loathing that the *Ancrene Riwle* encourages. The mystic who insists on that which has been excluded in medieval Christianity—namely, the feminine, the pervious flesh, and defilement—takes abjection for the sublime.

We could find many examples of female mystics who speak from the place of abjection in affective spirituality in England and on the Continent. Let us turn to one example, Angela of Foligno, to examine how the female mystic takes abjection for the sublime and for a place from which to speak. The text of her revelations leaves distinct traces of the translation from flesh to word and therefore provides a good case study for the discourse of abjection in female mysticism. In addition, it struggles with two languages—a conventional and an abject one—in its effort to apprehend divine mystery. It is the latter language, the language of abjection, that allows Angela of Foligno to inhabit the flesh and thereby transgress the terms of her own exclusion from language and from culture.

Angela of Foligno

Angela of Foligno (1248–1309) became known for the extravagance of her affective participation in Christ's Passion, including her fits of screaming and her graphic involvement in his suffering. At the age of thirty-seven, Angela experienced a conversion and soon set about renouncing and doing penance for her former life.[63] As she tells the story in *Le Livre de l'expérience des vrais fidèles,* she first seeks humility through a renunciation of the flesh and a self-loathing that ultimately leads her to desire a rather dramatic public humiliation:

> Et vellem ire per plateas et civitates nuda, et appendere ad collum meum pisces et carnes dicendo: "Hec est illa vilissima mulier, plena malitie et simulationis, et sentina omnium vitiorum et malorum."[64]
>
> (I wanted to go naked through the streets and cities and hang fish and meat from my neck and declare: "This is the vilest of women, full of wickedness and hypocrisy, and a cesspool of all vices and evil deeds."

Angela here imitates the practice of parading evil women naked through the streets as a form of punishment and a parody of the enclosed, privatized body found in the religious ideal for women.[65] Such a penitential practice assumes the ideal of the *Ancrene Wisse* and *Hali Meidenhad*—that the good female body is one which is sealed off and enclosed—to counteract the conspiracy of the feminine with the breachability of the flesh. The presumably rotting meat and fish hanging from her neck serves to remind Angela of the fleshly corruption she wishes to flee.[66] Yet this desire for public penance leads her to self-loathing and, finally, despair instead of to the desired humility (3d letter, 498). Angela of Foligno learns that such renunciation of the flesh is a form of pride. Hence she rejects this masochistic internalization of the religious ideal, which valorizes enclosure and the sealed body, for mystical abjection that draws upon the heaving powers of the flesh to experience rupture, discontinuity, and excess.

Angela describes her imitation of Christ as a state of being, or an ongoing action. It is a continual transformation into the Crucified and into "the feeling (or affection), as yet inexperienced, of the suffering of Christ" (135.296). What she means by this is that the senses—particularly of smell, touch, taste, and sight—are exploited to their fullest in the mystic's access to "an increase in fervor, joys and sweet fragrances, and new savorings" (135.296).

Angela of Foligno's transformation into the crucified Christ begins with his gift of a profound knowledge of himself. This gift comes in the form of his instruction to her that she place her lips on the wound in his side. Christ tells her that the fresh blood she drinks from his side will purify her, while she in return vows to suffer a death more shameful in all parts of her body for him (17.16). The typology of the Fall in this vision is unmistakable. Eve was tempted by knowledge into eating the fruit of the forbidden tree, causing the rupture in the unity of flesh and spirit. In Angela's vision it is the ruptured body of Christ that offers knowledge anew through tasting.[67] Angela later sees friars at Christ's side in different degrees of immersion or knowledge of Christ (135.294). She interprets this vision to mean that Christ reveals this knowledge by different signs manifested to differing degrees and in diverse ways (135.294). This knowledge, we learn elsewhere, begins in desire but it is limited by the devoted subject's abjection, that is, his or her recognition of his/her's own *incompletion*. The ritual of devouring, whether it is focused on the Eucharist or the sacramental drinking from the lateral wound of Christ, reminds the devoted subject that the way to perfection is strangely familiar because it was also the way to sin. An overflowing of the affections from a desire for knowledge leads to purification and sin alike.[68] That perviousness associated with the feminine and flesh thus becomes the means to perfection. The toppling of the heaving powers of the flesh into holiness signifies the kind of transgression that the imitation of Christ requires. This transgression is accomplished through abjection. Angela is scornful of the earnest soul that desires Christ but stops short of abjection:

> Set invenitur aliqua que dicit: "Ego amo Christum et volo diligere, et non curo si mundus non facit michi honorem. Set non tantum quod ego velim et desiderem verecundiam habere et esse dejecta(ta), set ego vivo continuo prelio et continuo timore quod homo non faciat michi et quod Deus non permittat." (178.410)

> (There are those who say: "I love Christ and I want to cherish him. I do not care if the world does not honor me, but not to the point that I want and desire to feel shame and abjection; on the contrary I live in continual conflict and fear of what man will not suffer me and what God will not permit me.")

These are the fears of the "tepid" soul that is reluctant to bear abjection "with patience, with joy, and with pleasure of body and soul." Without the desire for abjection, there is no possibility of an imitation of Christ because his life is an example of freely willed abjection (178.412). Yet as we shall see later, Angela never confuses Christ's voluntary abjection with passivity or victimization.

Angela's initiating experience at Christ's side is repeated in other meditations on Christ's Passion in *Le Livre de l'expérience*. In describing the complete absence of sadness she feels in the presence of the Passion, she recalls that often her soul is permitted to enter the wound in Christ's side and stroll about. During these periods, she experiences such incomparable delight and pleasure that it is impossible to describe or recount (66.140). In yet another example, a Passion play performed in the streets of Santa Maria fills her with such joy instead of sadness that she falls to the ground. By a feat of miraculous strength, she manages to withdraw from the crowd to a more secluded spot. There, stretching herself upon the ground, she loses all speech and all use of her limbs just before she finds herself once again entering the side of Christ (66.140).

The emphasis in all three accounts on a heightened sentience and profound knowledge are linked to the interiorization of Angela's soul in Christ's body. In a reversal of the Eucharist, Angela is subsumed into Christ's body in the course of contemplating his Passion. Unlike the tepid soul, Angela exhibits the surrendering of her will to Christ's suffering. More importantly, however, her entrance into the side of Christ is a variation on the gesture of doubting Thomas. The Gospel of John tells the story of Thomas, one of the twelve disciples who doubted the witness of the other disciples to Christ's resurrection. Only when Christ appears to him and instructs him to place his hand in his side does Thomas finally believe.[69] Yet Angela's immersion in Christ's side is also like Thomas's gesture, in that both are transgressions of the body. In a sense, both reenact Christ's own transgression of the prohibitions against defilement of the body in Leviticus.[70] The one gesture that stems from doubt is replicated in the other, which springs from compassionate belief. Angela's vision of immersion and the story of Thomas both offer interiorization as the practice leading to belief and revelation. This interiorization, in turn, is dependent on heightened sentience, that is, on the responsiveness of the flesh and senses to bring about self-transformation. Christ's wound is the signifier of the radical perviousness of the flesh that is necessary to personal conversion and mystical revelation. For Angela of Foligno, as for other women mystics, this meant transgressing the medieval taboo of the sealed female body.

This taboo of the female body is an extension of the taboos associated with the flesh, including fornication, concupiscence, and lust (which embraced all the sins of the flesh).[71] While Christ transgressed the Old Testament laws governing the flesh, particularly eating, the medieval Church resumed many of the taboos associated with sexuality.[72] Prohibitions against the flesh and the feminine theologized in the spiritual guides for women are duplicated in the decretals of canon law. Marriage taboos in particular attempted to regulate the sex lives of married couples by guarding against excessive carnality and the impurities associated with women's bodies.[73] In the context of such taboos against the flesh, the female mystic's *imitatio Christi* represents a dangerous and unsettling transgression. The female mystic's claim to spiritual perfection requires abjection through impurity and defilement. While medieval theology and canon law attempt to ward off abjection by placing boundaries on the feminine and by restrictions against impurity, the female mystic lodges her speech and her revelations squarely within the taboo. And, hence, within abjection itself.

The heightened sensitivity required by Angela's mysticism may be seen in a number of her visions in which she experiences ravishment, ecstasy, and desire. The scribe who records her visions, Fra Arnaldo, is less puzzled by these types of mystical rapture than he is by her accounts of feeling a divine sweetness in her suffering and persecution. When he contradicts her to say that such experiences are painful, she proceeds to prove him wrong with an example from her life. She tells him how she and a companion set out together in search of Christ at the local hospital among the poor, sick, and afflicted. There they distribute food and linen and proceed to wash the feet of the men and women, including the decomposed and putrid feet of the lepers. After washing their feet, she and her companion drink the water. Instead of revulsion, she is filled with an "immense sweetness . . . as if [we] had received communion:"

> Et videbatur michi recte quod ego communicassem; quia suavitatem maximam sentiebam, sicut si cummunicassem. Et quia quedam scarpula illarum plagarum erat interposita in gutture, ego conabar ad glutiendum eam, et reprehendebat me conscientia expuere sicut si communicassem, quamvis non expuerem ad ej[i]ciendum set ad deponendum eam de gutture. (53.106)

> (It seemed to me truly that I had communicated; indeed, I felt the greatest sweetness as if I had received communion. When a scab from the wounds remained in my throat, I tried to dislodge it. My conscience restrained me from spitting it out as though I had received the sacrament, although I did not remove it in order to expel it, but in order to dislodge it from my throat.)

Angela's lesson perhaps becomes lost for her modern reader in the horrifying detail of her example. Her own bodily reaction to this monstrous communion is to expel it, but her conscience prevents her from rejecting it. Eucharistic rapture fluctuates with physiological repulsion as defilement makes purification possible.

Some of the horror of Angela's claim to "divine sweetness" in this example is its perverse analogy to the Eucharist, yet it also brings out the traumatic nature of the Sacrament itself through a reversal. Piero Camporesi reminds us that the taking of the Sacrament probably filled the communicant with terror: "As he swallowed it, all the terrifying images connected with this act—the body of the purest lamb entering the filth of the digestive apparatus, the divine flesh polluted by contact with mucous membranes, the juices of the corruptible flesh and the rot of the bowels—must have returned to his mind and seized him with vertiginous horror."[74] This is, after all, the only sacrament that is received internally. While the Eucharist induces one kind of abjection due to the ingestion of the pure by the impure, Angela's Sacramental act revives the Levitican horror of defiling the body with the impure. In addition, though, Angela's Eucharist treads on a medieval taboo. Burchard, bishop of Worms (d. 1025), enumerates the forms of penance for the eating of scabs among other bodily pollutions.[75] Angela of Foligno's transgression of this taboo introduces defilement into the process of spiritual transformation. Whereas corporeal food is transformed into the person who swallows it, the person who swallows is transformed in the Eucharist into the received food.[76] In the case of the leper's scab as Host, Angela experiences a transformation into the divine flesh through the diseased body of the leper.

As we should recall, Angela recounts this story in order to show how pain and suffering become exquisite sweetness. The sweetness satisfies mystical desire that, like Original Sin, is expressed in a voraciousness. The carnal vestige of the Fall is, according to Augustine, *rerum absentium concupiscentia* "concupiscence for absent things," or desire.[77] Desire rooted in voraciousness is for Angela of Foligno the fount of corruption and perfection—through corruption to perfection.

The state of mystical abjection, then, is one of the "insistent presence of the flesh—uncontrollable affect." It is a state of violence, since the flesh resists reason and the good will, and of paradox, according to Bernard of Clairvaux's formulation: "Here is fullness without disgust; here is insatiable curiosity without restlessness; here is that eternal, inexplicable desire knowing no want."[78] We can see how Angela of Foligno experiences both violence and paradox in her conversionary experiences and in her visions of the Passion. Dedicating her chastity to Christ, Angela behaves in the manner of a wanton woman. She stands before the cross, strips off her clothes, and offers herself to Christ, promising to serve him in perpetual chastity (11.8–10). The violence of Angela's love stems from the tension between her fear and her desire and between "inestimable satiety" and a hunger such that "all the parts of my body were ruptured and my soul languished and desired to reach him" (75.156–58).

The voraciousness of the soul is exhibited in the body's fragmentation, which in turn imitates that of Christ on the cross. Angela's visions on the Passion focus on the suffering of Christ and the process by the which the soul is transformed into ("absorbed by") that suffering. Her meditations on the Passion focus on the wounds, ruptures, and dislocations in the body of Christ that pierce her own soul with compassion. In one such meditation on the deposition, she views the body of Christ bleeding freely as he is lifted from the cross. Yet she is even more struck by the terrible disfigurement of his limbs, at the dislocation of the joints, tendons, and bones, which seems to reveal to her even more than the wounds the secret of Christ's Passion

(135.292). The dislocation of his limbs transfixes the heart with compassion, causing a complete transformation of body and soul into the suffering of the cross. More than any other vision, Angela of Foligno declares, this offered the most perfect contemplation of his humanity and divinity and understanding of what the imitation of Christ means. Her scribe describes her as "completely crucified by the vision of the crucified" (135.292).

Miraculous bodily dislocation rather than the sealed and perfect body, then, is what signifies the secrets of the Passion. The desire for imitation is not a desire for passive suffering but a desire for the miraculous bodily dislocation that occurs to the soul which strives to "conform itself" to Christ. For example, the peace that Angela of Foligno experiences after swallowing the Eucharist, she says, can be discerned in her body's violent trembling (80.166). The physical marks of violence on Christ's body, its dislocation, are the outward signs of his physical pain and suffering, but more importantly for the mystic, they are the signs of the possibility of redemption. The fissures in the body "speak" to the fissured flesh, to its shame and disgrace, as well as to its capacity for self-transformation. To be crucified by the vision of the Crucifixion means, in Christ's words to Angela, to be "fixed on my passion and my death" (156.342). It also suggests the state of abjection in which the soul is caught between joy and sadness, intimacy and estrangement, satiety and incompleteness.

In one sense, the imitation of Christ involves embracing this "spectacle of torture" by fixing all the senses and affections of the flesh upon it. There is, however, another aspect of the Crucifixion that Angela of Foligno also experiences. In her study of Hans Holbein the Younger's painting, *The Body of the Dead Christ*, Julia Kristeva comments on the significance of the Crucifixion and burial as the caesura or break between Christ and his Father and life. It is a period of despair, a "hiatus," a severance from meaning.[79] Identification with this aspect of the Crucifixion emphasizes rupture and loss over union and transformation such as Angela describes in the vision above. She pursues this kind of imitation as well by entering Christ's tomb in a vision. There she finds him lying with his eyes closed as though he were dead. She kisses him and an indescribable odor emanates from his mouth. Finally, she presses her cheek against his, and he in turn presses her to him (74.154–56). Far from being disturbed by this experience, Angela reports that she felt an immense joy. This is the other side of the spectacle of torture. It is the rupture that, according to Kristeva, represents those separations that condition autonomy and subjectivity.[80] In identifying with this rupture, Angela identifies with the condition of her own subjectivity.

She also perversely insists upon the horror of the Crucifixion, Christ's disfigurement and death, rather than his triumph. Her response is to imitate

that horror, to embrace it with her own excess, whether that excess is enacted by a morbid sexual embrace in Christ's tomb or in the drinking of
leper's water. Much of the horror of her imitation of Christ lies in her insistence on the fleshly affections, on her blurring of the boundary between
humanus amor and *divinus amor,* which churchmen such as Jean Gerson
used to distinguish true visions from false ones.[81] The power of mystical
horror is the power of the feminine—the "heaving powers of the flesh,"
our Eve—which threatens to demystify God's transcendence and, worse, to
embarrass it.

More importantly, the insistence on the flesh in the mysticism of Angela and other female mystics is an insistence on the Word. After being
immersed in the crucified body of Christ, Angela of Foligno says that
Christ then showed her the Word:

> Et tunc etiam ostendit michi verbum, ita quod modo intelligo, quid est
> verbum, et quid est dicere verbum. Et dixit michi tunc: "Hoc est verbum
> quod voluit incarnari pro te." Et tunc etiam transitum fecit per me, et
> totam me tetigit et amplexatus est me. (p. 518)

> (And then he showed me the Word, and now I know what the Word is,
> and what it is to speak the Word. Then he spoke to me: "This is the
> Word which wished to be incarnated for you." And then the Word passed
> through me, touched me, and embraced me.)

Angela receives the Word like a sacrament in this vision. Elsewhere she
compares the incarnate words that speak in her soul with those paltry words
that are "exterior to the ineffable divine workings in the soul" (121.238).
Because of the inadequacy of language to convey the incarnate Word, she
claims that her discourse is blasphemy. Angela's vision reveals the abject in
language itself, which is the realm of the flesh. While she experiences the
abject in her vision when her flesh is visited, touched, and embraced by the
Word, she recognizes the inadequacy of spoken and written words to articulate this. Her scribe's frustration with his own efforts to record her revelations is the best proof of Angela's criticism of language. Again and again,
he listens carefully to her as she is rapt in her visions, records them, and
reads them back to her only to find that she cannot understand what he has
written. True, she says, the words vaguely recall those she spoke, but she
hardly recognizes her experience in his version of it. His account is obscure; it preserves the insignificant and completely ignores the marvelous
aspects of the revelation (34.42). For his part, the scribe acknowledges that
her revelations have been sifted like flour through the sieve of his writing,
which manages to preserve only the coarser remnants. The rest is too fine
for the *scriptor*'s sieve.[82]

Of course, it is a convention of mystical writings to complain of the inexpressibility of the mystical experience. Language is simply too dull to "get" the riddle of the Word. Angela is bound to blaspheme in her native Umbrian dialect, while her scribe's translation of her visions into Latin obscures the mysteries of which she speaks even more. Each articulation lapses further and further from the truth of the vision. The Word that passes through Angela leaves hardly a trace in the text of *Le Livre de l'expérience des vrais fidèles.*

Angela's criticism of those words that are exterior to divine mystery is not merely a convention of mystical discourse, however. It is a claim to a privileged language, the Word made flesh and uttered through the flesh. One gains a knowledge of this Word through continuous contemplation of the *liber vitae,* the Book of Life, which is the life and death of the crucified Christ.[83] The Word that speaks through the flesh, through abjection, is manifested through the body—through the trembling of limbs, cries, falling on the ground. Such a language does not deny the "intractable drives" of the flesh, nor does it rest securely on the prohibition of the sealed body. Without the sealed body, the border between flesh and spirit and letter and spirit is lost. Angela's vision of the Word that touches and embraces her anticipates Hélène Cixous's modern vision of the subversive potential of women's language: "Her flesh speaks true. She lays herself bare. In fact, she physically materializes what she's thinking; she signifies it with her body. In a certain way she *inscribes* what she's saying, because she doesn't deny her drives the intractable and impassioned part they have in speaking."[84]

The female mystic's language begins in transgression, but unlike Eve's transgression, it is not a transgression based on denial. It is more like the affirmative transgression described by Michel Foucault in his vision of an alternative to the Western model of knowledge and language:

> Transgression opens into a scintillating and constantly affirmed world, a world without shadow or twilight, without that serpentine "no" that bites into fruits and lodges their contradictions at their core. It is the solar inversion of satanic denial. It was originally linked to the divine or rather, from this limit marked by the sacred it opens the space where the divine functions.[85]

The serpentine "no" leads to the repression of the feminine and flesh and to a discourse safely ensconced in its tiered system of flesh and spirit, masculine and feminine, literal and figurative, and human and divine, and a religion protected by the ideal of the sealed female body. Angela's transgression functions at the place of the "limit marked by the sacred." Instead of assuming limitations in order to deny them, as medieval theology does, Angela of Foligno "affirms limited being" in order to transgress, to pass over into the divine union and knowledge, which is limitless.[86]

Angela's language, like the language of other female mystics who insist upon the flesh and the Word, is both intractable and subversive. Considering the exclusion of women from both the oral and written languages of the Church, this claim to a privileged language is an important one. As André Vauchez has argued, the imitation of Christ offers something different to the illiterate laywoman than it did to the male religious. It provides her a piety that she often expressed through the body and that she also interpreted—an instrument of power and a privileged communication.[87] Speaking from the place of abjection, Angela of Foligno and other female mystics seek to return language and words in particular to Aristotle's definition of them as "symbols of that which suffers in the soul."[88] Angela of Foligno implicates the flesh and the feminine in that suffering and, thus, in language itself. Here, too, she seeks to transgress the limits of a language that is hopelessly exterior and that excludes the marvelous. From the fissured flesh comes the female mystic's language of suffering, words derived from the wounds of the soul, utterance both intractable and marvelous.

While it is neither desirable nor feasible for scholars of medieval mysticism to adopt this language of abjection, it is possible for us to try to describe its practice. Our own language has too often relied on assumptions that, like Fra Arnaldo's sieve, merely sift the marvelous down to its coarser remnants. A recognition of how the flesh was understood to operate in mystical experience, especially affective mystical experience, is necessary to any feminist reading of the female mystics, as well as to any description of affective spiritual practices. Such a recognition enables us to see how a language of abjection offers women the possibility of transgressive speech. Perhaps more importantly, it forces us to rethink our own interpretive oppositions, such as those of body and soul, physical and spiritual, and literal and figurative. It helps us to see how our own positivistic ideas about the body and its relationship to language have informed our analyses of medieval spirituality. By paying attention to the mystic's struggle with two languages—the one conventional and the other abject—we should begin to wrestle with our own critical language for describing mystical experience.

The language of abjection also offers mystical scholarship a whole new area of study concerned with the practice of mystical discourse. In addition to our comparative and historical studies of themes, images, language, and movements in medieval mystical practice, we can finally examine the practice itself. This is especially important as mystical texts are becoming included in literature anthologies, such as the *Norton Anthology of English Literature* and Norton's *Literature by Women*. How do we talk about mystical texts, particularly in literary contexts? This is the kind of question that is already being raised in literature classes but that needs to be addressed by scholars of mysticism. This new language of mystical practice also recasts feminist questions regarding women's voices and writing, as we have seen in this essay.

Perhaps Arnaldo's sieve offers an appropriate metaphor for the way in which the languages of mystical scholarship might be practiced in the future. Instead of the one sieve, which sifts mystical texts through our historical and discursive methodologies, we should consider using two sieves, a second which would strain our language through the abject practices of mystical texts, as this essay has attempted to do. The one language serves as the sieve of the other. Together, the two languages of mystical scholarship might bring the marvelous a bit closer to the "coarse remnants" of our own analysis.

✻   ✻

Further Reading

Toril Moi provides a good introduction to feminist literary theories in *Sexual/Textual Politics* (London, 1985). Luce Irigaray makes her argument for female mysticism as a place from which patriarchy might be disrupted in her chapter on "La Mystérique" in *Speculum of the Other Woman*, trans. Gillian C. Gill (Ithaca, 1985): 191–202. For an introduction to Kristeva, readers may consult Toril Moi's *The Kristeva Reader* (New York, 1986), although Kristeva's theory of abjection is not included in this anthology. Moi says elsewhere that Kristeva's *Powers of Horror* "could be valuably appropriated for feminism," but this work has been largely neglected by feminists. Catherine Clément's theory of contagion and its relationship to the "masculine integrity of the body" is articulated in Hélène Cixous and Catherine Clément, *The Newly Born Woman*, trans. Betsy Wing, vol. 24 of *Theory and History of Literature* (Minneapolis, 1975). Also, Michel Serres discusses the issues of boundaries and the crossing of them in *The Parasite*, trans. Lawrence R. Schehr (Baltimore, 1982).

The issue of women's language occupying a place of disruption in patriarchy has been discussed by Catherine Clément ("Enslaved Enclave") and particularly by Hélène Cixous in "The Laugh of the Medusa," both of which are included in the anthology, *New French Feminisms*, ed. Elaine Marks and Isabelle de Courtivron (New York, 1980). Arguments for a returning of language to the body and to the feminine that are repressed in patriarchal discourse may be found in Chantal Chawaf's "Linguistic Flesh" *(New French Feminisms)* and both articles by Cixious cited above. Recently, Trin T. Minh-ha, *Woman, Native, Other: Writing Postcoloniality and Feminism* (Bloomington, IN, 1989), addresses the issue of women's writing and its relationship to the body, suggesting a Buddhist understanding of what it means to "write the body."

Feminist theory in medieval studies is still relatively new. A study of the body in the *Ancrene Wisse* that differs from my own is Elizabeth Robertson's "The Rule of the Body: The Feminine Spirituality of the *Ancrene Wisse*," in *Seeking the Woman in Late Medieval and Renaissance Texts*, ed. Sheila Fisher and Janet E. Halley (Knoxville, 1989). An interesting three-volume work covering theories of the body that also includes some excellent feminist essays from which I have quoted in this essay is *Fragments for a History of the Human Body*, ed. Michel Feher, Ramona Naddaff, and Nadia Tazi (New York, 1989). The first volume explores the relationship of the body to the divine; the second, the relationship of body to soul; and the third, the relationship between organ and function, particularly in social and political metaphors of the body.

Chapter 6

Texts That Speak to Readers Who Hear: Old English Poetry and the Languages of Oral Tradition

✳ John Miles Foley ✳

In this contribution to our joint inquiry on "Speaking Two Languages," I hope to call attention to a fundamental but too often unacknowledged characteristic of Old English poetry: that, although the poems come to us in manuscript form, they are encoded in an idiom that owes much to a prior and ongoing oral tradition. I say "characteristic" because by this point enough research and scholarship has appeared to establish beyond reasonable doubt that such an oral tradition existed in Anglo-Saxon England;[1] by the same token, I say "owes much" because we do not know (and probably shall never know) precisely how the idiom and the poems in question relate to that oral tradition. Given these two competing realities, we can afford to dismiss neither literary nor oral provenance from our considerations.[2] And, given the emphasis of this essay, I would argue that the critical tendency to overlook the role of oral tradition—even in manifestly written composition—has led to faulty assessments of the poetry at virtually all levels, from the philological through the aesthetic. In the spirit of this project, I would propose that the plurality of approach—dialogized approach, if you will—integral to the "two languages" motif include attention to a most basic pluralistic quality of Old English verse: its oral traditional as well as its written heritage and dynamics. This, in short, is the brand of bilingualism I shall be advocating.

In an attempt to make the case for the importance of oral tradition, the following brief overview will concentrate on three areas: (1) the history of relevant criticism; (2) the structural profile of our texts; and (3) aesthetic implications, especially as seen through reception theory, with emphasis on the work of Wolfgang Iser. The general thrust of the paper will thus be to take stock of where oral-formulaic theory and related methods have led us, to adumbrate at least the outlines of an oral traditional poetics, and then to ask what this poetics means to our reading—our own hearing—of the texts.

Particularly because these brief remarks are made alongside such a refreshingly heterogeneous array of other interpretive languages, I also feel compelled to stipulate that I shall attempt no "translation" into another critical idiom other than reception theory. The argument will proceed from its own history in Old English studies, with caveats and modifications as necessary, toward a new way of construing the inheritance from oral tradition, a perspective that explains the art of Anglo-Saxon poetry as in part a function of its oral traditional heritage—not, in other words, as something achieved despite the handicap of incipient textuality. In this connection it seems clear that we must explore the implications for oral tradition of Iser's ideas about representation and audience, with special attention to his observations on the text's array of signals and gaps of indeterminacy left to be solved by readerly (that is, audience) activity.[3] In short, only with a better appreciation of the audience(s) summoned by the works involved can we progress in our ability to speak and hear the language of oral tradition in Old English poetry.

Critical History

Virtually all research and scholarship on oral tradition and Old English poetry can be traced to Francis P. Magoun, Jr.'s 1953 article, "The Oral-Formulaic Character of Anglo-Saxon Narrative Poetry," and ultimately to the doctoral thesis by Albert Lord (1949) that prompted it and was later published as *The Singer of Tales* (1960).[4] Magoun assumed a simple one-to-one correspondence between the presence of formulas and the orality of a work. Transferring concepts and definitions directly from Lord's dissertation, and ultimately from Milman Parry's studies of the Homeric poems,[5] he claimed that "the recurrence in a given poem of an appreciable number of formulas or formulaic phrases brands the latter as oral, just as the lack of such repetitions marks a poem as composed in a lettered tradition" and that "oral poetry, it may be safely said, is composed entirely of formulas, large and small, while lettered poetry is never formulaic."[6]

This explanation of the formulaic style of *Beowulf* and other poems was challenged immediately, as scholars like Claes Schaar and Kemp Malone saw the Magoun school as threatening the great art of the poetry.[7] Such a reaction could easily have been predicted, both because the same sort of response had greeted Parry's original ideas in the ancient Greek arena and because, as Walter Ong has taught us more recently, perhaps nothing so disorients an "interpretive community" as a radical undermining of its chief communications technology.[8] But the reaction was in an important way a very healthy one: scholars like Schaar and Malone were demanding that verbal art remain their construction of verbal art and, again in their view, not be denigrated to mechanical shuffling of prefabricated parts. Although they may have overestimated the oralists' destructive intentions, it is not difficult to sympathize with their basic concerns.

At any rate, we now know that Magoun's original conception was too broad and too simple. Reports of oral poetries from around the world have brought what should have been welcome news: that oral traditions are phenomena fully as complex as their literary counterparts; that within each tradition there are many genres, each of which will exhibit different (though related) rules for composition; that literacy *can* play a role in the composition and reception of "oral poetry."[9] In many cases, however, the lines have been drawn as harshly on the oralist's as on the literary critic's side, and out-of-date polemics about such matters as the implications of formula density[10] still block the path toward a more finely tuned poetics and a realistic aesthetics. It is regrettably still a truism that we can proceed no further until the well-beaten, long-moribund horse is finally granted his richly deserved coup de grace.

Oral Traditional Structure

The chief reason that the Magoun school's version of the oral-formulaic approach did not achieve satisfactory results was its insensitivity to the complexities of oral traditional structure. Instead of "translating" the definitions and premises of the Parry-Lord model, itself based on ancient Greek and Yugoslav traditions, to the linguistic realities of Anglo-Saxon verse, Magoun and his adherents simply imported ideas and concepts that were thereby destined to remain foreign to the poetry for which they were now targeted. It was then only too easy for those who resisted orality, most notably Larry Benson, to point out that formulas seemed equally frequent in certainly written and putatively oral Old English poems. For Benson, the fact that his analysis of the (probably written) metrical preface to Alfred's *Pastoral Care*, *Riddle 35*, the *Phoenix*, and the *Meters of Boethius* showed about the same formulaic density as *Beowulf* and the Cynewulf poetry disqualified this measure as a litmus test for orality and thus returned Old English poetry to a familiar arena. The fundamental error in the underlying assumption—that there existed an Archetypal Formula somehow resistant to the idiosyncrasies of different languages and systems of versification—went unnoticed, or at least uncommented upon, and scholars essentially maintained an open argument about the significance of what amounted to an ancient Greek model of poetic diction for Old English alliterative poetry.[11]

With more distance on the problem than Magoun enjoyed, we can now inquire just what there is about Anglo-Saxon poetic phraseology and narrative patterning that *is* oral traditional (my subject in the present section) and then ask how these structures contribute to the art of the poetry, and also how they are to be understood from the perspective offered by reception theory (the subject of my concluding section). I shall cover structure or poetics under three headings: tradition-dependence; genre-dependence; and text-dependence.[12] The three areas apply to oral traditional works according to a natural gradation, with tradition-dependence addressing the gross anatomy of the work (the characteristics associated with the particular language in which it takes shape), genre-dependence treating the finer distinctions or typologies evidenced by various kinds of poems, and text-dependence supplying the most precise ground for analysis, encompassing as it does all of the concerns associated with the actual document that presents a work.

First, the nature of Old English prosody makes it prima facie unlikely that the caesura-bound, metrically encapsulated diction typical of ancient Greek and Serbo-Croatian epic verse will make up any large part of the phraseology. The Homeric hexameter and South Slavic *deseterac* (decasyllable) are recognizable and similar reflexes of the Indo-European epic line: they show a constant or slightly variable syllabicity, a true caesura (and therefore colonic structure), and increasing conservatism of pattern as one moves from left to right, beginning to end, in the line. These prosodic features, which function in symbiosis with traditional phraseologies, make for *traditional rules* that determine what kind of diction can be formed. Once formed, that diction may, according to usage, sound patterning, thematic attachment, and other factors, survive and become a viable part of a poet's (and a tradition's) compositional idiom; it may at some future time drop out in favor of other phraseology formed under the same rules; or it may amount to "nonce" diction[13] and never attain traditional status.

Whatever the fate of a given item of phraseology, it is admitted to the idiom, and continues to be a part of the idiom, only on the basis of its congruency with traditional rules. What is more, these rules are dependent not on archetypal parameters but on the individual features of the traditional prosody in question. Thus, for example, while the ancient Greek and Yugoslav oral epic lines are characterized by greater phraseological stability at the end, with the longest and least variable of items customarily in final position, Old English poetry does not exhibit this marked tendency—exactly because it obeys a very different set of traditional rules.[14]

Without regular syllabicity and without a true caesura, Anglo-Saxon verse will, for one thing, be a much more malleable medium. Because it emphasizes alliterating roots of words and other stressable morphs in its versification, the "formulaic" phrases will usually consist of a constant stressed item or two and a highly variable half-line context. Thus the tradition-dependent possibility (and observed fact, as some have proposed) presents itself that the phraseological patterning may consist not only of apparently combinable line-parts but also of a series of clustered morphs spread over a group of lines. Investigation of the Anglo-Saxon idiom has indeed yielded evidence of whole- and multiline patterns, clusters, collocations of alliterative pairs, and even metrical predispositions. All of these patterns are traditional in that they recur as extraprosodic phenomena in a variety of situations and function under the aegis of the traditional rules of Old English verse making.

The themes or type-scenes of Anglo-Saxon poetry might be thought to be less affected by the principle of tradition-dependence, and, as far as the narrative structure of themes is concerned, this is true. Sequences of ideas are, basically, sequences of ideas. But we should remember that all patterns, no matter what the poetry, must be expressed in actual phraseology, and here is where the variance begins. Because there exists in Old English verse little or nothing of what Parry called "economy," a one-to-one correlation between an idea and its expression (particularly among noun-epithet phrases), themes can take a much wider variety of forms than the examples adduced by Lord would predict.[15] The relationship between idea and verbal expression is still governed by traditional rules, so that the number of phrases available to the composing poet is of course not infinite (an important condition I shall address in the following section). But the central fact of the matter is that Anglo-Saxon themes also take a tradition-dependent form.

Genre-dependence, the second of the principles under the more general heading of oral traditional structure, can be treated very quickly. With this principle we are concerned that a given poem's genre be taken into account, so that comparisons of, say, riddles and hagiographies not be uncritically proposed. Such a caveat looms especially large for Old English poetry, not only because of the surfeit of genres that make up the corpus, but also because the oral-formulaic approach has unfortunately only rarely escaped its origins in epic. Myriad shorter genres from all parts of the world have been reported that seem to operate quite differently; without an extended narrative line and a length and depth that preclude even incipient textuality, phraseology and narrative multiformity simply do not function in the canonical way. In the Yugoslav oral tradition, for example, there are shorter "epics" that foster a kind of textuality; magical charms that (like the Anglo-Saxon *galdor*) depend more on sound patterning than do other genres; metrical genealogies and funeral laments that show some memorization as opposed to complete re-creation; and so on.[16] As observed near the beginning of this essay, oral traditions are complex collections of phenomena and are no more reducible to a single model than are literary traditions.

One of the most striking discrepancies among genres, and, as it turns out, a very telling one for the history of studies in oral tradition, is that between the Moslem and Christian epic poetries in the Yugoslav tradition.[17] The Moslem epics, selected by Milman Parry as his exclusive emphasis because they offered the best available comparand for the Homeric poems in terms of story pattern, length, and elaboration, commonly run to thousands of lines but show little if any evidence of a poet actively and individually placing his own personal signature on traditional materials. To put it another way, these poems—really performances—are not what we might call highly "textual." The Christian epics, on the other hand, especially those collected by Vuk Stefanović Karadžić in the mid-nineteenth century, are shorter in scope and also prove correspondingly more textual. It is quite usual for the Christian songs to show signs of a personal contribution to the traditional story, some mark of the singer's own imprint.[18] Thus the early doctrine that oral (or oral-derived) traditional poetry cannot by its very nature support "literary" composition obviously requires some rethinking; different genres and even subgenres provide different kinds of poetic and artistic opportunities.

The third area affecting any assessment of oral traditional structure is what I call text-dependence, a term that designates the individuality of the history and transmission of the work we propose to study and therefore provides the closest focus of the three criteria for comparative analysis. In the Anglo-Saxon period, although literacy was the possession of the professional and religious few, our extant poems must have encountered the literate sensibility in some fashion and were no doubt in many cases actually composed in writing. Perhaps the remarkable thing is not that written words should have inhabited the same world as their oral kin, but that the oral traditional idiom of phraseology and narrative patterns should have survived the encounter and been inscribed in the texts we have. At any rate, we do need to take into account the diglossic nature of the early part of the medieval period and to realize more fully than we have the many possibilities for poetic art that a transitional medium provides. Although the most crucial reason for the persistence of oral traditional forms after the advent of literacy cannot be addressed until I comment on the implications of those structures in the next section, it is well even at this point to emphasize that, unlike the *guslari* from whom Parry and Lord collected, the Old English poets are in many cases likely to have had a foot more or less firmly planted in each of two worlds.

Aesthetic Implications and Reception Theory

The most important problem associated with oral tradition and "literature," whether Anglo-Saxon or not, has always been what difference a work's orality or oral roots make to its interpretation. If it makes virtually no difference, as some have argued, then we need to know that; if it makes such a difference that aesthetic criticism of oral and literary works will have nothing in common, then we need to fashion a proper aesthetics. Because I view this issue as fundamentally a problem of reception, I shall follow the opening statement about referentiality with a brief illustration of how one can adapt the reception theory of Wolfgang Iser to the task of speaking and hearing the second language of Old English poetic texts.

As observed above, the approach through oral-formulaic theory in its classic form has often been seen as denaturing the poetic work, removing the author's guiding hand, and, in short, muting the (literary) art of great masterpieces. In the case of Western monuments like the *Iliad* and *Odyssey*, objections to such perceived malfeasance have been strenuous and frequent, and they have been nearly as common in studies of some of the medieval vernaculars.[19] Consider the following pair of quotations from a relatively recent study of Homeric epithets by Paolo Vivante:

> The very way a thing is named fills us with a satisfying sense of what it is. The feeling of beauty is not directly expressed, but it is always implicit.[20]

Who could argue with this articulate appraisal of Homer's "sense of form" (*idem*)? The epic *Kunstsprache* is heavily connotative and certainly means more than a phrase in isolation can denote. But then comes Vivante's justification of Homer as individual artist:

> Such lines as 'when the early-born rose-fingered dawn appeared' or 'at once speaking out he addressed winged words' are among the high points of Homeric poetry, although they are lines alleged to be most uncontroversially formulaic and traditional. We should try to recover these 'formulas' in their original value, look at them as if newly discovered. From an aesthetic point of view, it does not make the slightest difference whether they are traditional or not.[21]

It is easy, and I think only right, to join with Vivante in praising the role of form in the phraseology of the Homeric epics; the notion that the "essential idea" of "swift-footed Achilles" (*podas ôkus Achilleus*) is merely "Achilles" or of "blameless Aegisthos" (*amumonos Aigisthoio*, gen. s.) simply "Aegisthos" is inadequate aesthetically, even demeaning to the work of art. But can we at once hear this resonance in its true depth (that is, can we hear two languages?) and admit the real discoveries about structure made by Parry, Lord, and others by insisting that tradition does not matter? Most obviously, how could Homer have invented such an elaborate diction by himself? Less obviously, but perhaps more importantly, is the meaning he conferred in this great act of creation—a literary meaning, one supposes—the "end of signification"? And do we not run aground into similar shallows by asking the same questions of Old English and Serbo-Croatian poetry, by saying yes to art but no to tradition?

The resolution to this impasse, which has existed in some form since the initial debate between Parry and George Calhoun in the middle thirties,[22] lies not in choosing between literary finesse and oral mechanics but rather in recognizing that, in varying degrees, oral traditional poems have more-than-textual resources of meaning. How much more resoundingly do Homer's epithets or the *guslar's* themes or the *Beowulf*-poet's phraseology echo when we sense the possibility that their fields of meaning are not limited to this text, or a set of extant texts, but resonate against the unspoken tradition which they in part instance? By a process of signification I call metonymy, the oral traditional structures convey worlds of meaning that are institutionally associated with them, bringing to the fore associations that are always immanent, always impinging on the act of (re-) creating verbal art.[23]

The advantages of understanding oral traditional works in such a way are many. First, this view is true to the situation found in examining still living oral traditions: meaning principally inheres in rather than is conferred upon traditional art, again to varying degrees depending on genre and other factors. Second, it allows us to avoid having to choose between art and mechanism, a choice that was never viable or even realistic anyway. Third, it brings us one step closer to establishing an aesthetic context for the oral and oral-derived works we hope to interpret with new fidelity.[24] In short, understanding traditional structures not as chiefly denotative but as explosively connotative, not as confining but as metonymic, helps mark the path toward reinstatement of artistic complexity—a complexity achieved by indirection through the rich and textured resonance of simple forms.

At first sight, recourse to a text-based theory of interpretation like receptionalism might seem a curious path into the originally textless world of oral tradition. Even the oral-derived texts of Homer and *Beowulf* hardly fit into the same category with the works of prose fiction on which Wolfgang Iser relied for the formulation and illustration of his brand of Reception theory. Prima facie, a theory that takes as its principal concerns the text and the individual reader would seem quite inapplicable to the understanding of performance and audience in oral tradition, and only somewhat less so to oral-derived texts and their audiences in the ancient and medieval periods.

But what receptionalism offers is a direct and powerful way to come to terms with the metonymic dynamism of the oral traditional work. With certain adjustments in the critical parameters, we can take advantage of its focus on reader/audience participation and cocreation of the experienced work, and correspondingly deemphasize the literary, posttraditional values and assumptions that have become so much a part of our unconscious critical heritage—to the particular detriment of studies in oral tradition. We shall find that oral traditional texts or performances also serve as libretti for audience realization; that these "scores" imply readers or listeners as participants in a process; and that the oral performance or oral-derived text also consists of a "map" made up of explicit signals and gaps of indeterminacy that must be bridged in accordance with certain rules and predispositions.[25] What differs, of course, is the simple but far-reaching fact that the "text," that visible objective reality that derives authority from its uniqueness, is missing, and in its place we have at best one or more oral-derived texts, and at worst, a continuum of performances that resists reduction to a series of "texts."

Immediately, then, we must accept the premise that in speaking of oral traditional works we shall not be speaking of a single text and an individual "reader." As numerous studies have established,[26] all performances of a given song in the Serbo-Croatian epic tradition, for example, are formally equivalent versions of a tale that can never be textualized; some may be longer, fuller, or more satisfying than others, but against the background of the tradition at large, all equally are versions. As a first point of departure, therefore, we must extend our notion of the textual libretto to take account of the multiple "texts" typical of oral tradition and of the fact that all of them stand in the same basic relation to the larger song and are thus equally "authoritative."[27]

The other major point of differentiation has to do with the audience, the oral traditional counterpart of Iser's reader. For in addition to the variance in affective reading that arises from the idiosyncratic prior experiences of different individuals, we have now to deal with possibly even a greater number and variety of "readers" over a greater expanse of time, each of them encountering a different performance or version, at least in the case of oral tradition per se. The incongruencies among interpretations would seem to multiply under these circumstances, so that it is difficult to conceive of any kind of consistency across the many practitioners and audiences at any given moment or across the many generations through time.

But if the concepts of both "text" and "reader" seem pluralized beyond any useful purpose in this new arena, we have yet to take into account the unifying role of tradition. If the various performances that constitute an oral tradition were entirely without precedent, or if oral-derived texts existed wholly outside the tradition that spawned them, then the "reader" would indeed be without a horizon of expectation, a context for interpretation; the vacuum created by the lack of an authoritative object text would swallow up all points of reference, and the reader would in effect be overwhelmed by the unrelieved indeterminacy of the texts. However, with the immanent poetic tradition providing the points of reference by regularizing the relationship between structure and metonymic meaning, the process of interpretation can go forward. The tradition in effect makes each performance an authoritative "document," each textual structure a unique signal, by stipulating its significance, by institutionalizing its invariable, inherent meaning in the face of the ever-shifting superficial designs of performance, version, and so on. The riddle of the oral traditional text or performance is that every version (or instance of a phraseological or narrative structure) is both a thing in itself and the same thing; to lose sight of this consistent— because traditional—referentiality is to mis-"read" the text.

Just as the poetic tradition focuses the meaning of the apparent diversity of versions or texts, so it both simplifies and enriches the response of the audience. If each member of the group present at an oral performance, or serving as audience for an oral-derived work, were confronting the text without prior experience of its encoded significance, then we would expect a large and unintegrated range of interpretive responses. The variety in individual preparation would make for a corresponding variety in cocreation of the work and would generate critical dispute and no doubt an uneven regard for the work's literary quality.[28] But what could potentially be a crippling degree of heterogeneity in response is forestalled by the audience's earlier acquaintance with the work and its parts, for each of them brings to the process of interpretation a deep knowledge of how to "read" the text before him or her, of how to construe the traditional signals in their full metonymic, inherent meaning. While what we referred to as affective meaning in the case of literary works will still play a role in the decoding of the text or performance, it will be a much more modest role, since such individual variance will be limited by the individual's experience of the tradition—of translating structure into meaning. In fact, to put it positively (and since "affective meaning" is primarily a literary, posttraditional concept),[29] we may say that each member of the audience interprets the text according to a shared body of knowledge that is his or her inheritance. What passes down through the generations is thus not simply an idiom that allows convenient oral composition but the equivalent of a critical methodology, evolved and practiced by a "school" or "interpretive community"[30] unified by the act of (re-)making and (re-)"reading" traditional verbal art.

A few examples may help to explain the extratextual referentiality so much a force in oral traditional dynamics. To take the celebrated case of the noun-epithet phrase, a common element in ancient Greek, Serbo-Croatian, and Old English narrative poetry, we need no longer settle for either (1) the reduction of poetic meaning to an "essential idea" (for example, "swift-footed Achilles" = merely "Achilles" in convenient metrical form) or (2) the licensing of the poet to use each phrase with special situational overtones, different each time. Rather we understand Achilles's swift-footedness as the *typical detail*, the single facet that stands *pars pro toto* for the personality as a whole, the character too large to conjure textually but available for narrative duty through the metonymic implications of the phrase. There is nothing sacred about his swiftness of foot; true, he is fast and quick to react, but the appropriateness of the detail is a necessary rather than sufficient cause for the poet's (and tradition's) assignment and deployment of the epithet. The given details that make up epithets stand in nominal relation to the personalities they summon, with the institutionalized relationship between epithet and personality being the operative aspect. That is why "swift-footed Achilles" can sit sulking in his tent without offending Homer's (and his tradition's) aesthetic sense.

Although the structure of noun-epithet phrases in Serbo-Croatian epic is somewhat different, just as the principle of tradition-dependence would lead us to expect, their mode of conveying meaning is very similar. A phrase like *sužanj nevoljniče*, or "unwilling captive," offers a clear insight on metonymic referentiality, especially since in this case no specific person is named. But although the phrase can be applied widely to any number of individuals, its implications are highly focused. Most often it describes an imprisoned Turkish hero in a Christian ban's cell, a hero who was captured on his wedding night and is now shouting loudly enough to disturb the ban's wife and/or infant son. The unbearable noise will soon lead the wife to demand that her husband do something about the racket or to seek out the prisoner and strike a bargain for his release. All this and more is necessarily, institutionally implied in the very act of calling someone "sužanj nevoljniče;" as noted above, the consistency or "repetitiveness" of the traditional idiom is not claustrophobic but enormously reverberative.[31]

When we think of noun-epithet phrases in Old English, half-lines like "bearn Ecgþeowes" and "helm Scyldinga," two metonymic foci in *Beowulf*, spring to mind. But in order to illustrate the added complexity and resonance of traditional phraseology as employed in poems with an obvious Christian subject, I choose to look at "heofonrices Weard." The most familiar occurrence of this phrase is of course at line 1b of *Cædmon's Hymn*, where it identifies the Creator whom "nu sculon herian." But it may surprise even the professional Old English scholar that the same noun-epithet combination also occurs no less than twenty-three additional times, in poems as diverse as *Genesis A, Exodus, Daniel, Andreas, The Dream of the*

Rood, Elene, Juliana, the Psalms, *The Menologium, Judgment Day II,* and the *Charm for Unfruitful Land.*[32] That "heofonrices Weard" is an element in the traditional idiom cannot, in short, be questioned.

Conventional oral-formulaic theory would see this phrase as a metrical solution to the compositional problem of naming God in a just measure of verse, and with h-alliteration. This pseudo-explanation deprives "the guardian of the heavenly kingdom" of its poetic content, turning it into a mere filler, and must be dismissed. No more successful is the strictly literary approach, which will try to fashion a singular meaning for "heofonrices Weard" every time it appears, seeking to empower a poet who uses the common idiom with the ability to reinvent its signification according to personal designs. We come nearer the art of the poetry by positing a traditional, inherent signification for "the guardian of the heavenly kingdom" by understanding the phrase as a metonym that summons a characterization from the extratextual field of the poetic tradition at large. To the extent that some of the poems involved are shorter and more integral than, say, *Beowulf,* and taking into account the oral-derived nature of the texts that have survived to us, it is only reasonable to include a degree of individual poetic design in the overall aesthetic equation. But the fundamental meaning of "heofonrices Weard" will remain that given the phrase by its life in the poetic tradition, and it will be a meaning shared among all poets who employ the idiom (and thereby tap its referentiality).

In the case of Old English traditional phraseology, in which as we recall there exists no one-to-one relationship between idea and expression, phrases like "heofonrices Weard" do not have exclusive rights on the immanent characterization they summon to narrative or lyric present. In the familiar *Cædmon's Hymn,* for example, God is also named as "ece Drihten" (88 additional occurrences in the poetic corpus), "frea ælmihtig" (14), "moncynnes Weard" (2), and "halig Scyppend" (hapax legomenon). Each of these contributes its own resonance to the polyphony of the hymn, each bringing both a nominal (but of course appropriate) quality to the fore at the same time that it stands *pars pro toto* for the Christian God. The advantage of this kind of traditional "naming," which differs from literary and purely textual naming in that it institutionally summons a fully contextualized figure instead of simply denoting that figure, is that it depends on a limited set of signifiers: even in the Old English idiom, where economy is virtually unknown among the fixed as well as variable phrases,[33] the metonymic keys to the wordhoard are relatively (and precious) few. This limitation should be seen not as a constraint on poetic creativity but as a structural conduit through which extratextual meaning can flow—regulated, as it were, by the special relationship between metonyms and their ambient, immanent meanings. When Cædmon combines these various phrases for

God, in other words, he is neither mouthing metrical fillers nor manipulating diction in new and individual ways.[34]

The same general aesthetic principle of traditional referentiality informs other, less fixed aspects of the phraseology. At the least structured end of the spectrum, even mere observance of traditional rules for the composition of Old English poetry[35] conveys what speech-act theorists call "illocutionary force." The making of verses and lines according to poetic strictures on word-type placement (a traditional rule of far-reaching importance), for example, itself announces the kind of performance that is to follow and creates certain rough expectations on the part of the audience/reader. The map for successful construal of the work, in receptionalist terms, becomes successively more elaborate as the degree of structure increases and as the metonymic implications become concomitantly more focused. We notice, for example, the two related phrases used in *Cædmon's Hymn*: "heofonrices Weard" and "moncynnes Weard." Because of their similarity, which some would ascribe to a common "formulaic system,"[36] it may be that each has some added resonance, some extra dimension of traditional meaning that it would otherwise lack.

From "nonce" phraseology through formulaic systems to fixed phrases, the spectrum of Old English poetic diction brings into play a correspondingly diverse and complex set of inherent meanings. This network of signification provides the individual poet not with a ready-made collection of prefabricated phrases but with a ready-made method of communicating his artistic vision. To sever the vessel connecting metonym and meaning, as we have not seldom done by ignoring the oral traditional roots of this poetry, is to deprive it of artistic life.

The same holds true for the typical narrative structures called "themes" or "typical scenes."[37] Far from being mere counters that the composing poet shuffles dextrously in piecing together his story, these commonplaces serve as focal points for traditional meaning. Whatever the particular, momentary situation may be, the narrative metonyms call forth certain inherent significations from the unspoken entirety of the poetic tradition according to the same referential code under which other such structures yield meaning. Thus Magoun's "Beasts of Battle," Greenfield's "Exile," and Crowne's "Hero on the Beach," to take three early and prominent examples, do much more than fill out the narrative; they help to create it in full extratextual resonance, bringing the immanence of tradition to the individual text and individual moment.

Alain Renoir has been particularly persuasive in bringing to the fore what he calls the "context" of oral-formulaic structures. Ranging widely over ancient Greek, Latin, Old and Middle English, Old and Middle High German, and Old French works, he has argued for the replacement of the lost empirical facts of authorship, date, and other conventional literary tools with the oral-formulaic context assumed by even the latter-day writers employing the traditional idiom. This last emphasis is of special importance for the Middle Ages, of course, given the complex and bewildering interlaces of orality and literacy that prevailed at various times in various places. As Renoir puts it:

> In respect to those poems which rely on oral-formulaic devices whose nature and functions have been ascertained, however, we can occasionally approach the understanding which the less informed members of the intended audience would have had, although our understanding must regrettably prove more self-conscious and artificial than theirs. This may seem like a rather meager achievement, but it is infinitely better than the incomprehension which must necessarily guide much of our interpretation whenever we study these same poems without reference to the oral-formulaic tradition.[38]

Conclusion

In summary, then, I have attempted to offer a brief sketch of what studies in oral tradition have to offer to scholarship on and interpretation of Old English poetry. I consider oral tradition a "language" worth speaking—better, perhaps, a language worth *hearing*, and for the best of reasons: it gives us insights into aesthetics that can be gained in no other way and, therefore, uniquely enriches our understanding of poetic art in Anglo-Saxon. As we have seen, where there are opportunities there are also pitfalls, and the history of oral-formulaic theory is a chronicle of both successes and failures. But with a better grasp of the inevitable differences among various oral and oral-derived traditions, and specifically of the tradition-dependent nature of Old English phraseological and narrative structure, we shall be able to compose a more articulate poetics. From that poetics, and with the aid of reception theory, an aesthetics can be fashioned that takes account of the nourishing oral traditional roots of this poetry, that reinstates the referential richness and complexity that tradition has invested in the simplest of forms.

Perhaps we are now in a position to answer the nagging question of why Old English poets, many of them certainly literate, continued to use the traditional idiom after writing became available. After making due allowance for the realities of diglossia and specialized uses of literacy,[39] we come back to the innate value of the idiom as a signifying instrument. For the fact is that traditional phraseology and narrative structure comprised a network of signification known to and used by generations, a poetic code with well-established associations that was not easily displaced. It would be some time before (imported) written idioms, imbued with the new kind of literary meanings more appropriate to textual deployment, could compete successfully. To put it most simply, the oral traditional idiom persisted because—even in a written incarnation—it offered the only avenue to the immanent poetic tradition, the invisible but ever-present aesthetic context for all of the poems.

* *

Further Reading

Studies in oral tradition is an interdisciplinary area of inquiry, one that combines literary history and theory, linguistics, folklore, anthropology, and related disciplines in an effort to understand works of oral traditional art in cultural context. Although the general field includes many different kinds of approaches, historically the most important for medieval literature is the so-called Oral-Formulaic Theory (for an introduction, see my *The Theory of Oral Composition: History and Methodology*, Bloomington, 1988). Also known as the Parry-Lord Theory after its co-founders Milman Parry and Albert Lord (see especially Parry, *L'Epithète traditionnelle dans Homère: Essai sur un problème de style homérique*, translated in Parry, *The Making of Homeric Verse: The Collected Papers of Milman Parry* [Oxford, 1971], 266–324, and Lord, *Serbo-Croatian Heroic Songs [Srpskohrvatske junacke pjesme]* [Cambridge, MA, 1953-] and *The Singer of Tales* [Cambridge, MA, 1960]), this particular approach began as a structural examination of texts that attempted to isolate tectonic units typical of—and limited to—oral traditional poetry. The advent of the Oral Theory in Old English poetry can be traced to Francis P. Magoun's articles "The Oral-Formulaic Character of Anglo-Saxon Narrative Poetry" in *Speculum* 28 (1953): 446–67, and "The Theme of the Beasts of Battle in Anglo-Saxon Poetry" in *Neuphilologische Mitteilungen* 56 (1955): 81–90, and to Stanley B. Greenfield's discussion of the "exile" theme in "The Formulaic Expression of the Theme of 'Exile' in Anglo-Saxon Poetry" in *Speculum* 30 (1955): 200–06. From that point on, hundreds of books and articles have appeared, some advocating the Theory, some disagreeing with its methodology and conclusions (e.g., Larry D. Benson's "The Literary Character of Anglo-Saxon Formulaic Poetry" in *PMLA* 81 (1966): 334–41), and many suggesting modifications (summarized in Alexandra Hennessey Olsen's "Oral-Formulaic Research in Old English Studies: I" in *Oral Tradition* 1 (1986): 548–606, and "Oral Formulaic Research in Old English Studies: II" in *Oral Tradition*, 3 (1988): 138–90). For most scholars, the problem no longer seems as simple as oral versus literate, especially with the new appreciation of the complex, diglossic nature of early medieval England (e.g., Brian Stock's *The Implications of Literacy,* Princeton, 1983). As in the larger, comparative field (see my bibliography in *Oral-Formulaic Theory and Research* [New York, 1985] and updates in *Oral Tradition*), the key issues on the Old English horizon are the variety and comparability of oral traditions; the spectrum of oral, oral-derived, and written works; and the implications of oral traditional structure for the interpretation of the entire spectrum of verbal art.

Chapter 7

Working with Patristic Sources: Language and Context in Old English Homilies

✳ Clare A. Lees ✳

Old English prose has traditionally provided the stepping-stone to Old English poetry, whether viewed from the perspective of the student, the literary historian, or the scholar. The perils of *Cynewulf and Cyneheard* or Ohthere and Wulfstan, for example, often formed a student's introduction to Old English literature. The standard literary history, *A Critical History of Old English Literature,* by Stanley B. Greenfield, dutifully surveyed the prose in its first 64 pages but reserved the more valuable insights for the poetry and the remaining 162 pages. Greenfield's *History* offers one example of the model for even the best scholarly studies of the literature, where analysis of the prose forms the backdrop, the context, for a reading of the poetry.[1]

However, something very odd has been happening to this "poor relation" of Anglo-Saxon studies.[2] Ohthere and Wulfstan, together with the traditionally held finer examples of Old English homilies (for example, Wulfstan's *Sermo Lupi*), have been deleted from the teaching canon as now represented by Bruce Mitchell and Fred C. Robinson's *A Guide to Old English.*[3] Indeed, one recent undergraduate introduction to early medieval literature, Michael Swanton's *English Literature Before Chaucer,* refuses to discuss the prose whatsoever by employing a modern distinction between fiction and nonfiction.[4] In the absence of a full survey of what is taught under the heading of Old English in institutions of higher education, it is difficult to analyze this situation clearly.[5] Nonetheless, it seems to me that these recent textbooks and guides are pragmatic responses to the pressures of teaching in an already marginalized discipline.

On the other hand, Stanley Greenfield and Daniel G. Calder's *New Critical History* has a substantially enlarged section on the prose, by Calder, as well as a new and valuable chapter on Anglo-Latin literature, by Michael Lapidge.[6] There has also been considerable growth in the publication of scholarly editions of prose texts, and we have witnessed the inception of large-scale international projects such as the *Sources of Anglo-Saxon Literary Culture* (SASLC) and *Fontes Anglo-Saxonici: A Register of Written Sources Used By Authors In Anglo-Saxon England.*[7] These projects extend their ambit far beyond that of the prose, but both use the long-established technique of prose study—source analysis—as their methodology. Again, the explanations for this trend are to be found perhaps in the exigencies of life in a marginal subject in the academies. The sources projects elevate the profile of Anglo-Saxon studies by reinforcing its perception as a highly scholarly discipline. In the broader arena of the debate about the role of English studies within the humanities, these projects provide an answer to the question, Where do we go from here? with a conservative method that garners the best from the past and uses it to shape the future. The paradox is this: it would appear that we have all but stopped teaching Old English prose to our students at precisely the time when the methodology used to study it defines and justifies our professional commitment to Anglo-Saxon studies in general.

These two contemporary issues—the status of Old English prose in the curriculum and as an index of the professional interests of Anglo-Saxonists—have profound implications. The status of the prose, above all homiletic prose, has always been a precarious one within the curriculum and betrays, perhaps, an anxiety about the literary value of such works.[8] Rather than address this anxiety about Old English prose as "literature" critically, scholars have preferred to use the vocabulary of the literary historian. Hence, prose specialists use the techniques of the textual critic, the philologist, and the source analyst. Each demands a thorough training in traditional methods beyond a firm grounding in Old English and Latin: a training that can be supplied only at the graduate level. Indeed, SASLC and *Fontes* require a generation of scholars trained in just such methods for the successful establishment of data bases in the sources of Anglo-Saxon literary culture. For the foreseeable future at least, Anglo-Saxonists are in danger of speaking a language that only they can understand.

It is one of the current ironies of Anglo-Saxon studies that we have endorsed a commitment to two sophisticated information-processing projects, SASLC and *Fontes,* at a time when postmodern critical debate questions the merit of such traditional methodologies. The language of Anglo-Saxonists who do not evaluate critically their research paradigms is thus increasingly at odds with that used by our colleagues in departments of English. Unless we find a way of opening fruitful dialogue both with our colleagues and with our students, we run the risk of greater isolation as well as the label of antiquarianism. We now know more about Anglo-Saxon culture than ever before: a position that can only be strengthened by the textual information identified, collected, and analyzed by the sources projects. *Fontes* and SASLC will provide another resource for the scholar and student that, given the ambitions of both projects, inevitably brings with it another highly technical vocabulary. However, as any Anglo-Saxonist would agree, textual sources do not by themselves generate Old English literature nor do they adequately define Anglo-Saxon culture. By addressing the question of sources as *resources,* I wish to consider the implications of modern critical theory for the study of Old English homilies and for the teaching of Old English prose to our students.

My choice of subject is in part dictated by the observation that Old English homilies provide an excellent case study for the traditional patristic criticism that is now applied more comprehensively by the sources projects. But patristic criticism has never been a methodology confined to Anglo-Saxon studies and is, moreover, under scrutiny in other fields, as Lee Patterson's reassessment of Chaucer studies confirms.[9] Old English homilies therefore present just one example of the possibilities for medieval studies opened up by speaking the two languages of contemporary theory and traditional disciplines.

We do not, of course, actually speak two languages as defined by the title of this book but two varieties (more precisely, registers) of the same academic discourse that inhabit at present the two exclusive domains of postmodern theory and traditional philology. For the purposes of this paper and for reasons that will become clearer later, I propose to bridge these domains with a third "language," or approach, which combines theoretical insights into traditional historicism by Michel Foucault and Hans Robert Jauss with the more general issue of the social use of language. Jauss and Foucault provide me with the necessary theoretical apparatus to assess the research models of traditional scholarship, and each opens new avenues for future work.[10] In the second part of this paper, however, I choose to concentrate on an area of research suggested by developments in modern sociolinguistics. This combination of what might be loosely termed critical and linguistic theory is not as startling as it may seem initially, since advances in both "fields"[11] have consistently taken place side by side in this century, with mutually beneficial results. More specifically, philosophers and linguists alike have become increasingly interested in the use and meaning of utterances in context, or rather pragmatics. We can take J. L. Austin's *How To Do Things With Words* as an early example of this interest. Austin draws attention to a range of utterances that perform actions rather than assert; such utterances do not merely *say* something, they *do* something, as in the case of promising in the marriage ceremony (provided the relevant felicity conditions obtain). It is these performative utterances, or speech acts, that are not accountable for in traditional semantic terms.[12]

I shall not be concerned, however, with a speech act analysis of Old English homilies, although these texts, which were largely designed to be delivered on particular occasions, do provide material analogous to the one-

party talk of contemporary discourse analysis. Nor do I wish to enter the
debate about the applicability of speech act theory to so-called literary
texts, because the dichotomy between literary and nonliterary texts is as
difficult to maintain for Old English prose as for other works.[13] Instead, it
is the performative function of language in specific contexts that interests
me: the function of language use in the contexts of the homilies and in the
scholarly ways that we talk about them. And it is with a consideration of
context that pragmatics meets the work of Jauss and Foucault, since each
underlines the social and historical components of language use.[14]

Above all, any investigation of context in Old English—be it that of
traditional scholarly language or that of language use in Old English
texts—cannot afford to ignore the context of the classroom. It is for this
reason that I conclude my paper with a brief assessment of the teaching of
Old English prose in an attempt to revitalize its somewhat dry reputation.
Austin concludes his first study of speech acts with an apologia: "Here,
then, is an instance of one possible application of the kind of general theory
we have been considering; no doubt there are many others."[15] I offer
"Working with Patristic Sources" in the same spirit—as an outline of a
possible approach to medieval texts and their sources.

Research Models

It is no accident that the steering committees both of SASLC and *Fontes* comprise, for the most part, experts in the field of Old English prose.
Central to the study of these texts is the practice of source identification,
supported on the one hand by textual criticism and, on the other, by a
nineteenth-century model of philology, above all etymology.[16] By identifying the sources of prose texts (the argument runs) we are in a better position to know who read what, which helps to explain how that reading was
assimilated in the works of individual writers. This process not only provides a model of composition, especially homiletic composition, with
which to define the corpus; it also generates lists of sources, which can then
be checked against the manuscripts known to be available in Anglo-Saxon
England. By comparing the use of one lexical item (that of the source) with
another (that of the text), we are able to define more closely the semantic
range of Old English words, which can then be tested against their other
established uses.

The agendas of the international sources projects thus complement
those of the bibliographical handlist of extant manuscripts written or owned
in England up to 1100, the *Dictionary of Old English,* and the *Historical
Thesaurus.*[17] These collaborative projects legitimate at an institutional level

contemporary Anglo-Saxon studies and seek to reconstruct the language and culture, primarily from the written remains. Conducted almost exclusively by analyses of words and texts, these projects confer authoritative status on what is in fact only *one possible* reconstruction of an historical period.[18] It seems to me that the corporate goals of contemporary and future Anglo-Saxonists have been modeled on those of the traditional scholar of prose homiletic texts.

The traditional methods used to analyze Old English homilies and now enshrined in the international sources projects have been called into question only rarely.[19] I have looked in vain for a theoretical examination of the premises of source criticism; there is none. Nor, indeed, in all of the documents of SASLC and *Fontes* can I find a single definition of a source.[20] For, rather than examine the theoretical assumptions upon which source criticism is based, scholars have spent their energies refining its techniques. What we are presented with instead is a sophisticated terminology for dealing with sources; on theory, the practitioners of this methodology are silent. James W. Earl makes an important case for the psychoanalytic significance of silence in Old English literature in his essay in this collection; we should not ignore our own silences either. After all, however complex and tedious the compilation of evidence, identification itself is based on the very simple criteria of some form of verbal correspondence between text and source. The reluctance to speak critically about our methodologies demonstrates the confidence of a discipline so rooted in tradition that its processes are seen to be self-evident, transparent, and ideologically neutral.[21] In the light of the shift from meaning to method that has underpinned most postmodern theory, I shall here attempt to redress this imbalance in the study of Old English homilies and their patristic sources. My argument is a simple one: I examine the assumptions of traditional scholarship in order to demonstrate how they are instrumental in dictating the kinds of research that may be undertaken.

Like many traditional methodologies, source criticism attempts to preserve a crucial distinction between the object of knowledge (here, Old English homilies) and the knower (the traditional scholar). The source analyst assumes that the Old English homily can be understood only in terms of some larger historical context that it is the role of the scholar to reconstruct, *objectively*. We hypothesize, therefore, that each homily has its sources, if only in an ideal world where all relevant manuscripts have survived. The hypothesis has worked. We have found sources and will continue to do so until all have been recovered—the enterprise of the sources projects. This model of research is not only self-fulfilling, it is self-perpetuating, in that it provides an infinite combination of sources. This is already evident in the category distinctions employed by *Fontes*: certainly an immediate source; probably an immediate source; possibly an immediate source; certainly an antecedent source; probably an antecedent source; possibly an antecedent source; and analogue.[22] Such distinctions allow for considerable subjectivity in our decisions about the relations between text and source but are placed in a rigid methodological framework that assumes objectivity, even if it does not guarantee it. In such a way, then, we ensure the survival of the method, for our identifications will always require revision, our insights will always be necessarily partial. Another more immediately obvious implication of this model is that we will soon know more (if we do not already) about the sources of Old English homilies than did the writers themselves.

It would be most helpful if those involved in the sources projects acknowledged the limitations of their approach and its relationship to Anglo-Saxon studies in general, rather than simply outline the expected results. No one would deny that Old English homilies have their sources or that source criticism is a valuable research tool. Indeed, patristic criticism is particularly suited to the highly literate, bookish writers who produced these texts. Source analysis promotes too our understanding of the relationship between the Old English homilists and the Latin culture of western Christendom. But, what is at issue is the status of a source as a *fact,* and the implications of treating sources as facts for research purposes. When a source becomes a fact—in the same way that a date can become a fact—it can be incorporated into the framework by which we organize our knowledge of homiletic texts and used to dictate the placing of other sources (as facts) within the system. Let me demonstrate this point by examining the canon of Old English homilies.

Canon Formation

The most bookish of all the homilists is Ælfric, who seems to have been both an inspiration and mentor for his contemporary, Wulfstan. Without doubt, the methods of traditional source criticism have succeeded admirably for these two writers. From the pioneering work of Max Förster through to the discoveries of Cyril L. Smetana and Patrick H. Zettel, Ælfric's own remarks on his use of sources, interspersed throughout his works but most notably in the Preface to the First Series of Catholic Homilies, have been progressively refined.[23] The major contribution of traditional research is the identification of Ælfric's two main source collections; the homiliary of Paul the Deacon and the Cotton-Corpus hagiographical collection. These two collections now provide the starting point for any investigation of his homilies and facilitate an increasingly sophisticated interpretation of Ælfric's use of sources.

Using the same methods, a slightly different, though comparable, picture of Wulfstan has emerged, with attention now concentrated on the assembly of manuscripts conveniently known as the Commonplace Book.[24] Regularly contrasted with Ælfric and Wulfstan, by virtue of their use of apocrypha, eschatology, and sources in general, are the two main anonymous collections, Blickling and Vercelli. That these collections draw on qualitatively different sources has been recently confirmed by James E. Cross's important identification of the Pembroke sermonary.[25] Taking up the rear in the canon, we find the anonymous miscellaneous homilies: texts that are rarely found in coherent collections and that have an authorship and a manuscript circulation which cuts across the carefully maintained division between the writers of the second generation of the Benedictine Reform (Ælfric and Wulfstan) and the works of the pre-Reform collections (Blickling and Vercelli).

In other words, the homiletic canon is arranged according to our ability to identify sources and to determine dates and provenance. The broad binary division into the known *writers* (Ælfric and Wulfstan) and the unknown (anonymous) *texts* necessitates the use of comparison as the main evaluative tool. Judged particularly according to Ælfric's scholarly standards, anonymous works are regularly found wanting and are described as popular texts lacking a sufficient command of the source language, Latin.[26] Other anonymous works have yet to be admitted to the canon due to the absence of an identifiable or authoritative source.

The homiletic canon is also cemented by scholars' identification of dates and provenance. In addition to N. R. Ker's classification of manuscripts containing Anglo-Saxon and Angus Cameron's list of texts prepared for the *Dictionary of Old English,* there are a further three sets of sigla specifically for homilies, sermons and Saints' Lives.[27] The categories of manuscript sigla, however, present another methodological problem. We have an impressive sigla for the manuscripts of Ælfric's works (formulated by John C. Pope and Malcolm Godden but based substantially on the work of Kenneth Sisam and Peter Clemoes); another for the corpus of Wulfstan's texts (that of Karl Jost and Dorothy Bethurum, now in need of revision); and a third for the anonymous homilies (that of D. G. Scragg).[28] No doubt this is a necessary evil, but it does have significant consequences for the kind of study that we can undertake. Notably, the same manuscript can have a different siglum according to an individual scholar's priorities in assessing its contents.

The sigla for Ælfric achieves its aims: it is useful only for the scholar working on Ælfric. The manuscripts are arranged in a descending hierarchy of dissemination from Ælfric's putative original compositions and take into account his revisions, recensions, and later additions. As a result, we understand the chronology of Ælfric's works better than that of any other Anglo-Saxon writer. Scragg's sigla uses a different set of premises. Anonymous works are classified according to date of initial composition (in theory at least) or date of manuscript as well as by the number of anonymous items per manuscript; hence, Vercelli and Blickling are respectively A and B.[29] Scragg's work establishes a network of relationships among the anonymous corpus; Pope and Godden achieve the same for the Ælfrician corpus. These sigla are impressive works of scholarship and yet, as is well known, we have very few manuscripts that deal exclusively with Ælfrician texts or that can be definitively assigned to his circle. Many more manuscripts incorporate both Ælfrician and anonymous works and some date from within Ælfric's lifetime.[30] Unlike Ker's seminal survey, the present sigla make it difficult to move across this corpus in the way that the manuscript evidence suggests.[31]

Apart from the evident problems presented by these three sets of sigla, which each use an alphabetical classification, the core of homiletic manuscripts common to all of the sigla will signify a different set of relationships according to the siglum selected. Take the example of Cambridge, Corpus Christi College 41 (Ker 32), a rather poor copy of the Old English Bede that also includes a number of anonymous items written in the margins or on blank pages in the manuscript. By virtue of the apparent independence of these anonymous homilies, Scragg assigns the manuscript the siglum D. However, as Scragg himself points out, some of these works do share similarities of subject with other anonymous texts.[32] One such text is *De Passione Domini* (Ker 32.18 and Cameron B. 3.2.19), a translation and Passion narrative of Matthew 26 and 27, which is also the subject of a second independent translation extant in three versions: Oxford, Bodleian Library 340 and 342; Cambridge, Corpus Christi College 198; and Cambridge, Corpus Christi College 162 (Scragg's E, F, and G). EFG also provide contributory evidence for the rearrangement of Ælfric's Catholic Homilies into a single annual cycle and, accordingly, are given the sigla D, E, and F by Pope and Godden. In order to discuss the complex intertextuality of these manuscripts—of which *De Passione Domini* is only one example—the scholar is faced by the problem of using simultaneously two sets of sigla for the same manuscripts: DEFG (Scragg) and DEF (Pope and Godden) plus D (Scragg).[33] To devise yet another set of sigla is to ignore the important connections between this group of manuscripts and others in the homiletic canon.

Cambridge, Corpus Christi College 41 illustrates the practical problems that result from arranging homiletic manuscripts first into the known and the unknown and, second, by a chronology of date of composition or compilation. Despite Ashley Crandell Amos's convincing demonstration that dating criteria are notoriously unreliable, scholars have borrowed the techniques of the traditional philologist and have opted for a diachronic arrangement of the corpus.[34] The current arrangement of the homiletic canon, enshrined in its manuscript sigla, forms a developmental series that resists synchronic analysis of, in particular, the broader sociohistorical significance of the corpus as "textual events."[35] Furthermore, this series assumes an unproblematic relationship between textual events and our perception of them as a chronology. The artificiality of this diachrony is revealed at present by those marginal texts, such as *De Passione Domini,* which do not fit easily into the preestablished sequence. While apparently the result of an attempt to preserve the separateness of the past from the present, the homiletic canon is formed from our own modern priorities in ordering knowledge.

These observations bring me to the heart of the matter: it is one thing to reveal the assumptions of an established research paradigm and canon but quite another to suggest alternative models. Such models do, of course, exist, and two, in particular, address the related issues of canon formation and the negotiation between texts of the past and present perspectives. We now have the possibility of writing what is essentially literary history without recourse to the monolith of tradition and the impasse of selective chronology and binary systems. Jauss's aesthetic of reception directly recognizes the differences between past and present readings of a text with its dialectic of canon formation. This methodology examines the relationship among author, work, and public (reader/listener) at any given historical moment—the horizon of expectations.[36] Thus, all literary works can be accessed synchronically and diachronically through temporally constituted horizons of expectations and, moreover, are to some degree determined by them. The value of this approach for the Anglo-Saxonist is already evident in Martin Irvine's analysis of *The Dream of the Rood* and *Elene.*[37]

Reception theory enables us to bridge the gap between the known and unknown homilists dialectically rather than hierarchically even as we interrogate the strategies of Jauss's theory.[38] Even simply reversing the traditional terms of *dissemination from* to *reception of* will clarify our understanding of the textual circulation of homiletic manuscripts. Consider what happens to the triad of author, work, and public, at the moment of a homily's aesthetic reception in a manuscript: here homilies are rarely identified by authorship but more often by a rubric that locates each homily in the temporal framework of the Christian calendar (Sundays and Saint's days, for example). This moment of reception confronts Jauss's formulation of author and work with one between work and work and, in this textual reception, there are no anonymous homilies in Old English manuscripts—authorship is irrelevant. But what of the relationship between work and public (reader/listener)? Whether or not these homilies were actually delivered in church (and the debate is by no means resolved),[39] they maintain a rhetoric of oral delivery that is stripped of an original author. At this new moment of oral reception, when there are only speakers and listeners, all homilies are anonymous homilies and all are mediated through the trope of the voice of the preacher. This voice can itself defer to a patristic *auctor,* who is no more the author of the homily than the preacher.[40] At either of these moments—textual or oral—the event itself reorients the triad of author, work, and public and thereby modifies our understanding of its reception. Moreover, these communicative events participate in a process whereby the Church attempts to control the beliefs and behavior of its congregants, but it is by no means clear how this control is effected in Jauss's model of the social function of literature, which stresses the role of the reader (though not the listener) but does not examine the text as an agent of institutional practices.[41]

The communicative character of *literary* events is clearly acknowledged by Jauss, whose code model of reception is based on modern linguistic theory:

> The historicity of literature as well as its communicative character presupposes a dialogical and at once processlike relationship between work, audience, and new work that can be conceived of *in the relations between message and receiver as well as between question and answer, problem and solution.*[42] (my emphasis)

But what happens when these literary events are cast as *speech* events (as occurs in the reception of the homilies)? H. P. Grice and many others have been at pains to point out that communication is not simply a matter of encoding and decoding but also of pragmatic inference requiring some mutual knowledge between sender and receiver.[43] In other words, conversations normally exhibit some degree of coherence and continuity—what Grice calls the cooperative principle. Therefore, comprehension (the model in part underlying reception theory) involves both code and inferential models; as Dan Sperber and Deirdre Wilson put it (silently invoking Austin):

> Utterances are used not only to convey thoughts but to reveal the speaker's attitude to, or relation to, the thought expressed; in other words, they express "propositional attitudes", perform "speech acts", or carry "illocutionary force".[44]

Jauss, on the other hand, does not adequately account for inference in communicative events in his otherwise dynamic process of the moments in a work's reception.[45]

Reception theory offers a methodology that mediates between the past and the present; Foucault's archaeology is premised on the absolute difference of the past but, nonetheless, offers alternatives to the traps of a traditional approach. Writing history from an essentially antihistoricist perspective may seem a paradoxical enterprise, but Foucault's emphasis on archaeology resists the positivist connections of similarities, tradition, and influence in favor of acknowledging discontinuities, ruptures, and spaces.[46] Foucault asks us to address rather than to suppress difference—a potent corrective for the source analyst whose solution to the absence of a source is often that we have lost it. The implications for Anglo-Saxon studies are obvious. One starting point would be a reexamination of the Benedictine Reform itself, which scholarship, in its search for tradition and continuity, frequently formulates in terms of an earlier Continental reform movement. Another would be the question, What are the formations of the discourses of the tenth and eleventh centuries that permit the radically different use of sources in works that occupy the same archaeological space?[47] For it is clear from the evidence of the homiletic manuscripts that the texts of the Benedictine reformers are often to be found side by side with those of the pre-Reform, or non-Reform, writers. Foucault's analysis of archival discourses would also help us to understand how institutions, such as the Church, encode and enforce belief—a strategy far from clear in Jauss's theoretical model, as I have already suggested.[48]

What is less clear in Foucault's work, however, is the relationship between the subject and the archive. The archaeological method here raises similar questions about the role of the author to those raised about the listener in Jauss's aesthetic of reception. In Foucault's terms, the archive with its system of discursive practices creates the subject or author function.[49] Evidently there is space in these discourses for Ælfric—silenced in the reception of his homilies—to name himself in his Prefaces, if not as an author then certainly as a translator. Other writers, who do not exploit the genre of the preface, remain anonymous or use a Latin nom de plume (Lupi). How is this achieved? Foucault's archaeology relies in part (and for all his denials) on the *langue/parole* distinction of structural linguistics and shares with this brand of linguistic theory the criticism that the individual subject is made subservient to the formal system.[50] Foucault does not actually propose a theory of communication and, perhaps because of this, his system of discourses neglects the social and individual implications of the archive for the subject in the same way that structural linguistics ignores the situation of the speaker in favor of a constructed *langue*. There is little room here for a speaker or writer to express attitudes toward, or to engage in a dialogue with, various discourses. And yet, it is precisely the dialogue between the formal rhetoric of prefaces and that of homiletic writing that enables Ælfric to name himself in his Prefaces.[51] By examining issues such as these, we will be able to deconstruct the traditional and hierarchical division of the homiletic canon into named authors and unknown texts in terms of discursive formations, subject, and reception.

The studies of Jauss and Foucault offer but two possibilities for future research; it seems inherent to the postmodern critical climate that responses to traditional methods will celebrate a welcome plurality. But the fundamental problems raised by both suggest a need for the third "language" of linguistic theory. We need to look at the linguistic strategies of the homilies in their social and cultural contexts and, thereby, reconceptualize the project of source study—source analysis as a challenge to the new literary history, to paraphrase Jauss. It seems to me that applied pragmatics can begin to supply the missing link—at the very least by highlighting Anglo-Saxon attitudes toward language in their sociohistorical contexts.[52] Nowhere are these attitudes more immediately apparent than in the translation activities of the homilists.

Translation and Interpretation: Attitudes and Authority

The traditional model of identification of sources, followed by analysis, ignores, on a theoretical level, the central issue: identification is itself an interpretative act, both for the Old English homilist and for the modern scholar. On the macrolevel of the research paradigm, we have seen how the use of patristic sources has been a major interpretative factor in the formation of the homiletic canon. It goes *almost* without saying that source criticism is the preeminent technique at the microlevel of the individual text as well. The relationship between a source and the text has been presented as one of cause and effect; however, we can look at this relationship as an interpretative process in which the languages of both source and text play a major role.

Translation is the central activity of the homilists, who use a host of interpretative strategies when dealing with sources—direct (literal) translation, allusion, mistranslation, and mnemonic recall, to name but a few.[53] Such techniques demonstrate the complexities of the process whereby material in one language (Latin) is decoded and then encoded into another (Old English). Rather than examine the pragmatic effects of this process, traditional scholarship has been content to describe its results and then (arguing backward from the evidence) relate these results to an individual writer's competence in the source language. Thus, Ælfric's mastery of sources is adduced to be the result of his ability in Latin as well as his sensitive grasp of his native language. In contrast, several of the Blickling homilies, for example, have an apparently cruder use of sources and, therefore, a poor command of Latin and an insensitive use of English.[54] This model of translation ignores two important factors: firstly, the symbolic status of Latin as a "high" cultural language with English as its "low" counterpart; and, secondly, the competition for specific domains between these two languages.

In general terms, languages in contact borrow from one another selectively, and the nature of the selection depends on the primary interests of donor and receiver as well as on the structures of the relevant languages.[55] Therefore, the relationship between Latin and English may be usefully described as a dynamic process comprising three interrelated elements: the structure of donor and receiver languages; the functional distribution of these languages in Anglo-Saxon society; and the differing competencies of individual writers (or speakers) as a result of different attitudes and needs. Helmut Gneuss's work on Latin and Old English liturgical terminology provides just one example of this process in that the English terms are not always the direct equivalents for, or even direct borrowings from, the Latin. Gnuess's work is thus complemented by contemporary analyses of bilingualism and diglossia that have important implications for a redefinition of Old English translators and their linguistic resources.[56]

Old English homilies provide fruitful material for an investigation of the roles of Latin and English in the translation process both in terms of their respective domains and individual attitudes. One recurrent issue is that of the role of Latin as the sacred language of Scripture (itself a purely conventional notion) and the consequential problems of translating Scripture into English. Note, for example, how Ælfric carefully sets out criteria for scriptural translation in his Preface to Genesis so as to avoid theological error:

> . . . we ne durron na mare awritan on Englisc þonne ðæt Leden hæfð, ne ða endebyrdnysse awendan, buton ðam annum, ðæt ðæt Leden 7 ðæt Englisc nabbað na ane wisan on ðære spræce fandunge [sic]: æfre se ðe awent oððe se ðe tæcð of Ledene on Englisc, æfre he sceal gefadian hit swa ðæt ðæt Englisc hæbbe his agene wisan, elles hit bið swyðe gedwolsum to rædenne ðam ðe ðæs Ledenes wise ne can . . .[57]

> (. . . and we dare not write more in English than the Latin has, nor change the order, save in this alone, that Latin and English are not of one idiom in the disposition of their language: whosoever translates or teaches from Latin into English, he must always order it so that the English has its own idiom, else it be very misleading to read for those who do not know the idioms of Latin . . .)

and, indeed, concludes the Preface with the comments that he will undertake no other such translations.

However, Ælfric shows no traces of such hesitation about the difficulties of scriptural translation earlier in his career, when he regularly translated biblical lections in the Catholic Homilies.[58] But the status of English translations of biblical passages does pose problems for anonymous homilists and revisers of homiletic translations, as the case of the Passion narratives indicates. Two versions of the homiletic Matthew narrative, *In Dominica Palmarum,* in Bodley 340, 342 and Corpus 162, contain numerous minor lexical and morphological emendations in hands roughly contemporary with the main hands of the manuscripts. Many of these corrections conform to the fuller translation in the so-called West Saxon Gospels, indicating that the revisers of these texts worked with some idea of an orthodox and authoritative translation in mind.[59] The systematic examination of translations such as these would provide the beginning of a map of the functional distribution of Old English.

Of equal significance is the relationship between Ælfric's Latin and English Pastoral Letters. Contrary to prevailing views, the Old English Letters are not direct translations of the Latin: the English versions often address a different audience than do those of the Latin. This may be illustrated by evident changes in subject matter but also by the fact that Ælfric often signals a change in subject by a change in translation technique.[60] His sensitivity toward the different domains of English and Latin in the Pastoral Letters is a microcosm of Ælfric's attitudes toward the language of authority in general. For example, Ælfric *apparently* gives equal status to Haymo as *auctor* in the Latin Preface to the First Series of the Catholic Homilies:

> Hos namque auctores in hac explanatione sumus sequuti, videlicet Augustinum Hipponensem, Hieronimum, Bedam, Gregorium, Smaragdum, et aliquando Haymonem. (Thorpe, 1.14–15)

> (Therefore these writers have been followed in this exposition, namely Augustine of Hippo, Jerome, Bede, Gregory, Smaragdus, and sometimes Haymo.)

Reading this, we might be led to expect that Ælfric uses Haymo in the same way as his other *auctores,* if less frequently. However, in practice he rarely uses this derivative Carolingian without reference to a second authority, such as Bede.[61] Indeed, the best source analyses have revealed Ælfric's discriminatory use of Latin authorities.

However, before we can begin to understand the complex attitudes of Anglo-Saxon writers toward their vernacular and the prestigious cultural language of learned Latin, we must first reexamine our own attitudes.

General observations by commentators such as Milton McC. Gatch, who ponders,

> [W]hy it is that, compared with the products of continental centres, English palaeography and Latin learning seem to many scholars debased at the very time when Old English prose of stylistic and intellectual competence far in advance of any European vernacular was being produced in abundance

have to be set in a context that examines first the domains of this emerging vernacular and second its symbolic status when compared with that of Latin.[62] More specifically, one attitude toward Old English among modern scholars stresses its dependence on the more authoritative language, Latin, and underplays its linguistic autonomy. Mary Catherine Bodden's recent study of Anglo-Saxon self-consciousness about language in the Saints' Lives is a case in point:

> Our comments on historiographical skills and style *should assume that in large measure at least* they are adaptions of precedents and predecessors; our evaluation of their content *should assume* that it reflects the perceptions of earlier historians, not, *exclusively or even greatly,* the literal reality of contemporary circumstances.[63] (my emphasis)

Given the amount of rhetorical equivocation in this passage ("in large measure at least . . . exclusively or even greatly") as well as Bodden's neglect of the immediate contexts of such translations, one wonders why writers bothered to translate at all.

Mary Clayton's broader based analysis of vernacular homiliaries, on the other hand, has a fuller grasp of the issues largely because of her reintegration of Ælfric's homiliaries into the English milieu. She highlights, rightly in my view, the fact that Ælfric's use of English for the Catholic Homilies is in itself unremarkable. Rather, it is the range of uses to which Ælfric puts the vernacular that merits our attention, particularly his exploitation of the medium of preaching to provide *monastic* as well as *secular* instruction.[64] Even Clayton, however, does not take up the implications of her work. If it is unremarkable that Ælfric writes in the vernacular, then his practice of providing prefaces both in English and Latin becomes very remarkable. The precedents for the Latin Prefaces may be located within the practices of Carolingian homilists such as Hrabanus Maurus, but this does not adequately explain Ælfric's use of the *bilingual* address. Rather, the explanation may lie in the different subjects of the Prefaces. I note, in passing, that while Ælfric's full list of patristic *auctores* is to be found in the

Latin Preface to the First Series, he refers to a vernacular authority and king, Alfred, in the *English* Preface:[65]

> Þa bearn me on mode, ic truwige þurh Godes gife, þæt ic ðas boc of Ledenum gereorde to Engliscre spræce awende; na þurh gebylde mycelre lare, ac forþan þe ic geseah and gehyrde mycel gedwyld on manegum Engliscum bocum, þe ungelærede menn þurh heora bilewitnysse to micclum wisdome tealdon; and me ofhreow þæt hi ne cuþon ne næfdon þa godspellican lare on heora gewritum, *buton þam mannum anum ðe þæt Leden cuðon, and buton þam bocum ðe Ælfred cyning snoterlice awende of Ledene on Englisc, þa synd to hæbbenne.*

>   (Thorpe, 2.6–15; my emphasis)

> (Then it came into my mind, I trust through the grace of God, that I might translate this book from the language of Latin into the English tongue, not through boldness of great learning, but because I have seen and heard of much error in many English books, which unlearned men in their innocence consider as great wisdom; and it grieves me that they knew not nor had not evangelical doctrines in their writings, *save for those men only who knew Latin, and save for those books only which are to be had which King Alfred wisely translated from Latin into English.*)

Here authority is conferred on Ælfric's English homilies by the existence of an earlier set of translations sanctioned by royal power. Such examples of the relationship between language and power indicate that we need to look carefully at the specific question of authority in the translation process.

Ælfric's attitudes toward Latin and English are not necessarily shared by other homilists or, indeed, compilers of homiletic manuscripts. For example, the practice of citing authority is a technique common in the Catholic Homilies—even when citation refers only to a main source and conceals a complex pastiche of minor sources in the same work. Anonymous homilies can be quite different; citation is often restricted to a vague reference to a *boc,* which is itself frequently different to identify.[66] This is not simply a case of an anonymous writer's inability to translate the Latin accurately or with due respect. The Pembroke sermonary often acknowledges its authorities, which may be omitted in vernacular compositions.[67] Nor do I think that we can resolve this issue by pointing out the irrelevance of such citations in a preaching context, for this brings us back to Ælfric's own use of named authors. What we have here is material that suggests a different attitude toward the language of learning, Latin, and we must accordingly modify our astringent comments on the anonymous homilists' linguistic ineptitudes.

We might point instead to the use of common apocrypha by these anonymous writers as one symptom of this difference. Note, for example, the number of English versions of the so-called "Sunday Letter": a letter from heaven claiming to have been written by sacred means but, as its numerous versions indicate, clearly contaminated on earth. No version of the "Sunday Letter" exists in the Ælfrician corpus; Ælfric, moreover, makes explicit comments about the theological dangers of using other apocrypha popular in anonymous works, such as the Marian texts.[68]

We should, however, resist the temptation of a glib binary division in Ælfrician or anonymous attitudes toward either the language of authority or orthodox theological texts. Superficially, another symptom of difference in homiletic works is the prevalence of a technique such as *compilatio*. It is conventional to assume—albeit as a working hypothesis—that the Ælfrician and Wulfstanian texts use Latin sources. On the other hand, anonymous homilies may synthesize extracts from preceding vernacular texts; some are new versions of existing material arranged for a different liturgical occasion; others incorporate extracts from Ælfrician texts into a new framework.[69] This practice of working in English is not exclusive to the anonymous homilists. Wulfstan often composed in Latin, but some of his sermons are modeled on earlier Ælfrician homilies—his hand may also be detected in modifications of some sections of Ælfric's Pastoral Letters. Ælfric himself revised extracts of his own compositions.[70] Taken together with Martin Irvine's reformulation of the general significance of *compilatio* in this volume, the evidence testifies to the importance of the vernacular and the functions that it has taken over from the Latin. The situation of the homilists is a complex one, but, put briefly, the practice of compiling from previous works is a common rhetorical technique in Carolingian patristic texts. Many English homilies, *but not all*, work in the same vein by producing translated compilations from earlier Latin works.

Texts, Sources, and History

The attitudes of the homilists toward language and patristic authority are also influential in our assessment of that shifting and multifaceted series of events of broad sociohistorical concern known as the Benedictine Reform. Even when dealing with such orthodox policy documents as the *Regularis Concordia,* source criticism emphasizes not only dependence on Carolingian and Lotharingian materials but also English independence in matters of liturgical observance and monastic decorum.[71] While the Continental reforms of the previous century fostered by Charlemagne and his circle are clearly significant in providing documentary support and inspiration, they do not by themselves adequately describe the character of the Benedictine Reform. One puzzling aspect of this interrelationship is the absence of any coherent statement about education or monastic study in the *Regularis Concordia* when compared with its Continental counterpart, the

Admonitio Generalis. After all, one of the distinctive features of the English Reform is its use of the vernacular to promulgate and inculcate monastic policies.[72] The answer lies, perhaps, in the significance of an earlier, native and Alfredian, reform tradition that focused on the vernacular, for the educated elite of the tenth century.

Although the implications of the monastic reforms for vernacular education (vital for our understanding of attitudes) have concentrated on the proponents of the second generation of the Reform, Ælfric and Wulfstan, the progress of the Reform in England is by no means uniform. The movement had a limited reach, which centered primarily on Winchester as the principal ecclesiastical see as well as the seat of royal power. The regional character of the Reform is thus manifest along the Winchester/Worcester axis; even in such eminent sees as Canterbury its effects are muted.[73] Since the scriptoria of Canterbury and Rochester are active in producing homiletic manuscripts throughout this period, we must weigh carefully the import of the Reform against its documentary evidence and the attitudes displayed therein—a process that Antonia Gransden and Mary Richards have recently begun.[74] Circulated, if not always composed, under the broad aegis of the Reform, Old English homilies are as much responses to this movement as they are features of it.

The lesson of the sources of the *Regularis Concordia* is an important one, for it demonstrates that the Carolingian Reform is only partially imaged in its English counterpart. The old dictum that the Anglo-Saxons saw the present in terms of the past seems to me both intuitively one-sided and demonstrably wrong. That Old English homilists based their texts in large measure on earlier, sometimes late Antique, documents often disseminated via the Carolingian reforms does not mean that their perspective was exclusively retrospective, as claimed by Bodden and Godden.[75] Exegesis is without doubt an irresistably conservative genre, but these preachers were simultaneously addressing contemporary concerns, as numerous homilies indicate. Indeed, in the first instance, we need look no further than the *Sermo Lupi*.[76] Put simply, these writers formulated the past in terms of present priorities: the twentieth century gives far greater weight to patristic *auctores* than does the tenth.

One other legacy of twentieth-century scholarship that needs to be reexamined concerns historical periodization. The period of greatest activity in the production of homiletic manuscripts is not only the tenth but also the eleventh century. However, since our perception of the eleventh century is dominated by one major event, that of the Norman Conquest in 1066, the study of homiletic texts also divides at this point (despite efforts to move the date forward to 1100). It is well known that there were a number of regional efforts to promote and maintain English as a language of learning in the post-Conquest period: we think of the extension of the Anglo-Saxon Chronicle at Peterborough and the trilingual Canterbury Psalter of the twelfth century, for example. Later still, at the turn of the twelfth and thirteenth centuries, we find the "Tremulous" Worcester hand annotating a considerable number of Anglo-Saxon manuscripts, including homiletic works.[77]

Old English homilies and homiliaries were not simply read by monastic glossators but continued to be used, copied, and compiled up to the twelfth and early thirteenth centuries. The Lambeth, Trinity, and Vespasian homilies as well as the collection in Cotton Vespasian D. xiv, associated with Anselm and the reforms at Canterbury,[78] all contain versions of Old English, often Ælfrician, works. The practice of interpreting Ælfrician homilies, either by using extracts from his works in new compilations or by modifying his homiliary, dates from within twenty years of the earliest manuscripts of the Catholic Homilies but continues well into the next century. We need to look again at the canon of Middle English texts, which must now include the reception of Old English works, primarily at monastic centers, in the twelfth and thirteenth centuries. Such revisions of the canon can only clarify our understanding of the literary and linguistic situation post-Conquest; they will also modify our notions of the climate of learning in the twelfth century.

Belief

The discussion of the Benedictine Reform and the importance of reassessing the social history of text production brings me to one final matter—that of belief. However we might interpret the effects of the Reform, its central preoccupation was to extend the control of the monasteries over the observance of the faith in tenth and eleventh-century society (a view sadly neglected by the scholars). Old English homilies are above all didactic texts: whether explicating a biblical reading or expounding an article of faith, these works *overtly and covertly* promote the beliefs of their writers, their audience, and their readers, in contexts where all are engaged in an act of worship. They are therefore written examples of performative language use and are set in highly ritualized events reminiscent of some of Austin's earliest examples of performatives. Traditional examination of the beliefs manifested in the homilies has, as it were, leaked from the seams of a textual emphasis on sources.[79] However, I would like to suggest that source criticism can be used to illustrate how the homilists attempt to control the faith of their audience while claiming only to explicate it.

Even under the umbrella of Benedictine orthodoxy, we find evidence for different attitudes as well as different expressions of a Christian belief system. Ælfric's practice of structuring the Catholic Homilies according to the *temporale* is not simply a matter of following the earlier textual precedents of Carolingian homiliaries. On the contrary, his English Prefaces to the First Series culminates in an apocalyptic urgency (Thorpe, 2–9), which animates a recurrent stress in the homilies themselves on the conformity of liturgical practice. Throughout the Catholic Homilies, we find regulations for liturgical practice addressed both to the clergy and to the laity.[80] Ælfric's First Series homily for Palm Sunday, for example, outlines communal participation in the procession (Thorpe, 218.1–17), which is derived mainly from a description in the *Regularis Concordia*.[81] There are many other examples of how this Benedictine Reformer sought to control the path of Catholicism.

Orthodoxy can have its shades. An analysis of a common motif such as the penitential motif of binding and loosing sin (the Petrine prerogative of the priesthood) finds different expression in the works of Wulfstan and the works of Ælfric. Ælfric's use of the motif occurs in Christological discussion of the priesthood in the Catholic Homilies; Wulfstan reserves its analysis for the ears of the bishops alone and, accordingly, addresses the matter in Latin.[82] Into such a complex picture of belief and language use among the orthodox, it is sometimes difficult to find a place for the oddities of the anonymous homilies; but it is precisely in the use of, for example, the Seven Heavens apocryphon by these homilists that we will find a fuller understanding of Anglo-Saxon belief. Such studies will also clear the ground for a more detailed examination of the reception of Old English homilies, Benedictine or otherwise, in the eleventh and twelfth centuries in terms of their changing priorities in education and belief.[83]

Old English Prose in the Curriculum

Sometimes explicit, but always implicit, in my discussion has been the reexamination of modern attitudes toward Old English texts. This is a matter for the classroom as well as the study and, accordingly, in the last section of this paper, I reexamine the role of Old English prose in the curriculum. In the following discussion, I choose as my example a nonhomiletic work, Alfred's Preface to the *Cura Pastoralis*. While this is partly a matter of convenience—the text is still anthologized—it also reflects my feeling that our understanding of tenth- and eleventh-century homiletic practice can be enriched by Alfred's Preface, which clearly had a symbolic significance for the period.

At the risk of stating the obvious, the major hurdle that the student of Anglo-Saxon studies faces is learning the language. This was traditionally an unpalatable task, taught via grammar and translation classes, where the prose, generally held to be easier to translate, played an important role. On gaining a reading proficiency in Old English, the student graduated to the poetry, supplemented either overtly or covertly by the standard translations. Language study thereafter concentrated on the philological issues of literary texts or was channeled into history of the language courses. Study of the prose, as I have already suggested, was silently dropped from the lower reaches of the curriculum, to be resumed at a higher level. Recent developments in technological resources have made basic language learning a more exciting proposition for the student. Note the number of Old English courses designed for use in the language laboratory or on computer-assisted learning programs.[84] These courses represent a considerable advance over traditional methods; by allowing the student to proceed at her or his own pace, they provide tailor-made courses for the individual and liberate both student and teacher from the limitations of rote learning.

However, technical resources are at best simply tools for the teacher. The question that remains is how to integrate our knowledge of Anglo-Saxon into a format that draws together language and literary studies. It is by now a commonplace that developments in linguistics have fueled the debates about method, meaning, and intention in literary studies. From Saussure to Derrida, modern theory stresses the ability of language to talk about itself, to employ a metalanguage. Anglo-Saxon in the classroom offers the teacher the opportunity to explore some of these theories in practice. Since my preceding discussion was framed by research in applied pragmatics and sociolinguistics, I shall concentrate on that approach here.

One of the fundamental questions of sociolinguistics, that of the social organization of language behavior, has been usefully formulated by Fishman: "Who speaks (or writes) what language (or language variety) to whom and when and to what end?"[85] The relevance of this question to Anglo-Saxon studies is clear. The speech communities of pre-Conquest England were as complex and varied as those of contemporary societies. Anglo-Scandinavians lived side by side with Anglo-Saxon speakers, who, in turn, drew on a number of language varieties. In addition, these communities had contact, if only symbolic contact, with the language of Western Christendom, Latin. It is not an extravagant conjecture to assume that while many speakers had linguistic competence in only one language (Anglo-Saxon or Anglo-Scandinavian), others may have had a rough-and-ready knowledge of a second, nonnative, language; still others may have been bilingual or even trilingual—if not as speakers, then as readers.[86] Moreover, the written sources provide a wealth of material about the growth of the vernacular and the role of Latin, as I have already indicated. At the same time, the vast majority of speakers were functional illiterates; literacy was the privilege of a powerful elite. Nonetheless, John Miles Foley's work continues to show how the evidence of the written texts examined in the light of twentieth-century oral societies contributes much to our understanding of the theories of orality and literacy. We teach our students a language that no one now speaks, but the written remains pay eloquent testimony to their dead speakers. We do not need to lament with Barley that

> it is a sad fact that many Anglo-Saxonists tend to study their people not as thinking members of a social community but as generators of scribal errors and manuscript traditions.[87]

The skills of philology and textual criticism can be taught within a framework that discusses the social use of language and the issues of language contact and change from an integrated perspective, both synchronic and diachronic. Take the example of Alfred's Preface to the *Cura Pastoralis,* one of the few prose texts to preserve its place in the canon of Mitchell and Robinson. It is a pity that this version of the Preface is presented in quasi-normalized fashion, notably without full textual variants.[88] Textual variants are not the preserve of the traditional philologist—we can use them to demonstrate language change, inherent variation, and scribal reception, for example. However, we are more than compensated for this lacuna by the excellent translations and notes by Simon Keynes and Michael Lapidge, as well as by Allen J. Frantzen's guide to Alfred's works.[89]

Alfred's Preface provides the site for a range of issues: the formulation and implementation of a policy of language planning; the production, dissemination, and reception of a canon of educational materials; the status of the vernacular translation—be it prose or verse; the symbolic roles of Alfred as king, translator, and poet; the goals of the Church in establishing and controlling literacy; the attitudes of the English toward the Vikings; the complex intertextuality of the Preface's rhetoric; the interrelationship of the prose and verse Prefaces; the linguistic varieties of early Old English; and the vexed question of the *æstel,* to name but a few. Ælfric had good reasons for citing Alfred's translations in his own Preface. Moreover, Alfred's Preface presents to the student a microcosm of the problem that the contemporary Anglo-Saxonist faces—the reconstruction of a historical period from its written remains.

Alfred's Preface expresses the attitudes of one Anglo-Saxon toward the value of literature while it enacts its processes. As we all know, the vast majority of extant vernacular manuscripts preserve prose works; a substantial proportion of these manuscripts are homiliaries—in one form or another—that enjoyed a popularity and circulation among the educated elite far greater than that of the poetry. In comparison, the Old English poetic codices are low-prestige products, often poorly executed and compiled piecemeal. Jauss and other contemporary theorists remind us that the aesthetics of literature is socially and historically constructed and that any exploration of the writings of the Anglo-Saxons must take into account their attitudes toward literature. Despite the fact that we are urged beyond interpretation, beyond New Criticism, there can be little doubt that close reading will remain the prerogative of the classroom. Indeed, one of the advantages of teaching Old English is that the student is continually forced to take into account the text. We can acknowledge this as one of the positive advantages of speaking two languages. Yet, by deconstructing the distinctions between literature and writing, or by exploring the complex interplay between speech and writing, or even simply by asking the question, What is literature? we can introduce our students to a range of texts that do not have to account for their place in the canon by virtue of any demonstrable "literariness."

Conclusion

It seems to me that there are many things that we can do with sources other than identify, list, and classify them. At the beginning of this discussion I outlined some of the implications of the complex machinery of traditional source criticism, with especial reference to canon formation and the use of manuscript sigla. I suggested that there are alternatives to the positivist model of history on which source criticism is now based, giving the examples of Jauss, Foucault, and aspects of contemporary pragmatics. I then went on to explore the question of how Old English homilists interpret their sources, with a brief analysis of their attitudes toward language and authority. By revising the relationship among text, source, and cultural history, we can begin to reconceive our notions of the significance of the Benedictine Reform and the reception of Anglo-Saxon homiliaries post-Conquest. Early medieval homilies, moreover, provide fascinating evidence for the role of the preacher in directing belief. These issues prepare the ground for one possible approach to an historical sociolinguistics as well as a detailed examination between the relationship of language and power in Anglo-Saxon texts. This approach is by no means restricted to Old English homilies—I have in mind other "marginal" genres, such as the Laws, ecclesiastical handbooks, and the penitentials, for example. Nor is this approach restricted to the research library; the real effects of speaking two languages will be felt as we revise our teaching methods and offer our students the chance to find their own languages.

180 _Clare A. Lees_

* *

Further Reading

For reception theory see Ian Maclean's helpful introduction and bibliography in "Reading and Interpretation," in _Modern Literary Theory: A Comparative Introduction_, ed. Ann Jefferson and David Robey (London, 1986), 122–44, although Jauss, _Toward an Aesthetic of Reception_ is essential (see note 10 for full details). Foucault's work on archaeology begins with _The Order of Things: An Archaeology of the Human Sciences_ (London, 1970) and continues with _The Archaeology of Knowledge_ (note 10). One thoughtful and challenging assessment of historiography is that by White, _Tropics of Discourse_, but more directly relevant is Patterson's introductory chapter on New Critical and exegetical approaches to medieval studies in _Negotiating the Past_ (see notes 50 and 9, respectively). Frantzen and Venegoni, "Desire for Origins," (note 1), prepare the ground for a deconstruction of traditional Anglo-Saxon studies with a critical methodology based on Foucault's archive, a discussion developed further in Frantzen's _Desire for Origins_ (see note 5).

Trudgill's _Sociolinguistics_, on what might be loosely termed the language variation approach, is fairly representative of the many introductions to sociolinguistics; Milroy's "On the Sociolinguistic History" is a fine example of this methodology applied to sociohistorical linguistics (see note 52). Also promising is Jay Siskin, "A Medieval Semiotics of Translation," _Semiotica_ 63 (1987): 129–42—a semiotic model of translation (using fourteenth-century Hebrew and French), which has potential for translation studies in general. Ralph Fasold, _The Sociolinguistics of Society_ (Oxford, 1984), has invaluable introductions to bilingualism and diglossia, together with the issues of language attitudes and language contact (further studies are listed in note 55). Studies on literacy in Anglo-Saxon England are found in note 86. The standard works on pragmatics are those by Austin and Searle, but Levinson and Stubbs offer the clearest accounts of more recent developments (note 12 has full details). Ronald Carter and Paul Simpson have a helpful glossary of key terms in _Language, Discourse and Literature: An Introductory Reader in Discourse Stylistics_ (London, 1989). For the initiated, Sperber and Wilson propose radical insights into Grice's maxim of relevance, which have important consequences for communication theory (notes 43, 44). For examples of studies of speech act theory in Old English, see note 13.

Chapter 8

Medieval Textuality and the Archaeology of Textual Culture

✳ Martin Irvine ✳

Introduction: Considering the Literary Archive

An attempt to define medieval textuality necessarily entails the simultaneous study of the discursive and material dimensions of textual culture. That is, one must account for the systems of literary or textual language that formed the archive of discourse for medieval textual communities; these include the system of literary language, genres, styles, and rhetorical strategies that provided the ground of possibility for writing new texts and for interpreting those texts already received. One must also account for the material or physical form of texts in actual manuscripts; these include the material conditions of textual culture and the mode of signifying specific to the format, script, layout, and individuality of manuscript books. This essay will attempt to map out early medieval textuality in the hybrid Latin and English culture of Anglo-Saxon England by engaging "two languages" that have been considered contraries, namely, the descriptive language of traditional philology (oriented toward the particulars of textual and linguistic history) and a synthesis of recent theory that can be termed an extended archaeological model, articulated at the point where Foucault's archaeological method, historicized semiotics, and reception theory intersect (oriented toward the configuration of historically situated discursive systems).

One cannot engage these two "languages"—traditional practices and post-Foucauldian theory–however, without recognizing that they construct their objects at fundamentally different levels of analysis; therefore, my argument assumes that a dialogue cannot be set up between these "languages" as if they could speak across the same level, simply addressing in different ways neutral objects endowed with a prediscursive factuality. This would give the impression that critical theory simply completes or supplements traditional philology and literary criticism or (as is sometimes charged) critical theory merely translates the old concerns of traditional practices into a new metalanguage. On the contrary, the model of analysis that I am proposing here can be used to critique the ideological and episte- mological inadequacies of traditional philology and provide a rationale for the study of medieval textuality and literary culture reconceptualized at a level of analysis that was blocked and foreclosed by traditional philological discourse.

First, some background to the archaeological model of investigation I am proposing here. Foucault never completed his program of defining sys- tematically what he meant by "the archaeology of knowledge" or "the archive" of statements that form discourses,[1] but he provided many sugges- tions that can be extended to a study of early medieval textual culture. Recent studies by Gilles Deleuze, Hayden White, Roger Chartier, and Mark Poster (among others) have shown that Foucault's work leads to a systematic reconceptualizing of intellectual and social history—a large door that Foucault himself left ajar in *The Archaeology of Knowledge*[2]—and it is the aspect of Foucault's work I am interested in extending for the study of medieval textuality.[3] Deleuze has extended Foucault's notion of the archive in a way that exposes the heuristic potential of investigating systems of discourse as formed by archaeological strata or "fields or readability" that distinguish the discourses of an era,[4] in our case, literary texts in manu- script culture and the disciplines that promoted distinctive, historically de- fined kinds of literate practices. I would like to develop these suggestions further by showing that the aspect of Foucault's thought that entails a re- conceptualizing of literary and intellectual history intersects with, and can be usefully completed by, reception theory as formulated by Jauss[5] and a historicized semiotic theory along the lines suggested by Bakhtin and recent theories of the principle of intertextuality.[6]

For Foucault, discourses are systematized through a historical "ar- chive," and Foucault's second-order or transcendental use of this term should be distinguished from its ordinary meaning. The primary sense is equivalent to the sum total of textualized cultural history (the surviving documents of history), and the secondary sense used by Foucault designates the system of discursive rules and types of statement (*énoncé*) that autho- rize, in the way that linguistic rules authorize individual statements within a language, the discrete or individual discursive events (literary works, his- tories, law, and so on) considered as part of a larger system of discourse. For Foucault, the archive is formed of these discursive possibilities, and discourses are formed of groups of statements—"verbal performances" bearing subject, object, and concept relations and capable of repetition in other forms—stratified into synchronically discontinuous fields. The goal of archaeology is to disclose these discursive fields from within their own structure, as it were, showing how discourse functions in the larger sphere of the social institutions that regulate its use.

Like the historians of the Annales school, to whom he is often compared, Foucault redefines the "documents" of history, which are mainly written sources previously assumed to reveal a continuous, unified, rational consciousness expressive of individual human subjects and related referentially to objects, as "monuments," which are signifying traces of the past that must be reconstituted by archaeology to disclose their function within the fields of discourse that define a historical era.[7] Archaeology attempts to disclose the interior hierarchies and possible levels of articulation "within the very density of discourse."[8] For our purposes here, archaeological investigation of literary discourse—texts considered as monuments at the enunciative surface of an archive—can proceed across both horizontal and vertical relations: horizontal relations among various literary languages, styles, and genres, and vertical relations in an order of discourse analogous to the levels of linguistic and semiotic analysis (for example, the series "phoneme, morpheme, lexeme, sentence, text, discourse, archive"). In the study of literary history, then, it should be possible to disclose various stratified fields of discourse that formed the archive of possible genres and types of literary statement.

When these observations about discourse are inserted into the domain of social and literary history, the archaeological method requires further elaboration and clarification. Foucault's model of analysis, which presupposes a rigorous study of all forms of discourse on the synchronic level, is usefully completed by the theory of intertextuality, which parallels the notion of the archive in the presupposition that any text is a microcosm of a larger textual system, and by reception theory, which focuses on the social dimension of literary production and interpretation in a way parallel to Foucault's definition of discourse as social practice and archive as historical a priori. I shall elaborate on these principles in greater detail in the course of examining specific examples from Anglo-Saxon textual culture.

A study of medieval textuality and literary history reconceived as a project of archaeological analysis, however, entails a thorough reinterpretation of the primary archive that has traditionally been the domain of philology—languages, paleography, literary history—but reconceptualized at other levels of analysis. The data constructed by philology—identification of textual sources, editions of texts restored to an original version, descriptions of manuscripts and the history of scripts, linguistic history—are neither self-interpreting nor self-limiting with respect to the levels of analysis that may be brought to bear on them. Thus the investigator of medieval textual culture must be an archivist on two levels simultaneously—in the material archive of history and in the larger *system* of texts and discourse that formed the archive of possible statements, genres, and bodies of knowledge, the discursive conditions that made textual culture possible.

By adopting this extended archaeological model, I hope to provide a map for reading the textual culture of the early Middle Ages by studying this culture as a synchronic system with a structure observable in a series of transtextual and transgeneric discursive fields or levels. I will focus on texts from the early medieval and Anglo-Saxon era, a period largely neglected in most studies of literary theory and textuality. My analysis takes in a range of both Latin and Old English texts, since they were produced from the same libraries and scriptoria and were received by the same textual community. I will focus on Bede's narrative of Cædmon and the textuality of Cædmonian poetry, King Alfred's preface to his translation of Saint Augustine's *Soliloquies,* and the contents of the Parker Manuscript of the *Anglo-Saxon Chronicle* and Chronicle poems, especially the *Battle of Brunanburh.* Since Anglo-Saxon and Anglo-Latin textuality formed a major contribution to the literary archive in both senses of the term, providing textual exemplars at every level from the transmission of manuscripts to the major genres of literary culture, an investigation of early medieval textuality in Anglo-Saxon England can provide a model for the analysis of other eras in medieval history.

The description and analysis of Old English and early medieval Latin textuality begins with the historical investigation of the culture of the manuscript book, that is, with an archaeology of the text in both the traditional and Foucauldian senses, a study of the historical conditions—material, social, linguistic, institutional—that produced the culture of the text. An early medieval manuscript presupposes historically constituted conditions for textuality: (1) a textual community with knowledge of normative, literary Latin and the technology of manuscript book production; (2) an archive of possibilities for textual language and genres; and (3) a library or larger system of texts within which any text is read or composed.

I am using the term "textual community" here in a broader semiotic and receptionist sense than that used by Brian Stock in recent studies that have given this term currency.[9] A textual community is constituted by two aspects of the social function of texts that are as inseparable as the two sides of a sheet of parchment: a received canon and an interpretive methodology articulated in a body of commentary that accompanied the texts and instituted their canonicity. Canonical texts are those highly valued texts—especially supreme texts like Vergil's *Aeneid* and the Scriptures—to which a community refers for self-definition, authority, and authentification, texts that are the focus of an ongoing interpretive debate.

Anglo-Saxon and early medieval textual communities—in monastery, cathedral, and court centers—were constituted by *grammatica,* the discipline that governed literacy, the study of literary language, the interpretation of texts, and the writing of manuscripts. Consequently, the culture based on Latin manuscript books can be called grammatical culture. *Grammatica*, however, was not simply the source of literacy; as a discipline, it supplied a model for learning and knowledge, a system of discourses that constituted certain objects—texts, statements, meanings, values—as objects of knowledge as such. Grammatical discourse supplied the discursive conditions for textual knowledge of any kind, secular or religious. *Grammatica* was used by early medieval textual communities for self-definition and for circumscribing their own authority and power.[10]

Recent studies have shown that medieval textual communities were formed of literate, semiliterate, and illiterate members: those unable or just learning to read were expected to participate in textual culture, having the necessary texts, and their interpretation, read to them.[11] A manuscript book also presupposes a discursive system marked as literary, containing the genres, the styles, and the discursive regularities for the writing of new texts. The appearance of a book in grammatical culture also occurred within a library of larger intertextual system, which provided both the ground of possibility for a new text and the linguistic and textual space for its reception, intelligibility, and meaning in the community.

The Old English poems belong to two cultural archives simultaneously, orally based poetic tradition and Latin textual culture, and thus, when studied from the point of view of cultural reception, the texts of the poems engage two intertextual systems, two networks of discourse that provided the grounds for the production of new works and for their intelligibility and meaning as interpreted by those receiving them. The tradition of oral-formulaic composition and the genres transmitted in oral tradition were textualized through the technology of script and book production and through the network of Latin texts that formed the basis of grammatical culture in Anglo-Saxon textual communities. Old English poetic texts are constituted by an interplay between the textual memory of an oral culture, known to us only as a dialectical inverse of textual culture inscribed as a trace or absence within a text, and the culture of *grammatica*.[12] The interweaving of these two textual systems needs to be explored further, but what I want to emphasize here is the necessity of examining the Old English poems for the inscription of the textual culture that produced and received them, a subject that has not received the kind of attention given to the study of orality, a matter antecedent to the text itself.

At the level of textuality, then, most Old English poetical texts can be read as textual hybrids, formed from a dialogic interplay or interweaving of two literary languages: indeed, most of the poems in the Old English corpus, as we have them in their written form, presuppose a larger network of

Latin texts and textuality for their very articulation and intelligibility. This intertextual presupposition functioned on several levels that should be made clear before proceeding to a discussion of the literature.

The fundamental material level concerns manuscript culture itself, which was encoded as Latin and Christian textuality prior to its adaptation for English. The appearance of Old English texts at all is the result of the introduction of *grammatica* with the Roman missions to the British Isles: the Latin alphabet and a system of transcription enabled the Old English language to be written. The script used for Old English texts was adapted from the insular script used first for the Latin books of monastic textual culture. Scribes and readers were thus *litteratus* in Latin first before coming to books written in English, and even after the promotion of bilingual literacy by King Alfred and his successors, Latin texts and textuality supplied the models for most English texts, especially for Old English prose (for example, sermons, saints' lives, chronicles).[13]*Grammatica* and the technology of book production were the historical preconditions for the culture of the monastery and church, and, consequently, this culture was the historical precondition for the appearance of Old English texts. All manuscripts were thus initially encoded as instruments of grammatical culture, even after that culture had begun to be textually bilingual. The very fact that Old English poems were recorded in manuscripts signifies that they functioned within the library of textual culture.

This fact is demonstrated in the list of books donated to Exeter Cathedral by Archbishop Leofric around 1070: both Latin and English books were included in the bequest, but more important, Leofric included Latin literary works like Boethius, Prudentius, Sedulius, and Arator as well as the famous *Exeter Book* of Old English poetry; in other words, the English book of poems took its place in the general library of texts in use at Exeter. In the inventory of books and other treasures that Leofric donated, *The Exeter Book* (".i. mycel englisc boc be gehwilcum þingum on leoðwisan geworht") appears as an item directly following an entry for the English version of Boethius and a few items before the list of Latin literary texts. The English books functioned as part of Leofric's library.[14] English books (*Libri Anglici*) are also recorded in a separate category in the twelfth-century Durham library catalogue,[15] which preserves earlier conventions, and a similar "library" status would have been given to many English works following Alfred's program of translation.

Furthermore, on the level of textual relations at a primary archival level, there are very few poems in the extant Old English corpus that do not presuppose the existence of Latin texts, a fact demonstrated by the hundreds of source studies with which most Old English scholars have been preoccupied.[16] A quick scan of the contents of the *Anglo-Saxon Poetic*

Records produces few examples of extant poems that were composed without any prior experience of Latin textuality, and if we consider the poems at the level of textual reception, taking into account the date of their transmission in the manuscripts (the late tenth and early eleventh century), then nearly all of the poems become impossible to interpret as products of an oral and nontextual environment. Identifying sources and influences, however, remains at the level of discrete statements, the primary archive; it is not a study of intertextuality or the rules that generated the texts.

An archaeological study of the main compiled manuscript compilations of Old English poetry discloses an underlying intertextual system formed of an English and Latin literary archive. These are the Junius Manuscript (Oxford, Bodleian Library, Junius 11, s.x/xi), containing *Genesis, Exodus, Daniel, Christ and Satan,* the *Vercelli Book* (Vercelli, Biblioteca Capitolare, CXVII, s.x^2), containing homilies and *Andreas, Fates of the Apostles, Dream of the Rood* and *Elene,* the Beowulf manuscript (London, British Library, Cotton Vitellius A.xv, s.x/xi), containing *Beowulf, Judith* and prose works, and *The Exeter Book* (Exeter, Cathedral Library, 3501, s.x^2), containing a large compilation of poems, including *Christ, Guthlac, The Phoenix, Juliana, The Wanderer, The Seafarer* and many riddles. The editorial titles, of course, are not reliable guides to possible affiliations at the level of the cultural archive, but these codices do reveal that the textuality of grammatical culture is inscribed within the majority of Old English poems at each level from that of their physical form in the manuscripts to that of their (final) composition and reception within a textual community.

At the intertextual level, most Old English poetry and nearly all of the prose is *dialogic,* in Bakhtin's sense of the term: the Old English texts set up an interpretive dialogue with prior texts, and their own textuality is formed from an internal dialogue between the discursive systems that make up English and Latin literary discourse.[17] The resulting dialogical hybrid, formed of *utriusque linguae,* "both languages," is a distinctive feature of Old English textuality.[18] And here I mean "both languages" in two senses: Latin and English as ordinary languages, and the systems of literary discourse produced in those languages that were culturally encoded in very specific ways.

Bakhtin's model of textuality discloses essential features of Old English literature previously unseen or ignored: studied at the level of textuality, many Old English texts can be understood as interpretive rewritings of prior discourse, an ongoing dialogue between a writer, situated in a textual community, and the archive of statements that generates a dialogic response and in which a writer intervenes: in semiotic terms, every statement interprets others and is itself interpretable through and interpreted by additional statements. Many Old English texts presuppose Latin texts and discourse as a formally constitutive feature, linked as text and gloss, an explicit form of textual semiosis, the principle that the interpretation of a text will always take the form of another text. Or to change the textual metaphor, Old English poems are textual palimpsests that reveal another layer (even layers) of language beneath the manifest layer.

The hybrid textuality interwoven through most Old English poems is actually displayed at the discrete verbal level, the level of the primary archive, in three of the extant poems themselves. For example, the poem known as "Aldhelm," which was written in a tenth-century manuscript of Aldhelm's *De virginitate,* employs a lexicon formed of English, Latin, and Latinized Greek words arranged metrically in the Old English poetic line (I set off the Latin words in italics to expose more clearly the hybrid or macaronic textuality of the poem):

> þus me gesette   *sanctus et iustus*
> beorn boca gleaw,   *bonus auctor*
> Ealdelm, æþele sceop,   *etiam fuit*
> *ipselos* on æðele   Anglosexna,
> byscop on Bretene[19]

> (Thus he established me,   *the holy and just*
> man, wise in books,   *a good author*
> Aldhelm, the noble poet,   *who was once*
> *highest* among the noble   Anglo-Saxons,
> a bishop in Britain.)

The Old English *Phoenix,* based on the Latin poem attributed to Lactantius, concludes with similarly mixed poetic lines, following a consistent pattern of Old English in the first and Latin in the second half-line:

> Hafað us alyfed   *lucis auctor*
> þæt we motun her   *merueri,*
> goddædum begietan   *gaudia in celo*
> þær we motun   *maxima regna*
> secan ond gesittan   *sedibus altis*
> ligan in lisse   *lucis et pacis*

$$(667-72)^{20}$$

> (*The author of light*   has granted us
> that here we may   *merit,*
> obtain by good works,   *joy in heaven,*
> where we may seek out   *great kingdoms*

and sit upon   *lofty thrones,*
live in the grace   *of light and peace) . . .*

A similar strategy was used by the writer of the poem known as "A Summons to Prayer," one of a group of Old English poems written in a composite eleventh-century manuscript containing the *Regularis Concordia,* Wulfstan's homilies, laws, and other texts.[21] These experiments at linguistically hybrid poetry were an extension of the glossematic or hermeneutical style used by some Anglo-Latin writers.[22]

Some Anglo-Saxon writers and readers were capable of textual and linguistic code switching, manipulating two or more textual languages. This capability was evidently possible for some scholars very early on in Anglo-Saxon grammatical culture: Bede describes Tobias, bishop of Rochester (d. 726), a student of Theodore and Hadrian at Canterbury, as "a man equipped in the Latin, Greek, and English languages and in manifold learning."[23] Bede himself was known as a scholar of his own language, having translated a part of John's Gospel into English, and he "was learned" in traditional English poetry.[24] Hybridization could also work in the other direction, as Aldhelm's Latin verse, which exhibits an excessive use of alliteration, shows.[25] King Alfred is usually credited with initiating the use of English as an official, textual language, and his program of translation discloses the appropriation or co-opting of the values of Latin grammatical culture for English texts, a fact disclosed in his famous preface to the translation of Gregory's *Pastoral Care.* And of course the most famous example of high-level bilingual textual competence is Ælfric, who wrote with equal facility in Latin and English and even composed a grammatical handbook in English to introduce English speakers to textual Latin.

Other evidence from the verbal or primary archival level, like the use of Latin loan-words in the poems, could be added to these observations, but that would not explain the textual *system* itself, the rules for generating this hybrid or dialogical discourse, the textual conditions for its possibility. The poems usually considered anomalous curiosities like "Aldhelm" and the conclusion to *The Phoenix,* composed as a mixture of English and Latin, should be read as literary icons, disclosing, in the surface features of the language, deeper structures of discourse that are ordinarily invisible but everywhere present. In other words, we must look for the underlying discursive rules, the grammar of the system itself; that is, we must proceed to the second level of archival analysis, the level of discursive relations and the system of organization that made possible the discrete statements and individual texts. H. R. Jauss, in his major statement of reception theory, sums up this approach: "it must also be possible to take a synchronic cross-section of a moment in the development [of production and recep-

tion], to arrange the heterogeneous multiplicity of contemporaneous works
in equivalent, opposing, and hierarchical structures, and thereby to discover
an overarching system of relationships in the literature of a historical
moment."[26] What follows in this essay will be an attempt to define more
precisely the hybrid textuality of Old English literature by discovering the
"overarching system of relationships" that constituted the textual culture of
the period.

Textual Archaeology: Lexicon, Gloss, Compilation, Library, Encyclopedia

I would like to propose a way of analyzing Old English and early medieval Latin textuality by extending a procedure in the archaeological
method that entails applying the principle of linguistic and discursive levels, as distinguished in semiotic and linguistic analysis, to some of the dominant genres and systems of textual organization observable at the primary
archival level—like the notion of the wordhoard and the library as textual
system. This strategy defines more precisely the way an archaeology of
early medieval textuality could proceed.

Linguistics and semiotics depend on the ability to describe language at
the various levels of linguistic function, conventionally the phonological,
morphological, lexical, syntactic, semantic, sentence, and discourse levels.
Each level in a series is defined both by relations among like elements of
the same level and by vertical relations among levels, the elements of any
level understood to be included in those above it.[27] According to the seminal definition of Emile Beveniste:

> Linguistic entities being discrete, they admit of two types of relationships:
> between elements of the same level or between elements of different lev-
> els. These relationships must be clearly distinguished. Between elements
> of the same level, the relationships are *distributional;* between elements of
> different levels, they are *integrative.*[28]

For example, the sentence or propositional level includes all the functions
of the lower levels from phoneme to syntax and semantics. Linguistics ordinarily ends with the sentence level, and for the study of texts we must
rely on semiotics and discourse analysis to supply further gradations of distinctive levels of description: "it is in discourse . . . that language (*langue*)
is formed and takes shape."[29] The stratification of discursive levels as manifest in the texts and genres of a period can be examined to provide clues
for mapping out the larger fields of a textual system.

In other words, we can understand Anglo-Saxon textual discourse as being distributed along a series of levels, allowing various textual genres to function as models of discourse that disclose a larger underlying grammar, in the same way that the ending of *The Phoenix* can be read as an icon for the hybrid Latin-English textuality which constitutes the poem as a whole. This kind of analysis produces a description of transtextual and transgeneric models of "fields of readability" or strata in the cultural archive that supplied fundamental conditions for the writing and reception of new texts, a description of the ways textual culture was organized from within, as it were, in a series of synchronic discursive relations.

A survey of the main genres and types of discourse practiced in England by the end of the ninth century will reveal that literary culture can be described in at least five systematizing levels of discourse—what I will term here *macrogenres*—which can be elucidated by an archaeology of their material and discursive forms; that is, the literary system of language and texts was organized into various discursive levels functioning with distinctive horizontal and vertical relations. These macrogenres are the lexicon, the gloss, the compilation, the library, and the encyclopedia. Analogous to linguistic and semiotic levels, the higher levels in this series can be understood to embrace the lower, analogous to the features of distribution and integration observable among elements in the levels below the discursive.

For example, a glossary list, a set of glosses or notes transmitted with a specific text like Boethius, a compilation like *The Exeter Book,* the library at Wearmouth-Jarrow, and Isidore's *Origines sive etymologiae* presuppose larger systems of discourse, systems of linguistic and textual organization that functioned as ground or condition for the historically located cultural products. In semiotic terms, these texts are discrete instantiations (tokens) of abstract models of discursive organization (types, macrogenres). Thus, reading at the level of cultural systems, the Harley glossary, the widely distributed glosses on Prudentius or Arator, the grammatical compilation Bodleian Add.C.141, the Junius manuscript, and the library at Canterbury need to be understood as instances of larger discursive modeling systems, which the individual products presuppose as the ground of their possibility per se.

Furthermore, these macrogenres not only organized language and texts in a larger system but also functioned *within* individual works themselves, providing principles for composition and interpretation. Thus, Alfred's translations and the poems by Cynewulf, for example, will reveal that the principles of gloss, compilation, and the library function in a formally constitutive way for the composition and organization of *individual* texts. The textual principles writ large or macrotextually in the literary categories of

lexicon, gloss, compilation, library, and encyclopedia are also inscribed mi-
crotextually as organizing and interpretive principles in individual texts. I
would like to examine briefly each of these macrogenres and then present a
few examples to show how they are distributed throughout the literature.

The idea of a literary lexicon is supplied by the extending the notion of
the wordhoard to the level of discursive type, and thus forms the first archaeological stratum of early medieval textuality. In Old English poetry,
"wordhord" signifies not only the repertoire of language but the power of
language symbolic of the speaker's power.[30] As macrogenre, the cultural
lexicon functions at the level of *langue* rather that *parole*, competence
rather than performance. The literary lexicon is the ideal, organized dictionary of the writer and interpreter, in which words are marked for levels of
style and generic function. The poetic lexicon contains the formulae for
composition—context specific diction—as a system of abstract or ideal
patterns capable of metrical-syntactic variation. The lexicon distinguishes
poetic versus prose usage, specialized vocabulary for various trades, disciplines, sciences, and institutions (the various lexica of each discourse), historically accrued sense, and etymological force. For the Anglo-Saxon
textual community by the tenth century, the lexicon was bilingual and
therefore also included a system of substitutions or glosses in the sense of a
glossary list.[31]

The gloss was such a universally employed practice that one can easily
extract from the manuscripts the larger code that governed the compilation of glossaries and the writing of interlinear notes and marginal
commentary.[32] The gloss is essentially an interpretive supplement, a set of
expressions that attempts to disclose some latent or suppressed meaning in
an earlier set of expressions.[33] By the end of the eighth or beginning of the
ninth century, the layout of the most highly valued texts began to accom-
modate the practice of grammatical *enarratio*—textual interpretation—by
providing marginal and interlinear space for the transcription of glosses simultaneously with the main text. In semiotic terms, the glosses inscribed in
the space between the lines and around the text in the margins disclose that
a text is made intelligible or interpreted only through another text. What a
text means cannot be disclosed by simply copying the text over again either
on the same page or in another codex. The gloss or commentary as it was
presented on the page appears as an externalization of textual meaning, a
spatial dislocation or separation of text and meaning, a formal representation of interpretive supplementarity. The externality or marginality of commentary, an additional text extending a prior text in another textual space,
is formally reenacted in the writing of texts within the larger library: the
spatial dislocation of the gloss is recapitulated in the writing of other texts
in additional codices that supplement texts already in the library. The gloss

thus forms a node in the intertextual network: as the gloss supplements a text through an additional text, presenting an interpretation that is itself a text, so does the writing of a new text. Many Old English texts can thus be read as extended glosses on the Latin texts they supplement or interpret.

The literary principle of compilation took the concrete form of the miscellany and the anthology or compiled codex, but *compilatio* can also be seen as a macrogenre inscribed throughout a vast number of medieval texts. At the level of discursive type, the organizing principle of *compilatio* governed both the production of compiled codices and the composition of new texts. There were three common tropes used to describe the composition of a text from the archive of writings from the past; the bee who gathers the materials for honey from diverse flowers and fields; a gathering or arrangement of flowers from various fields; and *silva* (forest, lumber, raw materials) assembled from a "forest" of earlier works from which a new textual structure is built. Works that explicitly exemplify the principle of *compilatio* range from Clement of Alexandria's *Stromateis (Miscellanies)* to Aulus Gellius's *Attic Nights*, Macrobius's *Saturnalia*, and Isidore of Seville's *Etymologiae*. But many other early medieval works are also self-consciously compilations, like Cassiodorus's *Institutiones*, Aldhelm's *Epistola ad Acircium (De metris ac pedum regulis)*, Bede's grammatical treatises and even his *Historia ecclesiastica*, *The Anglo-Saxon Chronicle*, and Byrhtferth's *Manual*. The main principle of *compilatio* was the selection of materials from the cultural library so that the resulting collection forms an *interpretive* arrangement of texts and discourse.

The organizing principle of *compilatio* provided a model of composition and interpretation that touched nearly all medieval literary discourse. Isidore of Seville defines *auctor* as a derivation of the verb *augeo*, "increase" or "enlarge." An *auctor*, "author" or "orginator," is therefore an augmentor, one who expands writing.[34] He defines a *compilator* as a mixer and cites the tradition of calling Vergil a *compilator:* "*compilator*, one who mixes things said by others (*aliena dicta*) with his own words as paint dealers are accustomed to pound together various mixes in a mortar (*pila*). The Mantuan poet [Vergil] was once accused of this crime when, transposing certain verses of Homer, he blended them in with his own and was called a plunderer of the ancients (*compilator veterum*) by his rivals."[35] In classical and late Latin, *compilator*, "one who plunders or pillages," was frequently used as a term for a plagiarist, and it became commonplace to discuss how poets plundered one another's works in composing poetry.

The literary assumptions behind Isidore's definition of *compilator* are provided by Macrobius. The *Saturnalia* demonstrates that Vergil's works were interpreted through the intertextual network of the late imperial canon. All of the *Aeneid* is taken to be "a kind of mirror of Homer's work.''[36] All the poets are said to convert the words of others (*aliorum dicta*) to their own use, a practice that is called "plundering the library of earlier authors" (*se mutuo conpilarint bibliothecae veteris auctores*).[37] The writer is thus a *compilator bibliothecae*, a plunderer of the whole library of accumulated texts.

The principle of *compilatio* functioned at various textual levels from that of material and physical arrangement of a codex to that of the larger cultural library of texts and genres that supplied the systems of discourse capable of rearrangement, repetition, and interpretation. The manuscript form of texts compels us to investigate the relations established among texts at the level of their material or physical form in individual manuscripts. Texts arranged or grouped together in the physical divisions of a manuscript, that is in self-contained gatherings or booklets, must be examined at the most fundamental archaeological level, the material form of the codex.[38] The culture of the manuscript book is distinguished from that of the uniform printed book by the existence of a *material intertextuality* specific to the form that texts take in individual manuscripts. For example, the *The Battle of Brunanburh* and other Chronicle poems exist only in manuscripts of *The Anglo-Saxon Chronicle*, certain of which reveal the function of the poems at the material level of a compiled codex, and *The Dream of the Rood* exists in a unique copy in a compiled codex that also contains *Elene*, a poem on the finding of the Cross. These material facts have an important bearing on the meaning of the poems for Anglo-Saxon readers and cannot be ignored when considering the levels of intertextuality at work in Old English texts.[39]

A library assumes not only that there is an archive of texts available to a culture but that these texts are understood as part of a *system*. No text is read in isolation but as part of an organized system of texts. A subset of the library is the textual canon, the *auctores*, the authorized group of privileged texts. The library as discursive system is, of course, always larger than any one library: the cultural library is the repertoire of all discursive possibilities realized in texts. The library, considered as a distinct level for arranging discourse, is thus the ground of intertextuality, the conditions of possibility for the making of new texts and for the intelligibility and meaning of texts already organized in the library. Included in the library are books on the library itself, keys to the bookcase, as it were, like grammatical treatises, commentaries, and encyclopedias. Extant medieval booklists and library catalogues reveal some of the organizing principles used in medieval libraries.[40] The idea of the library as system emerges quite clearly from these surviving catalogues.

Finally, the encyclopedia functions transtextually and transgenerically as the sum of discourses that provide the possibilities for knowledge articulated in the discursive practices of various disciplines. The encyclopedia also supplies a system of correspondences, codes, and rules for interpretation that allow knowledge to be produced through texts. The distinguishing feature of the encyclopedia is its organization by discursive field rather than by work or genre. Encyclopedias known in the Anglo-Saxon period attempted to systematize and compile material from prior texts according to discursive practices: Cassiodorus's *Institutiones,* Isidore of Seville's *Origines sive etymologiae* and *De natura rerum,* Aldhelm's *De virginitate* and *Epistola ad Acircium,* Bede's *De natura rerum,* Rabanus Maurus's *De clericorum institutione,* and Byrhtferth's *Manual.*

In the case studies that follow, I will focus on the macrogenres of gloss, compilation, and library as major organizing structures in the literature of the Anglo-Saxon period.

Writing the Oral: Textual Culture and Orality

Grammatical culture eventually prevailed over oral culture in the early Middle Ages, but of course, an "oral residue," in Ong's terms, lingered in many of the genres of Old English long after their textualization. Recent studies have shown the profound effects that literacy and the technology of the book have had on oral cultures,[41] but I wish to investigate here the inscription of textual culture in the archive of Anglo-Saxon texts, rather than pursuing an afterimage of orality thought to be observable in the texts.

Many members of Anglo-Saxon society in the era of the text would have occupied a position somewhere along a sliding scale between complete ignorance of literate culture and full expertise in *grammatica* and matters of a textual competence.[42] However, an illiterate or semiliterate member of a textual community in a monastery, cathedral, or court—or an unlettered member of the ruling class in a society controlled by centers of power where writing prevails—was quite distinct from a member of a preliterate or nonliterate culture, Ong's "primary oral culture," a culture totally unaffected by the text.[43] Orality is thus unknown to us except as the dialectical other of grammactical culture.[44]

To place the question of orality and textuality in its historical context, let us first consider the textual culture of monasticism, the culture that introduced writing and the technology of the book in Anglo-Saxon England. The conditions for textual culture defined by monastic *grammatica* were sporadic and isolated in the seventh and eighth centuries but spread throughout England after the tenth century monastic reform movement, which was authenticated by the English kings themselves. Monastic *gram-*

matica, with its ideological affiliations with court and church centers, became normative, defining both textual culture and the role of its illiterate members.

Monastic meditative reading, *lectio divina*, was an extension of grammatical *lectio* and *enarratio* applied to the Scriptures and Christian literature. Benedict's *Rule* assumes that reading would be oral, indeed, that reading meant listening to a text read aloud, privately or publicly.[45] Monastic life was built around *lectio, lectiones,* and the work of the *lector,* who was considered so essential as to merit punishment for mistakes in pronunciation during the liturgy (*Rule of St. Benedict,* 45). *Lectio divina* meant reflective, private study (*meditare aut legere,* 48.23), in which the text was orally constituted and interpreted for its significance (8.3; 48.4–5, 10–23).[46] Reading was treated as part of the monks' daily manual labor (48.1–14), the most detailed instructions for which are those for Lent, when each member of the community received a book from the library which was to be read straight through (*per ordinem*). The *Rule* also assumes that books and records will be made, a library maintained, and writing materials available for every member of the community.[47]

The institutional and social force of *grammatica* in monastic culture is also demonstrated by the requirement that illiterate or unlearned members of the community participate in literate culture. Monastic culture is frequently characterized as being highly oral, based on oral reading and instruction, but this oral culture was essentially textual, and those unable or just learning to read had the necessary texts read to them: the prayers of the daily office and the Scriptures were read and chanted (8–19), the *Rule* itself was to be read to the whole community (66.8), the entire Psalter was to be read through once weekly (18.22–25), and other highly valued texts were read aloud at meals and at appropriate times in the liturgy (38; 9.8; 73.4). Before taking vows, the novice was required to have the *Rule* read to him three times during his novitiate (58.9–14), and the vows were made in the form of a promise written in his own hand. If he happened to be illiterate (*non scit litteras*), someone else could write it, but the novice himself needed to place his mark (*signum*) on the document, which he then placed on the altar with his own hand. The writing and the offering of the promise were to be done *manu sua,* "with his own hand" (58.19–20). Thus the initiation into the community required an acknowledgment of textual power, and writing was seen as intimately connected to the state of the soul, an externalized or visible sign of an inner intention.

Old English literature was composed, compiled, and transmitted in this textual environment, and the texts bear an inscription of a historically constituted textuality. This textuality, especially the poetry, indeed inscribes an orally based social past, but both constructs the written image of orality and cancels its pretextual valence in the act of inscribing it. By representing oral production in written discourse, orality becomes a *significatum* of textuality, an element of written discourse, or in Franz Bäuml's terms, a "fiction" of written culture.[48] The text knows, and can represent, oral culture; oral culture has no analogous knowledge of the text.

A larger question remains: what was the function of Old English poetic texts in the grammatical culture that commited them to writing? How was the newly textualized oral culture, most evident in the heroic texts, understood by the Anglo-Saxons themselves? Rather than accepting orality as a given even for the Anglo-Saxon textual community, I propose to question the function of *texts* of poetry, whose form bears an afterimage of oral culture, in an age of great textual sophistication. To what extent did a form of cultural nostalgia, and the ideological uses of nostalgia or historical myth making, motivate the writing, copying, and preservation of poetic texts in the late ninth through mid–eleventh centuries? The writing, copying, and compiling of Old English poetic texts must be examined for indications of a nostalgia for a lost, or at least historically prior, oral past, a past that knew the presence of the voice and the commemoration of racial heroes in a poet's performance. Too often the fact that Old English texts survive in tenth and eleventh-century manuscripts is accepted simply as a historical given rather than a historical problem in its own right.[49] Answers to these questions can be sought in an archaeology of the text.

Cædmon as Glossator: The *Illiteratus* in the Monastic Textual Community

Bede's hagiographic narrative of the poet Cædmon has long been a crux in the debate between proponents of oral culture and their critics, but the debate has overlooked a central feature of Bede's account, which surfaces only at the level of textuality and the historical investigation of textual communities—the necessity of an *illiteratus* participating in monastic, Latin textual culture. The example of Cædmon is of great interest but in precisely the reverse direction maintained by theorists of oral poetry: Bede's account of Cædmon and his "Hymn" itself recapitulate textual, grammatical culture rather than representing preliterate oral practice or the active presence of orality within the textual culture presumed to have superseded it.

According to Bede's narrative, Cædmon was an illiterate member of the monastic textual community—at first as lay laborer and then as monk—and Bede's account affirms that the inability to read did not exempt Cædmon from participating in literate culture. On the contrary, Cædmon had the texts of the Scriptures *read to him* as prescribed by monastic practice: "whatever he learned from the sacred writings through his translators he produced, after a short while, in the most pleasing poetical language and in his own language, which was English" ("quicquid ex divinis litteris per interpretes disceret, hoc ipse post pusillum verbis poeticis maxima suavitate et conpunctione conpositis in sua, id est Anglorum, lingua proferret"). The Old English version is also quite explicit about the textual nature of Cædmon's poetic gift: "swa hwæt swa he of godcundum stafum þurh boceras geleornode, þæt he æfter medmiclum fæce in scopgereorde mid þa mæstan swetnisse ond inbryrdnisse geglæged ond in Engliscgereorde wel geworht forþbrohte."[50] "Stafas" is the English equivalent of *litterae* (writings, texts), and Cædmon is instructed by "boceras," an even more explicitly textual reference than the Latin *interpretes*. And, of course, in his dream Cædmon is instructed to sing about the *principium creaturarum,* the first event in the master narrative of sacred history, the poem of which he re-members (*memoriter retinuit*) and recites the next day for the rest of the community. The leaders of the textual community (*multis doctoribus viris praesentibus*) listened to Cædmon's story of the dream and to his poem (*carmen*), and after determining that the gift of song was divine, the leaders explained other passages of sacred history and doctrine, bidding him to transfer this discourse (*sermo*) into poetry ("exponebantque illi quendam sacrae historiae sive doctrinae sermonem, praecipientes eum, si posset, hunc in modulationem carminis transferre").

Furthermore, the first thing Hild has Cædmon do after he joins the monastery is learn sacred history ("iussitque illum seriem sacrae historiae doceri"). Bede states that Cædmon listened to the texts read to him, and then Bede adds something distinctive of the monastic textual community: Cædmon is described as ruminating on the texts that were read for him before he turned them into poetry. The image of the clean animal chewing the cud (Lev. 11:3; Deut. 14:6) had become a traditional metaphor for monastic meditative *lectio* or *ruminatio.*[51] Although Cædmon remained *illiteratus* himself, he was expected to participate in textual culture and could meditate on texts read to him. Bede's description, of course, reveals more about the interpretation of the Cædmon story as a reiteration of grammatical culture than about any event that may lie behind it. But it is precisely the *representation* that is significant, that is, its textualized reception.

Viewed as an event assimilated into textual culture, Bede's account of Cædmon is not, in Magoun's words, "the case history of an Anglo-Saxon oral singer."[52] It is not a story of a lost, reconstructable, oral past, but an especially valuable disclosure of the textuality of grammatical culture at work in Old English poems. Cædmon's "Hymn," and whatever else he composed after listening to texts read to him, functioned as extended glosses on the central texts of the monastic textual community, supplementary texts that extended and interpreted the *sermo* of authoritative texts: Bede states that Cædmon added (*adiunxit,* OE *geþeode*) many words of poetry to what he remembered in his dream, and we can read this verb as characteristic of Cædmonian poetry as a whole—poems as additions or supplements. Bede's description of Cædmon's poems indicates that the genre closest to Cædmon's work was the Old English interpretive gloss, of which many survive in Latin manuscripts produced in Anglo-Saxon England. Cædmon's teachers were not interested in having Cædmon produce texts that *substituted* for the Scriptures or other Christian literature. He was not translating in the modern sense of supplying a substitute text that takes the place of the original for people who do not know the original language. Cædmonian poetry was a supplement, a set of glosses, for a textual community that was becoming textually bilingual but primarily constituted by Latin textuality or grammatical culture. In other words, Cædmon sang in a library, not a mead hall.

Cædmon's "Hymn" has been shown to be almost totally formulaic, composed in metrical units found elsewhere in Old English Christian poetry, but formulas that *already* reflected textual culture, Latin Christianity, before Cædmon composed his poem.[53] Earlier philologists saw the immediacy of the poet's voice and authentic primitive culture in the formula, the written record of which was a trail of improvisational, oral composition, poetic composition in the performance of the poem itself.[54] The Old English formula is now rightly understood as an abstract model for possible poetic statements, all of the instantiations of which are not recorded in the extant texts. Rather than providing an origin for poetry, the formula is an anonymous intertextual and transtextual unit drawn from a wordhoard, the poetic lexicon, a metrical and syntactical model whose very mode of being is that which is always already said before. A formula can only be such by being the model of an already-said in an iterable metrical environment. The "source" of a formula is not a prior text but the specialized lexicon of poetry and the underlying poetic grammar that governs it: an Old English poem is essentially mosaic of textual citations that have lost their origin. The fact of formulaic diction, then, leads to the anonymous intertextual archive. The formulaic structure of Cædmon's "Hymn" reveals not the identity of the poet in the spoken performance but the final anonymity of Old English poetry. Cædmon is a poet finally anonymous.

King Alfred's Description of *Compilatio*

King Alfred's versions of Augustine's *Soliloquies* and Boethius's *De consolatione philosophiae* in both form and content disclose the dialogical hybrid of Anglo-Saxon textuality, but I can only point out here the significance of Alfred's own attempt to describe composition as an act of interpretive compilation. Alfred's version of the *Soliloquies* has the outward form of a spoken dialogue but represents textual memory, *bocstafas*, writing, as the externalization of memory. At the beginning of the dialogue, Augustine reflects on the mind's inability to retain all that is entrusted to it. Reason (*sceadwisnes*) then commands the speaker to commit his thoughts to *bocstafas*, the written externalization of memory: "befæste hit þonne bocstafum and awrit it."[55] Wisdom is not simply a matter of transmitting oral tradition in writing: wisdom, in Alfred's works, has become an inscription of textual memory, interpreting—and locating itself in—the library.

The incipits and explicits in Alfred's version of the *Soliloquies* give the work the appearance of a florilegium or compilation rather than a translation.[56] The preface employs the *silva* metaphor—writing as compiling material from a "forest" of prior texts—but some of the explicits and incipits refer to the work as *þa blostma*,[57] "blossoms," "flowers," typical for a florilegium, and others as a selection of *cwidas*, "sayings," "words,"[58] In the preface to the work, Alfred's redeploys the trope of *silva* for an an extended allegory of writing as *compilatio*:

> Gaderode me þonne kigclas and stuþansceaftas, and lohsceaftas and hylfa to ælcum þara tola þe ic mid wircan cuðe, and bohtimbru and bolttimbru, and, to ælcum þara weorca þe ic wyrcan cuðe, þa wlitegostan treowe be þam dele ðe ic aberan meihte. Ne com ic naþer mid anre byrðene ham þe me ne lyste ealne þane wude ham brengan, gif ic hyne ealne aberan meihte; on ælcum treowo ic geseah hwæthwugu þæs þe ic æt ham beþorfte. Forþam ic lære ælcne ðara þe maga si and manigne wæn hæbbe, þæt he menige to þam ilcan wuda þar ic ðas stuðansceaftas cearf, fetige hym þar ma, and gefeðrige hys wænas mid fegrum gerdum, þat he mage windan manigne smicerne wah, and manig ænlic hus settan, and fegerne tun timbrian, and þær murge and softe mid mæge on-eardian ægðer ge wintras ge sumeras, swa swa ic nu ne gyt ny dyde.[59]

> (Then I gathered for myself staves, posts, and tie-beams, and handles for each of the tools that I knew how to use, and building-lumber and beam-lumber, and, for each of the structures I knew how to build, as many of the most beautiful trees that I could carry. I never came home with a single load without wishing to bring home the whole forest with me, if I could have carried it all. In every tree I saw something I needed at home. Therefore I instructed each of those who is able and has many wagons to direct himself to the same forest where I cut these posts; let him fetch more there and load his wagons with fine branches so that he can weave many a beautiful wall and build many an excellent house and build a fine town, and live therein with kinsmen happily and comfortably both in winter and summer, as I have not yet done.)

Alfred continues the trope for many more sentences, indicating that his earthly building from materials in the "wudu" (*silva*) of Christian writings is a preparation for an eternal dwelling. Earlier commentators on this passage missed Alfred's rhetorical gesture toward the Latin *silvae* tradition, the genre of the compiled miscellany of timber or matter (*silva*, Greek *hyle*) which can stand alone as a collection or provide raw material for other works. Although he knew the *blostma* metaphor,[60] Alfred chose the trope *silva* for his preface, which is an allegory of writing in the Christian textual community, the institution which Alfred earnestly desired to authorize as king and participate in as contributor. The Latin term *silva* is literally "forest," "woods," or "lumber," "building material taken from a forest," and the word acquired the philosophical sense of "matter" or "raw material" from which created things were made. The plural, *silvae*, was used early in Latin literary tradition for collections or miscellanies, and there were many metaphorical equivalents of *silvae* in late classical tradition, some of which were known to Alfred. The textual metaphor is clearly indicated in Alfred's use of verbs for building structures out of material from the forest, especially "windan" (weave) and "timbrian" ("build with timber).

Isidore of Seville provides a definition of *silva* closest to Alfred's use of the metaphor. In his chapter *De elementis*, an account of matter (*hyle*), Isidore relates that *hyle* means unformed *materia*: "consequently, poets call matter *silva*, and not inaptly, since raw materials are from the woods" ("Proinde et eam [hylen] poetae silvam nominaverunt, nec incongrue, quia materiae silvarum sunt").[61] Anglo-Saxon writers also exploited the literary sense of term. Aldhelm uses the phrase *densa latinitatis silva*, "thick forest of latinity," with reference to the language material from which he must deduce the metrical rules for his *De metris*.[62] Boniface, in the preface to his *Ars grammatica*, uses the same tropes as Alfred to describe his compilation of an authoritative *ars* from classical sources:

> As I enter into the ancient forest (*antiquam silvam*) of grammarians' intricate density to collect for you the best of each diverse fruits and the diffused fragrances of various flowers, which are found dispersed everywhere through the woodlands of the grammarians, for the daily nourishment of our diligent study and a fragrant garland of your youthful talent, so that I have presented to you the best and most necessary, piled together and shortened, packing them together by filling one pouch, as it were.[63]

Alfred expands this trope into an allegory of writing in the Christian textual community: he states that writing is a matter of finding the right *materia* or *silva* (OE *wudu*) to arrange into a spiritually rewarding compilation, assuming that writing itself is essentially an act of compiling earlier texts into a new interpretive arrangement. Alfred is thus signalling his literary role as *compilator bibliothecae*, a role he would follow in the writing of his version of Boethius's *De consolatione philosophiae*.

Brunanburh and the Chronicle Poems: Textualization, Ideology, Nostalgia

The heroic poem, The Battle of Brunanburh, which appears as the entry for 937 in 4 manuscripts of *The Anglo-Saxon Chronicle*,[64] represents the appropriation of traditional, orally rooted poetry by textual culture. The Chronicle poems disclose that by the tenth century the traditional lexicon and metrical form of heroic poetry had become newly encoded with a contemporary political, racial, and national value, capable of expressing a cultural ideology. The cultural function of traditional verse making—memorialization and eulogy—was transferred to and inscribed in the text of the Chronicle, a text compiled from earlier texts and firmly rooted in textual culture.[65] The contexts of the poems within *The Anglo-Saxon Chronicle* clearly indicate that Latin annals and histories as well as the Chronicle itself provided an essential intertextual frame for the poems. Furthermore, *Brunanburh* presupposes the textualization of history in annals and historical narratives, a textualization that is ideologically encoded for the creation of national myths of origin and dynastic succession.[66] But the larger social and political significance of *Brunanburh* is disclosed only by examining its function as part of a *compilatio* of historical narrative.

The Chronicle poems also reveal that the poetic form itself had become a vehicle for nostalgia, for the repetition of the heroic in the present. The traditional form was used to create an image of an unbroken tradition of national and racial heroic glory extending from the earlier kings in the Anglo-Saxon royal genealogy to the house of Alfred: the poetic medium for representing the heroic past was appropriated for representing a new "heroism" of the English kings in the creation of a national kingdom. *Brunanburh* memorializes an event that symbolized the solidification of English power by Athelstan and praises the heroic continuity of the Wessex dynasty.[67] *Brunanburh* and the Chronicle poems disclose the extent to which the writing of traditional, formulaic poetry in the tenth and eleventh centuries necessarily meant composing in a consciously archaizing form;[68] that is, writing poetry in the traditional form was an act of poetic nostalgia in the era of the text. The very form of the traditional diction, formulas, and meter was ideologically encoded to link the present to the heroic past. Poetic nostalgia thus became a vehicle for a larger ideological program served by the writing and disseminating of histories and historical praise poems.

The Chronicle poems need to be understood in the context of the annal entries as they appear in the manuscripts, and for my discussion here I will focus on the poems in the recension of the Chronicle in the Parker manuscript, Corpus Christi College, Cambridge, MS 173 (once owned by Archbishop Parker in the sixteenth century, known as manuscript A of *The Anglo-Saxon Chronicle*). This manuscript transmits the texts of *The Battle of Brunanburh*, *The Capture of the Five Boroughs*, *The Coronation of Edgar*, and *The Death of Edgar* in a separable gathering containing a continuation of the Chronicle, in various hands and dates, from 925–1072.[69] MS A of the Chronicle may have been copied and compiled at Winchester, the seat of the Wessex kings after Alfred, but if not there then certainly at a scriptorium with strong political affiliations with Winchester. Although it does not preserve the fullest text and is at least one or two removes from an original version, MS A clearly reveals a tenth-century compiler's attempt at making a coherent statement about the unified English nation won by the Wessex dynasty,[70] a statement that has an important bearing on the meaning and function of the poems included as Chronicle entries. Both the material and discursive levels of intertextuality are disclosed in this manuscript: the Chronicle poems in MS A are all found in a gathering of the continuation of the Chronicle inserted by a compiler in the second half of the tenth century.

CCCC 173 is a composite manuscript of five separable booklets (gatherings or units of gatherings capable of being rearranged or detached) and the compilation was worked on continually from the end of the ninth to the early twelfth century.[71] The last two booklets (a bifolium of episcopal and papal lists and four quires containing an eighth-century copy of Caelius Sedulius's *Carmen Paschale* with Old English glosses) are irrelevant to the plan of the tenth-century compiler who organized the manuscript to include the quire containing the Chronicle poems. The first three booklets contain (1) a genealogy of the West Saxon royal house to Alfred, the "common recension" of *The Anglo-Saxon Chronicle* to 891 (all by one scribe), and the first continuation of the Chronicle to 924, containing the only extant copy of the last campaigns of Edward the Elder (ff. 1–25, s. ix ex.–x. in.), (2) a quire containing a continuation of the Chronicle from 925–1070 (the Winchester hand, however, stops at 1001), which contains all the Chronicle poems in this manuscript, and the acts of Lanfranc, which were added at the end of the eleventh century after the manuscript had been taken to Canterbury (ff. 26–32, s. x med.–s.xi[2]), and (3) the laws of Alfred and Ine (ff. 33–52, s. x med.).

Booklet 1 was the earliest, and extends from genealogy of the house of Wessex (a preface to the Chronicle), to an affirmation of this dynastic authority in King Edward's victories and consolidation of power: the conclud-

ing entry (924) by the scribe who finished the first booklet records that
Mercia, Northumbria, the Scots, and the Welsh all accepted Edward as
"father and lord." The scribe stopped copying in the middle of the page (f.
25v), evidently where his exemplar ended. In the middle of the tenth century, during or after the reign of Athelstan, what is now booklet 3, containing the laws of Alfred and Ine, was joined to booklet 1, and thus the first
compilation of the manuscript sought to codify and glorify English rule
under the Alfredian dynasty. A second compiler, probably in the last quar-
ter of the tenth century, inserted the gathering that is now booklet 2 (the
continuation of the Chronicle with the Chronicle poems) between the first
two booklets, and it is clear that he was continuing the ideological program
of the first compiler. The original tenth-century form of the manuscript (the
genealogy, the chronicle to 924, and the laws of Alfred and Ine) represents,
as Parkes has stated, "a conscious attempt on the part of this compiler . . .
to preserve the tradition of the West Saxon royal house in its purest
form. . . . The form of the compilation of the Parker manuscript in the
mid-tenth century emphasizes the previous achievments of this dynasty."[72]
In a compilation that had already joined together three related textual
genres (genealogy, annal, laws) in promoting a historical myth of the English royal house, the second compiler added the continuation of the Chronicle with the poems whose traditional form was already encoded for
representing the heroic past and praising kings and warriors.

The Chronicle entries in booklet 2, from 925 on, are quite sparse except for the Chronicle poems, which constitute the bulk of the text in the
continuation copied in MS A. Although other manuscripts of the Chronicle,
produced in scriptoria with sources apparently unknown to the Winchester
scribes, preserve more historical information for the years after 925 as well
as the Chronicle poems, there is a single-mindedness to the Parker compilation that opens a window onto the function and meaning of the Chronicle
poems.[73] The first page of booklet 2 (f. 27r) begins with the entry for 925
and links the continuation with the political achievements of Edward the
Elder, with which the first booklet concluded: "925 In this year King Edward passed away, and Athelstan his son succeeded to the kingdom." *The
Battle of Brunanburh*, embedded between entries on the reign of Athelstan
(ff. 26v–27r), clearly becomes the main vehicle of memorialization and
praise for the king who consolidated power for the house of Wessex. There
is no change of layout for the poem, but the text is distinguished from the
other entries by the use of a medial point, which may have been added by a
later scribe, to mark half-line divisions in the poetry. This practice is continued with diminishing degrees of regularity in the other Chronicle poems
in this manuscript. The entry following the poem is Athelstan's obit,
which links him to Alfred and Edmund: "941 In this year King Athelstan

passed away on 27 October, forty years less a day after King Alfred died, and prince Edmund succeeded to the kingdom, and he was 18 years old. King Athelstan ruled 14 years and ten weeks." *Brunanburh*, as the first and longest of the Chronicle poems, provides a paradigm for the literary strategies at work in the continuation of the Chronicle.

The memorializing and eulogistic function of *Brunanburh* is signalled in the introductory statement, which incorporates the annal's "Her" ("in this place, at this annal entry, on this chronologically numbered line"), thus designating it as the entry for a specified year in the Chronicle. The introduction and conclusion to the poem provide an ideologically motivated historical frame that interprets the event commemorated, linking the poem to prior texts and to the first part of the Chronicle itself, which contains the dynastic genealogy and its fullfillment in the kingdom of Alfred and Edward the Elder:

> Her Æþelstan cyning,   eorla dryhten,
> beorna beahgifa,   ond his broþor eac,
> Eadmund æþeling,   ealdorlangne tir
> geslogon æt sæcce   sweorda ecgum
> ymbe Brunanburh.   Bordweal clufan,
> heowan heaþolinde   hamora lafan
> afaran Eadweardes,   swa him geæþele wæs
> from cneomægum,   þæt hi æt campe oft
> wiþ laþra gehwæne   land ealgodon,
> hord ond hamas.

(1–10)

> (In this year King Athelstan, lord of nobles,
> the ring-giver of men, and also his brother,
> Prince Edmund, won age-long glory
> at battle, with sword-blades,
> around Brunanburh. With hammer-forged weapons,
> the sons of Edward split the shield-wall,
> hacked open the war-linden, as was natural for them
> from their ancestry, that they ever at battle
> defended land, treasure, and homes
> against each enemy.)

The introduction situates Athelstan's victory in a heroic history of the Wessex dynasty ("sons of Edward") and represents the victory as a function of Athelstan's and Edward's inborn nobility ("as was natural for them / from their ancestry"). The reference to noble lineage ("cneomæg") recalls another text, the Chronicle itself and the genealogical preface on the first folio

of the Parker Chronicle (the first leaf of booklet 1), which traces the line of
Alfred back to Cerdic, the first Anglo-Saxon conqueror of Wessex, whose
genealogy goes back to Woden. The genealogy and the early annals of the
Chronicle trace the heroic lineage of the royal house of Wessex to these
early warrior-kings, who "were the first kings who conquered the land of
Wessex from the Welsh" (Preface).[74]

The conclusion locates the events of the poem in a grander racial and
national history and in the textualization of history represented in the
Chronicle and its sources:

> Ne wearð wæl mare
> on ðis eiglande   æfre gieta
> folces gefylled   beforan ðissum
> sweordes ecgum,   ðæs ðe us secgað bec,
> ealde uðwitan,   siððan easten hider
> Engle ond Seaxe   up becoman,
> ofer brad brimu   Brytene sohtan,
> wlance wigsmiðas   Weales ofercoman,
> eorlas arhwate,   eard begeatan.

(65–73)

> (Never before this
> was there greater slaughter on this island,
> people cut down by the sword's blade,
> according to what the books tell us,
> the old scholars, since the Anglos and Saxons
> came upon these shores from the east,
> sought Britain over the broad sea,
> proud war-makers, overcame the Welsh,
> the glorious nobles, to obtain the homeland.)

This passage is the most revealing of all: a formulaic poem refers to *written*
authority for knowledge of the past.[75] History in textual form is assumed to
be necessary for understanding the significance of Athelstan's victory over
the combined forces of the Scots and Danes: "according to what the books
tell us" (68). Which books? The poem refers the audience to the text of the
genealogical preface of the Chronicle, the Chronicle itself, and the Latin
texts, like Bede's *Historia,* upon which the Chronicle is based. For example, consider the following Chronicle entries from the Parker version, many
of which go back to Latin annals:

> [Preface] In the year when 494 years had passed from Christ's birth, Cer-
> dic and his son Cynric landed at Cerdicesora with five ships [genealogy of

Cerdic to Woden follows]. And six years after they landed, they conquered the kingdom of the West Saxons, and they were the first kings who conquered the land of the West Saxons from the Britons (Welsh) [genealogy of Wessex kings to Alfred]. (f. 1r)

519. In this year Cerdic and Cynric succeeded to the kingdom [of the West-Saxons (slightly later addition)], and in the same year fought against the Britons at a place called Charford [and from that day on the princes of the West Saxons have ruled (later addition)]. (f. 5v)

597. In this year Ceolwulf began to reign in Wessex, and he continually fought and contended either against the English, or the Britons, or the Picts, or the Scots [genealogy of Ceolwulf to Woden follows]. (f. 7r)

688. In this year Ine succeeded to the kingdom of the West Saxons, and he held it for 37 years [he built the monastery of Glastonbury (later addition)] [genealogy of Ine to Cerdic follows]. (f. 8v)

827 (829). . . . King Egbert conquered the kingdom of the Mercians and everything south of the Humber; and he was the eighth king who was called "ruler of Britain" (Bretwalda). (f. 12r)

855 [Reign of Æthelwulf, and his genealogy through Germanic kings and beyond to Adam.] (f. 13r)

Athelstan recapitulates heroic history by winning a battle that is represented as standing in a line of historic continuity with the first conquerors of the Welsh recorded to the Alfredian royal genealogy. The author of the poem knew the history of house of Wessex in its textual form, and the compiler who inserted the second booklet in its present place in the manuscript attempted to complete what the first compiler had begun by compiling a manuscript that would be a monument to the Alfredian dynasty.

The text of *Brunanburh* also tells us other things about the textuality of poetry in the tenth and eleventh centuries. The poem presupposes that English history already exists in written form and that these textual accounts of history, not the scop's perpetuation of national memory, are authoritative. *Brunanburh* inserts itself, both materially in the manuscripts of the Chronicle and discursively in Anglo-Saxon textuality, within written history, *historia* as the textual representation of *res gestae*. Furthermore, when read in its manuscript context, the poem reflects an ideological myth of Anglo-Saxon history as compelling as the ideologically encoded narrative in Livy (*ab urbe condita*, "from the founding of the city") and Vergil (the mythic, and therefore historically necessary, founding of Rome). The appropriation of a larger myth of the national past in the Chronicle, articulated in traditional, heroic form, functions to unite past and present, obliterating historical difference or discontinuity, and legitimizes the power of the house of Wessex as its genealogy is reaffirmed in each succession. The battle at Brunanburh is represented not as an isolated event but as part of an unbroken tradition of English victories that extends back to the original defeat of the native Welsh or Britons. Athelstan is represented as recapitulating deep history at the origins of a race of warrior-kings, much like the events in the *Aeneid* that served as exemplary types for events in imperial history. The nostalgic form of the poetry domesticates the past, and history becomes a style, a form of narrative myth making. Historicizing the past creates difference, distance, and discontinuities; nostalgia cancels historical distance and creates the ideologically powerful fiction of continuity, an image of an unbroken tradition of power and authority.[76]

Since most of the corpus of Old English poetry survives in copies that date from the time when the Chronicle poems were compiled in the second continuation of *The Anglo-Saxon Chronicle* and later, it should rightly be asked if the compiling, copying, and composition of poetry after the age of Alfred was motivated by nostalgia for an earlier, heroic past, a nostalgia for the earlier oral-poetic traditions of the people and nation, which, as the Chronicle reveals, had begun to conceive of itself as a nation with a deep history.[77] The first antiquarians of Anglo-Saxon poetry may well have been the tenth and eleventh century Anglo-Saxon scribes, editors, and compilers themselves. Certainly the text of *Beowulf* as copied and compiled in the early eleventh century—the only copy that survives—represents a nostalgic longing for the presence of the memorializing voice, the tribal voice that makes present the memory of heroes at the dynastic origins of English kings. In many respects, *Beowulf* is a written commentary on the heroic tradition transmitted in oral-formulaic poetry. Poetry, genealogy, historical myth making, and nationalism are thus intimately related; the Parker manuscript, through all the stages of its compilation, testifies to these aspects of Anglo-Saxon textuality.

Conclusion: The Archaeology of Textual Knowledge

I have been able to show only a few examples of the function of some major macrogenres in the Anglo-Saxon cultural archive, and my proposed set of macrogenres is not intended to be exhaustive or exclusive but heuristic, a model that can enable new discoveries to be made about medieval textuality. In light of the above examples, I would like to suggest some further implications of the extended archaeological model I have tried to develop here.

Although the model I have elaborated here depends upon some of the main strategies of poststructuralist thought, it is not merely a formalist exercise. The archaeological method, reception theory, and Bakhtinian semiotics converge at two important points: the investigation of discursive levels beyond those traditionally maintained by philology (underlying structures that disclose historical conditions for knowledge, meaning, and intelligibility) and the requirement that one must insert the various discursive systems into the realm of history and social practice. The archive as historical precondition for the system of discursive practices constitutive of knowledge, the "horizon of expectations" that establishes the conditions for the production and reception of texts, and the principle of dialogism as both social and formal ground for texts understood as microcosms of literary languages—these models of analysis also intersect in the assumption that discourse must ultimately be seen as ideological, mediating and reproducing social and institutional forces with their own historicity.

Strategically opposed to the agenda of traditional philology and constructing its objects at other levels, the archaeology of the text makes the problem of ideology and history part of the subject matter of literary investigation itself, rather than allowing ideology to obscure itself behind the seemingly neutral claims of various disciplines or the self-evident status often attributed to textual documents.[78] Furthermore, rather than leaving the details of textual history to the philologists, the archaeologist insists on a thorough, firsthand reexamination of all the available textual, linguistic, and historical evidence. For the textual system to disclose its various strata, the investigator uses the mass of details acquired through direct access to the primary archive to investigate (1) the system of discursive relations defined synchronically as preconditions for the appearance and reception of texts, (2) the function of a text in a network of intertextual relations, and (3) the text as inserted in history, the question of reception and ideology. I hope that this essay has illustrated in some way the kinds of results that are possible when the textual data of the primary archive are analyzed for the system that made them possible, in particular the discursive layers or archaeological strata into which various texts and bodies of discourse were organized within the archive that defined Anglo-Saxon and early medieval textual communities.

* *

Further Reading

For an introduction to the archaeological model, see Michel Foucault, *The Archaeology of Knowledge*, trans. A. M. Sheridan Smith (New York, 1972), and *The Order of Things: An Archaeology of the Human Sciences* (translation of *Les Mots et Les Choses*) (New York, 1970). The implications of Foucault's method are lucidly presented by Gilles Deleuze, *Foucault,* trans. Sean Hand (Minneapolis, 1988) and by Hubert L. Dreyfus and Paul Rabinow, *Michel Foucault: Beyond Structuralism and Hermeneutics,* 2d ed. (Chicago, 1983).

The principle of intertextuality has been widely discussed and applied in recent literary studies. The best starting point is Mikhail Bakhtin's *The Dialogic Imagination: Four Essays,* ed. Michael Holquist and trans. Caryl Emerson and Michael Holquist (Austin, 1981) and the interpretation of Bakhtin through semiotic theory in Julia Kristeva's work, *Semiotiké: Recherches pour une sémanalyse* (Paris, 1969), parts of which were translated in the collection *Desire in Language,* ed. Leon S. Roudiez (New York, 1980).

For semiotic theory in general, see Umberto Eco, *A Theory of Semiotics* (Bloomington, IN, 1976) and *Semiotics and the Philosophy of Language* (Bloomington, IN, 1984), and for useful explanations of key concepts in semiotics and poststructuralist theory see Oswald Ducrot and Tzvetan Todorov, *Encyclopedic Dictionary of the Sciences of Language,* trans. Catherine Porter (Baltimore, 1983) and A. J. Greimas and J. Courtés, *Semiotics and Language: An Analytical Dictionary,* trans. Larry Crist, et al. (Bloomington, IN, 1982).

On reception theory, see H. R. Jauss, *Toward an Aesthetic of Reception,* trans. Timothy Bahti (Minneapolis, 1982), "The Alterity and Modernity of Medieval Literature," *New Literary History* 10 (1979): 181–231, and "The Identity of the Poetic Text in the Changing Horizon of Understanding," in *The Identity of the Literary Text,* ed. Mario J. Valdés and Owen Miller (Toronto, 1985), 146–74.

Chapter 9

Epilogue: *De Scientia Interpretandi:* Oral Tradition and the Place of Other Theories in the Graduate Curriculum

✽ Adam Brooke Davis ✽

When I was asked to replace John Foley at the "Two Languages" colloquium, I became aware of an irony in my position: I would be speaking for him and yet, at the same time, speaking for graduate students, not because I was representing students as a group but simply because I was one. Now, given the opportunity to speak to the purposes of this collection in my own voice, as a graduate student, I find myself enmeshed in another irony. I have been asked to define the relations of the two languages in which my professional life will be conducted—the traditional disciplines of the medieval studies curriculum and oral-traditional theory—but I must do so prior to the professional practice that brings theoretical fluency out of the matrix of paradigm and rote.

Neither apprentice nor master of my trade, I find another irony proceeds from my indeterminate status. It may help to stage the "two languages" metaphor within another: I have not finished making my purchases in the bazaar of values, methods, materials, and ideologies that is the contemporary department of literature, where a thousand strange tongues are to be heard, although my arms—and my ears—are getting rather full. My personal assessment of the fair values of the various wares would lack credibility and relevance. But this ironic situation has its benefits: I am in a position to interpret some of the outlandish speech of those only visiting or just arrived in the bazaar and to report things few shoppers would share with a merchant. We have an operational pidgin we use amongst ourselves. You will have to decide for yourselves how far you trust someone who is, after all, an informer.

But I struggle with this metaphor, for while it conveys the bidirectional, material self-interest that is often neglected in discussions of theory and pedagogy, it reanalogizes itself too easily into a model of predator-and-victim. Further, it disregards the personal and institutional realities that

211

shape the students' choices of critical language, but in the end, its account of that selection squares with my own experience.

It is my intention, in the remainder of this essay, to grammatize the pidgin, giving some account of the rather mixed feelings I sense from my colleagues in graduate school as to the current state of the profession; the account will be inescapably biased by the selective filters of my attitudes, age, memory, field of acquaintance, and so forth. It is a view of productive eristics and pointless polemics, in response to which I sugggest a dialectal charity as a better choice in aporia than force or silence. From there I wish to speak in the language I have learned, oral-traditional theory, first (and briefly) about traditional disciplines, and then at greater length about some of the newer textual approaches with which it stands in highly problematic relation. Specifically, I hope to demonstrate how dialectal and dialectical charity can abolish a false dichotomy between orality and literacy that seems, on a short view, to assign oral-traditional studies to the classical disciplines, and to make its dialogue with textual theories impossible.

The Pidgin

There is a problem here connected with what journalists call "sourcing." Anonymous information is not the stuff of which responsible surveys of professional attitudes are made. Yet scholars-in-training grow understandably camera shy as they criticize their curricula, their institutions, and their advisers, or confess utter confusion as to what's expected of them in this rapidly changing field.[1]

And the changes are occurring more quickly than print can well record. A glance at the letters—and forum—sections of leading journals[2] indicates just how much uncertainty there is as to the presence, arrival, or departure of "theory" from literary studies. Medieval studies are no exception. One hears, and with about equal validity, that medievalists are just now beginning to avail themselves of the opportunities theory offers, that they have remained generally impervious to it, or that they lead the reaction against it. Theory was a fad, it is here to stay, it has only just begun to make itself felt. And which theory are we talking about, anyway?

That theory has created some sort of crisis, the existence of this book, if nothing else, would indicate. But Susan Stewart argues, in an issue of *Profession* devoted to "the state and boundaries of literary studies,"[3] that "crisis" is a construction dependent on some usually unarticulated notion of a natural or normal state of affairs. That ideal state of "natural relations" then legitimizes whatever is currently dominant. But Stewart's next point is hardly inevitable: "this rhetoric of wholeness calls forth a discourse of healing, pharmacy and remedy. But disciplines are not to be cured; the point is not to cover over the faults and contradictions of the social order, nor is it to ignore the incommensurable aspects of their own relation. Therefore the merger of such aspects would mark the discipline's demise." Stewart's model for literary studies is one of clash and conflict, a continuous undermining of any and all assumptions and orderings. She concludes with a metaphor, herself walking into a classroom, facing a blackboard: " 'I often don't understand what's written on the blackboard when I come in, or I recognize the terms, but not the connection, or someone's started to erase what's written. . . . Sometimes I like to start my class by explaining our relation to what's already on the blackboard. Or by asking what it means and who's listening when someone writes 'please don't erase.' "

On the surface, this seems like an apt description (and enactment) of the eristic environment within which we all work. However, all comparisons limp, and the vehicle of this metaphor is driving the tenor places it might not want to go. Stewart may have overestimated the general degree of enthusiasm for "a new order of things," at least among graduate students; from a purely pragmatic standpoint, those who are struggling to learn the rules of the game are not necessarily eager to see them changed, even if it makes them easier (which is open to doubt). And there are schools of thought subversive of subversion, thinking that the game was perhaps not quite as rigged as has been made out, or, alternatively, that the riggers have changed, but the rigging goes on just the same. Whoever wrote that poignant, naive request on a blackboard, which Stewart must, in the course of her professional duties, erase, either misunderstood the nature of the materials in question, assumed a code of material use whose conventions include a reasonable period for allowing dated material to remain undisturbed, or overestimated the generosity of future users. Blackboards are vehicles for ephemera. They do not stand very well for texts produced for posterity nor for a curriculum designed to rationalize and transmit groups of texts to the posterity.[4] Of course, these are old and traditional notions, but they are vigorous yet, and dirges over them may be a bit premature, for reasons that are contained in Stewart's own argument: if crisis be the natural state of things, how does a notion of "natural relations" come into being? Put another way, if there is no such thing as a crisis because there is no such thing as prelapsarian state, departure from which defines the crisis, how comes there such a general sense of crisis *right now,* a delusion so pervasive, Stewart feels called upon to disabuse us of it?

The answer is not far to seek; it lies not in the substance of what is being talked about in the academy, nor in the purposes for which it is being discussed, but in the *way* that discussion is conducted. Stewart's article is closely followed by Martin Mueller's;[5] he invokes, of all things, Saint Augustine's principle of charity in interpretation as a model for how the current strife in literary studies may most profitably be got through:

> The recovery of literature's central political dimension has been a major achievement of recent critical movements. But the achievement has come at a heavy price, for it has brought along with it a hermeneutics of suspicion and contempt, countered on the other side of the fence by a singularly meanspirited and strident complacency. . . . [The profession] needs a greater awareness and active acknowledgment of the simple truth that intelligence, insight, and integrity have been found, are now found, and will be found in the future in participants very far to one's political left and very far to one's political right.[6]

The sort of charity that Mueller calls for in literary studies amounts to a prescription for exactly the healing that Stewart deplores, yet it makes room for the productive conflict, the occasional abrasion creating "new objects of knowledge," which is for her the end of literary study.

"New objects of knowledge" are attractive; "the inevitability of a new order of things," with its oxymoron of liberation and coercion, less so. That is perhaps natural to education; certainly it was a flaw in my training that at no time was I required to demonstrate a general knowledge of events in literary theory beyond the New Criticism, but neither did I seek out the occasion to do so. I am excited by the opportunities and options theory makes available and skeptical of its claims and purposes, in about equal measures. Like a good many graduate students of my aquaintance, I suspect economic and emotional compulsions are exerted by partisans of various theories to make us "sign up"; in the presence of theorists, many of us feel that our role is to edit our speech to avoid saying the politically incorrect thing, and too many of us are consciously forming glossaries as we listen, knowing we had better get the buzzwords down, rather than feeling we are about to understand something important. The moral pleasure of *doing* something that comes with an understanding of one's methodology as part of a sociocritical model of literary study is central to the undeniably widespread, if in my view qualified, enthusiasm for theory that exists among graduate students. Virtually all of us have, at some point and to some degree, been troubled by the possible parasitism of academic literary study upon society. But often cognate with the pleasure in utility is a deep spiritual dissatisfaction with the new dynamo, a suspicion that one may be cooperating in the conversion of English departments into institutes of technical writing. The next problem to confront the graduate student will be the recovery of the aesthetic dimension of literature from the newly (re)valorized political.

There is no possibility of getting theory back into the box, and we can never again work under the idea that what we are doing is ideologically neutral. A new teaching assistant in Cornell's freshman composition program, during his orientation, asked what theory the department preferred that he teach. He was told to avoid theory at that level. His very appropriate response was to repeat his question. He understood that there is no tradition that is not at base ideological, and therefore exclusive of other ideologies, the more so it claims neutrality.

But then aren't all of our arguments ultimately ideological? Among equals, arguments about ideology quickly reach an aporia to be overcome only by force, whether we have it out among ourselves (the last one standing wins) or wait for Duke Theseus to impose it from without (often with a budget-cutting ax). For the graduate student, there is considerable risk in engaging in such a debate with a mentor, and there must be some examination of how one deals with one's mentor's language. Realistically, most of us keep our dissatisfactions to ourselves; for my part, I am occasionally unsure how to formulate my disagreement, or I am afraid to reveal some crucial ignorance, or I simply feel myself outmatched. It is no small part of charity to be cunning as serpents and harmless as doves.

The labyrinth is one model for the relation of the mentor's critical methods to the student's. Some of us make mentors out of the first personable, authoritative, or otherwise appealing person we find in there and consent to journey on together, at least a while. But one's mentor was already there, and arrived at the meeting place by a different route, and it seems likely that the forces that led by different ways to tangency will thereafter lead to divergence. Or shifting again to the languages metaphor, the one who taught you the paradigms will have little control over what you say with them, or whether you find new idioms, or join a group that develops its own patois. Most likely, your language at any moment stands on a scale of linguistic relationship running from identity through dialect, increasing perhaps with time to mutual unintelligibility. It is indeed likely you may learn yet another language, in which that of your first mentor is traceable only as an odd accent.

Failure to become a *critical* student of one's mentor's language leads, Jonathan Culler writes, to " 'limitations [of the methodology] that are not accessible to its own analytical tools. . . . Distinctions between truth and falsity, blindness and insight, or reading and misreading remain crucial, but they are not grounded in ways that might permit one definitively to establish the truth or insight of one's own reading.' "[7] Of course, one can sacralize the assumptions, restricting one's audience to a set of true believers in certain axioms. But that is questionable religion and certainly bad science. It can lead to a kind of orthodoxy test of which graduate students in a broad range of disciplines, from the highly traditional to the self-consciously theoretical, are aware and resentful. Better by far that the individual practitioner of a method maintain a dialectical relationship with its assumptions, by turns assimilating and interrogating, bringing them up for periodic review.

For myself, I am still at the stage of testing my competence. Of course the tests that signify are those that go to the limits of one's knowledge; you certainly have no claim to knowing a language until you have spoken understandably something you haven't heard said before in it. Although much remains to be done by practitioners who wish to look at text through oral-traditional theory in its present form, my own interest in the complex period of transition from orality to literacy will require me to examine oral traditional theory through text,[8] and to develop it in directions it has rarely sought before, for example, the psychology of runic inscription, the peculiar status of that variety of script and its relation to the texts it was developed to record (in an emphatically memorial way, on resistant materials), and the traditional matrices of those texts.

So in dealing with mentors as well as peers, the graduate student is structurally required to exercise a polyglossia never before needed. They are trained in theory, whether or not the student or teacher calls it that, and the commitment is regularly made, and some kind of informed consent expected, when they are still learning the language. Of course the decision is far from irreversible, and in the absence of the pettier kinds of departmental politics, the student can build a complex structure from diverse materials (though interdisciplinarity carries its own difficulties).[9] Nonetheless, the spiritual and intellectual strain of acknowledging and honoring (rather than humoring) other viewpoints is bound to wear. It is poignant to hear someone wish to be allowed again to be a *naive* reader, to spend less time learning to name her tools, and which ones "we" use. When the tools by which meaning is made are specific to a particular outlook with an explicit extraliterary agenda, they start to look like weapons. Weapons breed.

We have all lived with the danger created by regarding as inevitable a polarization of the world that turns out not to be inevitable, even when the sophistication of our destructive tools exceeds our cultural maturity. Stewart's is a similarly false bifurcation of literary-critical impulses into canon and strategy orientations. There is no medievalist in any institution anywhere who cares for Cotton Vitellius A. xv. to the exclusion of what its glyphs signify, though she may enjoy the exercise of her system of constructing significance more than its analysis. She may responsibly choose to leave that analysis to those who take pleasure in it. Indeed, that analysis itself is such a rigorous study that learning the full range of techniques and terminology might leave her little time for her original satisfactions. That she should acquaint herself with the questions relevant to practitioners of closely allied fields is no more than has been and will be expected of all professionals. To tell her that she must regularly use those methods and terms, and make politics her first interest, if she wishes to be heard at all, will not invite a cooperative response.

As teachers, it behooves us at least to understand the nostalgia for naive reading, free of conscious agenda; there is not much hope for us if we read as utterly alien the comment each of us has seen on an evaluation—"I used to like to read, but not when all we do is tear the stories apart." Further, I would ask that the nostalgia for naive reading not be confused with yearning for the days of hegemonic culture; the former was a pleasure defined by the absence of anxiety, the latter by the exercise of domination.

Hans Robert Jauss expressed forcefully the problem of what kind of readers we make ourselves into:

> Aesthetics occurs before there is cognition and interpretation of the significance of work, and certainly before all reconstruction of an author's intent. . . . Interpretation that bypasses this primary aesthetic experience is the arrogance of a philologist who subscribes to the error that the text was created not for readers but for him, to be interpreted by such as he.[10]

Even if our privately held aesthetics contain a notion of gestalt, we have a very difficult time talking about beauty, because it involves nonpublic judgments, questionable conclusions proceeding from private premises, and so we talk about texts as if beauty and pleasure had nothing to do with why people write and read them. But similarly, when we talk about what we do, I find it is the older scholars of the traditional disciplines who speak of joy and purpose, in that order; the younger rarely speak of joy at all. The old joy derived in large measure from a vaguely sensed but nonetheless commonly held sense of purpose connected with the transmission of Western traditions, an undertaking now seen as questionable, to put it mildly.

Joy may be recoverable through charity. Mueller's application of the principle of charity is what I wish to write from, toward, and for. I now turn from the pidgin I share with my peers. As I do so, I want to see if charity works, if it makes possible a discourse in which I disagree with people I respect about very fundamental things, as I make two explorations. First I wish to see how my own chosen method, oral tradition, relates to institutionalized approaches to scholarship. Then, and at greater length, I will try to articulate its position with respect to newer theoretical disciplines, contrasting it with textual studies, in order to discover what common ground there may be. I propose, in effect, to work through three languages toward a lingua franca.

Die Muttersprache

To the scholar dedicated to traditional methods and disciplines, oral tradition of course threatens "our" Homer and his artistry;[11] the disappearance of a unified author for texts or works that have long been regarded as the origin of Western eloquence involves the loss as well of certitude in the romantic idea of the vatic voice, the necessary dependence of integral art on an integral and inspired personality. If oral studies endanger the tradition of which the profession considers itself custodian, they pose a yet more insidious threat to the profession itself, seeming to make the text disappear as they undermine the very notion of textuality in a given work. A stemmatologist's "lost Latin intermediary,"[12] suspended in imagination between the received *Andreas* and the Greek *Praxeis*, loses what grasp it had on existence and plunges into the abyss when it is proposed that a Christian cleric in a literate (and indeed polyglot and polymath) environment, whether himself literate or not, could well have reconstituted the narrative according to traditional diction and thematic structures.[13] The patristic learning of Jackson Campbell[14] would seem to be undervalued as the disposition of the nails of the True Cross in *Elene* is interpreted according to a traditional treasure ethos, rather than as the irony of a writer wholly committed to material renunciation or, conversely, as the greedy fantasy of a relic enthusiast. From the standpoint of these conservative disciplines, oral tradition may seem to imply a trivializing primitivism, a reduction of the field to the sort of role playing one sees lampooned in a Kingsley Amis novel or conducted solemnly at a meeting of the Society for Creative Anachronism.[15]

The Languages of the Bazaar

In the other direction, and to those committed to rigorous receptivist approaches, especially insofar as the particular method is politically dedicated, oral tradition may appear to be engaged—at best naively and at worst consciously, culpably—in the construction and continuation of what Frantzen and Venegoni[16] have called the "originary myths" of traditional Anglo-Saxon studies and its version of Anglo-Saxon culture. Putatively disinterested inquires of a quasi-scientific character may be used to back-form a hypothetical Ur-language and prior culture. That version of history quickly loses its hypothetical character and becomes a validation of present social forms, with all their injustices. Philology *has* in the past served propaganda shamelessly,[17] and the faculty of major universities can still write publicly of the need to preserve the pure German language.[18] These are legitimate concerns and deserve careful response.

Oral tradition fits comfortably with neither the very old nor the very modern extreme. It does not regard medieval people as culturally continuous with us, differing only in the dialect they used and the materials they used it on (and perhaps in a few stray beliefs and customs). Nor can it settle itself into the receptivist spectrum, at one end caring about the text mainly as it is a space for the individual consciousness of the modern reader to occupy, or at the other, mainly as it is suited to the documentary needs of a utilitarian program of contemporary reform. Rather, it focuses on the technology of communication, and in so doing, allies itself perhaps more nearly with anthropology than with either traditional disciplines or contemporary theoretical approaches.

Whatever the roots of oral tradition in nineteenth-century romanticism may be,[19] and however unappetizing some of the philosophical fare of that time has now proven, I do not presently hear any Golden Age praising of the primitive as such. There may, occasionally, come what sounds like a lament over the decline of pristine illiteracy, but it is to be understood as in some instances a healthy corrective to cheirographic chauvinism,[20] a polemic response to the Derridean denial of the existence of a linguistic sign before writing,[21] or the grunt of a limnologist watching the data dry up and disappear: "There are not going to be many more dinosaurs."

Oral tradition also stands distinct from all those theories that Jonathan Culler,[22] in sheer exasperation, simply calls "theory," because it has provoked, and perhaps earned, charges of philosophical naiveté or blind positivism; oral tradition maintains a fairly flat-footed assumption that knowledge is possible and manifests a general lack of interest in principled philosophical skepticism. It is firmly and unapologetically grounded in Western empiricism, without which its methods fail. The earth is assumed to be as real as getting a little bit of it in one's eye. An even less salutary characteristic, and one I offer descriptively rather than programmatically, because it is certainly no necessary part of oral traditional studies, is that practitioners, as a group, show no great interest in criticizing scientific method per se, its sociopolitical determinants or implications.

On the other hand, by its very nature, oral tradition seeks a hearing for the voices silenced in a textual culture, demonstrating that epics even specialists have never read, (because these texts have never seen print), are aesthetically pleasing and socially useful within the cultures that produced them. Indeed, the early focus of oral-traditional studies on texts firmly within established canons—the *Iliad,* the *Odyssey, Beowulf*—served to show how co-optation by understandings alien to their origins transformed them. In this project, it is engaged in something consonant with the work of Clare A. Lees as here represented,[23] calling attention to the ways in which institutional specializations lead to curricular versions of culture whose status as disinterested reportage invites scrutiny. Put another way, oral tradition turns attention to verbal art and verbal communities considerably more than marginalized by high-culture paradigms. Karma Lochrie's work [24] must stand as a reminder that to focus exclusively on the poetry—most particularly within an oral tradition—threatens to institute a remasculinized canon whose deconstruction may meet with yet more resistance than last time if it seems to claim scientific sanction.

But I am not prepared to abandon all claims of scientific sanction for oral tradition, even as I acknowledge their limits. Oral tradition does not accompany other theories in the leap from the self-evident proposition that misunderstanding is possible to the conclusion that communication is impossible; exceptions to the rules of descriptive systems indicate not the absurdity of the attempt to describe but the insufficiency of the present model. Of course, the limited materials on which oral-traditional methods can be exercised liberate the practitioner from some of the difficulties that confront the careful theorist who attends to the *literary* text and its audience. A work produced within an oral tradition is by definition produced in *presence.* Derridean notions of author-absent-from-audience and audience-absent-from-author, upon which much contemporary theory rests,[25] are largely inapplicable when we are considering the oral-traditional reception of a text. The guarantor of meaning is *there,* not in the individual person of the "author,"[26] but in the complex of audience-and-singer. The latter is not in his present function sufficiently *autos* to be called "author." The values of an oral and traditional people are homogenous, and their system of meaning—at least within the reserved language of formulaic poetry—is purposefully consistent and stable, if immensely complex. Their communal activity is conservative, iterative, not innovative or exploratory.[27] These things have to be kept in mind in assessing the compatability of the theories that proceed from Derrida with those that proceed from Parry; *différance* can be made to apply to an oral-traditional lexicon only by speculations on the origins of language and the primal differentiation of paleolithic squeals as little informative as the disinclination to inquire into such matters. The reserved language of oral tradition obviously makes use of elements of the quotidian, transactional, "prosaic" lexicon, but meanings are not assigned according to a different system of denotation; rather, meaning is made according to a system that is connotative and associative, invoking much that is nonverbal and yet reliably invokable. The experience is per-

haps most nearly approximated by John Miles Foley's concept of metonymic association.[28]

Another consequence of oral tradition's view of itself as a scientific
methodology is that, unlike for example Marxist or feminist criticism, it
requires none but an intellectual commitment (that is, for its analytical exercise; the *experience* of oral tradition is, for participants, necessarily emotional). Oral tradition also differs from politically dedicated methodologies
in that it is not a reading predicted on resistance, a search for prevarication,
and complicity. Quite the contrary: to achieve maximum reading fluency
in the poetic lexicon, one must open oneself to the values it encodes. One
must recognize the meanings and the systems of meaning of another culture
as alien, learn what makes them alien, how they function, what their uses
are, what customs and values they support, and why it could seem worthwhile to support them. That is true if one is attempting to understand oral-
traditional culture analytically. That analysis is possible only from the
outside, and that those outside can never fully participate in the ritual aspects of oral traditions, must simply remain problematic for each scholar, at
each moment, reading each text. All this requires a rigorous personal discipline; it involves a humility I think useful in any scholarly, critical,
creative, or pedagogical undertaking. I am well aware of what kind of provocation I offer in recommending what Wlad Godzich criticized as the
ascesis[29] inherent in the aesthetic formulations to which Jauss responded,
but humility properly understood is neither an unbroken and self-effacing/
erasing reverentiality nor an absurd refusal of the relatively obvious episte-
mology on which deconstruction is founded. Rather, it is an admonition to
be articulate about the reasons for which one pays attention to one thing
and not another—which, I suppose, is the long and short of deconstruction,
the law, and all the prophets.

Humility has its uses. Each of us, as scholars pursuing various purposes by various methods, wishes to establish a certain set of operational
conditions, which will in turn suit or unsuit the texts in question to our
particular approaches. Obviously, a critique of disinterestedness is needful
here: in a kind of methodological arrogation, scholars describe their materials so as to adapt them to their own methods, declaring a thing wood and
not ivory, rather than going back for a different implement; our incomes
and identities depend on what we can pull into our spheres, and so we are
interested indeed. We may assert that much of the corpus of Old English
poetry is based on Latin texts, and, if we acknowledge orality at all, as
quickly dismiss it as "traces," "vestiges," and silences.[30] We will thereby
enable an analysis with all the elegance of an internally consistent system,
as self-contained as onanism and as free from interference by a thinking
Other. And exactly the same must be said of a methodologically naive treat-

ment of a text recorded in writing as if it were the product of a wholly prealphabetic brain.

What we need, and what cannot be found without recourse to dialect(ic)al charity, are alternatives to binary thinking about orality and literacy; the Anglo-Saxons, both individually and as a culture, are on the cusp: they also speak two languages, and the languages we use in approaching them had better be sensitive to that fact. We have here a genuine issue of descriptive rigor, the disposition of which will dramatically affect our results, and our students. Further, we have an opportunity for a mutual accommodation, a pluralism made possible not by squeamishness before the prospect of a firefight, nor by our unwillingness to test the descriptive limits of our respective methods, but a pluralism proceeding from a strict observance of those very limits. Instead of insisting on a simplex definition of a particular linguistic construction as either oral or literate, we may choose as more appropriate the categories "textual" and "nontextual."

A third possibility is thereby created: a *continuum* of capacity for textuality.[31] The individuals who form that continuum may have compartmentalized their language-linked textuality and nontextuality, coping with the necessity of cultural brinksmanship through a sort of diglossia.[32] Note that we have not left relative or subjective the question on which the appropriateness of our methods depends, but rather admitted its complexity, the thing that makes our work difficult and fascinating.

That the textuality that literacy enables finally wins out, we know. But in the struggle, we see Bede resorting to miracle to explain extempore production of satisfying verbal art, a mirror of the illiterate's awe of script in the nonlinguistic use of letters in the metrical charms of the *Exeter Book*. We need a model of medieval language that accounts for such data.[33]

A Chapter's-End Exercise

While we argue for a continuum of textuality in persons, we may argue for it in their linguistic artifacts as well. To take an example again from *Elene*, it is of value to understand the search for the Cross as a textual concern,[34] and that insight would be unavailable to an oral traditionalist determined to see nothing but oral tradition in the poem. That the textual concern takes the form of heroic agon, the object of which is rendered as a traditional treasure, is part of the enormously complex system of signification in that poem. It is true that the Cross in *Elene* is a "multivalent *signum*," but the assumption of literacy according to a binary model would obliterate the valence that is the primary emotional motor of the text for an audience with deep lexical loyalties. To assign the poem that status of commentary addresses one kind of historically constituted reception; acknowledging it as simultaneously a primary instantiation, a mimetic narrative encoding values for the nontextual as well as interpretation for the textual, speaks to another. It is difficult but essential to bear in mind the diachronic depth, the connotative complexity of the synchronic fact of the text as we receive it now, or conceive it in Bede's world.

In England, the native/pagan/Germanic complex adapted and adapted to the imported/Christian/Latin culture. What it could not survive (except as a rootless archaizing meter with no lexical depth) was literacy. Such has been the pattern in Yugoslavia: memorization of traditional songs, textuality, replaces traditional composition. Traditional narrative cannot serve as a mimetic vehicle for the abstract ideology of Marxism (though *epske pjesme* can comprehend the heroic agon of a soccer game). Nor can formulas be generated by traditional rules to fit new semantic spaces—tractors and collectives—or loan-words that may not fit native patterns of stress and syntax. While it would be a grave error to suppose that a *guslar* is merely a *scop* in a turban, the native Germanic tradition may have similarly hiccoughed as it went "from an adult, mature style of one kind to a faltering and embryonic style of another sort."[35] Looking at a clearly *textual* artifact, from a period of more than utilitarian literacy—

> Hwæt! Ic flitan gefræn   on fyrndagum
> modgleawe men,   middangeardes ræswan,
> gewesan ymbe hira wisdom;   wyrs deð se de liehð [. . .][36]

—we find metrical awkwardness, because the purpose at hand is not traditional, is analytic rather than mimetic. It is tempting to read it as burlesque; the co-opting of the native form is crude, as hearts-and-minds propaganda always is. But the nontextual poems of the chronicle produce sound and convincing compositions: praise is a traditional purpose. If Cædmon sings in a library, then, it is because the meadhall *is* his library, the place where he consults the encyclopedia of values.

A resolutely textual approach may speak of "new poems rewriting earlier texts," through the repetitive wordhoard and formulaic system, "a form of intertextuality."[37] And it is a form of intertextuality in a sense suddenly made all the richer and more rigorous when we introduce the possibility of a coincident reception by some element of mind residually oral. The audience's memories of prior occurrences, when they listen in this mode, in no way enable commentary on those prior hearings; those words were inscribed only in breath, and they are as gone as the hour of their speaking. The influence all runs in the other direction: the past hearings ring through the present, condition and enrich, enable the song of the moment. The traditional audience does not re-vise (that would be to re-see, a very text-bound idea), they do not correct their prior experience, the shape of the old poem as it resides in consciousness; they relive it, re-create it, hear, and celebrate it. Tradition cannot reform or criticize; or insofar as it does, it is in that measure textual. We can have it that way, but we must be clear and careful about the people by whose purposes we determine the relevant archive. Whether this precision is charity or merely détente, it is probably the best—perhaps the only—hope for providing a sound and articulated methodological background for the graduate students of the future and the languages they and their students will speak.

Notes

Preface

1. For example, Terry Eagleton, *Literary Theory: An Introduction* (Minneapolis, 1983); Raman Selden, *A Reader's Guide to Contemporary Literary Theory* (Lexington, 1985); Donald Keesey, *Criticism in Context* (Palo Alto, 1987).

2. Recent recollections include *Medieval Texts and Contemporary Readers*, ed. Laurie A. Finke and Martin B. Shichtman (Ithaca, 1987); and *Sign, Sentence, Discourse: Language in Medieval Thought and Literature*, ed. Julian N. Wasserman and Lois Roney (Syracuse, 1989). A volume of feminist criticism, *New Readings on Women in Old English Literature*, edited by Helen Damico and Alexandra Hennessy Olson, has just appeared (Bloomington, 1990). Despite its title, there is not much theory that is specifically contemporary in *Hermeneutics and Medieval Culture*, ed. Patrick J. Gallacher and Helen Damico (Albany, 1989).

3. Stephen G. Nichols, "Introduction: Philology in a Manuscript Culture," *Speculum* 65 (1990): 1–10, see 9.

4. On the dating, see Nichols's "Editor's Preface" to "The Legitimacy of the Middle Ages," *Romanic Review* 79 (1988): 1. See also the "Editor's Preface" to "Images of Power: Medieval History/Discourse/Literature," *Yale French Studies* 70 (1986): 1, a special issue edited by Kevin Brownlee and Stephen G. Nichols.

5. There is no Old English in either of the first two collections listed in note 2.

6. Ruth Waterhouse, " 'Wæter æddre asprang': How Cuthbert's Miracle Pours Cold Water on Source Studies," *Paregon* 5 (1987): 20.

7. Richard Altick, *The Art of Literary Research* (New York, 1965); James Thorpe, *The Principles of Textual Criticism* (San Marino, 1972).

8. Jerome J. McGann, "The Monks and the Giants: Textual and Bibliographical Studies and the Interpretation of Literary Works," in *Textual Criticism and Literary Interpretation*, ed. Jerome J. McGann (Chicago, 1985), 180–99.

9. Peter Travis, "Affective Criticism, the Pilgrimage of Reading, and Medieval English Literature," in Finke and Shichtman, *Medieval Texts*, 201; Travis's

comments are cited by Mary Carruthers in her review of this collection, *Studies in the Age of Chaucer* 11 (1989): 221–24.

10. Daniel Donohue, *Style in Old English Poetry: The Test of the Auxiliary* (New Haven, 1987); for the quote, see p. 3. Donohue invokes support for his inquiry into facts not only from Bede but even from Bruce Mitchell, "Linguistic Facts and the Interpretation of Old English Poetry," *Anglo-Saxon England* 4 (1975): 11–28.

11. An issue of *Critical Inquiry* examines the problem of pluralism; see especially Wayne C. Booth, "Pluralism in the Classroom," *Critical Inquiry* 12 (1986): 468–79; Hayden White, "Historical Pluralism," *Critical Inquiry* 12 (1986): 480–93; and, as an antidote to the excesses of theoretical enthusiasm, Joseph Epstein's review of Booth's *The Company We Keep* (Berkeley, 1989) in "Educated by Novels," *Commentary* 88.22 (August 1989): 33–39.

Chapter 1. Prologue: Documents and Monuments: Difference and Interdisciplinarity in the Study of Medieval Culture

1. See Raymond A. Wiley, ed., *John Mitchell Kemble and Jakob Grimm: A Correspondence 1832–1852* (Leiden, 1981). Gretchen P. Ackerman comments on Kemble's abrasive ways in "J. M. Kemble and Sir Frederick Madden: 'Conceit and Too Much Germanism'?" in *Anglo-Saxon Scholarship: The First Three Centuries,* ed. Carl T. Berkhout and Milton McC. Gatch (Boston, 1982), 176–81. For an admiring account of Kemble's historical method, see Patrick Sims-Williams, "The Settlement of England in Bede and the *Chronicle,*" *Anglo-Saxon England* 12 (1983): 1–41, see 4.

2. Henry Sweet, ed., *The Oldest English Texts,* Early English Text Society, Original Series 83 (London, 1885; reprint, 1966), v–vi.

3. For further commentary, see Allen J. Frantzen and Charles L. Venegoni, "The Desire for Origins: An Archaeological Analysis of Anglo-Saxon Studies," *Style* 20 (1986): 142–56.

4. Lee Patterson, *Negotiating the Past: The Historical Understanding of Medieval Literature* (Madison, 1987), 3.

5. Ibid., 1–39.

6. Anne Middleton, "Introduction: The Critical Heritage," in *A Companion to "Piers Plowman,"* ed. John A. Alford (Berkeley, 1988), 1–25; see 15–18.

7. John P. Hermann, *Allegories of War: Language and Violence in Old English Poetry* (Ann Arbor, 1989), 199–208. Allen J. Frantzen, *Desire for Origins: New Language, Old English, and Teaching the Tradition* (New Brunswick, 1990).

8. See D. W. Robertson, Jr., "Historical Criticism," in *English Institute Essays, 1950*, ed. A. S. Downer (New York, 1951); "The Doctrine of Charity in Medieval Literary Gardens: A Topical Approach Through Symbolism and Allegory," *Speculum* 26 (1951), reprinted in *An Anthology of "Beowulf" Criticism*, ed. Lewis E. Nicholson (Notre Dame, 1963, reprint, 1980), 165–88.

9. E. Talbot Donaldson, "Patristic Exegesis in the Criticism of Medieval Literature: The Opposition," in *Critical Approaches to Medieval Literature: Selected Papers from the English Institute, 1958–59*, ed. Dorothy Bethurum (New York, 1960; reprint, 1967), 1–26; this essay also appears in Donaldson's *Speaking of Chaucer* (New York, 1970), 134–53.

10. R. E. Kaske, "Patristic Exegesis in the Criticism of Medieval Literature: The Defense," in Bethurum, *Critical Approaches*, 27–60.

11. R. S. Crane, "Criticism as Inquiry; or, The Perils of the 'High Priori Road'," in *The Idea of the Humanities* (Chicago, 1967), 2.25–44; and "Critical and Historical Principles of Literary History," 2.45–156. There is a good discussion of Crane's views of the a priori assumptions of historical criticism in Gerald Graff, *Professing Literature: An Institutional History* (Chicago, 1987), 233–40.

12. Crane, "Criticism as Inquiry," 2.30.

13. Donaldson, "The Opposition," 18–20.

14. Derek Pearsall, "Poverty and Poor People in *Piers Plowman*," in *Medieval English Studies Presented to George Kane*, ed. Edward Donald Kennedy, Ronald Waldron, and Joseph S. Witting (Wolfeboro, NH, and Woodbridge, Suffolk, 1988): 167–85, see 180 for quote.

15. Traditional, simplistic ideas about the "revolt" are countered by Christopher Dyer, "The Social and Economic Background to the Rural Revolt of 1381," in *The English Rising of 1381*, ed. R. H. Hilton and T. H. Aston (Cambridge, 1984), 9–42.

16. See Donaldson's commentary on the tale in *Chaucer's Poetry: An Anthology for the Modern Reader* (New York, 1975), 1104–8. I leave to one side the possibility that *The Knight's Tale* also refers to the rising as the "cherles rebellyng" Saturn claims to inspire, l. 2459; see in *The Riverside Chaucer*, ed. Larry D. Benson (Boston, 1987), 58 and notes by Vincent J. DiMarco to this line, 838.

17. David Aers, *Chaucer, Langland, and the Creative Imagination* (London, 1980). See Peter W. Travis, "Chaucer's Trivial Fox Chase and the Peasants' Revolt of 1381," *Journal of Medieval and Renaissance Studies* 18 (1988): 195–220, who notes that Aers does not analyze Chaucer's response; see 215–16.

18. R. E. Kaske, "*Sapientia et Fortitudo* as the Controlling Theme of *Beowulf*," *Studies in Philology* 55 (1958): 423–57; reprinted in Nicholson, *Anthology*, 269–310. R. E. Kaske "*Sapientia et Fortitudo* in the Old English *Judith*," *The Wisdom of Poetry*, ed. Larry D. Benson and Siegfried Wenzel (Kalamazoo, 1982), 13–29, 264–68.

19. I discuss the source projects in "Value, Evaluation, and Twenty Years' Worth of Old English Studies," *Old English Newsletter,* Subsidia 18 (1989): 43–57.

20. Derek Pearsall, "Interpretative Models for the Peasants' Revolt," in *Hermeneutics and Medieval Culture,* ed. Patrick J. Gallacher and Helen Damico (Albany, 1989), 63–70, see 64.

21. Siegfried Wenzel, "Reflections on (New) Philology," *Speculum* 65 (1990): 11–18; see 13.

22. Giles Gunn, *The Culture of Criticism and the Criticism of Culture* (New York, 1987), 131.

23. Gunn, *The Culture,* 119–20. In *The Advancement of Learning* Francis Bacon defined the "three knowledges" as "Divine Philosophy, Natural Philosophy and Human Philosophy, or Humanitie." Quoted by Raymond Williams, *Keywords* (New York, 1983), 149 (cited by Gunn, 119).

24. John Higham, Leonard Krieger, and Felix Gilbert, *History* (Englewood Cliffs, NJ, 1965), 150–70, see 158 for quote.

25. See Graff, *Professing Literature,* 55–118. Richard Ohmann, *English in America: A Radical View of the Profession* (New York, 1976); Richard Ohmann, *Politics of Letters* (Middletown, CN, 1987). William E. Cain discusses the issue in a Marxist context in "English in America Reconsidered: Theory, Criticism, Marxism, and Social Change," in *Criticism in the University,* ed. Gerald Graff and Reginald Gibbons (Evanston, 1985), 85–104.

26. R. Howard Bloch, "New Philology and Old French," *Speculum* 65 (1990): 38–58, and "Naturalism, Nationalism, Medievalism," *Romanic Review* 76 (1986): 341–60.

27. Bruce Wilshire, *The Moral Collapse of the University: Professionalism, Purity, and Alienation* (Albany, 1990), 99–110.

28. Michel Foucault, "History of Systems of Thought," in *Language, Counter-Memory, Practice: Selected Essays and Interviews by Michel Foucault,* ed. Donald F. Bouchard, trans. Donald F. Bouchard and Sherry Simon (Ithaca, 1977), 199–204.

29. John Frow, *Marxism and Literary History* (Oxford, 1986), 187. Frow cites Tony Bennett, "Texts, Readers, Reading Formations," *Literature and History* 9 (1983): 218.

30. Gunn, *The Culture,* 120.

31. Northrop Frye, *Anatomy of Criticism: Four Essays* (Princeton, 1957), 6–7.

32. Roberta Frank, " 'Interdisciplinary': The First Half-Century," in *Words: For Robert Burchfield's Sixty-Fifth Birthday,* ed. E. G. Stanley and T. F. Hoad (Cambridge, 1988), 91–101.

33. See Patterson, *Negotiating*, 37, for comparable comments.

34. Frank, "Interdisciplinary," 100.

35. Graff, *Professing*, 6–7, 208, 238.

36. Frow, *Marxism*, 3.

37. Philippa Levine, *The Amateur and the Professional: Antiquarians, Historians and Archaeologists in Victorian England, 1838–1886* (Cambridge, 1986).

38. Ackerman, "J. M. Kemble," 177.

39. Stanley B. Greenfield and Fred C. Robinson, *A Bibliography of Publications on Old English Literature to the End of 1972* (Toronto, 1980), xiii: "weil sie kein selbständiges Interesse haben." A few studies of the glosses appear here under "Textual Criticism" (67–68).

40. I presented a version of this argument at the 1989 International Congress at the University of Western Michigan, Kalamazoo.

41. Ian Hodder, *Reading the Past: Current Approaches to Interpretation in Archaeology* (Cambridge, 1986), 164–78.

42. C. J. Arnold, *An Archaeology of the Early Anglo-Saxon Kingdoms* (London, 1988), 7.

43. Michael Shanks and Christopher Tilley, *Re-Constructing Archaeology: Theory and Practice* (Cambridge, 1987) and *Social Theory and Archaeology* (Albuquerque, 1988).

44. I derive this definition of typology from Shanks and Tilley, *Social Theory*, 79–82; see 149 for quote.

45. Shanks and Tilley, *Social Theory*, 148.

46. Early issues of *PMLA* contain many addresses about the place of literature and language in American education; some papers are excerpted by Gerald Graff and Michael Warner, eds., *The Origins of Literary Studies in America: A Documentary Anthology* (New York, 1989). See also Higham, Krieger, and Gilbert, *History*, 150–70, and Williams, *Keywords*, 243–45.

47. C. Stephen Jaeger, *The Origins of Courtliness: Civilizing Trends and the Formation of Courtly Ideals, 939–1210* (Philadelphia, 1985). See 7–9 for Jaeger's discussion of the idea of courtliness in scholarship.

48. Michael Nerlich, *Ideology of Adventure*, translated by Ruth Crowley, 2 vols. (Berlin, 1977; Minneapolis, 1987).

49. Quoted from *The Knight's Tale*, lines 1408–45, ed. Benson, *Riverside Chaucer*, 44–45.

50. John Dryden, "In Praise of Chaucer," in *Fables Ancient and Modern,* excerpted in *The Norton Anthology of English Literature,* ed. M. H. Abrams, *et al.,* 5th ed., 2 vols. (New York, 1986), 1.1850–51. Chaucer's text quoted from *The Parlement of Foules,* lines 22–23, ed. Benson, *Riverside Chaucer,* 385. See David Aers, "The *Parliament of Fowls*": Authority, the Knower and the Known," *The Chaucer Review* 16 (1981): 1–17. Aers elaborates on the role of production in the later Middle Ages in "Rewriting the Middle Ages: Some Suggestions," *Journal of Medieval and Renaissance Studies* 18 (1988): 221–40.

51. Shanks and Tilley, *Re-Constructing,* 16–17; see also 103–10.

52. Shanks and Tilley, *Social Theory,* 202.

53. Foucault's analysis of the will to truth rests on some of the views of the "Annales" historians and the "Frankfurt School." See David Held, *Introduction to Critical Theory: Horkheimer to Habermas* (Berkeley and Los Angeles, 1980), 29–39, on the "Frankfurt School," and Stuart Clark, "The *Annales* Historians," in *The Return of Grand Theory in the Human Sciences,* ed. Quentin Skinner (Cambridge, 1985), 179–98. The past and the future of the "Frankfurt School" is discussed by Douglas Kellner, *Critical Theory, Marxism and Modernity* (Baltimore, 1989).

54. Michel Foucault, *The Archaeology of Knowledge* and *The Discourse on Language,* trans. A. M. Sheridan Smith (New York, 1972), 220–23. Helpful commentary on Foucault is offered by Edward W. Said, *Beginnings: Intention and Method* (New York, 1975), 228–31, 279–343; Frank Lentricchia, *After the New Criticism* (Chicago, 1980), 188–210; and Paul A. Bové, *Intellectuals in Power: A Genealogy of Critical Humanism* (New York, 1986), 209–37, 229–310. I elaborate on ideas expressed here in Chapter 4 of *Desire for Origins.*

55. Foucault, *Discourse on Language,* 224.

56. Foucault, *Archaeology of Knowledge,* 6–7. My discussion of this issue has profited from discussion with Jeffrey Nealon.

57. Ibid., 7.

58. Mark Poster, "The Future According to Foucault: *The Archaeology of Knowledge* and the Intellectual History," in *Modern European Intellectual History: Reappraisals and New Perspectives,* ed. Dominick LaCapra and Steven L. Kaplan (Ithaca, 1982), 137–52; see 144–45.

59. Foucault, *Archaeology of Knowledge,* 8.

60. Hayden White, "Foucault Decoded: Notes from Underground," in *Tropics of Discourse: Essays in Cultural Criticism* (Baltimore and London, 1978), 230–60; see 239.

61. John Earle, *The Deeds of* Beowulf (Oxford, 1892), xviii.

62. Martin Biddle and Birthe Kjøbye-Biddle, "Repton 1984." Pamphlet distributed to International Society of Anglo-Saxonists at Repton Church, August 1985, 3.

63. M. O. H. Carver, "Anglo-Saxon Objectives at Sutton Hoo, 1985," *Anglo-Saxon England* 15 (1986): 139–52.

64. R. W. Chambers, *"Beowulf": An Introduction to the Study of the Poem with a Discussion of the Stories of Offa and Finn* (Cambridge, 1959), 508.

65. Quoted by Chambers, *"Beowulf,"* 417–18; on Lindqvist, see 510.

66. Gunn, *The Culture*, 131.

67. Patrick Wormald, "Bede, 'Beowulf' and the Conversion of the Anglo-Saxon Aristocracy," in *Bede and Anglo-Saxon England*, ed. Robert T. Farrell (Oxford, 1978), 32–95; see 36.

68. Arnold, *An Archaeology*, 9.

69. Richard Johnson, "What is Cultural Studies Anyway?" *Social Text* 16 (1986): 38–80.

70. Johnson, "What Is," 63.

71. Ibid., 62.

72. Frow, *Marxism*, 59.

73. Ibid., 234, quoting Leo Bersani, "The Subject of Power," *Diacritics* 8 (1978): 6.

74. Clifford Geertz, *The Interpretation of Cultures* (New York, 1973), 433–51. Quoted in Gunn, 105.

75. Frow, *Marxism*, 64–66; Gunn, *The Culture*, 93–115. A related discussion of interest to Anglo-Saxonists is Seth Lerer's forthcoming study, *Literacy and Power in Anglo-Saxon Literature* (Lincoln, NB).

76. James Clifford and George E. Marcus, eds. *Writing Culture: The Poetics and Politics of Ethnography* (Berkeley, 1986), 15.

77. See Wilshire, *Moral Collapse*, 99–108 and 244–49 for a discussion relating the purity of the disciplines to purification rituals.

78. The influence of M. M. Bakhtin on Gunn's discussion is clear; see *The Culture*, 130–46. See also Ken Hirschkop and David Shepherd, eds., *Bakhtin and Cultural Theory* (New York, 1990).

79. Paul Zumthor, *Speaking of the Middle Ages*, trans. Sarah White (Lincoln and London, 1986), 27.

80. Vida Dutton Scudder, *Social Ideals in English Letters* (New York, 1898), 7. I thank Matt Matcuk for bringing this quote to my attention.

81. Vida Dutton Scudder, *On Journey* (New York, 1937); quoted in Graff and Warner, *Origins of Literary Studies*, 176–77.

82. E. T. Leeds, *Early Anglo-Saxon Art and Archaeology* (Oxford, 1936; reprint, Westport, CN, 1970), 26.

83. John Ruskin, "Torcello," in *The Stones of Venice*, vol. 2, quoted from *The Works of John Ruskin*, ed. E. T. Cook and Alexander Wedderburn, 39 vols. (London, 1904), 10.20.

84. On the medievalism of Ruskin, William Morris and others, which emphasized the Middle Ages as a time of primitive and bracing originality, see Patterson, *Negotiating the Past*, 10–11 and notes 14–15.

85. Ruskin, "Torcello," 18.

86. Richard Ellmann, *Golden Codgers: Biographical Speculations* (New York, 1973), 47. Ruskin later modified some of his views on the Italian Renaissance, Ellmann notes, 49–50.

87. Ruskin, "The Nature of Gothic," in *The Stones of Venice*, vol. 2, ed. Cook and Wedderburn, *Works*, 10.193.

88. Mary Louise Pratt, "Fieldwork in Common Places," in *Writing Culture*, ed. Clifford and Marcus, 27–50.

89. Johnson, "What is," 63.

90. This observation has often been made about deconstructionists; see Frederick Crews, "Deconstructing a Discipline," in *Skeptical Engagements* (New York, 1986), 115–20.

91. Terry Eagleton, *Literary Theory: An Introduction* (Minneapolis, 1983); Edward W. Said, *The World, the Text, and the Critic* (Cambridge, MA, 1983).

92. Bové, *Intellectuals in Power*, 306.

93. Frow, *Marxism*, 231–35; Shanks and Tilley, *Social Theory*, 194–208, and *Re-constructing Archaeology*, 243–46.

94. Kellner, *Critical Theory*, 7.

95. I quote Lentricchia, *After the New Criticism*, 209.

Chapter 2. On Reading Eve: *Genesis B* and the Readers' Desire

1. Elizabeth Elstob, "An Apology for the Study of Northern Antiquities," *The Rudiments of Grammar for the English-Saxon Tongue* (1715; reprint, Menston, England, 1968). My references to the "Apology" are from a facsimile reprint is-

sued separately from the *Grammar* by the Augustan Reprint Society (UCLA, Los Angeles, 1956), Publication Number 61.

2. Ibid., 2.

3. I am grateful to Karma Lochrie for this astute observation.

4. See the section on further reading following this essay for specific references.

5. Alice Jardine, *Gynesis* (Ithaca, 1985), 32.

6. I refer here to Judith Fetterly's seminal study of the female reader, *The Resisting Reader: A Feminist Approach to American Fiction* (Bloomington, IN, 1978).

7. Patrocinio Schweickart, "Reading Ourselves: Towards a Feminist Theory of Reading," in *Gender and Reading: Essays on Readers, Texts, and Contexts*, ed. Elizabeth A. Flynn and Patrocinio P. Schweickart (Baltimore, 1986), 35.

8. Ibid., 50.

9. Christine Froula, "When Eve Reads Milton: Undoing the Canonical Economy," in *Canons*, ed. Robert Von Hallberg (Chicago, 1986), 164.

10. Ibid., 164.

11. Schweickart, "Reading Ourselves," 42.

12. Froula, "When Eve Reads Milton," 165.

13. Schweickart, "Reading Ourselves," 43.

14. See especially the essays by Martin Irvine and Clare Lees.

15. Schweickart, "Reading Ourselves," 47.

16. Adrienne Rich, *On Lies, Secrets and Silence: Selected Prose, 1966–78* (New York, 1979), 161.

17. In 1875 Edouard Sievers advanced the theory that *Genesis B* was a translation of an Old Saxon poem, and in 1894 he was proved right with the discovery of an Old Saxon fragment in the Vatican library. A close examination of the surviving Old Saxon, which corresponds to lines 791–817 of the Old English text, shows that the Old English poet translated almost word for word. The passage is cited in *The Junius Manuscript*, ed. G. P. Krapp (New York, 1931), 171. The text of *Genesis B* is inserted into the text of *Genesis A*, suggesting that someone has already taken the fragment and attempted to give it context within a whole. This text is at once an independent unit and a fragment. Also interesting to note is Krapp's editorial overview, where the poem is perceived a "to as large extent an interruption of the orderly paraphrase of *Genesis A*"(164).

18. See Laurie A. Finke's remarks on Augustinian doctrine and the idealized synthesis of words and things in "Truth's Treasure: Allegory and Meaning in *Piers Plowman*," in *Medieval Texts and Contemporary Readers*, ed. Laurie A. Finke and Martin B. Shichtman (Ithaca, 1987), 53.

19. Annette Kolodny, "Dancing Through the Minefield: Some Observations on the Theory, Practice and Politics of a Feminist Literary Criticism," *Feminist Studies* 6 (1980): 10–12.

20. Examples of source studies include: F. N. Robinson, "A Note on The Sources of the Old Saxon *Genesis*," *Modern Philology* 4 (1907): 389–96; S. J. Crawford, "A Latin Parallel for Part of the Later Genesis," *Anglia* 158 (1924): 99–100; Marcel Dando, "The Moralia in Job of Gregory the Great as a Source of the Old Saxon *Genesis B*," *Classica et Medievalia* 30 (1969): 420–39; Thomas D. Hill, "Satan's Injured Innocence in *Genesis B*, 360–2; 390–2: A Gregorian Source," *English Studies* 65 (1984): 289–90; see also the first part of J. M. Evans, "*Genesis B* and Its Background," *Review of English Studies*, n.s., 14 (1963): 1–16 and 113–23, for a good overview of source studies. Studies focusing on specific motifs, passages, or phrases include: John F. Vickrey, "The *Micel Wundor* of *Genesis B*," *Studies in Philology* 68 (1971): 245–54; G. C. Britton, "Repetition and Contrast in the Old English *Later Genesis*," *Neophilologus* 58 (1974): 58–73; J. R. Hall, "*Geongordom* and *Hyldo* in *Genesis B*: Serving the Lord for the Lord's Favor," *Papers on Language and Literature* 11 (1975): 302–7, and "Duality and the Dual Pronoun in *Genesis B*," *Papers on Language and Literature* 17 (1981): 139–45; David Yerkes, "*Genesis B* 318–320 Again," *English Language Notes* 13 (1976): 242–43; Karen Cherewatuk, "Standing, Turning, Twisting, Falling: Posture and Moral Stance in *Genesis B*," *Neuphilologische Mitteilungen* 87 (1986): 537–44. References to the third group of critics—and I stress that to some extent such grouping is arbitrary, in that the categories of interest overlap—will follow as I refer to them in the text.

21. J. M. Evans, cited above, lays out clearly the terms of this poem's doctrinal difference. He hypothesizes the kind of traditional teaching on the subject of the Fall that might have been available to the *Genesis B* poet and then lists the ways in which *Genesis B* diverges from it. I include here Evans's thorough and succinct summary of the poem's theological peculiarities:

> The temptation is undertaken not by Satan himself but by a subordinate devil who masquerades as an angel of God, not as a serpent. He tempts Adam first, claiming that God has sent him to tell Man to eat of the tree of knowledge. This tree, far from being beautiful as in Genesis, is evil and ugly; it is the tree of death. Having failed to convince Adam, the devil turns to Eve, who believes his story and eats the forbidden fruit to save Adam from divine retribution. Her motives are pure and there is no suggestion of any "love of her own power" or "proud presumption." When she has eaten the fruit she has a vision of heaven which convinces her that the "angel" was all he claimed to be. Adam, too, is assured of the mes-

senger's good faith and eats the fruit believing that he is obeying the instructions of God. After the devil has made a long speech of triumph Adam and Eve realize that they have been deceived. They repent immediately, praying that God will punish them and thus allow them to make amends. Adam reproaches Eve for her part in his Fall, but she placates him and they go off together to pray for divine guidance. Nowhere is there any hint that they refused to acknowledge their guilt or sought to transfer it to God. (4)

22. Rosemary Woolf, "The Fall of Man in *Genesis B* and the *Mystère d'Adam*," in *Studies in Honor of Arthur G. Brodeur*, ed. Stanley B. Greenfield (Eugene, OR, 1963), 189.

23. Ibid., 197.

24. Ibid., 189.

25. Ibid., 193.

26. Ibid.

27. Ibid., 194.

28. Ibid.

29. Ibid.

30. Ibid., 196.

31. Ibid., 197.

32. John Vickrey, "The Vision of Eve in *Genesis B*," *Speculum* 44 (1969), 91.

33. Ibid., 98.

34. My references to *Genesis B* are taken from *The Junius Manuscript*, ed. G. P. Krapp (New York, 1931). All translations from the Old English are my own; in-text references are to lines.

35. Vickery, "The Vision," 99.

36. Ibid., 98.

37. Ibid., 98.

38. Ibid., 99.

39. Alain Renoir, "The Self-Deception of Temptation: Boethian Psychology in *Genesis B*," in *Old English Poetry*, ed. Robert P. Creed (Providence, 1967), 55.

40. Maureen Quilligan, *Milton's Spenser: The Politics of Reading* (Ithaca, 1983), 228.

41. Robert E. Finnegan, "Eve and 'Vincible Ignorance' in *Genesis B*," *Texas Studies in Literature and Language* 18 (1976): 329.

42. Ibid., 329.

43. Ibid.

44. Ibid., 336.

45. Ibid., 330.

46. Ibid., 331.

47. Ibid., 333.

48. Ibid., 336.

49. Ibid.

50. Robert Finnegan, "God's *Handmægen* Versus the Devil's *Cræft* in *Genesis B*," *English Studies in Canada* 7 (1981): 6.

51. Ibid., 9.

52. Ibid.

53. Ibid., 11.

54. Margaret Erhart, "The Tempter as Teacher: Some Observations on the Vocabulary of the Old English *Genesis B*," *Neophilologus* 59 (1975): 443.

55. Ibid., 436–37.

56. Ibid., 441.

57. For an overview of some of the idealogical assumptions that have shaped the course and nature of scholarship in both poetry and prose see Allen J. Frantzen and Charles L. Venegoni, "The Desire for Origins: An Archaeological Analysis of Anglo-Saxon Studies," *Style* 20 (1986): 142–56.

58. J. M. Evans, "*Genesis B* and Its Background" (part 1), *Review of English Studies*, n.s. 14 (1963): 1.

59. Ibid., 5.

60. Ibid., 5–16.

61. Ibid., 16.

62. J. M. Evans, "*Genesis B* and Its Background" (part 2), *Review of English Studies*, n.s. 14 (1963): 119.

63. Ibid., 113.

64. Ibid., 120.

65. Ibid., 122.

66. Ibid., 113.

67. Ibid., 121.

68. Ibid., 115.

69. Michael Cherniss, *Ingeld and Christ: Heroic Concepts and Values in Old English Christian Poetry* (The Hague, 1972), 164–65.

70. Ibid., 165.

71. Ibid., 166.

72. I discuss the problematic role of peaceweaver at greater length in an examination of gender and interpretation in chapter 3 of *Language, Sign and Gender in Beowulf* (Carbondale, IL, 1990).

73. Jane Chance, *Woman as Hero in Old English Literature* (Syracuse, 1986), 74. Although I have put Chance in my "Germanic" category, I should point out that she sees the poem as working on both biblical and Germanic levels (67). I am interested here, however, in the primarily Germanic construct of peaceweaving.

74. Ibid., 75.

75. Ibid., 79.

76. Ibid.

77. Jacques Derrida, "Structure, Sign, and Play in the Discourse of the Human Sciences," in *The Structuralist Controversy,* ed. Richard Macksey and Eugenio Donato (Baltimore, 1972), 265.

78. Chance, *Woman as Hero,* 76.

79. Ibid., 78.

80. John Vickrey, "*Selfsceaft* in *Genesis B,*" *Anglia* 83 (1965): 166.

81. Thomas D. Hill, "The Fall of Angels and Man in the Old English *Genesis B,*" in *Anglo-Saxon Poetry: Essays in Appreciation,* ed. Lewis E. Nicholson and Dolores Warwick Frese (Notre Dame, 1975), 282.

82. Ibid., 282.

83. Ibid., 283.

84. Ibid., 284.

85. See also Pat Belanoff, "The Fall (?) of the Old English Female Poetic Image," *PMLA* 104 (1989): 822–31. Belanoff's study fits neither of my categories but rather studies Eve in the context of the overlay and "intermixing of Germanic

traditional poetry and Christian dogma, as well as other political and social forces''
(829) and as such begins a needed reappraisal of our means of appraising both Eve
and the Anglo-Saxon woman as she is represented in poetry.

86. Anne L. Klinck, ''Female Characterisation in Old English Poetry and the
Growth of Psychological Realism: *Genesis B* and *Christ I*,'' *Neophilologus* 63
(1979): 599.

87. Ibid., 601.

88. Ibid., 600.

89. See Froula's remarks on Isak Dinesen's short story, ''The Blank Page,''
at the end of ''When Even reads Milton,'' 164–72. The story offers multiple ways
of metaphorizing women's silence and the process of being silenced.

90. Cherniss, *Ingeld and Christ*, 165.

91. Teresa de Lauretis, *Alice Doesn't: Feminism, Semiotics, Cinema* (Bloomington, IN, 1984), 112.

92. Ibid., 120–21.

93. Michel Serres, *Hermes Literature, Science, Philosophy* (Baltimore,
1982), also discusses these kinds of narrative patterning in his chapter ''Language
and Space: From Oedipus to Zola,'' 39–53. Serres metaphorizes narrative as a *jeu
de l'oie* (goose's game), a board game where landing on a certain square will determine certain moves. Narrative possibilities and progress then become ''a set of
circulations within the social body'' (40). But the journey through the series of
spaces and obstacles remains clearly identified as an oedipal itinerary, that is, one
motivated by oedipal desire. Though, for example, Serres suggests that Penelope, as
weaver of the flux of events, might create the conditions for the itinerary, Ulysses
will be its navigator.

94. See chapter 1, ''Approaching Abjection,'' of Julia Kristeva's *Powers of
Horror* (New York, 1982), 1–31.

95. Ibid.

96. Ibid., 87

97. Ibid., 88.

98. Ibid.

99. See lines 309–10, 329, 353, and 537 for references to honoring the Word;
and lines 245, 405, 440, 528, 593, 600, 613, 730–31, 770, and 798 for the many
variations on this phrase.

100. See Evans, 113–15, for a discussion and enumeration of contrasts between Eve's action and intention.

101. Froula, ''When Eve Reads Milton,'' 153–54.

102. Kristeva, *Powers of Horror,* 126.

103. Woolf also comments on this unusual use of the adjective, but claims that it suggests a "lack of dignity" ("Fall of Man," 197) and verges on "nagging."

104. While following the apple's semantic progress in the poem, I became curious about its actual semantic resonance. When I looked through the many references in the *Microfiche Concordance to Old English* (Toronto, 1980), I discovered that, overall, apples are remarkably unstigmatized and put to a great variety of innocent uses. The most common contexts for them, for example, were charms, spells, and medicinal uses. The juice or rind of an apple, or cooked apples, might be used to dress wounds, heal sore veins and limbs; apples were also cited as the cause of gas pain. For a more detailed summary of my findings in the *Concordance* and an examination of further contemporaneous sources for discovering the semantic and discursive possibilities of the apple, see my article, "Of Apples, Eve, and *Genesis B:* Contemporary Theory and Old English Practice," forthcoming in *American Notes and Queries.*

105. Kristeva, *Powers of Horror,* 88.

Chapter 3. *Beowulf* and the Origins of Civilization

1. I have developed supporting details of this argument elsewhere: the analysis of tragedy in "Identification and Catharsis" in *Pragmatism's Freud,* ed. J. Smith and W. Kerrigan (Baltimore, 1986), 79–92; of the Anglo-Saxon conversion in "The Role of the Men's Hall," *Psychiatry* 46 (1983): 139–60: of Christian psychology in "Augustine, Freud, Lacan," in *Psychoanalysis and Religion: Postmodern Perspectives,* a special issue of *Thought* 61 (1986): 7–15; of the heroic age in "Apocalypticism and Mourning," *Thought* 57 (1982): 362–70; and the secularity and materialism of Anglo-Saxon culture in "Transformations of Chaos," *Ultimate Reality and Meaning* 10 (1987): 164–85.

2. Jameson's "political unconscious" might seem to offer a linkage between the insights of psychoanalysis and Marxism, the source of these criticisms. But that concept is as mystical in its Hegelian way as the Jungian collectivities from which it is also derived (via Northrop Frye) and cannot be counted a psychoanalytic concept.

3. Detailed argument of this point is forthcoming. In short, three factors have led me to doubt the traditionality of the text. (1) Recent debate over the dating of the poem by Kevin S. Kiernan, *"Beowulf" and the Beowulf MS* (New Brunswick, 1981); Colin Chase *The Dating of "Beowulf"* (Toronto, 1981); David N. Dumville, *"Beowulf* and the Celtic World," *Traditio* 37 (1981); 109–60; and Michael Lapidge, *"Beowulf,* Aldhelm, the *Liber Monstrorum,* and Wessex," *Studi Medievali,* 3d s., 23 (1982): 151–92, inter alios, suggests to me only that that problem is probably insoluble. There are now good arguments for dating the poem in every century from the seventh to the eleventh, in every part of England. Therefore, we

should not build theories and interpretations of the poem that depend too heavily on an eighth-century, or any other, date; and inversely, we cannot safely use the poem to help us interpret Anglo-Saxon history. (2) It is a hasty generalization to claim that epic is a traditional oral genre: "There exists in the oral tradition no epic as such, although epics are now being written," Jeff Opland says of the Bantus (*Anglo-Saxon Oral Poetry* [New Haven, 1981], 21–22). There are other oral cultures without epic as well—most conspicuously the Yugoslavian Christians, whose Muslim neighbors have produced the most studied oral epics of all. The issue then becomes, what evidence exists of specifically Anglo-Saxon oral epic? *Beowulf* is the single example of the genre, unless we credit the tiny fragments "Finnsburh" and "Waldere," which could as easily be lays like "Maldon." If there was no traditional oral epic, there would have been no epic-generic expectations in the *Beowulf* poet or in his audience. Therefore, the distinctive features of the poem's large structure—its use of digressions, for example—should not be regarded as traditional or typical, but rather as the invention of the poet. An older generation of scholars knew this; E. V. K. Dobbie says "Neither the Caedmonian poetry nor the heroic lays brought from the Continent could have afforded a sufficient model" for *Beowulf* (*Anglo-Saxon Poetic Records,* vol. 5 [New York, 1953], lv.). (3) The most telling argument, however, is the complete absence of any reference to our poem or its hero in any other medieval document. All the other characters except Unferth are more or less richly attested, but the silence regarding Beowulf himself is deafening. Dobbie again: "There is no reason for believing that [Beowulf] was anything more than a fictitious hero invented by the poet" (xxxiv). Applying Occam's razor to all three of these arguments, it is hard not to draw the conclusion that the poem is highly original in important respects.

4. Sigmund Freud, "Future of an Illusion," in *The Freud Reader,* ed. Peter Gay (New York, 1989), 690.

5. E.g., Robert Hanning, "*Beowulf* as Heroic History," *Medievalia et Humanistica,* n.s., 27 (1974): 77–102: the poet "completely reverses all tendencies toward harmony in heroic history, and offers instead a soured, ironic version of what has gone on before, embodying a final assessment of a world without God as a world in which time and history are themselves negative concepts" (88); and T. A. Shippey, *Beowulf* (London, 1978), 37–38, who observes "that the poet is demonstrating the inadequacy of heroic society; that he sees this the more forcibly for being a Christian; and that his rejection of overt finger-pointing first gives the pleasure of ironic perception, and second shows the glittering insidiousness of heroism, the way it perverts even the best of intentions." The latest major statement of this position is Bernard Huppé, *The Hero in the Earthly City* (Binghamtom, 1984).

6. J. R. R. Tolkien, "*Beowulf:* the Monsters and the Critics," in *An Anthology of Beowulf Criticism,* ed. Lewis Nicholson (Notre Dame, 1963), 77.

7. *The Wanderer,* quoted from *The Exeter Book,* ed. Elliott van Kirk Dobbie (*Anglo-Saxon Poetic Records,* vol. 3 [New York, 1936], 134.

8. James W. Earl, "The Role of the Men's Hall," 152.

9. Colin Chase, "*Beowulf*," in *The Year's Work in Old English Studies*, ed. Rowland L. Collins, *Old English Newsletter* 18 (1984): 96.

10. W. F. Bolton, *Alcuin and Beowulf* (New Brunswick, 1978).

11. See, for example, Hans Loewald, *Papers on Psychoanalysis* (New Haven, 1980), especially "Internalization, Separation, Mourning, and the Superego" and "The Waning of the Oedipus Complex"; Roy Shafer, *Aspects of Internalization* (New York, 1968); Joseph Smith, "Identificatory Styles in Depression and Grief," *International Journal of Psycho-Analysis* 52 (1971): 259–66; Richard Wolheim, "Identification and Imagination," in *Freud* (Garden City, 1974); Janine Chasseguet-Smirgel, *The Ego Ideal* (New York, 1985); and Mikkel Borch-Jacobsen, *The Freudian Subject*, trans. Catherine Porter (Stanford, 1988).

12. *Beowulf*, ed. Dobbie, 93–95.

13. This in spite of Rosemary Woolf's demonstration, "The Ideal of Men Dying with Their Lord in the *Germania* and 'The Battle of Maldon' *Anglo-Saxon England* 5 (1976), that there is no Germanic tradition of suicidal battle. The force of her argument does not diminish but enhances the ethic of suicidal heroism in "Maldon," because it is freely chosen. Note Richard Abels's argument in *Lordship and Military Obligation in Anglo-Saxon England* (Berkeley, 1988), that even in the eleventh century the Anglo-Saxon army was motivated by appealing to local ties of lordship rather than national loyalties.

14. Tacitus, *Germania*, trans. H. W. Benario (New York, 1967), 47.

15. E.g., Derek Freeman's anthropological defense of the theory in "Totem and Taboo: A Reappraisal," in *Man and His Culture: Psychoanalytic Anthropology after "Totem and Taboo,"* ed. Warner Muensterberger (New York, 1970), 53–78; René Girard's analysis of sacrifice and Greek tragedy in *Violence and the Sacred*, trans. P. Gregory (Baltimore, 1977); C. R. Badcock's sociobiological analysis in *The Problem of Altruism* (Oxford, 1986); Janine Chasseguet-Smirgel's revision of the classic theory in *The Ego Ideal*, esp. 76–93; and Borch-Jacobsen's deconstruction of Freud's concept of the ego in *The Freudian Subject*.

16. Sigmund Freud, *Group Psychology and the Analysis of the Ego*, vol. 18 of the *Standard Edition*, ed. James Strachey (London, 1953–78), 116, 125.

17. Ibid., 88–89.

18. Sigmund Freud, "The Ego and the Id," in *The Freud Reader*, ed. Peter Gay (New York, 1989), 641–42.

19. Freud, *Group Psychology*, 105.

20. Ibid., 125.

21. Freud, *Group Psychology*, 88.

Chapter 4. The Plot of *Piers Plowman* and the Contradictions of Feudalism

1. However, see some recent arguments for dialogism in *Piers Plowman* in M. M. Bakhtin's sense: David Aers, *Community, Gender, and Individual Identity: English Writing, 1360–1430* (London and New York, 1988), 40; and David Lawton, "The Subject of *Piers Plowman*," *Yearbook of Langland Studies* 1 (1988): 1–30.

2. I take "ideology" as consisting of "those myths through which individuals are reconciled to their given social positions by falsely representing to them those positions and the relationships between them as if they formed a part of some inherently significant, intrinsically coherent plan or process" (Tony Bennett, *Formalism and Marxism* [London, 1979], 116). "Hegemony" in Raymond Williams's sense has a comparable meaning: it "is a whole body of practices and expectations; our assignments of energy, our ordinary understanding of the nature of man and of his world. It is a set of meanings and values which as they are experienced as practices appear as reciprocally confirming. It thus constitutes a sense of reality for most people in the society." ("Base and Superstructure in Marxist Cultural Theory," *New Left Review* no. 82 [1973]: 9).

3. Cf. Raymond Williams: "the process of an author's development can be grasped as a complex of active relations, within which the emergence of an individual project, and the real history of other contemporary projects and of the developing forms and structures, are continuously and substantially interactive" (*Marxism and Literature* [Oxford, 1977], 196). On changes made by Langland on some forms of representation, see Charles Muscatine, *Poetry and Crisis in the Age of Chaucer* (Notre Dame and London, 1972), 71–109. Priscilla Martin's *"Piers Plowman": The Field and the Tower* (London, 1979) takes Muscatine's essay as a point of departure.

4. Pierre Macherey, *A Theory of Literary Production*, trans. Geoffrey Wall (Paris, 1966; London, 1978), 115.

5. For a time Louis Althusser described science and ideology as essentially different forms of knowledge (see, e.g., "Marxism Is Not a Historicism," in *Reading Capital*, ed. Althusser and Etienne Balibar, trans. Ben Brewster [Paris, 1968; New York, 1970], 127–28, 131, 133). This position was untenable (see, e.g., Bennett, *Formalism and Marxism*, 112). While James Kavanagh calls criticism "scientific" when it reads the symptoms of an ideology, this does not mean that critical discourse can somehow exist outside ideology, free of its own distortions, unmotivated by class interest. See "Marxism's Althusser: Toward a Politics of Literary Theory," *Diacritics* 12, no. 1 (Spring 1982): 27.

6. I.e., Jean Jacques Rousseau, *Discours sur l'origine et les fondements de l'inégalité parmi les hommes* (1755). See Derrida's *Of Grammatology*, trans. G. C. Spivak (Paris, 1967; Baltimore and London, 1974), 170–94. Deconstruction, of course, is not a theory.

7. See Anna P. Baldwin, *The Theme of Government in "Piers Plowman"* (Cambridge, 1981), 40–41.

8. Anna P. Baldwin, "The Historical Context," in *A Companion to "Piers Plowman,"* ed. John A. Alford (Berkeley, 1988), 67–68. James Simpson has now proposed that Langland often sees the "relations between man and God . . . in the terms of a profit economy ("Spirituality and Economics in Passus 1–7 of the B Text," *The Yearbook of Langland Studies* 1 [1987]: 87). Simpson uses "profit" very broadly to denote bribes, gifts, interest on loans, and profits from trade, which he refers to just briefly. "Profit economy" in such a broad sense has only a very limited descriptive value within economic history.

9. Baldwin, "Historical Context," 83.

10. For attempts to articulate the relationship between literature and ideology, see Bennett, *Formalism and Marxism,* 59, 122, 124–26, 128–29, 132–34, 140.

11. Baldwin, "Historical Context," 68.

12. William Langland, *Piers Plowman: The B Version,* ed. George Kane and E. T. Donaldson (London, 1975), 6.27–28. I follow the B text in this essay because, as Kane and Donaldson say in their Introduction, it is "the one form of *Piers Plowman* which at some moment in history its author might have considered finished" (212). Further references will be included in the text, cited by passus and line.

13. Baldwin, "Historical Context," 68.

14. Quoted by M. A. Moisa, "Fourteenth-Century Preachers' Views of the Poor: Class or Status Group?" in *Culture, Ideology, and Politics: Essays for Eric Hobsbawm,* ed. Ralph Samuel and G. S. Jones (London, 1982), 161.

15. Georges Duby, *The Three Orders: Feudal Society Imagined,* trans. Arthur Goldhammer (Paris, 1978; Chicago and London, 1980), 161. Cf. Jon Elster: "The impression of a voluntary and rational arrangement disappears when one observes that the lord provided protection mainly against other lords. . . . Feudalism, that is, may well have been a Nash equilibrium, in the sense that for each community subordination to the lord was optimal given that everyone else behaved similarly. Yet insubordination would also have been an equilibrium, for if all communities refused to sustain their lords there would be no predators to fear and no need for protection" (*Making Sense of Marx* [Cambridge, 1985], 488–89).

16. M. M. Postan, *The Medieval Economy and Society: An Economic History of Britain in the Middle Ages* (London, 1972), 156.

17. On the way in which a ruling ideology is installed only by "a very bitter and continuous class struggle," see Louis Althusser, "Ideology and Ideological State Apparatuses (Notes towards an Investigation)" (1969–70), in *"Lenin and Philosophy" and Other Essays,* trans. Ben Brewster (New York and London, 1971), 185. Trifunctionality was clearly contested: Rodney Hilton points out that leaders and followers alike in the Peasants' Revolution rejected "the concept of a society composed of a balance of hierarchically arranged estates" ("Social Concepts in the English Rising of 1381" (in German, 1975), *Class Conflict and the Crisis of Feudalism* [London, 1985], 225).

18. Baldwin, "Historical Context," 69.

19. Ibid., 72.

20. Ibid., 70.

21. By "relations of production" I mean the relations in which means of production (both the objects on which labor power works and the instruments that work on these objects) stand to the agents of production (individual human beings, institutions, corporations, etc.). See W. A. Suchting, *Marx: An Introduction* (New York and London, 1983), 76. Jacques Rancière defines them as "the social forms of appropriation of the means of production, which are class forms of appropriation": "On the Theory of Ideology (the Politics of Althusser)," trans. Martin Jordin, *Radical Philosophy* 7 (Spring 1974): 3.

22. Kohachiro Takahashi, "A Contribution to the Discussion" (1952), in *The Transition from Feudalism to Capitalism*, ed. Rodney Hilton (London, 1976), 81. Cf. John Merrington, "Town and Country in the Transition to Capitalism" (1975), in ibid., 179.

23. See Rodney Hilton, "Peasant Movements in England Before 1381," *Economic History Review*, 2d ser., 2 (1949): 135, and *Bond Men Made Free: Medieval Peasant Movements and the English Rising of 1381* (London, 1973), 174–75.

24. Baldwin, "Historical Context," 71.

25. Ibid., 76.

26. Ibid., 70.

27. Ibid., 71.

28. Ibid., 72.

29. M. M. Postan, however, whom Baldwin quotes in *Theme of Government*, 62, speaks of "the capitalist or quasi-capitalist economy in demesne or monastic granges." While Baldwin takes up the Peasants' Revolution (70–72), she remains oblique on its having been exactly a conflict between feudal and capitalist elements. See E. A. Kosminsky, *Studies in the Agrarian History of England in the Thirteenth Century*, trans. Ruth Kisch (Oxford, 1956), 357.

30. Myra Stokes, *Justice and Mercy in "Piers Plowman": A Reading of the B Text Visio* (London and Canberra, 1984); Robert Adams, "Piers's Pardon and Langland's Semi-Pelagianism," *Traditio* 39 (1983): 367–418.

31. Stokes, *Justice and Mercy*, 168.

32. Ibid., 60.

33. Ibid., 211.

34. Ibid., 257.

35. Seriatim: Anne Middleton, "Narrative and the Invention of Experience: Episodic Form in *Piers Plowman*," in *The Wisdom of Poetry: Essays in Early English Literature in Honor of Morton W. Bloomfield*, ed. L. D. Benson and Siegfried Wenzel (Kalamazoo, 1982), 92; A. J. Colianne, "Structure and 'Foreconceit' in *Piers Plowman* B: Some Observations on Langland's Psychology of Composition," *Annuale Mediaevale* 22 (1982): 106; Steven Justice, "The Genres of *Piers Plowman*," *Viator* 19 (1988): 305; and John Norton-Smith, *William Langland* (Leiden, 1983), 126. Many earlier scholars like Jusserand and Saintsbury would have joined S. B. James in describing the form of the poem as "rambling inconsequence": "The Mad Poet of Malvern, William Langland," *The Month* 159 (1932): 223.

36. See Robert Adams, "The Nature of Need in *Piers Plowman* XX," *Traditio* 34 (1978): 286, 296.

37. Adams, "Piers's Pardon," 377.

38. Ibid., 416.

39. Ibid., 417.

40. Ibid.

41. Ibid., 385, 391.

42. Ibid., 390–92, 396–97.

43. Ibid., 382.

44. Ibid., 380.

45. Adams, "Piers's Pardon," 375–76. "Granting to the first [objection] that [God] gives out of his mercy and grace [when he extends grace to the *viator* who disposes himself for grace by doing the best that is in him]: because he mercifully established and keeps such a law; but by the established law [i.e., God's having covenanted to accept as meritorious the *viator's* best efforts] he necessarily gives grace as a consequent necessity." (My translation.)

46. Macherey, *Theory of Literary Production*, 141.

47. Adams, "Piers's Pardon," 402–03.

48. Ibid., 413.

49. Adams is candid enough about the ideal nature of the critical object—its abstraction, that is, from history: "Strictly speaking, no late medieval theologian taught such a theory. . . . Still, there is a striking similarity between, say, the teaching of Ockham . . . and the much less sophisticated approach of Cassian" (ibid., 370).

50. Ibid., 380.

51. The lap of Abraham is full of people who are there until Christ "bettre wed for us waage þan we ben alle worþi" (16.277). This does not emphasize the value of obeying the best law one knows.

52. "Piers's Pardon," 382. Adams makes this deemphasis explicit, in his suspicion "that Langland set less store by the sacrament than did many of his contemporaries." "At present, then, the only safe generalization about Langland's sacramental theology is [Gordon] Whatley's: 'Langland's conception of Christianity is at bottom ethical and social rather than sacramental or mystical' " (Adams, "Langland's Theology," in Alford, *Companion to "Piers Plowman,"* 99, 102). Adams's contribution to the *Companion* partly reiterates in a briefer form his views from *Traditio.*

53. Adams, for example, seems not to distance himself from the question that he imputes to Piers, when the laborers will not work unless they are "heiʒliche hyred" (6.312): "Why should some be given a free ride by the decency and industry of others?" ("Piers's Pardon," 414). Adams recurs to his metaphor: wasters "enjoy a free ride on the backs of honest laborers" (415). Stokes is somewhat more strident: "Although the Marxist rhetoric of the down-trodden proletariat had not yet developed in Langland's day, he has here, especially at [6.]313 and 317, anticipated it, catching the authentic note of self-righteous whining against the 'bosses' " (*Justice and Mercy,* 212). Cf. Lee Patterson, *Negotiating the Past: The Historical Understanding of Medieval Literature* (Madison, 1987), 39.

54. For an instance of such naturalizing, see Stokes's remark that "the beauty of the natural law . . . is that it is its own very efficient policeman. Nothing could be more impressive in its terrifying unnegotiability than the prompt and violent assault on the miscreants by Hunger" (*Justice and Mercy,* 203). But if Postan is correct that reclamation of marginal lands in earlier years had produced the conditions for subsequent depopulation (when exhaustion of the land combined with unfavorable weather to reduce the food supply), then industriousness itself had been one of the conditions for natural disaster.

55. Diane Macdonell, *Theories of Discourse: An Introduction* (Oxford, 1986), 3.

56. Macherey, "An Interview with Pierre Macherey," trans. Colin Mercer and Jean Radford, *Red Letters* no. 5 (Summer 1977): 234.

57. Macherey, *Theory of Literary Production,* 36.

58. Bennett, *Formalism and Marxism,* 26. Bennett locates Macherey's identification of disjunctions in the text against the background of Russian formalism, which showed how "the old and the new, the defamiliarized and the defamiliarizing coexist within the text as different levels" (56).

59. After his persuasive critique of certain currently influential forms of "historicism" in medieval studies (*Negotiating the Past,* 3–39), Patterson taxes Marxism with a totalizing character: "Marxist totalization inevitably subordinates

local and contingent actions to the historical character of the whole; . . . it endows the critic's knowledge of the totality with the capacity to predetermine the historical context that brings the cultural object into being and that consequently governs its interpretation" (47). However, students and opponents of Althusser alike deny that "the historical context" is any such totalizable whole. The literary work refers to an object that "is multiple, a thousand separate, hostile, and discontinuous realities," writes Macherey. Even if history were totalizable, the critic could not find its reflection in the text, where there are always "gaps and contradictions" (*Theory of Literary Production*, 99, 100). Having evidently assumed that Althusser imputes a unified character to an "ideological state apparatus," Raymond Williams and E. P. Thompson argue that the incorporative activity of institutions "is in practice full of contradictions and of unresolved conflicts" (Williams, *Marxism and Literature*, 118); that "values no less than material needs will always be a locus of *contradiction*, of struggle between alternative values and views-of-life" (Thompson, *"The Poverty of Theory" and Other Essays* [London and New York, 1978], 175). But Althusser never advances the ISAs as totalizable: rather, as Michael Sprinker points out, they "are not only at stake in, but are themselves constantly traversed by class struggle" (*Imaginary Relations: Aesthetics and Ideology in the Theory of Historical Materialism* [London, 1987], 229). If an ISA cannot be summed up, then, given even the simplest base-superstructure model, no unified knowledge of history is possible. Nor, in Althusser's view, is history unified by its movement toward a telos or as the activity of a unified subject (and thus by a movement that the critic could somehow grasp in its entirety): see Sprinker, *Imaginary Relations*, 231. The New Historicist view is similar: "so many cultural codes converge" upon a text "that ideological coherence and stability are scarcely possible" (Louis Montrose, "Professing the Renaissance: The Poetics and Politics of Culture," in *The New Historicism*, ed. H. A. Veeser [New York and London, 1989], 22). Against Macherey, who claims no means of predicting in advance (1) the specific nature of a writer's project, (2) the conventions actually adopted, or (3) the specific dislocations that result, Patterson's complaint that "the text serves not as the source of the [Marxist] historian's knowledge but merely as an occasion for its deployment" (*Negotiating the Past*, 48) would be unfounded.

60. The work of David Aers, for all its shrewd observation, does not always seem to take account of this. That is, it is at times reflectionist. On the one hand, Aers claims that passus 6 displays the "new work ethos," as if the ordinary language of politics and economics entered fiction unchanged. On the other, Langland's "recreation of traditional perspectives and neo-Franciscan perspectives in [passus 20] constantly leads to an imaginative *withdrawal* from the field of material production" (*Community, Gender, and Individual Identity*, 44, 67; his emphasis). This seems close to holding that some parts of the poem reflect history while others do not. It seems ungrateful to disagree with Aers, who with great learning and energy over the last decade has worked to open *Piers* to economic and political history. Yet some of his major points are unconvincing. The "conflicting ideologies" on poverty that he sees as attractive to Langland were both deployed by the aristocracy, although under changing circumstances. The relevant question would

seem to be the strategies by which the discrepancy was hegemonically resolved. Langland was ambivalent about "market-centered relations" (48–49), which captured his imagination yet threatened to dissolve "fundamental pieties and forms of life" (49). Production for the market, however, on occasion appears actually to have strengthened feudal relations. (See E. A. Kosminsky, "Service and Money Rents in the Thirteenth Century," *Economic History Review* 5 no. 2 [1935]: 42–45.) Finally, Aers seems to me to offer no clear account of the function of *Piers* within feudal contestation.

61. I assume here, with Macherey, the meaningfulness of the notion of a "social formation": "Social formations are specifically articulated, complex structures in dominance, whose contradictions are overdetermined, displaced, and condensed instantiations of the reciprocal effectivity" of "economic, political, ideological, and scientific-theoretical" practices (Kavanagh, "Marxism's Althusser," 30).

62. On some of the difficulties implicit in this notion, however, see Raymond Williams, "Base and Superstructure in Marxist Cultural Theory," 15–16. For other criticism of Macherey, see, e.g., Terry Eagleton, "Pierre Macherey and the Theory of Literary Production," *Minnesota Review* 5 (1975): 142.

63. Macherey, *Theory of Literary Production*, 91.

64. The ideological project might better be called preconscious in Freud's sense, not unconscious—that is, descriptively, not dynamically, unconscious. Francis Mulhern, commenting on Macherey's notion of the "silent," or sparse and laconic, nature of the literary text, compares Freud's joke-work rather than the dream-work: see "Marxism in Literary Criticism," *New Left Review* 108 (1978): 83–84. History acts within the text not as "a model but as a motor" (Macherey, "History and Novel in Balzac's *The Peasants*," trans. Warren Montag, *Minnesota Review*, n.s., 26 [1986]: 111).

65. See Hilton, "Social Concepts," 219.

66. Contrast, however, E. D. Kirk, "Langland's Plowman and the Recreation of Fourteenth-Century Religious Metaphor," *Yearbook of Langland Studies* 2 (1988): 6.

67. Piers, then, is only metaphorically a *hyne*. The narrator of *Pearl* calls all Christians God's "homly hyne" (line 1211; *The Poems of the "Pearl" Manuscript*, ed. Malcolm Andrew and Ronald Waldron [Berkeley and Los Angeles, 1978]).

68. See Rodney Hilton, *The English Peasantry in the Later Middle Ages* (Oxford, 1975), 21.

69. David Aers, "*Piers Plowman* and Problems in the Perception of Poverty: A Culture in Transition," *Leeds Studies in English*, n.s., 14 (1983): 14.

70. Justices of the peace, for example, find that common laborers accept higher wages from new masters than the "duos denarios per diem et cibum" they are able to receive on their own manor: Bertha Haven Putnam, ed., *Proceedings*

Before the Justices of the Peace in the Fourteenth and Fifteenth Centuries, Edward III to Richard III (London, 1938), 111. (The lawful wage, of course, is not always twopence.) "Pees" also, with his "hewen" (4.55), appears to be a peasant employer. That the half-acre is capitalized, however, is not entirely clear. At points it sounds communist: Piers will share the food with all those who help him produce it (6.65–69). (Contrast, however, 20.275–77, where the poet denies that Plato and Seneca believe "That alle þynges vnder heuene ouȝte to ben in comune.") 13.373–74 may glance at capitalized agriculture.

71. Hilton, "Social Concepts," 218.

72. Harvey, Conclusion, in *The Peasant Land Market in Medieval England,* ed. P. D. A. Harvey (Oxford, 1984), 341. "The formation of some large holdings seems to have been a consistent feature of the local land market" (343). Cf. Zvi Razi, *Life, Marriage and Death in a Medieval Parish: Economy, Society, and Demography in Halesowen, 1270–1400* (Cambridge, 1980), 145–46.

73. "There were perhaps more freemen than villeins in the topmost layer of village society, i.e. among the few villagers with holdings of two or more virgates": Postan, *Medieval Economy,* 145. Cf. J. A. F. Thomson, *The Transformation of Medieval England, 1370–1529* (London and New York, 1983), 21.

74. See John Hatcher, *Plague, Population, and the English Economy, 1348–1530* (London, 1977), 68.

75. Labor was in short supply for several reasons, not simply that the plagues had reduced the numbers of smallholders (who had always had to work for wages in order to make ends meet) or because vacant holdings had been added to their own tenancies by some peasants, who thus came to need workers. With many holdings vacant, peasants who had previously been obliged to work for wages had the opportunity to hold land on favorable terms: Rodney Hilton, *The Decline of Serfdom in Medieval England* (London, 1969), 32–33; "Social Concepts," 219.

76. Postan suggests that the main pressure for the legislation came not from the seigneurial group, "who by now derived the bulk of their revenues from rents," but from smaller gentry who still cultivated their home farms. "This at any rate is how the clash of interests is presented in the only contemporary discussion of the issues available to us: that in a parliamentary petition of 1368" (*Medieval Economy,* 152). This does not mean that, economically, the lesser gentry were hit harder by the smaller labor pool than the greater landholders, who faced the problem of vacant holdings (174).

77. Hilton, *Decline of Serfdom,* 36; cf. his "Social Concepts," 218.

78. See, e.g., Hilton, "Peasant Movements," 122, 130–31, 135; Hilton, *Bond Men,* 154; and Merrington, "Town and Country," 179. Passus 6 may exaggerate the antagonism between the peasant employer (the plowman-husbandman) and the hired laborer. Hilton suggests that "Their antagonism could be compared rather to a family quarrel than to the hostility arising from a social gulf": *English Peasantry,* 51.

79. See Morton W. Bloomfield, *"Piers Plowman" As a Fourteenth-century Apocalypse* (New Brunswick, 1962).

80. Cf. Stephen A. Barney: "The closest poem to *Piers* is *Wynnere and Wastour*" ("Allegorical Visions," in Alford, *Companion to "Piers Plowman,"* 130). With *Winner and Waster [W&W]* (*A Good Short Debate between Winner and Waster,* ed. Israel Gollancz [1921; reprint, Cambridge and Totowa, NJ, 1974]), line 6, cf. *Piers* 10.17–22, 13.228–34; with *W&W* 13–17, cf. *Piers* 6.324–25; with *W&W* 21, cf. *Piers* 10.44–50; with *W&W* 281, cf. *Piers* 5.336; with *W&W* 282, cf. *Piers* 7.91; with *W&W* 300–307, 441–44, cf. *Piers* 12.51–52, 15.136–48; with *W&W* 310, cf. *Piers* 13.348; with *W&W* 370–74, cf. *Piers* 13.264–70; with *W&W* 407–8, cf. *Piers* 5.30–31; with *W&W* 436, cf. *Piers* 5.391; with *W&W* 460 ad fin., cf. *Piers* 2.213–35; with *W&W* 480–95, cf. *Piers* prol.226–31. For some recent discussion of similarities between the two poems, see S. S. Hussey, "Langland's Reading of Alliterative Poetry," *Modern Language Review* 60 (1965): 168–69; Elizabeth Salter, "The Timeliness of *Wynnere and Wastoure,*" *Medium Aevum* 47 (1978): 57 and Thorlac Turville-Petre, "The Prologue of *Wynnere and Wastoure,*" *Leeds Studies in English,* n.s., 18 (1987): 20–21. Hussey discusses some differences (167–68).

81. In a forthcoming essay, however, Professor Carter Revard will advance new reasons for believing that *W&W* alludes specifically to the Statute of Treasons of 1352 and for linking the composition of the poem to a visit by the Black Prince to Chester in 1353 (personal communication).

82. However, for a different explanation for the series of genres in *Piers,* see Justice, "Genres of *Piers Plowman,*" n. 35 above.

83. See also, for example, 10.263 and Patience's closed "bouste" (13.152).

84. See also instances where a reforming force is simultaneously external and internal: e.g., 3.284, 315, 321–22; 15.553–55; 16.231–2; 17.212–28.

85. This power operating in objective space is at once offset by the capacity of "kynde wit" to establish clerks (prol.114).

86. For a consideration of the passages where this requirement occurs, see B. J. Harwood, "Langland's *Kynde Knowyng* and the Quest for Christ," *Modern Philology* 80 (1983): 242–55, and earlier work cited there (242, 246); see also Hugh White, *Nature and Salvation in "Piers Plowman"* (Cambridge, 1988), chap. 2.

87. Cf. Theology at 2.138–39 and Wit at 9.59–60. (Wit envisages Kynde as a creator clearly external to his creatures, who are nevertheless endowed with Inwit, which then becomes decisive: "he [Inwit] let hire [i.e., Anima] at his wille, / For after þe grace of god þe gretteste is Inwit.")

88. He argues this again at 12.277–79. Cf. 15.457–58.

89. Cf. 11.115–18; 12.277–79.

90. Cf. esp. the episode of Need, an unmistakably internal imperative, something felt (20.37), equivalent to suffering (20.46–47): "nede haþ no lawe" (20.10).

91. Cf. 13.257, 259, 397–98.

92. I have attempted to support this view of passus 12 in " 'Clergye' and the Action of the Third Vision in *Piers Plowman*," *Modern Philology* 70 (1973): 279–90; and "Imaginative in *Piers Plowman*," *Medium Aevum* 44 (1975): 249–63.

93. Anima, in making the will decisive (15.200, 210), assigns a particular privilege to another internal entity. The relation between the *voluntas* and *liberum arbitrium* for Langland is open to debate.

94. Cf. 19.71–83.

95. Macherey, *Theory of Literary Production*, 123, 79.

96. Ibid., 115.

97. From his patient study of C.5.1–104 ("the poet's most candid bit of autobiography"), E. T. Donaldson concluded that Langland held minor orders as either acolyte or *tonsuratus* and "might have earned his living praying for the souls of the living rather than for those of the dead" (*"Piers Plowman": The C-Text and Its Poet* [1949; n.p., 1966], 199, 214). In the course of a month, Langland would evidently make a circuit of these patrons, who were not necessarily wealthy.

98. The difficulty is not simply that of smoothing out of account artisans, retailers, and freeholders. With respect to the latter objection, however: despite the presence of retailers and the others, the dominant form of the social relations of production in fourteenth-century England was feudal: "Nothing could be clearer than that the prime mover of the economy until the 16th-century at the earliest was the struggle for rent" (Rodney Hilton, "Warriors and Peasants," *New Left Review* 83 [1974]: 94). *Piers* represents a scattering of nonagricultural phenomena plainly enough, mostly dishonest practices within retail trade: see, e.g., 3.76–86; 5.197–223; 13.357–58, 360–61, 379–82; 14.292; 19.401–3. However, retail trade does not presuppose one form of the relations of production rather than another. Neither does the use of commercial capital in wholesale trade (13.391–95). (See Maurice Dobb, *Studies in the Development of Capitalism* [New York, 1947], 121; and Merrington, "Town and Country," 177.) The considerable satire at the expense of the privatization of knowledge (e.g., prol.211–16) or sale of the sacraments (e.g., prol.63) is likewise neutral with respect to social formation, like dishonest consumer lending (5.237–52) and the details of cloth finishing (15.450–53).

99. See George Kane, *"Piers Plowman": The Evidence for Authorship* (London, 1965), 26–27, 71.

100. William Langland, *Piers Plowman: The C-text*, ed. Derek Pearsall (Berkeley and Los Angeles, 1979), 5.54, 65–66, 70–71, 66, 78).

101. Baldwin, "Historical Context," 69.

102. See, e.g., Patience's utopian counsel: "Forþi cristene sholde be in co-mune riche, noon coueitous for hymselue" (14.201).

103. Donaldson, *C-Text and Its Poet,* 110. Donaldson went on to say that Langland's "doctrine of the individual tends inevitably toward the radical" (ibid. 111). No doubt a text taking as its problematic the need for individual conviction lends itself to ideologies of humanism and liberalism.

104. See J. S. Critchley, *Feudalism* (London, 1978), 16–17.

105. Postan reports that in Langland's west Midlands until 1340 at least "serf-dom in its various degrees was the lot of most of the countryfolk" (*Medieval Economy,* 147).

106. In 18.76–78, Langland asserts that only a knight, not a "harlot," is lit-erally able to lay violent hands upon another knight. At points—e.g., 20.146—the poet appears to make more of the legal difference between free and villein status than peasants always did.

107. See 6.38, 45; 15.310; 19.460–62. The same caution is implicit in his satire of "louedayes" (10.312).

108. See Moisa, "Preachers' Views," 161–71. Donaldson believed that *Piers* achieves a balance between "Gregory and Cato" (*C-Text and Its Poet,* 134). Aers concluded that the poet turns from the "ethos" of compelling the able-bodied poor to work toward the traditional ethic of indiscriminate generosity, although "there are signs that Langland still wavered" ("Problems in the Perception of Poverty," 18–20). See also his "Good Shepherds of Medieval Criticism," *Southern Review* 20 (1987): 179; and his *Community, Gender, and Individual Identity,* esp. 50–62.

109. In his excellent study, "Poverty and Poor People in *Piers Plowman,*" Derek Pearsall points out that, even in the face of social change, later parts of the poem preserve poverty as "part of the providential order" because they block out "nontraditional types of indigence from the concept of poverty: poorly paid work-ers, the unemployed, rebellious vagabonds" (*Medieval English Studies Presented to George Kane,* 174).

110. See Postan, *Medieval Economy,* 144.

111. Thomson, *Transformation of Medieval England,* 18.

112. Ibid., 22.

113. As reported by Hilton, *Decline of Serfdom,* 32.

114. May McKisack, *The Fourteenth Century, 1307–1399* (Oxford, 1959), 420.

115. Barry Hindess and Paul Q. Hirst, *Pre-Capitalist Modes of Production* (London, 1975), 241. See also 189–91, 237–38, 241–42. Cf. Maurice Dobb, "A Reply," in Hilton, ed., *The Transition from Feudalism to Capitalism,* 63; Takahashi,

"Contribution to the Discussion," 71–72, 84–87; and Elster, *Making Sense of Marx*, 169 (with the relevant quotation from Marx, *Capital*, vol. 3), 204, 761–62.

116. "Feudalism or *Feodalité* and *Seigneurie* in France and England" (1979), in Hilton, *Class Conflict and the Crisis of Feudalism*, 231, 238.

117. On this point, however, see Simon Clarke, "Althusserian Marxism" in Clarke et al., *One-Dimensional Marxism*, 56–58.

118. See Hindess and Hirst, *Pre-Capitalist Modes of Production*, 226.

119. See, for example, Postan, *Medieval Economy*, 149, and Thomson, *Transformation of Medieval England*, 34.

120. See Putnam, *Proceedings*, cxxiii; Hilton, *Decline of Serfdom*, 36; and "Social Concepts," 219.

121. Perry Anderson, *Passages from Antiquity to Feudalism* (London, 1974), 152.

122. I have argued a view of the nature of this problematic in "Langland's *Kynde Knowyng* and the Quest for Christ" (n. 86 above).

123. This is of course the function of all myth, in Claude Lévi-Strauss's view: see "The Structural Study of Myth" (1955), in *Structural Anthropology*, trans. C. Jacobson and B. G. Schoepf (Garden City, NY, 1967), 221, 226. "Literature displays these conflicts by adding to them an imaginary resolution": Macherey, "Problems of Reflection," trans. John Coombes, in *Literature, Society, and the Sociology of Literature*, ed. Francis Barker et al. (n.p., 1977), 53. Patience and the Samaritan in *Piers* can be partly explained as mediating figures also.

124. I owe a large debt to R. James Goldstein for a painstaking reading of an earlier version of this essay that saved me from many errors. For those that remain, I am solely responsible.

Chapter 5. The Language of Transgression: Body, Flesh, and Word in Mystical Discourse

1. Carolyn Walker Bynum, *Holy Feast and Holy Fast: The Religious Significance of Food to Medieval Women* (Berkeley, 1987), 40.

2. Luce Irigary, *Speculum of the Other Woman*, trans. Gillian C. Gill (Ithaca, 1988), 191.

3. Sarah Beckwith poses this same question in her investigation of the construction of femininity and subjectively particularly in *The Book of Margery Kempe* in "A Very Material Mysticism: The Medieval Mysticism of Margery Kempe," in *Medieval Literature: Criticism, Ideology, and History*, ed. David Aers (Brighton, 1986), 34–57.

4. For a discussion of the two types of mysticism, see Clarissa W. Atkinson, *Mystic and Pilgrim: The "Book" and the World of Margery Kempe* (Ithaca, 1983), 203–7; and Beckwith, "Very Material Mysticism," 37–41.

5. Julia Kristeva, *Powers of Horror: An Essay in Abjection,* trans. Leon S. Roudiez (New York, 1982).

6. Good descriptions of affective spirituality may be found in Carolyn Walker Bynum, *Jesus As Mother: Studies in the Spirituality of the High Middle Ages* (Berkeley, 1982), 129–54; and Atkinson, *Mystic and Pilgrim,* 129–56.

7. Bynum distinguishes between the external and internal, or psychomatic, manipulation of the body, the former being more predominant in male spirituality and the latter, in female piety, "The Female Body and Religious Practice in the Later Middle Ages," in *Fragments for a History of the Human Body,* ed. Michel Feher, Ramona Naddaff, and Nadia Tazi (New York, 1989), part 1, 164–65.

8. For example, the Grey Friar William Melton refused to allow her to hear his sermons and threatened to shame anyone who supported her publicly from his pulpit. Kempe is also arraigned before the archbishop of York twice for her disturbance of the people. See Hope Emily Allen and Sanford B. Meech, eds., *The Book of Margery Kempe,* Early English Text Society 212 (London, 1940), 152, 123–28, and 131–35.

9. See Richard Kieckhefer, *Unquiet Souls: Fourteenth-Century Saints and Their Religious Milieu* (Chicago, 1984), 98; for an account of this shift from the evangelical to the interior models of *imitatio Christi,* see André Vauchez, *Les laïcs au Moyen Age: Pratiques et expériences religieuses* (Paris, 1987), 455–60.

10. See Vern Bullough, "Medieval Medical and Scientific Views of Women," *Viator* 4 (1973): 485–501.

11. Aristotle attributed matter to the mother and form to the father, while Galen argued that both father and mother provided seeds to the fetus. Yet like Aristotle, Galen views the mother chiefly as a provider of the food, or material, of the body. See Bynum, "Female Body and Religious Practice," 182.

12. See Barbara Newman, *Sister of Wisdom: St. Hildegard's Theology of the Feminine* (Berkeley, 1987), 172. For this same idea in Margaret of Oingt, see Bynum, *Holy Feast and Holy Fast,* 265–66.

13. See Newman, *Sister of Wisdom,* 182–83.

14. *Homilia 28 in Festum Annunciationis, Patrologiae cursus completus: series latina,* ed. J.-P. Migne (Paris, 1841–64), 174, col. 160b. Hereafter the *Patrologiae Latinae* will be abbreviated *PL.* Newman discusses this idea further in *Sister of Wisdom,* 183–94.

15. See Bynum, "Female Body and Religious Practice," 185.

16. Hildegard of Bingen uses this association to justify women's exclusion from the priesthood, claiming that women had a more privileged position as brides of Christ, rather than as his representatives; see Bynum, "Female Body and Religious Practice," 179–80. Bynum argues elsewhere that the male mystic's imitation of Christ constituted a symbolic reversal (of soul to body and masculine to feminine), while the female mystic's imitation was an extension of her physicality; see *Holy Feast and Holy Fast,* 277–96.

17. Bynum lays out the medieval assumptions that accompany these equivalences in "Female Body and Religious Practice," 176–88; André Vauchez argues that the *imitatio Christi* represented something different for men and women in that it offered women a "privileged communication," which they expressed through their bodies; see *Les laïcs au Moyen Age,* 202.

18. Simone de Beauvoir, *The Second Sex,* trans. and ed. H. M. Parshley (New York, 1952), 751.

19. Beckwith, "Very Material Mysticism," 36.

20. Ibid., 54.

21. Jean-Pierre Vernant, "Dim Body, Dazzling Body," in Feher, Naddaff, and Tazi, *Fragments for a History of the Human Body,* Part 1, 20.

22. Bynum, for example, argues for the fluidity of gender imagery in the Middle Ages, in "Female Body and Religious Practice," 185–88, and for the medieval understanding of the person as a psychosomatic unity, 162.

23. Vernant, "Dim Body, Dazzling Body," 20.

24. See Bynum's argument, "Female Body and Religious Practice," 162; see also Jacques Le Goff's discussion of "The Body and Ideology in the Medieval West," in *The Medieval Imagination,* trans. Arthur Goldhammer (Chicago, 1988), 83–85; for medieval ideas about sexuality, see Danielle Jacquart and Claude Thomasset, *Sexuality and Medicine in the Middle Ages* (Princeton, 1988).

25. See Donald Weinstein and Rudolph M. Bell, who find that 42 percent of female saints experienced conflicts concerning their sexual lives compared with only 19 percent of male saints. They conclude that the differences bespeak "cultural prejudice and social reality" without distinguishing between chastity and sexuality in women's *vitae,* in *Saints and Society: The Two Worlds of Western Christendom, 1000–1700* (Chicago, 1982), 97–98. Jane Tibbetts Schulenburg suggests a more complicated relationship between chastity and female sexuality, one that involves women's manipulation of restrictive social practices, in "The Heroics of Virginity: *Brides of Christ and Sacrificial Mutilation,*" in *Women in the Middle Ages and the Renaissance,* ed. Mary Beth Rose (Syracuse, 1986), 29–72; see also Schulenburg, "Female Sanctity: Public and Private Roles, ca. 500–1100," in *Women and Power in the Middle Ages,* ed. Mary Erler and Maryanne Kowaleski (Athens, GA, 1988), 102–25.

26. Peter Brown, *The Body and Society: Men, Women, and Sexual Renunciation in Early Christianity* (New York, 1988), 259–84; and Bynum, "The Female Body and Religious Practice," 162.

27. For Bernard's contribution to medieval piety, see Bynum, *Jesus As Mother,* 125–69; Atkinson, *Mystic and Pilgrim,* 137–38; and Kieckhefer, *Unquiet Souls,* 90–91.

28. Brown, *Body and Society,* 341–447.

29. Augustine, *De Genesi ad litteram,* bk. 10, chap. 12, par. 20, *PL* 34, col. 416.

30. Augustine, *De civitate dei,* bk. 14, chap. 2–3, *PL* 41, cols. 403–7.

31. For a good summary of the Pauline view, see Brown, *Body and Society,* 47–49.

32. Ibid., 418.

33. *De civitate dei,* bk. 14, chap. 3, *PL* 41, col. 406; bk. 14, chap. 2, *PL* 41, col. 405.

34. Augustine, *De Trinitate,* bk. 12, chap. 10, 15, *PL* 42, col. 1006; and *De civitate dei,* chap. 14, par. 27, *PL* 41, col. 435.

35. See Brown, *Body and Society,* 424.

36. *Enarratio in Psalmum 140,* par. 16, *PL* 37, cols. 1825–26; my translation.

37. Bernard of Clairvaux, *Sermo de conversione ad clericos,* chap. 7, par. 12, *PL* 182, col. 841d; *Bernard of Clairvaux: Selected Works,* trans. G. R. Evans (New York, 1987), 74.

38. Ibid., chap. 6, par. 10, *PL* 182, col 840b–c; Evans, *Bernard of Clairvaux,* 76.

39. Bernard of Clairvaux, *Sermo de conversione,* chap. 6, par. 11, *PL* 182, cols. 840–41.

40. Quoted in Julia Kristeva, *Tales of Love,* trans. Leon S. Roudiez (New York, 1987), 159.

41. For this idea in Augustine, see D. W. Robertson, *A Preface to Chaucer: Studies in Medieval Perspectives* (Princeton, 1962), 80–81.

42. See Evans, *Bernard of Clairvaux,* 75.

43. Quoted in Kristeva, *Tales of Love,* 156. From *De gratia et libero arbitrio,* bk. 2, *PL* 182, cols. 1003–4.

44. Kristeva, *Tales of Love,* 157.

45. See Bernard of Clairvaux, *Sermones in Cantica Canticorum*, 20, 6, *PL* 183, col. 870.

46. Bernard of Clairvaux, *De gratia et libero arbitrio*, chap. 12, par. 41, *PL* 182, col. 1023; *Sermones in Cantica Canticorum*, 50, 4, *PL* 183, col. 1022. Bernard says that there are three kinds of affection: one that is an offspring of the flesh and does not submit to divine law; one that obeys reason; and one that is seasoned wisdom, which savors the sweetness of God.

47. Bernard of Clairvaux, *Sermones in Cantica Canticorum*, 20, 7, *PL* 182, col. 871: " . . . toto corde diligere, est omne quod blanditur de carne propria vel aliena, sacrosanctae carnis ejus amori postponere." Quoted in Kristeva, *Tales of Love*, 153.

48. For this idea, see Bernard of Clairvaux, *Sermones in Cantica Canticorum*, 27, 6, *PL* 183, cols. 915–16; also *De gratia et libero arbitrio*, chap. 10, pars. 32–33, *PL* 182, cols. 1018–19. Etienne Gilson is responsible for drawing attention to this idea in Bernard and tracing it to Augustine. See *The Mystical Theology of St. Bernard*, trans. A. H. C. Downes (London, 1940), 33–59. See Kristeva's discussion in *Tales of Love*, 29–30.

49. Bynum, "Female Body and Religious Practice," 186; see also Jacquart and Thomasset, who summarize the medieval medical view that the openings in the female body make it particularly windy and vulnerable to external influence, in *Sexuality and Medicine*, 66.

50. J. T. Muckle, ed., "The Letter of Heloise on Religious Life and Abelard's First Reply," *Mediaeval Studies* 17 (1955): 246. Heloise cites Macrobius's work, *Saturnalia*, bk. 7, chap. 6.16–17; 18. For a discussion of the problem of windiness in women and its treatment, see Beryl Rowland, ed., *Medieval Woman's Guide to Health: The First English Gynecological Handbook* (Kent, 1981), 105–9.

51. For a discussion of the ideals of physical and spiritual integrity, see John Bugge, *Virginitas: An Essay in the History of the Medieval Ideal*, Archives internationales d'histoire de idées, séries minor 17 (The Hague, 1975), 115–33. Schulenburg points out how the distinction between physical and spiritual *integritas* becomes problematic for Augustine when he addresses the subject of rape, in "Heroics of Virginity," 35.

52. Bella Millett, ed., *Hali Meidenhad*, Early English Text Society 284 (London, 1982), 5. "Ant hwet is lufsumre þing ant mare to herien bimong eor[ð]lich[e] þing þen þe mihte of meiðhad bute bruche ant cleane, ibrowden on himseoluen, þe make[ð] of eor[ð]lich mon ant wummon . . . ?" *Hali Meidenhad*, 5–6; also 6.

53. Ibid., 7. This represents an addition to the source for this passage, Gregory's *Regula Pastoralis*, which implicates both sexes in fleshly frailty, see 7, line 23 and notes.

54. Millett, *Hali Meidenhad*, 8. Even the famous descriptions of the disfigurement of the female body caused by marriage and childbirth represent for the *Meidenhad* author a kind of fleshly perversion. See his descriptions, 17–18.

55. For examples and discussion, see Bynum, *Holy Feast and Holy Fast,* 211, 274; and "The Female Body and Religious Practice," 165.

56. *Aelred of Rievaulx's De Institutione Inclusarum,* ed. John Ayto and Alexandra Barratt, Early English Text Society 287 (London, 1984), 9, 1.

57. See Brown, *Body and Society,* 354 and 349.

58. J. R. R. Tolkien, ed., *Ancrene Wisse: The English Text of the Ancrene Riwle, ed. from MS Corpus Christi, Cambridge 402,* Early English Text Society 249 (London, 1962), 39. *The Ancrene Riwle* trans. M. B. Salu (London, 1955), 32.

59. Salu, *Ancrene Riwle,* 46, 51.

60. Kristeva, *Powers of Horror,* 5, 4, and 11; 9–10; see Kristeva's discussion, 2–3 and 7–8.

61. See Kristeva's analysis of this difference, *Powers of Horror,* 90–132.

62. Ibid., 127.

63. Peter Dronke, *Women Writers of the Middle Ages* (Cambridge, 1984), 216.

64. Angela of Foligno, *Le livre de l'expérience des vrais fidèles: Texte latin publié d'après le manuscrit d'Assise,* ed. and trans. M.-J. Ferré and L. Baudry (Paris, 1927), 3d letter, 494. Hereafter all references will be cited in the text by paragraph and page number. All translations are my own.

65. Ibid., 495n. Bynum notes, too, that the "good female body is closed and intact; the bad woman's body is open, windy and breachable," in "Female Body and Religious Practice," 212, n. 98.

66. See this idea in Bynum, *Holy Feast and Holy Fast,* 143.

67. Wolfgang Riehle discusses the relationship between knowing and tasting in mystical discourse in *The Middle English Mystics,* trans. Bernard Standring (London, 1981), 104–10. See also Bynum, *Holy Feast and Holy Fast,* 151.

68. See Kristeva's discussion of this idea in Bernard, in Kristeva, *Tales of Love,* 123–25.

69. Elaine Scarry examines the "transformed relation between body and belief" in Christianity as it is exemplified in Thomas's doubt in *The Body in Pain: The Making and Unmaking of the World* (Oxford, 1985), 215.

70. As Kristeva points out, the Old Testament defines abjection as the external threat to the subject by setting up food and sexual taboos designed to defer abjection, in *Powers of Horror,* 90–112.

71. See Jacque Le Goff's discussion of these same aspects of the flesh and medieval taboo, *Medieval Imagination,* 94–98.

72. For some of the biblical and theological taboos regarding marriage and homosexuality, see James Boswell, *Christianity, Social Tolerance and Homosexuality: Gay People in Western Europe from the Beginning of the Christian Era to the Fourteenth Century* (Chicago, 1980), 91–117, 137–206.

73. See Le Goff for an example from Burchard, *Medieval Imagination*, 99–100. The problem of women's impurity is examined in medical literature in Jacquart and Thomasset, *Sexuality and Medicine*, 76–78.

74. "The Consecrated Host: A Wondrous Excess," in Feher, Naddaff, and Tazi, *Fragments for a History of the Human Body*, 228.

75. *Decretorum libri XX*, bk. 19, chap. 84, *PL* 140, col. 1002.

76. See this idea in Camporesi, "The Consecrated Host," 229–30.

77. *Enarratio in Psalmis 118*, 7, 4, *PL* 37, col. 1522.

78. Quoted in Kristeva, *Tales of Love*, 164.

79. Kristeva, "Holbein's Dead Christ," in Feher, Naddaff, and Tazi, *Fragments for a History of the Human Body*, 261–65.

80. Ibid., 261.

81. Vauchez discusses Gerson's distinction in *Les laïcs au Moyen Age*, 273.

82. Angela of Foligno, *Le livre de l'expérience*, 34, 40. Nevertheless, the scribe asserts that it is true because Christ himself has approved it (34, 42).

83. Angela identified this as the way to humility, 183, 428.

84. "The Laugh of the Medusa," in *New French Feminisms: An Anthology*, ed. Elaine Marks and Isabelle de Courtivron (New York, 1980) 251.

85. Michel Foucault, *Language, Counter-Memory, Practice: Selected Essays and Interviews*, trans. Donald F. Bouchard and Sherry Simon (Ithaca, 1977), 37.

86. This idea is also from Foucault, *Language*, 35. Foucault's formulation of this new knowledge and language is influenced by Buddhism, according to Uta Liebmann Schaub, "Foucault's Oriental Subtext," *PMLA* 104 (May 1989): 306–16.

87. Vauchez also argues that feminine mysticism was subversive because it contributed to the split between mystical love and intellectual knowledge, between faith and reason, *Les laïcs au Moyen Age*, 247.

88. *Peri Hermenias I*, trans. Harold P. Cooke, Loeb Classical Library (Cambridge, MA, 1938) 114–15.

Chapter 6. Texts That Speak to Readers Who Hear: Old English Poetry and the Languages of Oral Tradition

1. On the history of the oral-formulaic approach as a whole, see John Miles Foley, *The Theory of Oral Composition: History and Methodology* (Bloomington:

IN, 1988), especially 65–74 on Old English; on Old English in particular, Alexandra Hennessey Olsen, "Oral-Formulaic Research in Old English Studies I," *Oral Tradition* 1 (1986): 548–606; and "II," *Oral Tradition* 3 (1988): 138–90. Bibliography is available in Foley, *Oral-Formulaic Theory and Research* (New York, 1985), with updates in the journal *Oral Tradition*.

2. I hope the assumption here is implicitly obvious, but I also want to make explicit my conviction that the approach through oral tradition is compatible with all of the other approaches advocated in this volume.

3. See especially Wolfgang Iser, *The Implied Reader: Patterns of Communication in Prose Fiction from Bunyan to Beckett* (Baltimore, 1974); also Iser, *The Act of Reading: A Theory of Aesthetic Response* (Baltimore, 1979), and *Prospecting: From Reader Response to Literary Anthropology* (Baltimore, 1989). Of related interest for those investigating oral tradition and the work of Jacques Derrida is Dennis Tedlock's perspective, "Beyond Logocentrism: Trace and Voice Among the Quiché Maya," in *The Spoken Word and the Work of Interpretation* (Philadelphia, 1983), especially 248–49, 258. The comparative examples cited later in the paper are drawn from the ancient Greek and Yugoslav traditions, chosen because they are the only traditions other than Old English with which I am able deal in the original languages.

4. See note 1 above for apposite bibliography.

5. See *The Making of Homeric Verse: The Collected Papers of Milman Parry*, ed. Adam Parry (Oxford, 1971), a compilation of all of his published and heretofore unpublished writings. He defines a *formula* as "an expression regularly used, under the same metrical conditions, to express an essential idea" (13).

6. Magoun, "Oral-Formulaic," 84.

7. Another important dimension of this reaction is the work of Adrien Bonjour, who argues for a compromise between the Magoun school and the literary critics, especially in relation to the poet's manipulation of traditional thematic patterns (e.g., Bonjour, "*Beowulf* and the Beasts of Battle," *PMLA* 72 [1957]: 563–73; and "Quelques considérations sur *Beowulf* et la théorie orale," in his *Twelve "Beowulf" Papers* [Neuchatel and Geneva, 1962], 165–72). The history of studies of *themes*, defined by Lord as "the groups of ideas regularly used in telling a tale in the formulaic style of traditional song" (*The Singer of Tales* [Cambridge, MA, 1960], 68) begins with Stanley Greenfield ("The Formulaic Expression of the Theme of 'Exile' in Anglo-Saxon Poetry," *Speculum* 30 [1955]: 200–206) and Magoun ("The Theme of the Beasts of Battle in Anglo-Saxon Poetry," *Neuphilologische Mitteilungen* 56 [1955]: 81–90; following Lord's 1949 dissertation, which became *The Singer of Tales*.

8. See Walter Ong, *Orality and Literacy: The Technologizing of the Word* (London and New York, 1982), especially 75–77; as well as *The Presence of the Word: Some Prolegomena for Cultural and Religious History* (New Haven, 1967); and *Interfaces of the Word: Studies in the Evolution of Consciousness and Culture* (Ithaca, 1977).

9. See, for example, the oral poetries reported in Ruth Finnegan, *Oral Literature in Africa* (Oxford, 1970) and *Oral Poetry: Its Nature, Significance, and Social Context* (Cambridge, 1977), as well as Albert Lord, "Perspectives on Recent Work on Oral Literature," *Forum for Modern Language Studies* 10 (1974): 1–24, and "Perspectives on Recent Work on the Oral Traditional Formula," *Oral Tradition* 1 (1986): 467–503.

10. See now Lord, "Perspectives on Recent Work on the Oral Traditional Formula," 479–81, where he denies the certainty of the formulaic test for orality and then notes that "there seem to be texts that can be called either transitional or belonging to the first stage of written literature" (479).

11. Nor was this problem confined to Old English studies; early attempts to take account of the poetics of an individual tradition (e.g., Patricia Arant, "Formulaic Style and the Russian Bylina," *Indiana Slavic Studies* 4 [1967]: 7–51) were rare.

12. For a full presentation of the material outlined here, see Foley, *Traditional Oral Epic: The Odyssey, Beowulf, and the Serbo-Croatian Return Song* (Berkeley, 1990), chapters 3, 6, and 9.

13. I owe this term to Constance Hieatt ("On Envelope Patterns [Ancient and—Relatively—Modern] and Nonce Formulas," in *Comparative Research on Oral Traditions: A Memorial for Milman* Parry, ed. John Miles Foley [Columbus, OH, 1987], 245–58).

14. Here we encounter the (in some ways unfortunate) circumstance that the original comparison made by Parry and Lord was between ancient Greek and Yugoslav oral epic. For the basic similarities in prosody, and the consequent similarities between the two phraseologies, made for a parochial idea of traditional diction that was then unthinkingly extended to very different poetries, with predictably mixed results. Had one of the original comparands been Old English, for example, the focus on a single kind of traditional phraseology—the caesura-bound, encapsulated sort—would have been less exclusive.

15. Lord, *Singer*, 68–98. In fact, there is a wide spectrum of thematic structure even in the Serbo-Croatian epics (see Foley, *Traditional Oral Epic*, chap. 8).

16. On the shorter narrative songs, Foley, "Literary Art and Oral Tradition in Old English and Serbian Poetry," *Anglo-Saxon England* 12 (1983): 183–214; on charms, Barbara Kerewsky-Halpern and Foley, "The Power of the Word: Healing Charms as an Oral Genre," *Journal of American Folklore* 91 (1978): 903–24; on metrical genealogies, Kerewsky-Halpern, "Genealogy as Genre in a Serbian Village," in *Oral Traditional Literature: A Festschrift for Albert Bates Lord*, ed. John Miles Foley (Columbus, OH, 1981), 301–21; on funeral laments, Kerewsky-Halpern, "Text and Context in Serbian Ritual Lament," *Canadian-American Slavic Studies* 15 (1981): 52–60.

17. For lengthier and more explicit discussion, see Foley, "Literary Art and Oral Tradition," and *Immanent Art: Toward an Aesthetics of Traditional Oral Epic* (Bloomington, IN, 1991), chaps. 3 and 4.

18. Of course, any text collected from oral tradition bears an evanescent relationship to the ongoing tradition, in that, however, unique it may prove, it may well exert no effect whatever on the larger tradition. Intertextual relations, even among the Christian epic songs, thus obtain primarily through the always intervening, always immanent tradition rather than text-to-text.

19. In addition to Old English (for bibliography, see note 1), one might cite the extended exchange between Joseph Duggan and William Calin on the Old French *chansons de geste*. See Duggan, "La Théorie de la composition orale des chansons de geste: Les faits et les interprétations," *Olifant* 8, no. 3 (1981): 238–55, and "La Mode de composition des chansons de geste: Analyse statistique, jugement esthétique, modèles de transmission." *Olifant* 8, no. 3 (1981): 286–316; Calin, "L'Epopée dite vivante: Réflexions sur le prétendu caractère oral des chansons de geste," *Olifant* 8, no. 3 (1981): 227–37, and "Littérature médiévale et hypothèse orale: Une divergence de méthode et de philosophie," *Olifant* 8, no. 3 (1981): 256–85.

20. Paolo Vivante, *The Epithets in Homer: A Study in Poetic Values* (New Haven, 1982), 118.

21. Ibid., 169.

22. On their joust over contextual meaning and utility, see Calhoun ("The Art of Formula in Homer: ΕΠΕΑ ΠΤΕΡΟΕΝΤΑ," *University of California Publications in Classical Philology* 12 [1935]: 1–25) versus Parry ("About Winged Words," *Classical Philology* 32 [1937]: 59–63; reprint in Parry, *The Making of Homeric Verse*, 414–18).

23. Some early versions of these ideas are available in, e.g., Foley, "The Price of Narrative Fiction: Genre, Myth, and Meaning in *Moby-Dick* and the *Odyssey*," *Thought* 59 (1984): 432–48; see further Foley, *Immanent Art*.

24. And is thus in harmony with ground-breaking work of Alain Renoir (especially *A Key to Old Poems: The Oral-Formulaic Approach to the Interpretation of West-Germanic Verse* [University Park, PA, 1988]) on, as he puts it, "oral-formulaic context."

25. I thus second Richard Bauman's description of the link between reader-response theory and his own approach through story, performance, and event: "the focus is on the role of the reader, no longer as a passive receiver of the meaning inherent in the text, but as an active participant in the actualization—indeed, the production—of textual meaning as an interpretive accomplishment, much like the members of an oral storytelling audience" (*Story, Performance, and Event: Contextual Studies of Oral Narrative* [Cambridge, 1986], 113).

26. Most memorably Lord: "Each performance is the specific song, and at the same time it is the generic song. The song we are listening to is 'the song'; for each performance is more than a performance; it is a re-creation" (*Singer*, 101).

27. As an expository convenience (and as a compromise with the tyranny of the individual reader/unique text syndrome that has become our sole model for interpreting works of verbal art), I use "reader" to designate the audience for an oral (or oral-derived) traditional performance (or document) and "text" as that performance or document itself.

28. Not surprisingly, Homer and other oral and oral-derived works have generated just these sorts of critical disputes and uneven opinions of their quality, chiefly because of the diversity of their audiences over the centuries.

29. The concept of one individual's contribution, understood as importantly different from that made by other individuals, applies chiefly to a situation involving a unique text (unencumbered by traditional referentiality) and a group of diversely prepared readers (unburdened by a sense of immanent signification). Compare the range of authors and readers discussed in Ong, "The Writer's Audience Is Also a Fiction," *PMLA* 90 (1975): 9–22.

30. Compare Brian Stock (*The Implications of Literacy* [Princeton, 1983], 88–240) on "textual communities."

31. It may be well to mention in passing that "repetition," a concept that presupposes a linear field of reference and a textual environment, is impertinent to traditional structures in their role as metonymic links to extratextual meaning.

32. *Gen* 1363b, 1484a, 1744b, 2073a; *Exo* 486b; *Dan* 12a, 26a, 457a; *And* 52b, 58a; *DrR* 91b; *Ele* 197b, 445b, 718b; *Glo* 611a, 789b; *Jln* 212b; *P*90.1 2b; *P*91.7 2b; *P*98.10 4b; *Mnl* 4b; *Jg2* 70a; *MCh1* 20b (based on Jess B. Bessinger and Philip H. Smith, ed. and programmer, *A Concordance to the Anglo-Saxon Poetic Records* [Ithaca, 1978]). Note that *Dan* 457a, "halig heofonrices weard," which occurs near the end of a four-line hypermetric passage, is the only instance in which the core phrase does not fill a half-line. This verse-phrase congruence is less the evidence of a "formula" than the issue of traditional rules (see Foley, *Traditional Oral Epic*, chap. 9). Abbreviations of Old English texts are those used in the *Concordance*.

33. Recognized as early as Donald K. Fry, "Variation and Economy in *Beowulf*," *Modern Philology* 65 (1968): 353–56.

34. Of course, this textual power to spark extratextual meaning does not at all depend on Cædmon's nonfictionality; even if he is construed as a wholly fictional character in Bede's text, the hymn still taps the ambient tradition. From a receptionalist point of view, it is the audience rather than the speaker or writer whose perceptions and operations are examined.

35. See Foley, *Traditional Oral Epic*, chap. 9.

36. While the "formulaic system" (see Parry, *The Making of Homeric Verse*, 275–85, and, for Old English, especially Fry, "Old English Formulas and Systems," *English Studies* 48 [1967]: 193–204; John D. Niles, *"Beowulf": The Poem and Its Tradition* [Cambridge, MA, 1983], 121–37; and Anita Riedinger, "The Old

English Formula in Context," *Speculum* 60 [1985]: 294–317) is a useful synchronic description, from a diachronic perspective traditional rules are more fundamental to the formation and maintenance of phraseology.

37. See note 7 above.

38. Renoir, *A Key to Old Poems*, 177.

39. See especially Stock, *The Implications of Literacy*, and Franz H. Bäuml, "Varieties and Consequences of Medieval Literacy and Illiteracy," *Speculum* 55 (1980): 237–65.

Chapter 7. Working with Patristic Sources: Language and Content in Old English Homilies

1. Stanley B. Greenfield, *A Critical History of Old English Literature* (New York, 1965). The revised version, Stanley B. Greenfield and Daniel G. Calder, *A New Critical History of Old English Literature* (New York and London, 1986), 38–121, also discusses the prose before the poetry. Daniel G. Calder, "Histories and Surveys of Old English Literature: A Chronological Review," *Anglo-Saxon England* 10 (1982): 201–44, contains intermittant observation on the fluctuations of the prose in the canon, but Allen J. Frantzen and Charles L. Venegoni, "The Desire for Origins: An Archaeology of Anglo-Saxon Studies," *Style* 20 (1986): 142–56, is more rigorous.

2. Frantzen and Venegoni, "Desire for Origins," 149.

3. Bruce Mitchell and Fred C. Robinson, *A Guide to Old English*, 4th ed. (Oxford, 1986). In *On Old English: Selected Papers* (Oxford, 1988), Mitchell, acknowledging the pressure on Old English in the curriculum in British universities, comments: "The generous response of the Old English community to the third and fourth editions has led the authors and the publishers to contemplate a fifth edition, in which we hope to rectify one or two of the more obvious omissions such as the absence of an Ælfric homily or saint's life. However, it is impossible to include every text which every teacher regards as essential without making the book prohibitively expensive. So those who, quite understandably, regret the absence of Ohthere and Wulfstan, *Sermo Lupi*, or *The Battle of Brunanburh*, may think it worth while [sic] preparing their own classroom version" (330).

4. Michael Swanton, *English Literature Before Chaucer* (London, 1987), xii.

5. But see Robert F. Yeager, "Some Turning Points in the History of Teaching Old English in America," *Old English Newsletter* 13, no. 2 (Spring 1980): 9–20, and the results of the 1989 survey of South Atlantic MLA (SAMLA) institutions, reported by Allen J. Frantzen in *Desire for Origins: New Language, Old English, and Teaching the Tradition* (New Brunswick, 1990).

6. Greenfield and Calder, *New Critical History*, 5–37.

7. An index of the resurgence of scholarly interest in the prose may be gained from the relevant sections in the standard bibliographies for recent years—*Anglo-Saxon England, Old English Newsletter,* and the Old English chapter in *The Year's Work in English Studies.* The two sources projects were first announced in *Old English Newsletter* 19, no. 1 (Fall 1985): 22–23; the *Newsletter* carries regular annual progress reports on both projects.

8. Frantzen and Venegoni, "Desire for Origins," 148.

9. Lee Patterson, *Negotiating the Past: The Historical Understanding of Medieval Literature* (Madison, 1987), 3–39.

10. Michel Foucault, *The Archaeology of Knowledge,* trans. A. M. Sheridan Smith (London and New York, 1972); and Hans Robert Jauss, "Literary History as a Challenge to Literary Theory," in *Toward an Aesthetic of Reception,* trans. Timothy Bahti, (Brighton, Sussex, 1982), 3–45.

11. See Roberta Frank, " 'Interdisciplinary': The First Half-Century," in *Words: For Robert Burchfield's Sixty-Fifth Birthday,* ed. E. G. Stanley and T. F. Hoad (Cambridge, 1988), 91–101, and Frantzen's essay in this collection for a reappraisal of scholarly "fields" and "disciplines."

12. J. L. Austin, *How To Do Things With Words,* 2d ed., ed. J. O. Urmison and Marina Sbisa (Oxford, 1976). Austin's initial distinction between performatives and constatives (assertions, statements, descriptions of states of affairs) was collapsed in the course of *How To Do Things With Words* in favor of a more general theory of speech acts; see 132–64. Austin's work is developed by John R. Searle in *Speech Acts: An Essay in the Philosophy of Language* (Cambridge, 1969). For more recent general discussion see Stephen C. Levinson, *Pragmatics* (Cambridge, 1983), especially 5–34; and Michael Stubbs, *Discourse Analysis: The Sociolinguistic Analysis of Natural Language* (Oxford, 1983). I wish to thank Paul Simpson and Penelope Harvey for their expert advice on pragmatics and its relationship to sociolinguistics.

13. Speech act analyses of Old English texts already exist: see, for example, Ann Harleman Stewart, "The Diachronic Study of Communicative Competence," in *Current Topics in English Historical Linguistics,* ed. Michael Davenport, Erik Hansen, and Hans Frede Nielsen, Odense University Studies in English, vol. 4 (Odense, 1983), 123–36; and "Inference in Socio-Historical Linguistics: the Example of Old English Word-Play," *Folia Linguistica Historica* 6 (1985): 63–85. In the former, Stewart excludes the homilies and sermons from her data on the basis of their institutionalized language (124). I take the opposite view: the conventional discourse of such texts, our knowledge of the institution of the early Church and its practices, as well as the large corpus, make homilies a prime candidate for pragmatic analysis. Despite the fact that Austin explicitly excluded literary texts from his formulation of speech act theory, studies of literary texts have proliferated. For two opposing evaluations of the somewhat uneasy relationship between speech act theory and so-called literary texts, see John R. Searle, "The Logical Status of Fic-

tional Discourse," *New Literary History* 6 (1975): 319–32 (who distinguishes between "serious" and "fictional" discourse); and Stanley Fish, "How To Do Things With Austin and Searle: Speech Art Theory and Literary Criticism," in *Is There a Text in This Class? The Authority of Interpretive Communities* (Cambridge, MA, 1980), 197–245 (who stresses the institutional nature of all discourse, literary or otherwise).

14. The notion of context is often taken to be static and unproblematic in sociolinguistics; for a more challenging definition of context as a dynamic process of which linguistic interaction forms an integral part (using contemporary ethnography as evidence) see Penelope Harvey, *Power, Identity and the Politics of Language Use*, forthcoming. A similar situation prevails in traditional explication of medieval manuscript contexts, discussions of which are all too often treated as separate from, even prefatory to, consideration of content. Two articles in a recent issue of *Speculum* devoted to the "New Philology" appeared to late for me to take them fully into account. Suzanne Fleischman's "Philology, Linguistics, and the Discourse of the Medieval Text" (*Speculum* 65 [1990]: 19–37) and Gabrielle M. Spiegel's "History, Historicism, and the Social Logic of the Text in the Middle Ages" (*Speculum* 65 [1990]: 59–86) use only evidence from medieval French; both essays complement my discussion.

15. Austin, *How To Do Things*, 164.

16. For a comprehensive analysis of the research models and their relationship to traditional philology, see Frantzen, *Desire for Origins*, ch. 3.

17. For the manuscripts see Helmut Gneuss, "A Preliminary List of Manuscripts Written or Owned in England up to 1100," *Anglo-Saxon England* 9 (1981): 1–60, now in the process of revision (*Old English Newsletter* 20, no. 1 [Spring 1986]: 19). The *Historical Thesaurus* of English is announced in *Old English Newsletter* 13, no. 1 (Fall 1979): 10–11, and the *Dictionary* project is regularly reported in the *Old English Newsletter*. For a more general discussion of this project and other developments in Old English language see Antonette di Paolo Healey, "Old English Language Studies: Present State and Future Prospects," *Old English Newsletter* 20, no. 2 (Spring 1987): 34–45.

18. My remarks on possible reconstruction are similar to Eleanor Searle's in "Possible History," *Speculum* 61 (1986): 779–86, but are more indebted to Jerome Bruner's discussion of the psychological constructs of possible worlds in *Actual Minds, Possible Worlds* (Cambridge, MA, and London, 1986), especially 44–54, 93–105.

19. Exceptions are Colin Chase, "Source Study as a Trick with Mirrors: Annihilation of Meaning in the Old English 'Mary of Egypt,' " in *Sources of Anglo-Saxon Culture*, ed. Paul E. Szarmach with Virginia Darrow Oggins, Studies in Medieval Culture, vol. 20 (Kalamazoo, MI, 1986), 23–33; and Ruth Waterhouse, "Wæter æddre asprang: How Cuthbert's Miracle Pours Cold Water on Source Study," *Parergon* 5 (1987): 1–27.

20. The reader may wish to refer to Roger Dragonetti, *Le Mirage des sources: L'art du faux dans le roman médiéval* (Paris, 1987). Dragonetti's study of sources in the medieval romances underlines the radically different nature of this genre from that of patristic homiletics, which is the subject of my study. There are no theoretical studies of the premises of source study in relation to Old English prose works, and these works use patristic writers in quite a different way from some other, more widely read, medieval writers. Medievalists too speak different languages and should acknowledge difference rather than suppress it in favor of surface similarities.

21. As Frantzen and Venegoni argue, *Desire for Origins*, 143.

22. "Guidelines for Contributors" (7), circulated by *Fontes* in a revised version, March 1987.

23. The most influential of Max Förster's articles on the sources of Old English is "Über die Quellen von Ælfrics Exegetischen Homiliae Catholicae," *Anglia* 16 (1894): 1–61. See also Cyril L. Smetana's "Ælfric and the Early Medieval Homiliary," *Traditio* 15 (1959): 163–204, and "Ælfric and the Homiliary of Haymo of Halberstadt [sic]," *Traditio* 17 (1961): 457–69; and Patrick H. Zettel, "Saints' Lives in Old English: Latin Manuscripts and Vernacular Accounts: Ælfric," *Peritia* 1 (1982): 17–37. The history of the identification of sources for the prose has yet to be written, but see Milton McC. Gatch, "Beginnings Continued: A Decade of Studies of Old English Prose," *Anglo-Saxon England* 5 (1976): 225–43, for an overview of work in this area. For the Catholic Homilies see *The Homilies of the Anglo-Saxon Church: The First Part, Containing the Sermones Catholici, or Homilies of Ælfric,* vol. 1, ed. Benjamin Thorpe (London, 1844; reprint, Hildesheim, Germany, 1983), 1, lines 14–18. All subsequent references to the First Series are to this edition, by page and line number.

24. The standard study remains Dorothy Bethurum, "Archbishop Wulfstan's Commonplace Book," *PMLA* 57 (1942): 916–29; see also *The Homilies of Wulfstan,* ed. Bethurum (Oxford, 1957), 98–101. In a series of conference papers, Professor Cross has recently identified the importance of one manuscript in relation to Wulfstan's work and is editing Copenhagen Gl. Kgl. S. 1595 with Jennifer Morrish for Early English Manuscripts in Facsimile. I am grateful to Professor Cross for this information.

25. *Cambridge Pembroke College MS 25: A Carolingian Sermonary used by Anglo-Saxon Preachers,* ed. J. E. Cross, King's College London Medieval Studies, vol. 1 (London, 1987).

26. See, for example, Milton McC. Gatch, "Eschatology in the Anonymous Old English Homilies," *Traditio* 21 (1965): 117–65; Judith Gaites, "Ælfric's Longer *Life of St. Martin* and its Latin Sources: A Study in Narrative Technique," *Leeds Studies in English,* n.s., 13 (1982): 23–41; and Mary Clayton, "Blickling Homily XIII Reconsidered," *Leeds Studies in English,* n.s., 17 (1986): 25–40.

27. N. R. Ker, *Catalogue of Manuscripts Containing Anglo-Saxon* (Oxford, 1957); and Angus Cameron, "A List of Old English Texts," in *A Plan For The*

Dictionary of Old English, ed. Roberta Frank and Angus Cameron (Toronto, 1973), 25–306. All references to Ker's *Catalogue* and to Cameron's *List* are given by the editors' names and follow their system of manuscript description.

28. For Ælfric, see *Ælfric's Catholic Homilies: The Second Series Text,* ed. Malcolm Godden, Early English Text Society, s.s. 5 (London, 1979); *Homilies of Ælfric: A Supplementary Collection,* vol. 1, ed. John C. Pope, Early English Text Society, o.s. 259 (London, 1967); Kenneth Sisam, "MSS. Bodley 340 and 342: Ælfric's *Catholic Homilies,"* *Studies in the History of Old English Literature* (Oxford, 1953), 148–98; Peter Clemoes, "The Chronology of Ælfric's Works," in *The Anglo-Saxons: Studies in Some Aspects of Their History and Culture Presented to Bruce Dickens* (London, 1959), 212–47. For Wulfstan, see Karl Jost, *Wulfstanstudien,* Schweizer Anglistische Arbeiten 23 (Berne, 1950); and Bethurum, *The Homilies of Wulfstan.* For the anonymous homilies, see D. G. Scragg, "The Corpus of Vernacular Homilies and Prose Saints' Lives before Ælfric," *Anglo-Saxon England* 8 (1979): 223–77.

29. Scragg, "Corpus of Vernacular Homilies," 225–35.

30. The most authoritative manuscripts of the Catholic Homilies are (using the sigla of Pope and Godden): London, British Library Royal 7 C. XII (A); Cambridge, University Library Gg. 3. 28 (K); and Cambridge, Corpus Christi College 188 (Q). For discussion see Sisam, "MSS. Bodley 340 and 342," 165–78; Pope, *Homilies of Ælfric,* 6–9; and Godden, *Ælfric's Catholic Homilies,* xx–xxi. Examples of manuscripts compiled during Ælfric's lifetime and including significant collections of anonymous works are: Oxford, Bodleian Library 340 and 342 (D, *saec.* xi$^{in\cdot}$); Cambridge, Corpus Christi College 198 (E, *saec* xi); and Cambridge, Corpus Christi College 162 (F, *saec* xi$^{in\cdot}$). The dating of these manuscripts was established by Ker but, in the case of Corpus 162, recently revised by David Dumville, "Beowulf Come Lately: Some Notes on the Palaeography of the Nowell Codex," *Archiv* 225 (1988): 49–63 (especially 59–63).

31. Ker's *Catalogue,* however, presents additional problems for those working on the relationship between Anglo-Latin and Old English texts; this will be partially remedied by Lapidge's list of Anglo-Latin manuscripts (in preparation for *Fontes* and SASLC). Martin Irvine's essay in this volume proposes a different theoretical model for Anglo-Latin/Anglo-Saxon texts, which enables us to reconceptualize their interrelationship, even if it does not solve the practical problems of reference to manuscript descriptions.

32. Scragg, "Corpus of Vernacular Homilies," 237.

33. For a more detailed discussion see Clare A. Lees, "Liturgical Traditions for Palm Sunday and their Dissemination in Old English Prose" (Ph.D. diss., University of Liverpool, 1985), 110–27, 154–220 (in the process of revision for publication).

34. Amos is as skeptical of dating the prose as the poetry; see *Linguistic Means of Determining the Dates of Old English Literary Texts* (Cambridge, MA,

1980), 171–77. It should be noted, however, that there has been greater success in the dating of homiletic manuscripts than the poetic codices, largely because the homilies often exist in multiple and variant versions that enable the formulation of a chronology on the basis of content *and* linguistic features. The best examples of this approach are by D. G. Scragg: "The Compilation of the Vercelli Book," *Anglo-Saxon England* 2 (1973): 189–207; and "The Homilies of the Blickling Manuscript," in *Learning and Literature in Anglo-Saxon England: Studies Presented to Peter Clemoes on the Occasion of his Sixty-Fifth Birthday,* ed. Michael Lapidge and Helmut Gneuss (Cambridge, 1985), 299–316. See especially his correlation of the digraph [io] both with internal and external textual and codicological evidence in the Vercelli texts.

35. Although similar to Jauss's "literary events" ("Literary History as a Challenge," 20–25), the term "textual event" (which is analogous to the widely used "speech event" of contemporary discourse analysis) is most lucidly discussed by J. G. A. Pocock in "Texts as Events: Reflections on the History of Political Thought," in *Politics of Discourse: The Literature and History of Seventeenth-Century England,* ed. Kevin Sharpe and Steven N. Zwicker (Berkeley, Los Angeles, London, 1987), 21–34. As Pocock points out, texts are both events and actions that are played out in a diachronic and synchronic process governed by three variables— language, author, and readers. A text is therefore not a static moment fixed by its manuscript context but a locus for a series of unfolding events (which are simultaneously actions) in a matrix of discourses.

36. Jauss, "Literary History as a Challenge," 20–45.

37. It is instructive to compare the theoretical approach of Martin Irvine's "Anglo-Saxon Literary Theory Exemplified in Old English Poems: Interpreting the Cross in *The Dream of the Rood* and *Elene*," *Style* 20 (1986): 157–81, with that of M. R. Godden, "Ælfric and the Vernacular Prose Tradition," in *The Old English Homily and Its Backgrounds,* ed. Paul E. Szarmach and Bernard F. Huppé (Albany, 1978), 99–117. Godden's influential analysis of Ælfric's response to, and rejection of, some vernacular anonymous texts is conceived of hierarchically, not dialectically. Deriving from an uncritical reading of Ælfric's expressed intentions, Godden seeks to identify those vernacular works of which Ælfric disapproved and thus, with Ælfric, effectively silences them. It is not surprising that such an approach is in part responsible for the widely held view that Ælfric writes *against* anonymous collections such as Blickling and Vercelli. For a more balanced view of Ælfric's unusual treatment of, for example, the Marian apocrypha from the same perspective, see Mary Clayton, "Ælfric and the Nativity of the Blessed Virgin Mary," *Anglia* 104 (1986): 286–315.

38. As Waterhouse also notes, "Wæter æddre asprang," 20. This is a major study of narrative and reader-response theory in relation to Old English hagiography, whose carefully detailed observations on the various versions (Latin and English) of the Life of Cuthbert provide important complementary evidence for the broader issues that my own work seeks to explore. My discussion of Jauss and

Foucault here has benefited substantially from conversations with James W. Earl and Allen J. Frantzen.

39. The fullest discussion is by Mary Clayton, "Homiliaries and Preaching in Anglo-Saxon England," *Peritia* 4 (1985): 207–42, especially 214–42; but see also Milton McC. Gatch's largely unsubstantiated comments on preaching during the Prone in his *Preaching and Theology in Anglo-Saxon England: Ælfric and Wulfstan* (Toronto, 1977), 37–59. Further details on Carolingian preaching are supplied below, note 72.

40. Ælfric, for example, refers to Gregory in *Dominica Prima Post Pasca* (Thorpe, 230) and *Dominica Secunda Post Pentecosten* (Thorpe, 328), and to Augustine in *De Fide Catholica* (Thorpe, 274).

41. Jauss, "Literary History as a Challenge," 39–45.

42. Ibid., 19.

43. See especially H. P. Grice, "Meaning," *Philosophical Review* 66 (1957): 377–88; and "Logic and Conversation," in *Syntax and Semantics 3: Speech-Acts,* ed. P. Cole and J. L. Morgan (New York, 1975) 41–58.

44. Dan Sperber and Deirdre Wilson, *Relevance: Communication and Cognition* (Oxford, 1986), 10–11.

45. Jauss does examine some of the processes of inference in his account of the reader, but he emphasises literary aesthetics ("Literary History as a Challenge," 39–41) and neglects, for my purposes, communicative competence. Moreover, Jauss's sketch of oral reception in *Toward An Aesthetic of Reception,* 76–109, is at best crude: see, for example, his *Modus dicendi,* 84.

46. Foucault, *Archaeology of Knowledge,* 7–13.

47. For the formation of discourses see ibid., 31–39, especially 34: "What one must characterize and individualize is the coexistence of these dispersed and heterogeneous statements; the system that governs their division, the degrees to which they depend upon one another, the way in which they interlock or exclude one another, the transformation that they undergo, and the play of their location, arrangement, and replacement."

48. See, for example, Foucault's potent analysis of knowledge *(connaissance/ savoir),* science, and ideology; *Archaeology of Knowledge,* 181–87.

49. Foucault, "What is an Author?" in *Language, Counter-Memory, Practice,* ed. Donald F. Bouchard, trans. Bouchard and Sherry Simon (Ithaca, 1977), 113–38.

50. For Foucault's comments on structuralism see, for example, *Archaeology of Knowledge,* 199–203. Hayden White offers a perceptive analysis of Foucault's work and its relationship with structuralism in "Foucault Decoded: Notes from Underground," in *Tropics of Discourse: Essays in Cultural Criticism* (Baltimore and London, 1978), 230–60 (see especially 230).

51. I presented a detailed version of this argument, "Ælfric: Art, Artifice, and the Problem of Signification," at the Theory and Method of Anglo-Saxon Studies session at the 1989 International Congress at the University of Western Michigan, Kalamazoo.

52. The term "applied pragmatics" is Levinson's (*Pragmatics*, 374–78) and refers to the relationship between pragmatics and, for example, sociolinguistics or psycholinguistics. Although much of my subsequent discussion falls under the general heading of sociolinguistics, the methodology used by many sociolinguists correlates linguistic features (e.g., grammatical and phonological) with social indices such as race, age, or class or with situational characteristics such as degree of formality or topic (often in an attempt to account for language variation or change). Peter Trudgill's *Sociolinguistics: An Introduction to Language and Society* (Harmondsworth, Middlesex, 1974; rev. ed., 1983) offers the standard approach. A similar, more sophisticated application is used by Suzanne Romaine in *Socio-Historical Linguistics: Its Status and Methodology* (Cambridge, 1982), a study that amply demonstrates its limited appeal to those interested in sociohistorical linguistics. See rather J. Milroy, "On the Sociolinguistics History of /h/-Dropping in English," in *Current Topics in English Historical Linguistics*, 37–53. Levinson's (non-) definition of pragmatics is a useful guide to my own work: "the term *pragmatics* covers both context-dependent aspects of language structure and principles of language usage and understanding that have nothing or little to do with linguistic structure. It is difficult to forge a definition that will happily cover both aspects" (*Pragmatics*, 9).

53. The extent to which memory plays a role in the composition of homiletic texts has yet to be fully appreciated, but see the pioneering work by J. E. Cross, "Ælfric—Mainly on Memory and Creative Method in Two *Catholic Homilies,*" *Studia Neophilologica* 41 (1969): 135–55; and "The Literate Anglo-Saxon—On Sources and Disseminations," *Proceedings of the British Academy* 58 (1972): 67–100.

54. For examples of the Blickling homilies see Gaites, "Ælfric's Longer *Life of St. Martin*"; Clayton, "Blickling Homily XIII"; and Lees, "The Blickling Palm Sunday Homily and its Revised Version," *Leeds Studies in English*, n.s., 19 (1988): 1–30. Peter Clemoes's view that "Ælfric's command of the text of his sources was complete. His Latin did not let him down" in "Ælfric," in *Continuations and Beginnings: Studies in Old English Literature*, ed. Eric Gerald Stanley (London, 1966), 176–209 (186) is representative of the views of many Ælfrician scholars.

55. As formulated by Joshua A. Fishman, "Societal Bilingualism: Stable and Transitional," in *Language in Sociocultural Change*, ed. Anwar S. Dil (Stanford, 1972), 135–52. The classic study on bilingualism is C. A. Ferguson, "Diglossia," *Word* 15 (1959): 325–40, subsequently refined by Fishman; see also his "Bilingualism With and Without Diglossia: Diglossia With and Without Bilingualism," *Journal of Social Issues* 32 (1967): 29–38. The most recent study is by Suzanne Romaine, *Bilingualism* (Oxford, 1989).

56. See Helmut Gneuss, "Linguistic Borrowing and Old English Lexicography: Old English Terms for the Books of the Liturgy," in *Problems of Old English*

Lexicography: Studies in Memory of Angus Cameron, ed. Alfred Bammesberger (Regensburg, Germany, 1985), 107–29; and "Liturgical Books in Anglo-Saxon England and their Old English Terminology," in Lapidge and Gneuss, *Learning and Literature in Anglo-Saxon England,* 91–141. Broadly speaking, bilingualism refers to an individual's ability to use more than one language variety in any given society, whereas diglossia refers to the functional distribution of language varieties in such a society. Fishman has a useful definition: "diglossia exists not only in multilingual societies which officially recognise several 'languages,' [sic] and not only in societies that utilize highly divergent and even genetically different vernacular and classical varieties, but also in societies which employ separate dialects, registers, or *functionally differentiated language varieties of whatever kind"* ("Societal Bilingualism," 136; his emphasis).

57. *The Old English Version of the Heptateuch, Ælfric's Treatise on the Old and New Testament and his Preface to Genesis,* ed. S. J. Crawford, Early English Text Society, Original Series 160 (London, 1922), 79–80, lines 95–101; see also 80, lines 113–16. Ælfric makes similar comments in the prayer that concludes the Second Series of the Catholic Homilies (Godden, *Ælfric's Catholic Homilies,* 345) and in the Latin Preface to the Lives of Saints: *Ælfric's Lives of Saints,* ed. Walter W. Skeat, vol. 1, Early English Text Society, Original Series 76, 82 (London, 1881, 1885; reprint as 1 vol., 1966), 4, lines 29–33. Translations from Old English and Latin both here and subsequently are my own.

58. The extent of Ælfric's use of translated pericopes is unfortunately masked in Thorpe's edition, but see Arthur S. Napier, "Nachträge zu Cook's Biblical Quotations in Old English Prose Writers I," *Archiv* 101 (1898): 309–24; and "Nachträge zu Cook's Biblical Quotations in Old English Prose Writers II," *Archiv* 102 (1899): 29–42.

59. Dorothy Horgan, *"The Dream of the Rood* and a Homily for Palm Sunday," *Notes and Queries* 227, n.s., 29 (1982): 388–91; and Lees, "Liturgical Traditions," 120, 180–97.

60. Compare, for example, Ælfric's First Old English Letter to Wulfstan (*Die Hirtenbriefe Ælfrics,* ed. Bernhard Fehr, BaP 9 [Hamburg, 1914; reprint, with supplementary introduction by Peter Clemoes, Darmstadt, 1966]), Brief II, 72–75, sections 8a–12, with the corresponding sections in his First Latin Letter, Brief 2, 35–36, sections 4–8. Sections 8 and 12 of the Old English letter include direct quotation from their Latin equivalents in sections 4 and 8. The intervening sections in the English develop the themes of the Latin (possibly for a less specialized audience) and represent a departure from the Latin.

61. As Pope, for example, indicates in *Homilies of Ælfric,* 169.

62. Gatch, "Beginnings Continued," 242. Gatch's remarks should be treated with some caution: both David Dumville, "English Square Miniscule Script: The Background and Earliest Phases," *Anglo-Saxon England* 16 (1987): 147–79, and Michael Lapidge in, for example, "The Hermeneutic Style in Tenth-Century Anglo-

Latin Literature,'' *Anglo-Saxon England* 4 (1975): 67–111; and "Some Latin Poems as Evidence for the Reign of Athelstan," *Anglo-Saxon England* 9 (1981): 61–98, increasingly stress the revival of Latin learning and the developments in English scripts in the tenth and eleventh centuries.

63. Mary Catherine Bodden, "Anglo-Saxon Self-Consciousness in Language," *English Studies* 68 (1987): 24–39 (at 35). For a more extreme version of this view see Bengt Lindström, "The Old English Translation of Alcuin's *Liber de Virtutibus et Vitiis,*" *Studia Neophilologica* 60 (1988): 23–35, at 23: "Translators from Latin into Old English usually failed to do justice to their originals. Not only is the characteristic concision of the Latin language lost in the translations but occasionally the sense is lost, too, and one had to seek enlightenment from the originals."

64. Mary Clayton, "Homiliaries and Preaching," 240–41.

65. For a fuller discussion of Ælfric's use of Alfredian works see Godden, "Ælfric and the Vernacular Prose Tradition," 102–05.

66. Although this is frequently the case with named authors as well; compare, for example, W. H. Hulme, "The Old English Gospel of Nicodemus," *Modern Philology* 1 (1904): 579–614 (especially 610, line 1), with Ælfric, *In Letania Maiore* (Thorpe, 244).

67. See, for example, Cross, *Cambridge Pembroke College MS 25*, 140–41.

68. For full details see Dorothy Whitelock, "Biship Ecgred, Pehtred and Niall," in *Ireland in Early Medieval Europe: Studies in Memory of Kathleen Hughes*, ed. Dorothy Whitelock, Rosamund McKitterlick, and David Dumville (Cambridge, 1982), 47–68; and Clare A. Lees, "The 'Sunday Letter' and the 'Sunday Lists,' " *Anglo-Saxon England* 14 (1985): 129–51. See also Clayton, "Ælfric and the Nativity of the Blessed Virgin," for Ælfric's comments on the Marian apocrypha.

69. For examples see M. R. Godden, "Old English Composite Homilies from Winchester," *Anglo-Saxon England* 4 (1975): 57–65; D. G. Scragg, "Napier's 'Wulfstan' Homily XXX: Its Sources, Its Relationship to the Vercelli Book and Its Style," *Anglo-Saxon England* 6 (1977): 197–211; Clare A. Lees, "Theme and Echo in an Anonymous Old English Homily for Easter," *Traditio* 42 (1986): 116–42; and "The Blickling Palm Sunday Homily."

70. Wulfstan's use of Ælfrician homilies is discussed by Bethurum, *The Homilies of Wulfstan*, 27–36 and by Gatch, *Preaching and Theology*, 19–21; for Wulfstan's use of the Pastoral Letters see Jost, *Wulfstanstudien*, 133–48, and Clemoes in his introduction to Fehr, *Die Hirtenbriefe Ælfrics*, cxxxix–xlii. Useful comments on Ælfric's revision of his own work can be found in Clemoes, "Chronology," 230–40, 246–47, and in Clayton, "Homiliaries and Preaching," 236–40. Ælfric, however, rarely used vernacular works other than those of the Alfredian reforms; see Godden, "Ælfric and the Vernacular Prose Tradition," 105.

71. Thomas Symons, "*Regularis Concordia:* History and Derivation," in *Tenth-Century Studies: Essays in Commemoration of the Millennium of the Council of Winchester and Regularis Concordia,* ed. David Parsons (London and Chichester, 1975), 37–59 (see especially 43–59).

72. For comments on the absence of educational policy see *Regularis Concordia: The Monastic Agreement of the Monks and Nuns of the English Nation,* ed. and trans. Thomas Symons (New York and London, 1953), xxxv. While there are a number of Carolingian provisions for preaching in the vernacular, there is some doubt as to their interpretation—especially since the majority of extant homiletic manuscripts are written in Latin. Rosamund McKitterick, *The Frankish Church and the Carolingian Reforms, 789–895* (London, 1977), 81–90, implies that such preaching would comprise largely translation and simplification but derives part of her argument from Old High German and English evidence. Roger Wright's controversial account of Latin and vernacular romance, *Late Latin and Early Romance in Spain and Carolingian France,* Arca Classical and Medieval Texts, Papers and Monographs 8 (Liverpool, 1982), proposes style switching—possibly as a result of Alcuin's reforms of Latin pronunciation (118–22). Whatever the case, there can be little doubt that writers such as Wulfstan and Ælfric extended native traditions by writing in English as part of a planned educational policy—evidence for which is also provided by Helmut Gneuss's investigation into the Winchester school: "The Origin of Standard Old English and Æthelwold's School at Winchester," *Anglo-Saxon England* 1 (1972): 63–83. However, it should be noted that the *Regularis Concordia* is written in Latin (the dominant monastic language but, perhaps, it also reflects the prestige of the document) and survives in English only in the form of an interlinear gloss.

73. See Nicholas Brooks, *The Early History of the Church at Canterbury* (Leicester, 1984), 255–310.

74. For Antonia Gransden's important and revisionist study of the reform see "Traditionalism and Continuity during the Last Century of Anglo-Saxon Monasticism," *Journal of Ecclesiastical History* 40 (1989): 159–207. For a regional case study see Mary P. Richards, *Texts and Their Traditions in the Medieval Library of Rochester Cathedral Priory,* Transactions of the American Philosophical Society 78 (Philadelphia, 1988).

75. Bodden, "Anglo-Saxon Self-Consciousness in Language," and M. R. Godden, "Ælfric and Anglo-Saxon Kingship," *English Historical Review* 102 (1987): 911–15 (especially 913–14).

76. Bethurum, *The Homilies of Wulfstan,* 255–60.

77. For discussion see Pope, *Homilies of Ælfric,* 185–88; Ruth Evans, "Worcester Glosses in an Old English Homily," *Notes and Queries* 224, n.s., 26 (1979): 393–95; and William Schipper, "A Worksheet of the Worcester 'Tremulous' Glossator," *Anglia* 105 (1987): 28–49.

78. Rima Handley, "British Museum MS. Cotton Vespasian D. xiv," *Notes and Queries* 219, n.s., 21 (1974): 243–50; and Richards, *Texts and Their Traditions*, 89–94.

79. A good example of this kind of approach is Gatch's work on eschatology in *Preaching and Theology*, 66–116.

80. For addresses to the clergy, see the case of the controversial "Silent Days" notices: Joyce Hill, "Ælfric's 'Silent Days,' " in *Sources and Relations: Studies in Honour of J. E. Cross*, ed. Marie Collins, Jocelyn Price, and Andrew Hamer, *Leeds Studies in English*, n.s., 16 (1985): 118–31; and Roberta Frank, "A Note on Old English *Swigdagas* 'Silent Days,' " in *Studies in Honor of Rene Derolez*, ed. A. M. Simon-Vandernbergen, Seminarie voor Engelse en Oud-Germaanse Taalkunde (Rijksuniversiteit-Gent, 1987), 180–89.

81. See *Regularis Concordia Anglicae Nationis*, ed. Thomas Symons and Sigrid Spath, in *Consuetudinum seculi X/XI/XII monumenta non-Cluniacensia*, ed. K. Hallinger, Corpus Conseutudinum Monasticarum 7.3 (Siegburg, 1984), 105–8; and Lees, "Liturgical Traditions," 9, 15–16.

82. See Lees, "Binding and Loosing: An Analysis of Old English Homiletic Motifs," forthcoming.

83. A fruitful start has been made by Mary P. Richards in "MS Cotton Vespasian A. XXII: The Vespasian Homilies," *Manuscripta* 22 (1978): 97–103; and "Innovations in Ælfrician Homiletic Manuscripts at Rochester," *Annuale Mediaevale* 19 (1979): 13–26.

84. Constance B. Heiatt and O. D. Macrae-Gibson, "Progress in Computer-Assisted Learning: Beginning Old English/Learning Old English," *Old English Newsletter* 20, no. 2 (Spring 1987): 26–27. See also N. J. Marples and O. D. Macrae-Gibson, *A Critical Discography of Readings in Old English* (Kalamazoo, 1988). New computer-assisted learning programs are also being developed by Marilyn Deegan, University of Manchester, and Patrick Conner, West Virginia University.

85. Fishman, "The Sociology of Language," *Language in Sociocultural Change*, 1–15 (quote at 2).

86. Connie C. Eble, "Ælfric and Bilingualism in Anglo-Saxon England," in *The Fourth LACUS Forum 1977*, ed. Michel Paradis (Columbia, SC, 1978), 423–31, provides only a superficial outline of bilingualism; see instead the brief but suggestive article by J. Milroy, "The History of English in the British Isles," *Language in the British Isles*, ed. Peter Trudgill (Cambridge, 1984), 5–31. M. T. Clanchy, *From Memory to Written Record: England 1066–1307* (London, 1979), and Brian Stock, *The Implications of Literacy: Written Language and Models of Interpretation in the Eleventh and Twelfth Centuries* (Princeton, 1983) are two more orthodox studies of language and literacy in the medieval period (largely excluding

pre-Conquest evidence). For general information see rather D. D. Bullough, "The Educational Tradition in England from Alfred to Ælfric: Teaching *Utriusque Linguae*," *La Scuola nell'Occidente Latino dell'Alto Medioevo*, Settimane di studio del centro italiano di studi sull'alto medioevo 19 (1972): 453–94, 547–54; and C. P. Wormald, "The Uses of Literacy in Anglo-Saxon England and its Neighbours," *Transactions of the Royal Historical Society* 27 (1977): 95–114, neither of whom consider the issues of diglossia or bilingualism. I exclude her the question of knowledge of Greek, which on current evidence would be restricted to a more limited audience: the most recent discussion is Mary Catherine Bodden, "Evidence for Knowledge of Greek in Anglo-Saxon England," *Anglo-Saxon England* 17 (1988): 217–24.

87. Nigel F. Barley, "Old English Colour Classification: Where do Matters Stand?" *Anglo-Saxon England* 3 (1974): 15–28 (quote at 19), also quoted in a different context by Mitchell, *On Old English*, 327.

88. Mitchell and Robinson, *A Guide to Old English*, 188–91; in this respect *Sweet's Reader*, revised by Dorothy Whitelock, *Sweet's Anglo-Saxon Reader*, 15th ed. (Oxford, 1967), offers a more satisfactory text.

89. *Alfred the Great*, ed. and trans., Simon Keynes and Michael Lapidge (Harmondsworth, Middlesex, 1983), 122–27; and Allen J. Frantzen, *King Alfred*. (Boston, 1986), 22–42.

Chapter 8. Medieval Textuality and the Archaeology of Textual Culture

1. In this essay I will be concerned primarily with Foucault's method as outlined in *The Archaeology of Knowledge*, trans. A. M. Sheridan Smith (New York, 1972) and practiced in *The Order of Things* (New York, 1970).

2. Foucault, *Archaeology of Knowledge*, see part 3, chap. 5, "The Historical *a priori* and the Archive"; part 4, chap. 1, "Archaeology and the History of Ideas"; and part 4, chap. 6, "Science and Knowledge."

3. See Gilles Deleuze, *Foucault*, trans. Sean Hand (Minneapolis, 1988); Hayden White, "Foucault Decoded: Notes from Underground," in *Tropics of Discourse: Essays in Cultural Criticism* (Baltimore, 1978), 230–60, and "Foucault's Discourse: The Historiography of Anti-Humanism," in *The Content of Form: Narrative Discourse and Historical Representation* (Baltimore, 1987), 104–41; Roger Chartier, "Intellectual History or Sociocultural History? The French Trajectories," in *Modern European Intellectual History: Reappraisals and New Perspectives*, ed. Dominick LaCapra and Steven L. Kaplan (Ithaca, 1982), 13–46, *The Cultural Uses of Print in Early Modern France*, trans. Lydia G. Cochrane (Princeton, 1987), and *Cultural History: Between Practices and Representations*, trans. Lydia G. Cochrane (Ithaca, 1988); Mark Poster, "The Future According to Foucault: *The Archaeology of Knowledge* and Intellectual History," in LaCapra and Kaplan, *Modern European Intellectual History*, 137–52. Foucault's thought is also usefully outlined in Hubert L.

Dreyfus and Paul Rabinow, *Michel Foucault: Beyond Structuralism and Herme-neutics*, 2d ed. (Chicago, 1983).

4. See Gilles Deleuze, "Strata or Historical Formations: the Visible and the Articulable (Knowledge)," in *Foucault*, 47–69.

5. See H. R. Jauss, *Toward an Aesthetic of Reception*, trans. Timothy Bahti (Minneapolis, 1982).

6. I am referring to Bakhtin's principle of literary dialogism, presented in *Problems of Dostoevesky's Poetics*, trans. Caryl Emerson (Minneapolis, 1984) and in the essays collected in *The Dialogic Imagination*, ed. Michael Holquist, trans. Caryl Emerson and Michael Holquist (Austin, 1981), and to Julia Kristeva's now classic definition of intertextuality in *Semiotiké: Recherches pour une sémanalyse* (Paris, 1969).

7. See Foucault, *Archaeology of Knowledge*, 7–9, 137–39; and Poster, "Future According to Foucault," 144–45.

8. Foucault, *Archaeology of Knowledge*, 171.

9. See Brian Stock, *The Implications of Literacy: Written Language and Models of Interpretation in the Eleventh and Twelfth Centuries* (Princeton, 1983), 88–240 and passim. The term is similar to Stanley Fish's notion of an "interpretive community," though I am using the term "textual community" in a far more historicizing sense. See the essays in Fish's *Is There a Text in the Class: The Authority of Interpretive Communities* (Cambridge, MA, 1980).

10. On the nature of the literary culture defined by *grammatica*, see my "Bede the Grammarian and the Scope of Grammatical Studies in Eighth-Century Northumbria," *Anglo-Saxon England* 15 (1986): 15–44, and my forthcoming book, *Grammatica and Textual Culture: Literary Theory in the Early Middle Ages*.

11. See Stock, *Implications of Literacy*, "Medieval Literacy, Linguistic Theory, and Social Organization," *New Literary History* 16 (1984): 13–29, and "History, Literature, Medieval Textuality," *Yale French Studies* 70 (1986): 7–17; these articles and other related studies have been collected in Stock's *Listening for the Text: On the Uses of the Past* (Baltimore, 1990). M. T. Clanchy's *From Memory to Written Record: England 1066–1307* (London, 1979) is also useful for defining the social implications of literacy. Both Stock and Clanchy discuss eras later than the Anglo-Saxon, but the social power of literacy was already well underway in late-ninth- through eleventh-century England, the period in which the copies of all extant Old English texts were produced. On early medieval literacy, Rosamond McKitterick's *The Carolingians and the Written Word* (Cambridge, 1989) is essential. See also Franz H. Bäuml, "Varieties and Consequences of Medieval Literacy and Illiteracy," *Speculum* 55 (1980): 237–65.

12. See Franz H. Bäuml, "Medieval Texts and Two Theories of Oral-Formulaic Composition: A Proposal for a Third Theory," *New Literary History* 16 (1984): 31–50.

13. See D. A. Bullough, "The Educational Tradition in England from Alfred to Ælfric: Teaching *Utriusque Linguae*," *Settimane di studio del Centro italiano di studi sull' alto medioevo* 22 (1975): 453–94.

14. The Leofric bequest has been edited most recently by Michael Lapidge, "Surviving Booklists from Anglo-Saxon England," in *Learning and Literature in Anglo-Saxon England: Studies Presented to Peter Clemoes,* ed. Lapidge and Helmut Gneuss (Cambridge, 1985), 64–69, and can also be found in Max Förster's introduction to the facsimile edition of *The Exeter Book of Old English Poetry,* ed. R. W. Chambers et al. (London, 1933), 28–29.

15. See Gustav Becker, ed., *Catalogi bibliothecarum antiqui* (Bonn, 1885), 242. Booklists from Anglo-Saxon England also mix Latin and English books; see Lapidge, "Surviving Booklists," 99–140.

16. Abundant evidence for the dominance of source study can be found in Stanley B. Greenfield and Fred C. Robinson, *A Bibliography of Publications on Old English Literature to the End of 1972* (Toronto, 1980) and the annual bibliographies in *The Old English Newsletter* and *Anglo-Saxon England.* Two other recent projects, The Sources of Anglo-Saxon Literary Culture (in the United States) and Fontes Anglo-Saxonici (in Great Britain) will attempt a systematic tabulation of literary sources; this knowledge will be valuable for future research but remains on the positivistic, and primary archival, level.

17. For an application of intertextual analysis to Old English texts, see my "Anglo-Saxon Literary Theory Exemplified in Old English Poems: Interpreting the Cross in *The Dream of the Rood* and *Elene,*" *Style* 20 (1986): 157–81.

18. Major features of bilingual culture in ninth through eleventh-century England have been treated by Bullough, "Educational Tradition in England." On the question of literacy and its function, see also C. P. Wormald, "The Uses of Literacy in Anglo-Saxon England and Its Neighbors," *Transactions of the Royal Historical Society,* 5th ser. 27 (1977): 95–114.

19. From Cambridge, Corpus Christi College, 326, s.x^2, Canterbury; edited in *The Anglo-Saxon Poetic Records (ASPR)* 6: 97–98.

20. *ASPR* 3:112.

21. Cambridge, Corpus Christi College, 201; the poems in this manuscript have been edited in *ASPR* 6: 177–87.

22. See Michael Lapidge, "The Hermeneutic Style in Tenth-Century Anglo-Latin Literature," *Anglo-Saxon England* 4 (1975): 67–111, and Michael Winterbottom, "Aldhelm's Prose Style and its Origins," *Anglo-Saxon England* 6 (1977): 39–76.

23. "virum Latina Greca et Saxonica lingua atque eruditione multipliciter instructum." *Historia ecclesiastica,* 5.8, ed. Bertram Colgrave; and R. A. B. Mynors, *Bede's Ecclesiastical History of the English People* (Oxford, 1969), 474. Cf.

5.23 (p. 556), where Tobias is praised as being "learned in ecclesiatical and general literature and is said to have learned Latin and Greek so thoroughly that they were as well known to him as his native speech."

24. See Cuthbert's "Letter on the Death of Bede," Colgrave and Mynors, *Bede's Ecclesiastical History,* 580–82.

25. See Michael Lapidge, "Aldhelm's Latin Poetry and Old English Verse," *Comparative Literature* 31 (1979): 209–31.

26. From the essay "Literary History as a Challenge to Literary Theory," in *Toward an Aesthetic of Reception,* 36.

27. On the principle of descriptive levels, see Emile Benveniste, "The Levels of Linguistic Analysis," in *Problems in General Linguistics,* trans. M. E. Meek (Coral Gables, 1971), 101–11; and A. J. Greimas and J. Courtés, *Semiotics and Language: An Analytical Dictionary,* trans. Larry Crist, et al. (Bloomington, IN, 1982), 170–73. My model of discursive levels and macrogenres is an extension of Benveniste's theory and of Umberto Eco's work on semiotics interpreted through Foucault's model of archaeology; see Eco, "Metaphor, Dictionary, and Encyclopedia," *New Literary History* 15 (1984): 255–271, and *Semiotics and the Philosophy of Language* (Bloomington, IN, 1984). This procedure is presupposed by Foucault as a necessary step in archaeological description (see *Archaeology of Knowledge,* 106–117).

28. Benveniste, "Levels of Linguistic Analysis," 105–6.

29. Ibid., 111.

30. The formula "wordhord onleac" occurs five times in extant corpus (*Beowulf* 259; *Andreas* 316, 601; *Widsith* 1; *Meters of Boethius* 6.1) and twice in other forms ("wordhord onwreah" [*Vainglory* 3], "wordhordes cræft" [*Order of the World,* 19).

31. For examples, see *Anglo-Saxon and Old English Vocabularies,* 2d ed., 2 vols. ed. Thomas Wright and Richard Paul Wülcker, (London, 1884; reprint Darmstadt, 1968). See also J. D. Pheifer, "Early Anglo-Saxon Glossaries and the School of Canterbury," *Anglo-Saxon England* 16 (1987): 17–44.

32. On glosses transmitted in the Anglo-Saxon period, see Michael Lapidge, "The Study of Latin Texts in Late Anglo-Saxon England: The Evidence of Latin Glosses," in *Latin and the Vernacular Languages in Early Medieval Britain,* ed. Nicholas Brooks, (Leicester, 1982), 99–140; Gernot Wieland, *The Latin Glosses on Arator and Prudentius in Cambridge University Library MS GG.5.35* (Toronto, 1983) and "The Glossed Manuscript: Classbook or Library Book?" *Anglo-Saxon England* 14 (1985): 153–73.

33. See Ælfric's definition of "glossa," adapted from Isidore of Seville, in *Ælfric's Grammatik und Glossar,* ed. Julius Zupitza (1880; reprint Berlin, 1966), 293.

34. *Etymologiae sive Origines,* 10.2, ed. W. M. Lindsay, 2 vols. (Oxford, 1911).

35. Ibid., 10.44.

36. *Saturnalia* 5.2.13, ed. James Willis, 2 vols. (Leipzig, 1963, 1970).

37. Ibid., 6.1.3.

38. For examples see P. R. Robinson, "Self-Contained Units in Composite Manuscripts of the Anglo-Saxon Period," *Anglo-Saxon England* 7 (1978): 231–38.

39. The importance of reading Old English texts within a network of manuscript-specific relations among texts has also been argued by Fred C. Robinson, "Old English Literature in its Most Immediate Context," in *Old English Literature in Context: Ten Essays,* ed. John D. Niles (Cambridge and Totowa, NJ, 1980), 11–29.

40. A major compendium of medieval library catalogues is Gustav Becker, ed., *Catalogi bibliothecarum antiqui* (Bonn, 1885). For catalogues and booklists from Anglo-Saxon England, see Lapidge, "Surviving Booklists," 99–140. The system of organization followed in early medieval libraries is treated by Rosamund McKitterick, *The Carolingians and the Written Word* (Cambridge, 1989), 165–210.

41. See especially Walter J. Ong, *Orality and Literacy: The Technologizing of the Word* (London, 1982), and "Orality, Literacy, and Medieval Textualization," *New Literary History* 16 (1984): 1–11; and Stock, *Implications of Literacy.*

42. See Katherine O'Brien O'Keefe, "Orality and the Developing Text of Cædmon's *Hymn,*" *Speculum* 62 (1987): 1–20 and her forthcoming book, *Visible Song: Transitional Literacy in the Reading and Writing of Old English Verse.*

43. See Ong, *Orality and Literacy,* 31–77.

44. This point is discussed by Eugene Vance in "Roland and the Poetics of Memory," in *Textual Strategies: Perspectives in Post-Structuralist Criticism,* ed. Josuè V. Harari (Ithaca, 1979), 374–403, and in a revised form in chapter 3 of Vance's *Mervelous Signals: Poetics and Sign Theory in the Middle Ages* (Lincoln, 1986), 51–85.

45. *Lectiones sanctas libenter audire* (listen readily to holy readings), *Rule* 4.55. See also 8–18, an outline of the readings for the Office and liturgical year. References to the *Regula Benedicti* are to the edition by Adalbert de Vogüé, *La Règle de saint Benoit,* 6 vols., Sources Chrétiennes 181–86 (Paris, 1971–77).

46. See Denys Gorce, *La 'Lectio Divina' des origenes du cenobitisme à St. Benoit et Cassiodorus* (Paris, 1925); and Jean Leclercq, *The Love of Learning and the Desire for God,* trans. K. Misrahi (New York, 1974), 18–30, 87–95.

47. See *Rule of St. Benedict* 32.1–3; 33.3; 48.15; 54.1; 55.18–19; 58.19–20.

48. Bäuml, "Medieval Texts and Two Theories," 42–44.

49. Kevin Kiernan, in "The Eleventh-Century Origin of *Beowulf* and the *Beowulf* Manuscript," in *The Dating of "Beowulf"* ed. Colin Chase (Toronto, 1981) and *"Beowulf" and the "Beowulf" Manuscript* (New Brunswick, 1981), has questioned the historical meaning of the *Beowulf* manuscript in important and thought-provoking ways. The controversy this book generated has obscured the significance of the kind of question Kiernan raised. Some of the implications of Kiernan's argument have been taken up by David Dumville in a recent study: see "Beowulf Come Lately: Some Notes on the Paleography of the Nowell Codex," *Archiv für das Studium der neueren Sprachen und Literaturen* 140 (1988): 49–63.

50. Bede, *Historia ecclesiastica*, 4.24; all references to this text are from Bertram Colgrave and R. A. B. Mynors, eds. *Bede's Ecclesiastical History of the English People* (Oxford, 1969). References to the Old English Bede are from *The Old English Version of Bede's Ecclesiatical History of the English People,* ed. Thomas Miller, 2 vols. Early English Text Society, o.s. 95 (London, 1890; reprint London, 1959).

51. See Leclercq, *Love of Learning,* 90; and Timothy Fry, et al., eds., *The Rule of St. Benedict* (Collegeville, MN, 1981), 446–47 and references there.

52. Francis P. Magoun, "Bede's Story of Caedmon: The Case History of an Anglo-Saxon Oral Singer," *Speculum* 30 (1955): 49–63.

53. See Magoun, "Bede's Story of Caedmon," and Donald Fry, "Caedmon as a Formulaic Poet," in *Oral Literature: Seven Essays,* ed. Joseph Duggan (Edinburgh and London, 1975), 41–61.

54. For a history of formulaic theory, see John Miles Foley, *The Theory of Oral Composition: History and Methodology* (Bloomington, IN, 1988).

55. From Thomas A. Carnicelli, ed., *King Alfred's Version of St. Augustine's Soliloquies* (Cambridge, MA, 1969), 49, 17–18; subsequent references will be made to Carnicelli's edition by page and line numbers.

56. The form of Alfred's text has recently been examined by Milton McC. Gatch, "King Alfred's Version of Augustine's *Soliloquies,"* in *Studies in Early Old English Prose,* ed. Paul Szarmach (Albany, 1986), 17–46. For a useful study of Alfred's work, with valuable suggestions about the significance of Alfred's preface, see Allen J. Frantzen, *King Alfred* (Boston, 1986), 67–88. See also Paul Szarmach, "The Meaning of Alfred's *Preface* to the *Pastoral Care,"* *Mediaevalia* 6 (1980 [1982]): 57–86.

57. Explicit to book 1: "Her endiað þa blostman þære forman boce" (Carnicelli, 83.13); incipit to book 2: "Her onginð seo gadorung ðære blostmena þære æftran bec" (Carnicelli, 83.14); explicit to book 2: "Hær endiað þa blostman þære æfran bec þe we hatað Soliloquiorum" (Carnicelli, 92.13).

58. Beginning of book 3: Nu þu hefst þa cwydas geendod þe þu of ðisum twam bocum alese (Carnicelli, 92.14–15); explicit to book 3: "Haer endiað þa

cwidas þe Ælfred kinig alæs of þære bec þe we hatað on < Ledene de uidendo deo and on Englisc be godes ansyne >'' [conjectural emendation, Wülker] (Carnicelli, 97.17–18).

59. Carnicelli, 47–48.

60. Gatch rightly attempts to associate Alfred's timber metaphor with the more common ones but is unaware of the *silvae* tradition; see "King Alfred's Version," 23–25.

61. *Etymologiae sive Origines,* 13.3.1.

62. *De metris et enigmatibus ac pedum regulis (Epistola ad Acircium),* in Aldhelm, *Opera,* ed. Rudolf Ehwald, *Monumenta Germaniae Historica, Auctores Antiquissimi,* 15 (Berlin, 1961), 78. The standard English gloss for *silva* in Old English sets of glosses was "wudu"; see Wright and Wülcker, *Anglo-Saxon and Old English Vocabularies* 1: 139, 325.

63. "ut antiquam perplexae silvam densitatis grammaticorum ingrederer ad colligendum tibi diversorum optima quaeque genera pomorum et variorum odoramenta florum diffusa, quae passim dispersa per saltum grammaticorum inveniuntur, ad cotidianum scilicet tui diligentis studii pastum et odoriferam coronam ingeniosae pubertatis et ut optima quaeque et necessariora quasi in unum cumulando farciens marsuppium coacervata et circumcisa tibi obtulerim." Boniface, *Ars. grammatica,* ed. G. J. Gebauer and Bengt Löfstedt, CCSL 133B (Turnhout, 1980), 9.

64. The manuscript context of *Brunanburh* and the other Chronicle poems is presented by Alistair Campbell in his edition of *The Battle of Brunanburh* (London, 1938), 1–41.

65. See J. M. Bately, "World History in the Anglo-Saxon Chronicle: Its Sources and Its Separateness from the Old English Orosius," *Anglo-Saxon England* 8 (1970), and the introduction to her edition of *The Anglo-Saxon Chronicle: A Collaborative Edition,* ed. David Dumville and Simon Keynes (Cambridge, 1986), 3.MS A.

66. Cf. the suggestive remarks on annals by Hayden White, "The Value of Narrativity in the Representation of Reality," *Critical Inquiry,* 7 (1980): 5–27, reprinted in *The Content of Form: Narrative Discourse and Historical Representation* (Baltimore, 1987).

67. On the history of Athelstan's reign, see F. M. Stenton, *Anglo-Saxon England,* 3d ed. (Oxford, 1971), 339–56.

68. On the intentionally archaic language in *Brunanburh,* see Campbell, 8–15.

69. I have studied the manuscript in microfilm and in the facsimile edited by Robin Flower and Hugh Smith, *The Parker Chronicle and Laws,* Early English Text Society, o.s. 208 (London, 1941). References to the poems are from the standard edition in *ASPR* 6. For a description of the manuscript and important observations about its historical context, see M. B. Parkes, "The Paleography of the Parker

Manuscript of the *Chronicle*, Laws and Sedulius, and Historiography at Winchester in the Late Ninth and Tenth Centuries," *Anglo-Saxon England* 5 (1976); 149–71. See also Campbell, *The Battle of Brunanburh*, 1–15. On the coherence of the texts in the Parker manuscript, see the suggestions by Robinson, "Old English Literature in its Most Immediate Context," 27–30. The textual background provided in the introduction to vol. 2 of J. Earle and C. Plummer, *Two of the Saxon Chronicles Parallel*, 2 vols. (Oxford, 1892–99; reprint with additions by Dorothy Whitelock, Oxford, 1952) has been superseded by Dorothy Whitelock's introduction to the Chronicle in *English Historical Documents: c. 500–1042*, 2d ed. (London, 1979), 109–25, and by recent editions in the series *The Anglo-Saxon Chronicle: A Collaborative Edition*, ed. David Dumville and Simon Keynes; see especially vol. 3: MS A, ed. J. M. Bately. Dumville has recently written a strong critique of the traditional provenance associations of the manuscripts; see his forthcoming *Wessex and England from Alfred to Edgar: Six Essays on Political, Cultural, and Ecclesiastical Revival* (Woodbridge, 1991).

70. An interesting debate on the question of the Chronicle as propaganda has been conducted over the past three decades; I am posing the question in terms of the ideological function of discursive systems as opposed to intentional propaganda. See especially J. M. Wallace-Hadrill, "The Franks and the English in the Ninth Century: Some Common Historical Interests," *History* 35 (1950): 202–18; Janet L. Nelson, "The Problem of Alfred's Royal Annointing," *Journal of Ecclesiastical History* 18 (1967): 145–63; R. H. C. Davis, "Alfred the Great: Propaganda and Truth," *History* 56 (1971): 169–182; and J. M. Bately, "The Compilation of the Anglo-Saxon Chronicle: Vocabulary as Evidence," *Proceedings of the British Academy* 64 (1978): 93–129.

71. My discussion of the manuscript follows Parkes, "The Paleography of the Parker Manuscript," Bately's edition of MS A, and also relies upon an examination of details visible in the facsimile edition.

72. Parkes, "The Paleography of the Parker Manuscript," 167.

73. For the manuscript sources of the poems, see *ASPR* 6, xxxii–xliii and the apparatus for each poem.

74. On the historical traditions behind the genealogy and early annals, see Stenton, *Anglo-Saxon England*, 19–31; Kenneth Sisam, "Anglo-Saxon Royal Genealogies," *Proceedings of the British Academy* 39 (1953): 287–348; Bruce Dickens, *The Genealogical Preface to the Anglo-Saxon Chronicle* (Cambridge, 1952); and David Dumville, "The West Saxon Genealogical Regnal List: Manuscripts and Texts," *Anglia* 104 (1986): 1–32.

75. In this respect, *Brunanburh* is close to "pseudo-oral-formulaic" poems like the *Nibelungenlied*, which also refers to written texts; see Bäuml, "Medieval Texts and the Two Theories," 43–44.

76. A similar strategy was at work in many later Carolingian historical works and poems, which may well have influenced the Anglo-Saxon chronicle writers and

poets. A Latin verse geneology of the Carolingian dynasty was composed at the accession of Charles the Bald in 843 (*Monumenta Germaniae Historica, Poetae, 4,* 141–45) and a Saxon poet at a Carolingian monastery composed a five-book poem on the deeds of Charlemagne based on annals and Einhard's *Vita Karoli Magni* (*Monumenta Germaniae Historica, Poetae, 4,* 58–72).

77. A similar mythologizing of political and racial origins is at work in Cassiodorus's *History of the Goths* and Isidore of Seville's *History of the Goths, Vandals, and Suevi.*

78. For a valuable critique of the ideological and methodological foundations of traditional philology, see especially Allen J. Frantzen and Charles L. Venegoni, "The Desire for Origins: An Archaeology of Anglo-Saxon Studies," *Style* 20 (1986): 142–56 and Allen J. Frantzen, *Desire for Origins: New Language, Old English, and Teaching the Tradition* (New Brunswick, 1990); see also Jerome J. McGann, "The Monks and the Giants: Textual and Bibliographical Studies and the Interpretation of Literary Works," in *Textual and Literary Interpretation* (Chicago, 1985) and Lee Patterson, *Negotiating the Past: The Historical Understanding of Medieval Literature* (Madison, 1987). *Speculum* 65 (1990), a special issue devoted to the "new philology," appeared after I had completed work on this essay. Although the rubric "new philology" seems to announce a movement within medieval studies of universal importance, the articles in the issue are quite narrowly focused and exclude most of the subjects under discussion the present collection. Nonetheless, the contributions to the *Speculum* issue by Stephen G. Nichols, "Introduction: Philology in a Manuscript Culture," 1–10, and Gabrielle M. Spiegel, "History, Historicism, and the Social Logic of the Text in the Middle Ages," are especially relevant for the way they question the modern reading of medieval literary culture.

Chapter 9. Epilogue: *De Scientia Interpretandi:* Oral Tradition and the Place of Other Theories in the Graduate Curriculum

1. There are those who dare; particularly David J. Herman, "Academic Writing," *PMLA* 104 (1989): 898, and in the forum in the same issue, G. Burns Cooper's comments, 899–900. Both bring out the irony that theory now finds itself involved in: while it was meant to displace elitist and exclusionary discourses in the academy, it has developed a jargon of its own with these same vices and stands accused of seeking more consciously to silence and exclude ideological opposition than ever the former hegemonies did; on this last matter in particular, see also, in the same forum, remarks by Elizabeth Coleman (897).

2. And by citing such omnibuses of technical opinions briefly put, rather than more substantial articles, I hope to overcome some of the problem, mentioned above, of anonymous sources; the practice has the additional virtue of bringing in precisely those voices that, due to their lack of experience and knowledge, or for reasons some might attribute to conspiracy, go unheard.

3. Susan Stewart, "The Interdiction," *Profession 89* (1989): 10–14.

4. It does stand well for the arguably worthwhile purpose of teaching people how to make of things what they will.

5. Martin Mueller, "Yellow Stripes and Dead Armadillos," *Profession 89* (1989): 23–31.

6. Ibid., 29. The principle of charity is also central to the model of argument in the textbook used in our composition classes (John C. Bean and John D. Ramage, *Form and Surprise: Writing and Thinking Across the Curriculum* [New York, 1986]). Prior to outlining his or her own solution to a chosen problem, the student must summarize the opposition view in a way that assumes reason, understanding, and goodwill. I have occasionally found it necessary or expedient, where the student felt that such concessions undermined the primary argument, to point out that ostentatious displays of goodwill at least create the appearance of reasonableness on the writer's part and so facilitate whatever fundamentally aggressive discourse the student may be committed to.

7. This is Jonathan Culler's remark on Paul de Man's note to Hans Robert Jauss; see *On Deconstruction* (Ithaca, 1982), 275.

8. In this regard, I wish to emphasize the developing character of oral-traditional studies. Larry Benson's "The Literary Character of Anglo-Saxon Formulaic Poetry," *PMLA* 81 (1966): 334–41, forced reform of oral theory as then practiced; since then, Francis P. Magoun's "The Oral-Formulaic Character of Anglo-Saxon Narrative Poetry," *Speculum* 28 (1953): 446–67, is to be seen as a triggering event for oral-traditional studies in Old English, and certainly not as a presiding spirit. Theory is reshaped again by testing it against text, as in John Miles Foley's emphasis on internal tradition dependence in his forthcoming prolegomenon to an oral-traditional aesthetics, *Traditional Oral Epic* (Berkeley, 1990). But extension and refinement of oral theory is not the same as its retheorization, an ongoing acknowledgment of its status *as* theory, which should include its articulation with poststructural models of semiosis, as recommended by Martin Irvine (in a private communication at the original conference). Given the space limitations and the present state of my own studies, I can hardly do more toward that end here than point to my own developing dissertation, proceeding as it does from James P. Holoka's "The Oral Formula and Anglo-Saxon Elegy: Some Misgivings," *Neophilologus* 60 (1976): 570–76, which emphasizes the very different results that proceed from inquiries that restrict the range of textuality that may be brought to the reading of a particular composition. Sarah Jane Feeny's dissertation (University of Missouri, in progress) confronts these complexities directly, examining the use of Irish materials by Spenser, a literate sojourner among an oral and traditional people. I hope at some point to use her work for a model in converting my lecture "Aggressive Verbal Display and the American Literary 'Southwest Humor Tradition' " into an article.

9. See Stanley Fish, "Being Interdisciplinary is So Very Hard to Do," *Profession 89* (1989): 15–22 for an exploration of the issues of disciplinary rigor, intra- and interdepartmental politics and economics.

10. Hans Robert Jauss, *Aesthetic Experience and Literary Hermeneutics,* trans. Michael Shaw, Theory and History of Literature, vol. 3 (Minneapolis, 1982), xxix.

11. There are some such: Douglas Young's "Never Blotted a Line? Formula and Premeditation in Homer and Hesiod," *Arion* 6 (1967): 279–324; and Geoffrey S. Kirk, *Homer and the Oral Tradition* (Cambridge, 1976), which more responsibly acknowledges the complexities of the question.

12. George Philip Krapp, *Andreas and the Fates of the Apostles: Two Anglo-Saxon Narrative Poems* (Boston, 1906), xxi.

13. Suggested in Albert B. Lord, "The Nature of Oral Poetry," in *Current Issues in Oral Literature Research: A Memorial for Milman Parry,* ed. John Miles Foley (Columbus, 1986).

14. Jackson Campbell, "Cynewulf's Multiple Revelations," *Medievalia et Humanistica* 3 (1972): 257–77.

15. Robert P. Creed, in "The Making of an Anglo-Saxon Poem," *ELH* 26 (1959): 445–54, speculated that the ability to make traditional verse by traditional methods might be at least partially recoverable; apt criticisms are found in Robert P. Stevick's "The Oral Formulaic Analyses of Old English Verse," *Speculum* 37 (1962): 382–89.

16. Allen J. Frantzen and Charles L. Venegoni, "The Desire for Origins: An Archaeology of Anglo-Saxon Studies," *Style* 20 (1986): 142–56.

17. Frantzen and Venegoni present a rogues' gallery of such.

18. Dr. Herbert Galton, "Viele deutsche Ausdrücke sind vom Austerben bedroht," letter to *Die Presse* (Vienna), 7–8 July 1989.

19. For example, the *oeuvre* of the brothers Grimm, Karl Lachmann (*Liedertheorie* [1816] in *Betrachtungen über Homers Ilias* [1837–41; reprint, Berlin, 1847]); or Vasilii V. Radlov, *Proben der Volkslitteratur der nördlichen türkischen Stämme,* vol. 5: *Der Dialekt der Kara-Kirgisen.* St. Petersburg: Commisionare der Kaiserlichen Akademie der Wissenschaften, 1885; soon to be available in English, thanks to Gudrun Boettcher).

20. Albert B. Lord, *The Singer of Tales* (Cambridge, MA, 1960), 124–38.

21. Walter J. Ong, *Orality and Literacy: The Technologizing of the Word* (London and New York, 1982), 75–77.

22. Culler, *On Deconstruction,* 8. In this essay, by "theory" I will mean those approaches that emphasize the text as the creature of the methods brought to bear upon it and that, in consequence, are driven to describe and criticize their own methods, as distinguished from traditional approaches which objectified text and regarded their methods as transparent and undemanding of scrutiny. Under this broad definition I would certainly gather all the viewpoints represented in this volume, including oral tradition.

23. Particularly Lees's pointed notice that the division between known and anonymous homilists correlates with affirmative and dismissive assessments of their value, judgments that reinforce "anxiety about literary value" and in turn, exclusive curricular emphases on poetry versus prose, belletristic versus utilitarian text. The creation of the journal *Oral Tradition* was in large measure intended to address precisely these problems of cultural centrism, with special issues on, for example, Hispanic balladry (2.2–3, May–October 1987), and Arabic and Oceanic traditions edited by specialists in these fields (both forthcoming).

24. Of most interest to me in Lochrie's study in this volume is the commitment to discuss aesthetic experiences and spiritual states for which institutional discourse has no language. Similarly, oral tradition can assist in the recovery of text lost to a high-culture paradigm. The origin of oral-traditional theory in the explication of male-oriented narrative has not diverted the attention of some of its current practitioners from women's song (e.g., Barbara Kerewsky-Halpern's extensive studies, and Lee Edgar Tyler's forthcoming book on Germanic charm traditions).

25. Culler, *On Deconstruction*, 100–101.

26. As Plato represents it in the *Phaedrus*. The disingenuous representation is part of a deliberate, cheirographically based reconstitution of language; see Eric A. Havelock, *A Preface to Plato* (Cambridge, MA, 1963).

27. At least in the standard view since Havelock *(Preface to Plato)*, which I regard as effectively unchallenged in regard to long narrative. It is the purpose of my own work to ascertain more precisely the capacity for analytic thought, per genre and tradition, of an oral literature.

28. As used in his contribution to the present volume. Whether the experience of traditional verbal art is available to literates at all remains problematic; I am inclined to think those who attend to the sound as much as to the analytic content of poetry may know something of it, if they familiarize themselves thoroughly with the body of poetry in a given tradition. It may also be that those who have a deep personal commitment to a church with a rich verbal ritual effectively participate in an oral subcommunity.

29. Introduction to Jauss, *Aesthetic Experience*, ix–x.

30. Ursula Schaeffer confronts the problem of discussing the orality of written texts directly ("A Song of Myself: Propositions on the Vocality of Old English Poetry," in *Anglistentag 1988 Göttingen*, ed. Heinz-Joachim Müllenbrock and Renata Noll-Wiemann [Tübingen, 1989], 196–208). While determining the relative distance at which a given composition lies from an oral tradition will continue to be necessary, and the methods of such determinations will require further refinement, what comes under analysis is the semiotic framework invoked by such a composition.

31. Even Albert Lord now acknowledges the possibility of a transitional text: "Perspectives on Recent Work in Oral Literature," in *Oral Literature: Seven Essays*, ed. Joseph J. Duggan (Edinburgh and New York, 1975).

32. As the term is used by Brian Stock in *The Implications of Literacy: Written Language and Models of Interpretation in the Eleventh and Twelfth Centuries* (Princeton, 1983), 24, 30–87.

33. A topic to be treated in the course of my dissertation on the nonnarrative genres in the Anglo-Saxon oral tradition, now in progress. Current findings on the amulet functions of script are contained in my paper, "The Non-Linguistic Use of Classical Languages in the Minor Genres of Old English," presented at the Twenty-Fifth International Congress on Medieval Studies in Kalamazoo, May 1990. Very promising directions are now pointed by such careful work as Franz H. Bäuml, "Varieties and Consequences of Medieval Literacy and Illiteracy," *Speculum* 55 (1980): 237–65; and Katherine O'Brien O'Keeffe, "Orality and the Developing Text of Caedmon's *Hymn*," *Speculum* 62 (1987): 1–20.

34. Martin Irvine, "Anglo-Saxon Literary Theory Exemplified in Old English Poems: Interpreting the Cross in *The Dream of the Rood* and *Elene*," *Style* 20 (1986): 157–81.

35. Lord, *Singer of Tales*, 134.

36. *Solomon and Saturn* 2.179–81, taken from The Anglo-Saxon Poetic Records, vol. 6, *The Anglo Saxon Minor Poems*, ed. Elliot Van Kirk Dobbie (New York and London, 1942), 38. Jackson Campbell notes, in "Learned Rhetoric in Old English Poetry," *Journal of English and Germanic Philology* 63 (1966): 190 n. 4), that "This curious poem is full of metrical peculiarities, only some of which are due to bad textual transmission." Ward Parks's "The Traditional Narrator and the 'I Heard' Formulas of Old English Poetry," *Anglo-Saxon England* 16 (1987): 45–66, speaks to the traditional purposes invoked by such an introductory strategy; see especially p. 51, with its note to Alain Renoir's discussion of the place of such observations in aesthetic criticism.

37. Irvine, "Anglo-Saxon Literary Theory," 158–59.

Contributors

Adam Brooke Davis is a graduate student at the University of Missouri-Columbia writing a dissertation on oral tradition and non-narrative genres of Old English poetry.

James W. Earl teaches in the Department of English at the University of Oregon; he has written on Old and Middle English literature and on psychoanalysis in *PMLA, Psychiatry,* and elsewhere.

John Miles Foley directs the Center for Studies in Oral Tradition and holds the Byler Chair in the Humanities at the University of Missouri-Columbia. He edits the journal *Oral Tradition* and is the author of *The Theory of Oral Composition* (1988), *Traditional Oral Epic* (1990), and several other books.

Allen J. Frantzen teaches in the Department of English at Loyola University of Chicago. He is the author of *The Literature of Penance in Anglo-Saxon England* (1983), *King Alfred* (1986), and *Desire for Origins: New Language, Old English, and Teaching the Tradition* (1990).

Britton J. Harwood teaches Middle English literature and literary theory in the Department of English at Miami University. His book, *"Piers Plowman" and the Problem of Belief,* is forthcoming. His study of *The Canon's Yeoman's Tale* appeared in *PMLA* in 1987; an essay on *Sir Gawain and the Green Knight* is forthcoming from *PMLA*.

Martin Irvine teaches Old and Middle English at Georgetown University. His book, *Grammatica and Textual Culture: Literary Theory in the Early Middle Ages,* is forthcoming. His articles on Old and Middle English have appeared in *Speculum, Anglo-Saxon England, Semiotica,* and elsewhere.

Clare A. Lees teaches Old and Middle English literature and linguistics at Fordham University. Her studies of Old English homiletic prose have appeared in *Anglo-Saxon England, Traditio,* and *Leeds Studies in English.*

Karma Lochrie teaches Old and Middle English literature at Loyola University of Chicago. Her articles on Old English poetry have appeared in the *Journal of English and Germanic Philology* and elsewhere; she is completing a feminist study of Margery Kempe and late medieval spirituality.

Gillian R. Overing teaches Old English, linguistics, and women's studies in the English Department of Wake Forest University. She is the co-editor of *Teaching Writing: Pedagogy, Gender, and Equity* (1987) and author of *Language, Sign, and Gender in "Beowulf"* (1990).

Index

abjection, 54–55, 59, 62, 116–117, 128–129, 131–133, 135, 137–138
Achilles, 79, 151
Adam, 36, 42, 44, 47–50, 51, 58–61, 63
Adams, Henry, 7, 78
Adams, Robert, 95, 97–99
Admonitio Generalis, 174
Ælfric, 162–164, 167–176; attitudes toward language, 170–172; manuscript classification of works, 163–164; pastoral letters, 170–171; prefaces, 162, 167, 168, 169; use of sources, 162–163, 167, 173, 176
Aelred of Rievaulx, 126
Aeneid, 193–194
Aers, David, 4, 15, 101
affectivity, 123
Alcuin, 46, 78
Aldhelm, 188, 189
Aldhelm, 188, 189, 193, 201
Alfred, 186, 204–206; preface to *Pastoral Care,* 143, 176–179, 189; *Soliloquies,* 199–202
almsgiving, 109–110
ambiguity, 76
ambivalence, 66, 74–77, 79, 83, 87, 88
Ambrose, Saint, 128
American Philosophical Association, 8
Amos, Ashley Crandell, 164
Ancrene Wisse, 126–127, 130
Anderson, Perry, 111
Angela of Foligno, 129–138, visions of, 133–136
Anglo-Saxon Chronicle, 175, 193, 194, 202–208
Anglo-Saxon studies, and cultural studies, 26–30; current research in, 4–5, 158–161; as discipline, 11–14; history of, 1–3, 71; and originary myth, 70–71, 218–219
antiquaries, 11

anxiety of influence, 68
apocrypha, 172–173, 176
apple (in Eden), 38, 54–55, 58, 61, 239n104
archaeology, 11–13, 16, 19
archaeology of knowledge, as method, 17–18, 30, 167–168, 182–184, 190–191; *See also* Foucault.
archive (Foucault), 167–168, 181–184, 208–209
aristocracy, paradigms of, 14–15, 21–22, 26–27
Aristotle, 79, 119, 124–125, 138
Arnold, C. J., 12, 22
Athelstan, 204–207
auctor, 166, 170, 171–172, 193, 194
Augustine, Saint, views of flesh, 120–121, 128, 134
Austin, J. L., 159, 160, 166
author, 99, 167, 220

Bacon, Francis, 7
Bakhtin, M. M., 182, 187–188, 231n78
Baldwin, Anna P., 92–95, 99, 108
Barley, Nigel F., 178
Battle of Brunanburh, 194, 202–208
Battle of Maldon, 78, 79, 81, 85–86
Bäuml, Franz, 197
Bede, 170, 189, 195, 197. See also *Cædmon's Hymn*
belief, issues of, 175–176
Benson, Larry, 143
Benveniste, Emil, 190
Beowulf (character), 79–82, 84–85
Beowulf, 65–88; audience of, 69–70, 83, 84, 85; authorship of, 67, 68, 72, 87; critical approaches to, 4, 19, 27–28, 67, 71–72, 75, 87; difficulty of, 68–69;

manuscript, 20; originality of, 67, 239n3; originary value of, 69–70, 208; signification in, 48; silences in, 66, 70–71, 73, 76, 88; and Sutton Hoo, 12, 15–16, 20–22, 27, 28, 71; and oral forms, 143, 148, 151–152; women in, 71, 74–75

Benedictine reform, 167, 174–176

Bernard of Clairvaux, theory of body, 120–124, 125, 127, 128, 134

Bersani, Leo, 24

Biddle, Martin, 19

bilingualism, 168–169, 172, 178, 189

Black Death, 94, 101, 110

Blicking Homilies, 163, 168–169

Bloch, R. Howard, 8

Bloom, Harold, 68, 75, 88

Bloomfield, Morton, 102

Bodden, Mary Catherine, 171, 174

body, constructions of, 116–117, 124–125; female, 119–120, 122, 124–127; fissures of, 120–123, 128; medieval views of, 118–122; metaphors for, 39, 52–56; as sealed, 125–126, 128, 135

Bolton, Whitney F., 78

Boniface, 201

Book of Life, 137

Bové, Paul, 31

Brown, Peter, 119, 120

Burchard of Worms, 134

Bynum, Carolyn Walker, 115, 119

Byrhtferth's *Manual,* 195

Byrhtnoth, 78, 81–82, 84, 85, 86, 193

Cædmon's Hymn, 151–155, 197–199, 223

Calder, Daniel G., 157–158

Calhoun, George, 148

Campbell, Jackson, 218

Camporesi, Piero, 133

Canterbury, 174, 175

capitalism, 95, 111

Carolingian theology, in Anglo-Saxon England, 171–174

Carver, Martin, 19

catharsis, 65, 75, 79

Chambers, R. W., 20–21

Chance, Jane, 48–49

charity, 109–110, and discourse, 214, 217

Chase, Colin, 78, 82

chastity, 126

Chaucer, Geoffrey, *Knight's Tale,* 15; *Nun's Priest's Tale,* 4; *Parlement of Foules,* 15

Chaucer criticism, history of, 3–4, 159

Cherniss, Michael, 48–49

Christ, suffering of, 117–119, 127, 131, 134–136

Christianity, psychology of, 65; cultural values of, 69–71

civilization, origins of, 72

Cixous, Helene, 137

Clayton, Mary, 171–172

Clemoes, Peter, 163

Colianne, A. J., 96

comitatus, 46, 48, 81–82, 85

compilatio, 173, 193–194, 200, 202

computers, 177

conception, theories of, 117–118

Conybeare, John Josias, 19

countertransference, 73, 75

courtly love, 14–15

Crane, R. S., 3–4

Cross, James E., 163

cross-signification, 58, 60. *See also* signification

Crucifixion, 118–119, 135

Culler, Jonathan, 215, 219

culture, analysis of, 65–66

cultural studies, 22–26; dialogic nature of, 24–25; and literary criticism, 23–24; and material culture, 24

Cynewulf, 191

de Beauvoir, Simone, 118

de Lauretis, Teresa, 52–54, 59

De Passione Domini, 164, 165

Deleuze, Gilles, 182

Derrida, Jacques, 50, 92, 219, 220

desire, in the reader, 38, 40–41, 42; in Eve, 42, 60; cultural, 53

dialogism, 185, 187

Dictionary of Old English, 160, 163

differance, 220

difference, and identity, 13, 23, 25; and *Genesis B,* 39, 52

diglossia, 169

disciplines, academic, conflict in, 213; as discourse, 16–18, 22–23; history of, 7–10, 22–23; and identity, 13–14, 25; and professionalism, 7–12; values of, 5–8

discourse, rules of, 16–17, 182–183, 270n47
disillusionment, 76
documents, and monuments, 12–13, 16–20; and consciousness, 183
Donaldson, E. Talbot, 3, 4, 108, 111
Dream of the Rood, 12, 165, 194
Duby, Georges, 93

Eagleton, Terry, 31
Earle, John, 19
economic history, 92, 94–95
elegy, 73, 76–77
Elene, 165, 194, 218, 222–223
Ellmann, Richard, 29
Elstob, Elizabeth, 35–36, 38
empiricism, 219
encyclopedia, 191, 194–195
English Department, history of, 1, 7–8
ennaratio, 192, 196
epic, Christian, 146; as law, 67–68; Moslem, 146; Serbo-Croation, 144, 146, 150–151; and superego, 68, 79
epic verse, 144–145
epithets, 147–148, 150–151
Erhart, Margaret, 45
ethnography, 30
Eucharist, 131–132, 133–134, 136
Evans, J. M., 41, 45–47, 49
Eve, ambiguity of, 40, 52, 57–58; Christian views of, 41–45; as constructed, 39–41, 52–53, 57; Germanic views of, 45–51; mental powers of, 42–45, 51, 55, 57–62, 131, 137; as peaceweaver, 47–50; and will, 121–123
events (textual), 166, 182, 269n35
exegesis (patristic criticism), 2–5, 98–99, 162
Exeter Book, 186, 187, 222

female subjectivity, 50–53, 60, 62, 63
feminist criticism, 7, 36–38, 63, 116–117, 139–140, 221
feudalism, 93–95, 110–112
fields, academic, 10–11
"fieldspeak," 11
Finnegan, Robert E., 44–45
flesh, 117–124, 127; Augustine's views of, 120–121; Bernard's views of, 121–123. *See also* body.

florilegium, 200–201
Fontes Anglo-Saxonici, 158–159, 160–162, 278n16
food, 39, 52, 115
food loathing, 54–55, 59, 128
Förster, Max, 162
Foucault, Michel, 12, 32, 137–138, 159, 160, 179; *Archaeology of Knowledge,* 17–18, 167–168, 182–183; *Discourse on Language,* 16–17
Frank, Roberta, 10
Franks Casket, 12
Freud, 55, 65–66, 67, 68, 83, 87
Froula, Christine, 37, 58
Frow, John, 8, 11, 24, 31
Frye, Northrop, 9–10

Gatch, Milton McC., 171
Geertz, Clifford, 24
Genesis A, 233n17
Genesis B, 35–63; allegory in, 50–51; critical history of, 39–51; language in, 39, 54–58, 60, 62–63; and Law, 55–56; orthodoxy of, 44, 46, 52–53; Satan as hero, 81; signification in, 39, 52–53, 54, 56–57, 60–63; sources of, 39, 41–42, 46; as translation, 39, 233n17
genre dependence, 145–146
glosses, 12, 191, 192–193
Gneuss, Helmet, 169
Godden, M. R., 163, 174
Godfrey of Admont, 118
Godzich, Wlad, 221
graduate programs, and critical theory, 212–216; faculty-student relations, 215–216
Graff, Gerald, 7, 11
grammatica, 184–186, 195–196
Grandson, Antonia, 174
Greenfield, Stanley B., 157–158
Grice, H. P., 166
guilt, 65, 70, 83
Gunn, Giles, 5, 7, 9, 21
guslar, 146, 148, 223

Hali Meidenhad, 125, 130
Harvey, P. D. A., 101
Haymo of Auxerre, 170–171
Heloise, 124
Hermann, John P., 3

hermeneutic circle, 5, 20–21
heroism, in *Beowulf*, 71, 72–73, 79–83, 84, 86–87; in *Anglo-Saxon Chronicle*, 202–207
Hildeburh, 48
Hildegard of Bingen, 118
Hill, Thomas D., 50, 51
Hilton, Rodney, 111
historical criticism, 2, 4
Historical Thesaurus, 160
History Department, 7
Hodder, Ian, 12
Holcot, Robert, 97–98
Homeric epic, 144, 147–148
homilies, Old English, manuscripts of, 163–166; method of study, 159, 161–162, 169–170, 178–179
humanities, origins of, 7
humors, bodily, 124–125

idealism, 82–83, 84, 85
identification, 65, 75, 78–79, 84, 85, 86–87
identity, personal, and academic disciplines, 5, 6, 8–9, 30
ideology, 91–92, 100, 107–108, 112, 215, 242n2; in language, 99, 100, 108
imitation of Christ, 117–119, 120, 123–124, 126–127, 130, 135, 138
individual, in psychoanalytic reading, 65–66, 68, 78–79, 86, 87
innovation, in critical tradition, 1–3, 32–33, 212–215
intertextuality, 182–184, 187, 194, 210, 223–224
"Institute for Social Research" (Frankfurt School), 31, 230n53
internalization, 75
interdisciplinary studies, 8–12, 15
Irigaray, Luce, 52, 115, 118, 119
Iser, W., 147, 148, 149
Isidore of Seville, 191, 193, 195, 201

Jaeger, C. Stephen, 14
Jameson, Fredric, 66
Jauss, Hans Robert, 159–160, 165–168, 182, 189–190, 217, 219, 221
Johnson, Richard, 23–24, 30–31
Judith, 4

Juliana, 42
Justice, Steven, 96

Kane, George, 108
Karadzic, Vul S., 146
Kaske, R. E., 3
Kellner, Douglas, 31
Kemble, John Mitchell, 1, 9, 11–12
Kempe, Margery, 117
Ker, N. R., 163–164
Keynes, Simon, 178
Klinck, Anne L., 51
Kolodny, Annette, 40
Kristeva, Julia, 52, 54–55, 59, 62, 116–117, 123, 128, 129, 135

laborers, shortages of, 101
landowning classes, 101
Lacan, Jacques, 67
Langland, William, class of, 108, 110. See also *Piers Plowman*
language, as "mother tongue," 35; eventfulness of, 38, 39; performative functions of, 160
langue, parole, 167–168, 190, 192
Lapidge, Michael, 157, 178
Latin, as patriarchal language, 36; as sacred language, 169
Leeds, E. T., 28
LeGoff, Jacques, 93
Leofric, 186
library, idea of, 184, 190–192, 194
literacy, 177–178, 185–186, 195–196, 277n11
literary conventions, 100
literary criticism, neutrality of, 6–8, 32, 220–221; as scientific, 9, 74–75. *See also* theory, critical.
literary history, and economic history, 92, 93–95, 99
Lord, Albert, 142, 145
Lundqvist, Sune, 21

Macdonell, Diane, 99
Macherey, Pierre, 91, 98, 100, 102
Macrobius, 124, 193–194
Magoun, Francis P., 142, 143, 198
Malone, Kempe, 142

Manuscripts
—Cambridge, Corpus Christi College, MS
  41, 164; MS 162, 170; MS 173, 203–206
—Dublin, Trinity College, MS. D.4.1, 108
—Exeter, Cathedral Library, MS 3501, 186,
  187
—London, British Library, Cotton Vespa-
  sian D.xiv, 175; Cotton Vitellius A.xv,
  187
—Oxford, Bodleian Library, Additional
  C.141, 191; Bodley MS 340, 170; Bodley
  MS 342, 170; Bodley 423, 126; Junius
  MS 11, 187, 191
—Vercelli, Biblioteca Capitolare, MS
  CXVII, 187
manuscript culture, 184–186, 194–195
manuscript sigla, categories of, 163–165
Marxist criticism, 7, 8, 15, 28, 67, 100,
  112–114, 221, 246–247n59
McKisack, May, 110
Meters of Boethius, 143
metonymy, 148–149, 151, 152, 221
Middle English, and Old English, 175
Middleton, Anne, 3, 96
Milton, *Paradise Lost*, 37, 43–44
Mitchell, Bruce, 157, 178
Modern Language Association, 14
money economy, 94–95
Mueller, Martin, 214, 217
mysticism, female, and patriarchial
  discourse, 115–116, 118–119; traditions in
  study of, 115–119; and penance, 130;
  teaching of, 138–139

naming, 152–153
Nerlich, Michael, 15
Nerman, Birger, 20
New Criticism (formalism), 2–3, 179
Norman Conquest, 175
Norton-Smith, John, 96
nostalgia, 197, 202

objectivity, 75–76
Oedipal criticism, 52–56, 62
Oedipus complex, 83, 87–88
Ohmann, Richard, 7
Old English. *See* Anglo-Saxon
Ong, Walter, 142, 195

oral formulaic theory, 87, 141–143, 145,
  152, 154, 199
orality, 185, 195–197, 198–199, 222–223
oral tradition, aesthetics of, 145–149, 154,
  217; and contemporary theory, 216–221;
  critical history of, 141–143, 155–156;
  dynamics of, 150–151; nationalism of,
  219; referentiality of, 150–154; scientific
  assumptions of, 219–221; structure of,
  143–146; and textuality, 145, 218–219,
  222
origins, desire for, 72
Ottar Vendel-Crow, 20
overdetermination, 74

Parry, Milman, 142–143, 146–148
patriarchy, language of, 35–36; and
  Beowulf, 75
patristic criticism: *see* exegesis
Patterson, Lee, 2, 159
Paul, Saint, view of flesh, 120
peaceweaver, 41, 48–50, 60, 61
Pearsall, Derek, 4, 5
peasant, status of, 101–102, 110
"Peasants' Revolt": *See* Rising of 1381
Peirce, C. S., 36
Pembroke semonary, 163, 172
penitential motif, 176
philology, 165, 178, 182; history of, 1–2,
  30, 209, 219, 220–221, 284n78
Philosophy Department, history of, 8
Phoenix, 143, 188–189, 191
Piers Plowman, 91–112; Anima, 96–97,
  103, 106; critical history of, 3, 91, 95;
  dream vision in, 102, 105; fictionality of,
  92–93; genres of, 102–103, 111; half
  acre, 94, 100–102, 104; Holy Church,
  104; Hunger, 94, 102, 111; pardon in,
  97–98, 105; penance in, 96, 98–99; political allusions in, 92–93; sources of, 97;
  structural patterns of, 96–97, 103–107;
  Tree of Charity, 97, 98, 106, 112; Truth,
  93, 98, 102, 104–105; unconscious
  project of, 100, 103, 111
Piers the plowman (character), 97, 98, 101,
  106–107, 111–112
plowman, 101
poetry, Old English, canon of, 220; critical
  history of, 3, 157; dialogism of, 185–190;

manuscript contexts, 178–179, 194; oral components of, 144–146; and oral-textual culture, 185–186; and the past, 68–69, 202–203, 207–208; verse forms of, 144–145, 151–153
political criticism, hegemony of, 31–32
Pope, John C., 163
Poster, Mark, 18
poverty, 109–110; idealization of, 4
pragmatics, 168, 271n52
primal horde, 83
progress, paradigm of, 14
projection, 73
prolepsis, 5, 76, 102
prose, Old English, place in cannon, 157–158; in curriculum, 176–179
prosody, 144
psychoanalytic criticism, 66, 68, 88–89
psychoanalysis, 54, 65–66

Quilligan, Maureen, 43

Rabanus Maurus, 46, 171, 195
reader in oral text, 149–150; in feminist discourse, 36–37, 40
reader-response criticism, 36–37, 68
reading, 196–198, 217
Reception theory, 146–149, 154, 165–167, 189–190, 210, 219, 223
reflectionist criticism, 99, 247n60. *See also* Marxist criticism.
Regularis Concordia, 173–174, 176, 189
relations of production, feudal, 108–109, 110, 244n21
Renoir, Alain, 43–44, 57, 153–154
rent, 94, 110–111
resistance, 73
Richards, Mary P., 174
Riddle 35, 143
Rising of 1381 ("Peasants' Revolt"), 4, 5, 94, 102, 110
Rich, Adrienne, 38
Robertson, D. W. R., Jr., 3–4
Robinson, Fred C., 157, 178
Rochester, 174
Rome, 207–208
Roosevelt, Theodore, 7
Rousseau, Jean Jacques, 92
Rule of St. Benedict, 196

rumination, 198
runic inscriptions, 12
Ruskin, John, 28–30
Ruthwell Cross, 12

Said, Edward W., 31–32
Salter, Elizabeth, 103
Schaar, Claes, 142
Schweickart, Patrocinio, 36–37
Scragg, D. S., 163–164
Scudder, Vida Dutton, 27–28
semiotics, 24, 188, 190–191, 210
Semi-Pelagianism, 95, 97, 100
Shanks, Michael, 13, 14, 16, 31
signification, 39, 41, 48, 56, 58, 59, 60, 63, 219; in oral tradition, 152–153
silva (forest) metaphor, 200–202
Sisam, Kenneth, 163
Smetana, Cyril L., 162
sociolinguistic theory, 159–160, 167, 177–178, 180
Solomon and Saturn, 223
Sources of Anglo-Saxon Literary Culture, 158–159, 160, 278n16
source studies, 5, 161–162, 168, 179
specialization, in academy, 9–10, 220
speech act theory, 160–161, 265n13
Sperber, Dan, 166
Statute of Laborers, 94, 101–102, 110
Stewart, Susan, 212–213
Stock, Brian, 184
Stokes, Myra, 95–99
Summons to Prayer, 189
Sunday letter, 173
Sutton Hoo, 12, 15–16, 20–22, 27, 28, 71
Swanton, Michael, 157
Sweet, Henry, 1, 9

taboo, 59, 128–129, 132, 134
Tacitus, 81, 82
teaching Old English, 157–160, 179
text dependence, 146
textual community, 184–185, 198, 199
textual culture, 195–197
textuality, 183–184, 185, 189
theory, critical. *See* archaeology of knowledge, cultural studies, feminist criticism, intertextuality, Marxist criticism, oral tra-

dition, psychoanalytic criticism, reception theory, semiotics
Thorpe, Benjamin, 172
three estates, model of, 93–94
Tilley, Christopher, 13, 14, 16, 31
Tolkien, J. R. R., 71–72
Torcello, 28–29
tradition dependence, 144–145
tragedy, 65, 75, 79
transference, 73, 75
translation, as interpretation, 168–169, 170
translators, anonymous, 170, 172–173
transgression, 55, 131–132, 137–138
tribal culture, 69, 72
"two languages" motif, 11, 25–26, 35–36, 65–66, 82–83, 116–117, 129, 139, 159, 181–182, 211, 224
type scenes, 145, 153
typology, 13, 14, 16, 21

Vauchez, Andre, 138
Venice, 28–29
Vercelli Book, 12, 163, 187
Vernant, Jean-Pierre, 119
Vickery, John, 42–43, 44, 50

villenage, 108–109
Vivante, Paolo, 147

Wanderer, 76–77
Wenzel, Siegfried, 5
Wessex, dynasty of, 204–208
White, Hayden, 18
Wilshire, Bruce, 8
Wilson, Deirdre, 166
Winchester, 174, 204
Winner and Wastour, 102–103
woman, and flesh, 117–118, 122, 136, 138
women's studies, 7, 25
Worcester, 174
wordhord, 152, 190, 192, 199, 223
Wormald, Patrick, 21
Woolf, Rosemary, 41–42, 44, 48
Wrenn, C. L., 20, 21
writing, project of, 100, 110
Wulfstan, 162–163, 167, 173
Wülker, Richard, 12
wyrd, 68 (fate)

Zettel, Patrick H., 162
Zumthor, Paul, 26